The Federal Trade Commission
since 1970

The Federal Trade Commission since 1970

Economic regulation and bureaucratic behavior

Edited by
KENNETH W. CLARKSON
and
TIMOTHY J. MURIS

Law and Economics Center and
University of Miami School of Law

CAMBRIDGE UNIVERSITY PRESS

Cambridge
London   New York   New Rochelle
Melbourne   Sydney

Published by the Press Syndicate of the University of Cambridge
The Pitt Building, Trumpington Street, Cambridge CB2 1RP
32 East 57th Street, New York, NY 10022, USA
296 Beaconsfield Parade, Middle Park, Melbourne 3206, Australia

First published 1981

Printed in Canada
Typeset by Progressive Typographers, Inc., Emigsville, Pa
Printed and bound by The Hunter Rose Company Ltd., Toronto

Library of Congress Cataloging in Publication Data
Main entry under title:
The Federal Trade Commission since 1970.
Bibliography: p.
Includes index.
1.United States.   Federal Trade Commission –
Addresses, essays, lectures.   2.Trade regulation –
United States – Addresses, essays, lectures.   I.Clarkson,
Kenneth W.   II.Muris, Timothy J.
KF1611.F43   353.0082'6   80–27652
ISBN 0 521 23378 X

Contents

v

Contributors

WILLIAM BREIT, Department of Economics, University of Virginia, Charlottesville, Virginia 22901

KENNETH W. CLARKSON, Law and Economics Center and University of Miami School of Law, Coral Gables, Florida 33124

LOUIS DE ALESSI, Law and Economics Center and University of Miami School of Law, Coral Gables, Florida 33124

DORSEY D. ELLIS, JR., College of Law, University of Iowa, Iowa City, Iowa 52242

KENNETH G. ELZINGA, Department of Economics, University of Virginia, Charlottesville, Virginia 22901

CHARLES J. GOETZ, School of Law, University of Virginia, Charlottesville, Virginia 22901

MARK F. GRADY, College of Law, University of Iowa, Iowa City, Iowa 52242

WESLEY J. LIEBELER, School of Law, University of California, Los Angeles, California 90024

DONALD L. MARTIN, Law and Economics Center, University of Miami, Coral Gables, Florida 33124

TIMOTHY J. MURIS, Law and Economics Center and University of Miami School of Law, Coral Gables, Florida 33124

RICHARD L. PETERSON, Credit Research Center, Krannert Graduate School of Management, Purdue University, West Lafayette, Indiana 47907

GEORGE L. PRIEST, School of Law, University of California, Los Angeles, California 90024

WARREN F. SCHWARTZ, Law Department, Georgetown University, Washington, D.C. 20057

Preface

To those who study or work in government regulation of business, the Federal Trade Commission (FTC) has been of intense interest for over a decade. Regarded in the 1960s as dormant and ineffective, in the 1970s the FTC quickly became a major agency focusing on problems that affect most American consumers and businesses. Our method, conclusions, and suggestions should interest scholars and practitioners in law, economics, political science, public administration, and other disciplines who analyze the operation and impact of the FTC in particular or of government agencies in general.

This book is the first comprehensive attempt to understand the "revitalized" FTC. The study originated in a desire to identify both the impact of the FTC's many projects and the underlying forces that motivated the agency's behavior. Supported by a grant from the Law and Economics Center, we recruited several scholars in the summer of 1977, all with extensive experience in law and economics.

We begin by focusing on the forces external to the agency that determine the parameters within which FTC decision makers operate. Thus, this book concerns institutions and how people react to them. For example, we discuss the extent to which the Congress and the courts affect the FTC. We then examine the impact of several substantive issues that characterize FTC actions since 1970. These issues were chosen to reflect both the types of activities that the Commission pursues and those in which the Commission claims it has made major accomplishments. Finally, we examine how the external forces, the internal operations of the FTC, and the incentives of FTC staff explain agency behavior.

Our research methods were varied. We extensively used the economic literature focusing on government behavior. We read every congressional hearing and report that focused on the Federal Trade Commission during the 1970s. We also examined volumes of internal Commission documents available from various public sources. We supplemented these written materials through extensive interviews with past and present chairmen, commissioners, directors, bureau chiefs, other top FTC staff, members of Congress, congressional aides, Office of Management and Budget staff, and Civil Service Commission officials. To guarantee frank exchange, we agreed in most cases to avoid quotation. A few footnotes cite interviews (without identifying the sources) when we received important information from at least two reliable sources that was otherwise unavailable in public documents.

All research must end, and we stopped our analysis as of December 1, 1979, with some chapters stopping before then as indicated within their text. The December 1979 cutoff occurred when the FTC was under extreme political attack, threatening for a time to result in legislation curtailing the agency's power. The threat did not become reality. For reasons discussed at length in the book, the provisions Congress adopted leave the FTC as a potent and largely unchecked force.

Throughout our study, we received considerable support. We wish to thank the Law and Economics Center, which generously supported the project, and the authors who contributed individual chapters to this volume. We especially want to thank the numerous personnel at the FTC, Congress, and executive agencies for their candid information about the Commission. We would also like to acknowledge the valuable research assistance of Randy Chartash, Daniel DeWolf, Helen Hauser, Ronald Perkowski, and especially Andrew Caverly. We extend special thanks to our colleagues, Louis De Alessi and Patrick Gudridge, who reviewed extensive portions of the manuscript, and to Judy Miley, who often improved the presentation of our ideas. Finally, we would like to thank Linda Craig and Deebee Watkins for their invaluable administrative and secretarial contributions.

K.W.C.
T.J.M.

1 Introduction

TIMOTHY J. MURIS AND KENNETH W. CLARKSON

Of all the regulatory agencies, the Federal Trade Commission (FTC) is one of the most important, both in its power to influence American business transactions and in its potential to reveal vital information about the regulatory process. Regarded in the late 1960s as inactive and ineffective, the current FTC, buttressed by substantial grants of power from Congress and the courts, is no longer content to concentrate on cases and enforcement dealing with single small firms or narrow areas of law. Rather, it has attacked whole industries, challenging both their structure and practices. Because it can impose wide-reaching rules with the force of law, the FTC has been called "the second most powerful legislative body in the United States . . . [with the power] to alter the structure of an industry."[1]

Two 1969 reports, both highly critical of the FTC, sparked this new approach to regulation. Understanding these reports and their impact is important because of their ultimate effect on the FTC. Section I of this chapter provides this background and briefly summarizes some of the steps the FTC has taken to achieve its current prominence. Section II then presents the plan of study.

I. Transformation of the FTC: 1969–70

A. The Commission until 1969

Two aspects of the FTC's history before 1969 help place the critical reports of that year in context. First, the Commission concentrated on trivia, focusing on small firms and narrow points of law.[2] Second, scholars often studied the Commission,[3] reaching similar conclusions. The Commission, they charged, lacked direction, was poorly managed, and was inadequately staffed. It was political, obsessed with trivia, and woefully inefficient. Nevertheless, many critics added that, as bad as the Commission was, it was improving. For example, the Hoover Commis-

1

sion, in referring to an often-cited Commission failure in planning, stated:

> Until recently, the Federal Trade Commission had for years allocated its energies on the hit-or-miss basis of complaints with relatively little attempt to assess the significance of the particular proceeding in the light of its limited resources and the over-all objectives of the statutes. Now it has begun to plan its program to use its resources more effectively.[4]

B. Nader and the ABA

In 1969, the Nader and American Bar Association (ABA) reports appeared, echoing the previously discussed failures of the Commission. Rather than conclude that the FTC was improving, however, they declared that the Commission had reached bottom with no sign of change.

Work on the Nader report had begun a year earlier, in the summer of 1968, with seven volunteers called Nader's Raiders. Six were students, or recent graduates, of law school. Although consumerist Ralph Nader himself had little to do with the actual writing, he lent his name and financial assistance to the enterprise, thereby helping to generate considerable favorable publicity. The January 6, 1969, report concluded that the FTC was a failure and in near total disarray.[5] The FTC had, the authors charged, systematically failed to detect violations, relying instead on consumer and competitor complaints; failed to establish priorities, attacking instead trivia; failed to enforce its statutes, relying instead on voluntary enforcement; and failed to seek the necessary resources and authority, remaining instead content with its nearly worthless efforts.

To the authors, the problem could be summarized in one word: people. Partisan politics and geographic locations determined hiring, not merit. Preferences went to Democrats, nonminorities, and southerners (particularly those from Tennessee, the home state of FTC Chairman Dixon as well as of Congressman Joe Evins, whose subcommittee oversaw the FTC budget). Further, individuals from prestigious schools were so discriminated against that the report concluded that "bright men need not apply" to the FTC.[6]

Rather than abolition, the authors recommended that the Commission be reformed to protect the consumer. Without systematic regulation, they believed that corporations would seriously harm consumers. They recommended increased regulation of modern advertising techniques, better Commission-wide planning, new programs for the ghetto consumer, more information disclosure, criminal penalties for violations of FTC law, and tighter restrictions on the power of the chairman.

Numerous newspaper editorials and magazine articles discussed the study and the reactions of government officials.[7] At congressional hearings, the report's charges generally received a sympathetic ear.[8] Praise came even from within the Commission. Although Chairman Dixon blasted the report as "a summer vacation smear project," Commissioner Elman, long a foe of Dixon, commended the authors for performing a public service in revealing many of the Commission's weaknesses.[9] Further, the report and responses to it encouraged President Nixon to ask the American Bar Association to study the FTC.[10]

Reacting quickly to Nixon's request, the ABA released its report in September 1969. Although more moderate in tone, as well as more scholarly and authoritative than the Nader Report, the 16 practitioners and scholars who comprised the ABA's special commission were just as critical of the FTC as was the Nader Report. The ABA group concluded that:

It should be the last of the long series of committees and groups which have earnestly insisted that drastic changes were essential to re-create the FTC in its intended image. The case for change is plain. What is required is that changes now be made, and in depth. Further temporizing is indefensible. Notwithstanding the great potential of the FTC in the field of antitrust and consumer protection, if change does not occur, there will be no substantial purpose to be served by its continued existence; the essential work to be done must then be carried on by other governmental institutions.[11]

Specifically, the report criticized the Commission for ineffective direction, noting that, despite an increased budget, all statistical measures showed decreased FTC activity. The report pointed to mismanagement as the cause of excessive delay and criticized the focus on trivia. Regarding consumer protection, the report condemned the overcommitment to statutes designed to protect specific industries, such as the textile, fur, and wool acts. Regarding antitrust, the report recommended a reevaluation of Robinson-Patman Act cases, a major FTC antitrust activity. Further, the report recommended procedural reforms, such as the delegation of authority from the Commission to its staff, thereby decreasing delay and preventing the Commission from acting as both judge and prosecutor.[12]

C. The FTC responds to its critics

Apparently in response to the barrage of criticism, two important events occurred in 1969. First, the Commission closed some 600 of its investigations.[13] Although similar to previous purgings of active investigations, this step apparently signaled a shift in attitude and approach: What had been acceptable in the 1960s might be discouraged in the 1970s. Second, President Nixon appointed a new chairman, Caspar Weinberger. In his "Consumer Message" to Congress, presented in the fall of 1969, Nixon stated that "the time has now come for the reactivation and revitalization of the FTC"[14] and that Weinberger was committed to such action. Weinberger considered his mandate from the White House to be "carte blanche,"[15] allowing for major reorganization and wholesale personnel changes. Further, he knew that the mandate of the Nader and ABA reports supported such changes. Although Weinberger resigned from the Commission after only about six months, he acted on both fronts.

Weinberger reorganized the work of the Commission along its two major functions: *antitrust,* for which he created the Bureau of Competition to replace the Bureau of Restraint of Trade, and *consumer protection,* for which he created the Bureau of Consumer Protection to replace the Bureau of Deceptive Practices. He abolished some of the previously existing bureaus, most notably the Bureau of Textile and Furs, which, according to the ABA Report, received far too large a commitment of the Commission's resources. Commission reorganization appears to be a favorite activity of new chairmen, not only because it gives the appearance of activity and purposefulness, but, more important, because it allows a reshuffling of top staff positions. The Weinberger reorganization, however, distinguished itself from many other Commission reorganizations. It improved staff morale by implying that the promise seen in the Nader and ABA reports would be fulfilled.[16] Further, this reorganization indicated that the Commission would deemphasize at least some of the agency's most criticized activities. In addition, it appeared to reinforce the consumerist movement that was then rapidly expanding.[17] Finally, the reorganization facilitated a task that the critics had called essential: hiring new people while eliminating the "dead wood."

This major shift in personnel began under Weinberger, who had to contend with both civil service regulations and powerful congressional friends of some incumbent staff members. Although attorneys do not have extensive civil service protection and thus can be dismissed with relative ease, a lawyer with military experience can be removed only "for such causes as will promote the efficiency of the [civil] service."[18] Weinberger's reorganization facilitated the removal of both veterans and nonveterans by, in effect, abolishing their jobs, concentrating on the top staff. Nonveterans were given 30-day notices. Because of their civil service protection, veterans had to be reassigned, reclassified, or offered retirement. By offering some veterans unattractive positions and persuading others that retirement or resignation was mutually beneficial, Weinberger was able to avoid serious problems with the civil service.

Neither did Congress prove to be a major obstacle. Although some members of Congress apparently tried to protect their FTC friends by cutting the FTC budget, their pressure was generally ineffectual because Weinberger wanted less, not more, money from Congress.[19] In all, 18 of the 31 top-level staff members were discharged.[20]

Upon replacing Weinberger in September 1970, Miles Kirkpatrick began transforming the remainder of the professional staff. Largely through his executive director, Basil Mezines, he replaced nearly a third of the middle- and lower-level staff. Consequently, the average age of the staff dropped, and many of the new attorneys were graduates of the more prestigious law schools.[21] During Kirkpatrick's two-year chairmanship, many of these new staff members were committed to the tenets of consumerism, including the need for greater regulation of advertising and for deconcentration of major industries.[22]

The consensus emerged that the Commission was "revitalized" during the Weinberger and Kirkpatrick years.[23] Consumer protection was probably the most publicized activity. As described in Part II of this book, innovative regulatory techniques were applied to advertising. Simultaneously, new emphasis was given to expanding Section 5 of the Federal Trade Commission Act, a step that led to the proposal of several major trade regulation rules during the chairmanship of Lewis Engman. The agency did not slight antitrust, however. In April 1972, the FTC filed a pathbreaking complaint to break up the cereal industry because four firms allegedly had a "shared monopoly." In general (Part II again provides greater detail), Commission antitrust shifted to an attack on the structure of American industry, as revealed by the cereals case, investigations of several concentrated industries, and development of the line-of-business program. Moreover, the Robinson-Patman Act (Section 2 of the Clayton Act), a mainstay of FTC antitrust before 1970, was (and continues to be) deemphasized. Despite occasional Robinson-Patman Act complaints and efforts to transform Robinson-Patman matters into cases under Section 5 of the FTC Act, the Commission no longer engages in massive Robinson-Patman enforcement.[24]

During the chairmanship of Lewis Engman, which began in early 1973 and continued for almost three years, the agency deemphasized consumer protection relative to antitrust, although in absolute terms budgets for both activities grew. The major antitrust initiative involved a suit to break up the eight largest domestic oil companies. Other important investigations of concentrated industries began, and the major case against Xerox ended. The most significant consumer protection development involved the proposal of numerous trade regulation rules designed to transform the practices of entire industries.

Calvin Collier became chairman in 1976. During his one-year tenure, no new trade regulation rules were proposed, and the Commission basically attempted to get control of the numerous major projects it had undertaken. President Carter then appointed Michael Pertschuk as chairman. With Pertschuk came further reorganization (as usual) and new efforts to expand Section 5 of the Trade Commission Act beyond traditional consumer protection and antitrust concerns to allow scrutiny of problems such as the alleged political power of large corporations. To date, the major initiative under Pertschuk has been the proposal of a rule to regulate and in some instances eliminate advertising directed at children.[25]

As the FTC prepared for the 1980s, the agency indeed seemed a potent force. In 1970, its budget of approximately $21 million was used to enforce 11 statutes. By the end of 1979, with the budget approaching $70 million, the Commission had enforced 16 new statutes and had created or proposed more than 60 programs and 40 rules to regulate American business. Further, the Bureau of Consumer Protection had taken bold measures to regulate advertising, credit practices, and warranties, as well as attempting to remedy problems that state regulation caused in the eyeglass and funeral industries. The Bureau of Competition had initiated the largest case in the Commission's history in an effort to break up the nation's largest oil companies.

It is time to evaluate the performance of this powerful agency. What has been the impact of the FTC's efforts? Can we explain why the agency acts as it does? It is to these questions that this study is directed.

II. The plan of this study

The remainder of the book is divided into three parts. Part I identifies the constraints originating from external factors, such as Congress and the courts, that influence FTC decision makers. Only by understanding the environment in which the Commission exists can we begin to understand the agency's behavior. Further, knowledge of the impact of existing institutions on the Commission will assist us in determining how changes in the agency's environment are likely to affect its performance. Part II then examines several substantive activities that the FTC has undertaken since 1970. We chose the activities to reflect both the range of matters that the Commission pursues and those specific activities that the Commission considers its major accomplishments.[26] Finally, Part III analyzes some of the reasons for FTC actions and discusses a number of possible reforms.

In our analysis, we assume that FTC decision makers are not motivated by a single concept of the public interest; rather they employ their own self-interested view of the public welfare. The choices they make are designed to further their own satisfaction or utility subject to the constraints that limit options available to them.[27] Of course, the preferences of the relevant decision maker influence the choices made, and individuals have different preferences. To the extent that different constraints provide different opportunities, however, knowledge of the relevant constraints allows us to predict patterns of behavior without knowing the identities and preferences of specific individuals. At least, we can exclude certain alternatives from the set that the FTC is likely to follow. Thus, unlike other studies of the FTC,[28] we are not exclusively concerned with a description of what the Commission does. Moreover, we do not explain FTC activity solely on the identity of particular chairmen, commissioners, or top-level staff.

The method we employ uses both law and economics. It blends the discipline of law, which creates and interprets constraints, with the discipline of economics, which deduces individual decisions under alternative constraints. Part I employs legal analysis to identify the constraints imposed by the array of regulations emerging from the Office of Management and Budget, the Justice Department, Civil Service Commission, and other executive agencies, as well as by Congress, the courts, state and local governments, business organizations, and consumer groups.[29] Legal analysis is particularly suited for this task, because understanding these constraints often requires a technical knowledge of the language of a statute, its legislative history, the regulations promulgated thereunder, and the relevant court decisions. Part II combines legal analysis and economic theory. Legal analysis is first applied to specify the precise form of the Commission's regulation, rule, or activity. Then economic theory is used to predict the consequences of the FTC's action. Many chapters test the validity of the predictions. Finally, Part III focuses on the relationship between Part I and Part II. In particular, we attempt to explain FTC actions, such as those discussed in Part II, as a consequence of the opportunities defined in Part I.[30]

Thus, the Commission's statutory powers are interpreted in the context of formal and informal legislative, administrative, and judicial contacts that establish FTC constraints. Once the opportunities available to agency decision makers are identified, economic theory is employed to predict how the FTC will act. These predictions are then compared with actual FTC actions, particularly those discussed in Part II. In short, this book uses legal analysis and economic theory to examine the outcomes of particular FTC activities and to begin to explain why FTC decision makers behave as they do.

Part I

The institutional setting

Introduction

This part identifies and evaluates the constraints that determine the options (opportunity sets) available to decision makers within the Commission. These constraints are imposed on the Commission by external forces within the legislative, executive, and judicial branches of government. (The Commission's organizational structure, personnel policies, and operating procedures also affect the options of FTC officials and are discussed in Chapter 15.)

The legislative branch potentially exerts power over the Commission by controlling its budget, changing its statutory authority, and applying pressure via oversight and other ad hoc monitoring. Chapters 2 and 3 examine the Commission's statutory authority and its relationship with Congress. The courts review most major FTC actions and, consequently, could limit the Commission's power under the broad language of the FTC Act. Chapter 4 considers this judicial constraint. Next, Chapter 5 discusses the relation of other parts of government to the FTC. The President appoints the commissioners and designates the chairman, the Office of Management and Budget has the final word on the FTC budget before it is submitted to Congress, the Civil Service Commission (recently changed to the Office of Personnel Management) has authority over many FTC employees, and several other agencies either directly or indirectly affect the Commission.

To define these constraints, we examined statutes, cases, hearings, and various other documents. Although these sources were useful, we did not confine ourselves to them. We extensively interviewed present and former government officials from both inside and outside the FTC. These interviews helped fill the gaps left by the official documents and assisted in determining whether what appeared to be serious constraints actually had minimal effect on the Commission.

As will become apparent from these chapters, what emerges is a picture of a largely unconstrained agency. Although appearing effective, most means of controlling Commission actions are virtually useless, owing to lack of political support and information, lack of interest on the part of those ostensibly monitoring the FTC, or FTC maneuvering. In short, throughout much of the 1970s, within wide parameters the Commission could do what it wanted with only a minimum of outside interference.

2 Statutory powers

TIMOTHY J. MURIS

Much of the Commission's current prominence stems from its broad statutory powers that have dramatically increased in the 1970s as Congress entrusted new authority to the "revitalized" FTC. By 1979, the Commission exercised authority under 27 separate statutes.[1] Our discussion divides these powers into three categories: The statutes as of 1969, statutes added in the 1970s, and the many statutes, called special statutes, that apply only to specific industries or problems, as contrasted to the more general statutes discussed in the first two categories.

I. Powers as of 1969

The heart of the Commission's power lies in Section 5 of the Federal Trade Commission Act.[2] Under that section as originally written in 1914, the Commission had the power to prevent unfair methods of competition in commerce. In 1938 the Commission received the power to prevent unfair or deceptive acts or practices in commerce.[3] Although there may not be a legal distinction between the two, within the Commission it is usually thought that antitrust involves unfair methods of competition, whereas consumer protection involves unfair or deceptive acts or practices. As we will see in Chapter 4, by 1969 the courts had become very lenient in deferring to the Commission's judgment of what activities violated the general language of Section 5. Commentators noted, however, the FTC's limited remedies. As of 1969, the Commission's power either to proceed on an industry-wide, rather than on a case-by-case basis, or to force companies to return to consumers money that was illegally obtained was in doubt. Further, the Commission had limited ability to enjoin illegal practices, and its basic remedy, the cease and desist order, was criticized as a mere slap on the wrist.

Another important part of the original Federal Trade Commission Act, Section 6, gives the agency broad powers to investigate not only for law

13

enforcement, but also for the many economic reports that it has produced. Besides the many special statutes discussed below, the Clayton Act is the remaining substantive statute effective in 1969 that is still important to the Commission.[4] Under Sections 3, 7, and 8, the Commission can prevent and eliminate unlawful tying arrangements, corporate mergers, and interlocking directorates, respectively. Further, Section 2 of the Clayton Act, as amended by the Robinson-Patman Act, empowers the Commission to prevent unlawful price and related discriminations. As discussed in Chapter 1, this statute accounted for much of the Commission's antitrust work in the 1960s, although not in the 1970s.

Few corporations of any significance are exempt from the FTC's powers, except those regulated by other agencies, such as banks, airlines, and trucking firms. As of 1969, some observers feared that the Commission's power to reach only practices "*in* commerce," as opposed to the more far-reaching standard of "*in or affecting* commerce," hampered its effectiveness. As we shall see next, however, in the 1970s Congress removed this and several other possible limitations on the FTC's powers.

II. 1970s: expansion of powers

Aside from special statutes, three congressional acts passed in the 1970s significantly increased the Commission's powers. First, the Alaska Pipeline Act of 1973[5] doubled the penalties for violating FTC orders to $10,000, empowered United States district courts to grant mandatory injunctions and other equitable relief to enforce Commission orders, and granted the Commission greater powers to appear on its own behalf in federal court. In addition, this act expanded the Commission's information-gathering power and allowed it to seek temporary injunctions and restraining orders whenever it has reason to believe both that any law that it enforces is being, or is about to be, violated and that, pending final FTC action, the injunction would be in the public interest.

Next, in January 1975, the Federal Trade Commission Improvements Act became law (along with the Magnuson-Moss Warranty Act, a special statute that will be discussed below). In providing procedures for the Commission to prescribe substantive rules for unfair or deceptive acts or practices, the act confirmed the Commission's power to issue industry-wide rules, a power that has led some to call the agency the second most powerful legislature in Washington.[6] Further, the Commission received the power to go to federal court to recover civil penalties for knowing violations of the FTC Act. Violators of FTC law with actual knowledge, or knowledge fairly implied on the basis of objective circumstances, face a penalty of up to $10,000 for each violation even if they are not themselves subject to a Commission cease and desist order. As an example of the significance of this power, in late 1975 the Commission initiated a pilot enforcement program dealing with practices such as bait and switch, door-to-door selling problems, and selling damaged or defective merchandise without disclosing the defect.[7] Under this program, the FTC notified selected businesses throughout the country of the potential penalty of $10,000 per violation for engaging in the practices. Thus, the Commission gained a potentially potent remedy with which to influence business conduct without first having to obtain a cease and desist order against each firm.

The Improvements Act made other changes. Congress empowered the Commission to sue in federal district court for various forms of redress, including restitution on behalf of consumers who have been injured by acts or practices that the Commission had found to be unfair or deceptive. Further, Congress changed the Commission's commerce jurisdiction from *"in* commerce" to *"in or affecting* commerce," and again extended the Commission's power to represent itself in court.

Finally, the Hart-Scott-Rodino Antitrust Improvements Act of 1976 added a new section, Section 7A, to the Clayton Act, requiring notification to the Commission and to the assistant attorney general in charge of the antitrust division of certain contemplated mergers or acquisitions. The Act also facilitated the ability of the Commission to enjoin certain mergers before a full-scale hearing is held on the merger's merits. The Commission has recently promulgated detailed regulations pursuant to this legislation.

Before 1970, rule making, greater injunction power, consumer redress, civil penalties, expanded commerce jurisdiction, premerger notification, and increased ability of the Commission to represent itself in court were said to be necessary for optimal enforcement. Thus, in the 1970s, Congress remedied what had appeared to be defects in Commission authority.

III. Special statutes

A. *As of 1969*

The heavy amount of Commission activity under three special statutes requires their mention: the Wool Products Labeling Act of 1940, the Fur Products Labeling Act of 1951, and the Textile Fiber Products Identification Act of 1958.[8] These statutes have typically been used to inhibit rivals of certain producers. For example, the wool act protects producers of virgin wool from competition of other fibers.[9] Although once heavy resource users, they were little-utilized in the 1970s. In fiscal 1969, the Commission spent about $1.7 million (or about 10 percent of its entire budget) on these statutes, whereas in fiscal year 1978 the Commission estimated that it would spend only about $327,000 (or about 0.5 percent of its total budget).[10]

Three noteworthy special statutes were passed in the late 1960s. The

Fair Package and Labeling Act of 1966, covering consumer commodities other than food, drugs, therapeutic devices, and cosmetics, requires the Commission to issue disclosure regulations concerning the contents and identity of the product, such as the net contents and the manufacturer's name and place of business. The Federal Cigarette Labeling and Advertising Act of 1966, amended in 1969 to require a warning on cigarette packages, instructs the Commission to submit annual reports to Congress regarding cigarette labeling, advertising, and potential legislation. Finally, the Truth in Lending Act of 1968 requires all consumer creditors to make detailed written disclosures concerning charges and related aspects of the transaction.[11]

B. 1970s: special statute legislation increases

The Commission significantly increased its power through special statutes during the 1970s. Many important statutes involved credit transactions. First, the Fair Credit Reporting Act, effective in 1971, regulates the confidentiality, accuracy, and use of the information that consumer reporting companies, such as credit bureaus, compile. Next, the Equal Credit Opportunity Act, which became effective in late 1975, forbids creditors from discriminating against applicants on the basis of sex or marital status. Any violation of the act or its implementing regulations is a violation of the FTC Act. Third, the Fair Credit Billing Act, an amendment of the Truth in Lending Act that became effective in late 1975, regulates billing practices, such as billing errors. The Consumer Leasing Act of 1976, another amendment to the Truth in Lending Act, requires disclosure of relevant costs for certain leases of personal property to consumers. Finally, the Fair Debt Collection Practices Act of 1977 concerns the practices of persons who regularly collect debts.[12]

Two other major special statutes of the 1970s, the Magnuson-Moss Warranty Act and the Energy Policy and Conservation Act, do not involve credit. The Warranty Act authorizes the Commission to develop regulations for written and implied warranties. The Commission has spent considerable resources on this act, mostly to promulgate regulations, and Chapter 14 considers the act and regulations in detail. Among other aspects, the Energy Act requires the FTC to specify the form and content of label disclosures for products such as air conditioners and dishwashers. This act also promises to be a heavy resource user.[13]

Although difficult to determine precisely, the percentage of Commission resources for fiscal year 1978 spent on special statutes exceeded 6 percent (or about $3.6 million) and, at least in the short run, continued growing.[14] Special statutes, albeit different from those prevalent in the late 1970s, are still a noticeable part of Commission enforcement.

IV. Conclusions

Congress has conferred broad powers upon the Commission. Although the 1969 critics could argue that the Commission needed increased power to become "truly" effective, such power is now part of the FTC's arsenal.

3 Legislative constraints

KENNETH W. CLARKSON

This chapter discusses congressional constraints on the FTC. Section I discusses the major methods of congressional constraints. Section II then turns to the nature of congressional incentives to control the FTC, focusing on the interest groups that influence Congress and the Commission. Finally, Section III considers the legislative veto, the most widely discussed means of modifying congressional control of the FTC.

I. Congressional authority and monitoring

Congressional authority, oversight, and monitoring of the FTC comprise four major categories. First, Congress may shape the agency through the annual authorization and appropriation process.[1] Second, Congress can engage in overall surveillance of the agency through questionnaires, investigations, and hearings. Third, Congress may focus at any time on specific issues, a process we refer to as "ad hoc monitoring." Finally, Congress may change the legislative authority of the Commission.[2]

A. *Congressional authorization and appropriation*

Some scholars contend that, in terms of influence and the ease with which that influence can be employed, control over the budget is Congress's most effective constraint over agencies.[3] By this view, Congress influences agencies both by adjusting the total funds appropriated to the agency as well as by allocating expenditures within various agency programs. For example, Congress may encourage particular policies by "earmarking" funds or discourage other policies by limiting the use of funds or the number of agency personnel. Specific FTC examples include congressional earmarking of separate funds for truth-in-lending enforcement in fiscal years 1969 and 1970 and for the study of the oil industry following the energy crisis of 1973–4.[4]

18

In fact, however, since 1970 Congress has significantly increased the FTC budget. Further, Congress has frequently approved supplemental appropriations. Table 3.1 shows that since fiscal year 1970, FTC budget requests have been equal to or below the amount that Congress authorized except for fiscal years 1979 and 1980.[5] In fiscal year 1979, although Congress appropriated less for consumer protection than the Commission requested, the total appropriation for all activities exceeded the total requested. Fiscal year 1980 is the first year that the total appropriation was less than the amount requested. The agency did not receive large budget increases in 1979 and 1980, however, probably reflecting a political environment that had become unfavorable to the FTC. We discuss this environment in more detail later in this chapter and in Chapter 15.

Using the overall budget level to reward and punish the FTC is a very crude means of control. Even if it effectively controlled the FTC's overall budget, Congress can only rarely use its control to direct the allocation of resources *within* the FTC. An understanding of the operation of the Commission and of the budget process reveals significant congressional limitations in shaping the direction of the FTC's programs. The Commission's budget is divided among maintaining competition, consumer protection, and "other" (economic support, compliance, and administration comprise most of this category). Within the two major categories – maintaining competition and consumer protection – there are hundreds of activities. Thus, Congress could not effectively stop or expand a particular activity either by dictating the Commission's total budget or by dictating its budget by mission. Instead, it would have to specifically address the activity at issue. Further, obtaining and digesting the voluminous information necessary to judge the merits of individual activities would be so complicated and costly that close congressional supervision of specific Commission projects is unlikely.

Even when knowledge about specific programs is available and understandable, Congress would need to update it continually. Thus, Congress may overcome the first hurdle, acquiring adequate information about the hundreds of individual FTC activities with which to specify actual resource levels of both dollars and personnel to each activity. Nevertheless, circumstances change. Unless the Congress has continued access to information necessary to modify Commission activities accurately, misallocation of public resources is unavoidable. Most important, these powers would effectively turn Congress into an administrative agency, an impossible transformation.

There are, of course, exceptions to the rule that the Congress is ineffective in changing specific FTC resource allocations. In 1975, when the Commission curtailed its investigations of the condominium industry, Congress forced continued Commission effort by appropriating resources

Table 3.1. *Budget requests, appropriations, and actual expenditures, fiscal years 1970–80 (thousands of dollars)*

Fiscal year	Maintaining competition	Consumer protection	Economic activities	Administration, executive, direction, and other expenditures	Total
1970					
Request	$ 7,795[a]	$10,853[a,b]	—	$1,282	$19,940
Appropriation	8,720[a]	11,050[a,b]	—	1,230	21,000[c]
Actual expenditure	8,389[a]	10,294[c]	—	2,103	20,786
1971					
Request	8,968[a,b]	10,915[a,b]	—	1,492	21,375
Appropriation	8,658[a]	10,995[a]	—	2,277	21,930[c]
Actual expenditure	7,689[a]	12,729[a]	—	2,052	22,470
1972					
Request	9,430[a]	12,151[a]	—	2,345	23,926
Appropriation	8,466[a]	13,307[a]	—	3,319	25,092
Actual expenditure	5,609	12,131	$2,266	5,986	25,092
1973					
Request	9,660[a]	14,538[a]	—	2,875	27,073
Appropriation	7,006	14,865	3,425	5,134	30,430
Actual expenditure	6,149	13,694	2,533	7,829	30,205
1974					
Request	7,335	13,838	3,671	5,246	30,090
Appropriation	8,332	14,394	3,995	5,619	32,340[c]
Actual expenditure	9,427	15,217	2,557	5,122	32,334
1975					
Request	9,900	16,436	4,770	6,998	38,104
Appropriation	12,382	17,702	3,402	5,512	38,998[c]
Actual expenditure	12,296	16,981	3,003	6,648	38,983

1976					
Request	15,511	19,878	4,135	6,125	45,649
Appropriation	17,672	19,061	4,074	6,284	47,091[c]
Actual expenditure	15,968	18,739	3,745	6,618	47,199
1976 Transition quarter					
Appropriation	4,418	4,765	1,019	2,219	12,421[c]
Actual expenditure	4,153	4,878	974	2,541	12,543
1977					
Request	23,309	18,685	4,197	6,642	52,833
Appropriation	23,293	19,714	3,953	7,720	54,680[c]
Actual expenditure	25,893[d]	22,284[d]	5,299[d]	1,204	54,680
1978					
Request	24,327	22,936	4,156	8,124	59,543
Appropriation	29,030[d]	27,357[d]	5,763[d]	—	62,150[c]
Actual expenditure	26,488[d]	27,019[d]	5,129[d]	652	62,100
1979					
Request	29,746[d]	30,932[d]	5,807[d]	—	66,485
Appropriation	31,189[d]	29,539[d]	6,022[d]	—	66,750
Actual expenditure	27,100[d]	28,854[d]	5,381[d]	3,965	65,300
1980					
Request	32,510[d]	30,347[d]	6,164[d]	—	69,021
Appropriation	31,427[d]	30,957[d]	5,372[d]	—	67,756[c]
Actual expenditure	—	—	—	—	—

[a] Includes economic activities.
[b] Includes truth in lending.
[c] Includes supplemental.
[d] Includes administration and executive direction.

Source: The Budget of the United States Government, App. A, fiscal years 1970 through 1980.

specifically for law enforcement in this industry.[6] This effort is notable in that it stands virtually alone and involved resources of less than 0.2 of 1 percent of the FTC's total budget.[7] A more typical example involves occupational licensure, one of the agency's most controversial activities. Planned occupational licensure program expenditures have grown both absolutely and relatively (when compared to total consumer protection spending of which occupational licensure is a part). Thus, in fiscal year 1976 the request was $580,000, or 3.5 percent of the consumer protection mission. In fiscal year 1977 the FTC request for the occupational licensure program had grown to $787,000, or 5.1 percent of the consumer protection mission. By fiscal year 1978 the expenditure was $1,197,000, or 6.1 percent of the consumer protection mission, and by fiscal year 1979 it was $1,480,000, or 7.2 percent of the consumer protection mission.[8]

Because Congress lacks complete information, it in effect gives the agency the power to reallocate (or "reprogram") its resources to meet changing economic and social conditions. Reprogramming is clearly within the scope of Commission alternatives. The actual appropriation language is extremely general, permitting great flexibility. In fiscal year 1979, for example, the initial authorization of the FTC was "for necessary expenses of the Federal Trade Commission . . . $64,750,000."[9] Further, the Controller General of the United States has stated that he was "not aware of any statute or regulation which requires committee approval of reprogramming by the FTC."[10] Some Congress members have been concerned about the ability of the agency to shift its funds from one activity to another. In fiscal year 1975 the appropriations committee considered that "except as provided in existing law, funds provided in the act shall be available only for the purpose for which they were appropriated."[11] Still, the FTC's reprogramming power remains intact and frequently exercised.

B. Oversight

Besides the budget process, Congress also oversees the FTC through the General Accounting Office (GAO) and congressional committees. An examination of the record since 1970 reveals no evidence that Congress effectively used these activities to constrain the FTC.

Although several of the GAO's inquiries have resulted in issued reports,[12] the congressional response to identified problems was perfunctory at best. Probably the most obvious example of this lackadaisical attitude occurred in 1974, when Congress directed the GAO to work with the FTC to resolve some important problems associated with the Commission's line-of-business program. The GAO's March 1975 report on problems concerning the FTC's management of the program, made to the Committee on Appropriations, was apparently ignored. Congressional hearings indicated that the only questions concerning the line-of-business program focused on total expenditures and the confidentiality of the data. There is no reference to GAO's criticisms in the hearings, and the Commission did not alter its line-of-business program.[13] In fact, no evidence indicates any substantial lessening in FTC line-of-business activities from outside pressures, including those that sought to use Congress to abolish or reduce the scope of the program.

As to congressional committees, in 1975 and 1978 two detailed questionnaires were sent to the Federal Trade Commission.[14] The answers to the 1975 questions alone filled approximately two regular file drawers. Although the agency spent considerable time in carefully answering these questions, they were more of a nuisance than an effective check on agency action. Our investigations revealed no changes in FTC substantive actions because of this oversight.

The oversight committee occasionally holds hearings regarding the Commission. Although recently more hostile toward the FTC, generally these hearings focus only on progress reports of various FTC programs, often trying to assess why there is delay in certain cases or rules. For example, in 1976 oversight hearings examined FTC effectiveness in eliminating unfair and deceptive advertising practices. The data and testimony of FTC officials amounted to a mere description of FTC progress.[15]

Regardless of the form of its actions, the oversight committee faces the same information problems that confront the appropriations committee. Even if Congress members or staffers acquire some information about a program, the Commission can pool several experts on the subject, who in total (and often individually) know more about the topic than do the Congress members or their staffs. For this and the reasons discussed above, one should not expect the oversight committee to be an effective and continuous constraint upon the FTC.

C. Ad hoc monitoring

Ad hoc monitoring involves informal contacts with the Commission, formal hearings, and congressional inquiries. Although little is known about informal contacts between members of Congress and the Commission, FTC officials of course treat Congress members and other individuals with the deference that their positions deserve. The influence of Congress members merely as individuals over the FTC's programs, however, appears normally limited. A politically powerful Congress member with a personal and close relationship to one or more commissioners or top staff members, such as the Bureau of Competition or the Bureau of Consumer Protection directors, has a significantly increased probability of raising specific matters of his choosing before the Commission. This type of influence, however, is not limited to congressional members. Anyone who has the ear of one of these FTC officials could similarly influence the FTC's agenda. Informal contacts appear to become particularly important only in periods of general political hostility toward the Commission, a condition discussed at more length in Section I.D. Chairpersons of the FTC oversight and appropriations committees, as well as other Congress members influential in legislation affecting the FTC, then possess unusual influence, and accordingly receive unusual deference from the FTC.

More visible forms of ad hoc monitoring involve formal hearings and other official congressional inquiries that focus on particular issues. Several such inquiries took place during the 1970s. Chairman Collier's confirmation hearings, for example, focused extensively on his expected enforcement (or lack of enforcement) of the Robinson-Patman Act.[16] Several Congress members, backed by small business groups, strongly favored continuation of Robinson-Patman cases. Despite their extensive questioning on this issue and the existence of a special committee to pressure the FTC, enforcement of the Robinson-Patman Act remained minimal after Collier's appointment as chairman of the Commission.

Recently, the Congress has attempted to monitor the Commission more closely. Federal Trade Commission appearances before the Congress from fiscal years 1970 through 1978 increased dramatically. Table 3.2 shows that for the first half of the 1970s the number of hearings for appropriations, supplementals, and other reasons was relatively constant and below 30 per year. Beginning in 1975, however, the number of congressional hearings increased by more than one-third. These hearings greatly increased the time and effort of the Commission in responding to congressional inquiries and thus have some constraining effect if valuable opportunities are forgone. Nonetheless, only rarely, if ever, have these hearings resulted in the Commission bringing or not bringing a case or establishing a rule.

An examination of hearings involving the funeral rule shows the Commission spending more time with Congress without stopping its activity. Industry representatives appearing before Congress were generally funeral directors who were also officers in industry organizations such as the National Funeral Directors Association.[17] They objected to FTC interference and rule making, claiming that such actions were unnecessary because few consumers complained about the funeral industry. Industry representatives asserted that the rule would not only increase the cost of funerals but also reduce the number of funeral homes by 25 percent, driving smaller homes out of business. They also questioned the authority of the FTC to preempt state law, alleging that certain practices in the Commission's rule-making proceeding were unfair. Furthermore, the funeral

Table 3.2. *FTC appearances before Congress, 1970–9*

Year	Purpose	Number of appearances
1970	Appropriations and supplementals	2
	Others	25
	Total	27
1971	Appropriations and supplementals	2
	Others	24
	Total	26
1972	Appropriations and supplementals	2
	Others	16
	Total	18
1973	Appropriations and supplementals	2
	Others	26
	Total	28
1974	Appropriations and supplementals	4
	Others	24
	Total	28
1975	Appropriations and supplementals	2
	Others	46
	Total	48
1976	Appropriations and supplementals	3
	Others	51
	Total	54
1977	Appropriations and supplementals	3
	Others	39
	Total	42
1978	Appropriations and supplementals	4
	Others	45
	Total	49
1979 (through September)	Appropriations and supplementals	2
	Others	38
	Total	40

Source: Based on Congressional Information Service (CIS) listings. The CIS index classifies the hearings according to the date the publication is issued, so these figures do not correspond directly to the calendar years they are listed under. For example, a hearing held in late 1975 would probably be in the CIS 1976 index because the transcript of that hearing was not published until 1976.

directors claimed that the FTC action aroused suspicion even of reputable funeral homes.

Openly hostile toward the agency, the Congress members focused on FTC expenditures of $450,000 from January 1, 1975, until the September 1976 hearings in order to develop a program in response to fewer than a dozen complaints about the funeral industry.[18] The committee members were also upset because the Commission consulted very few state officials. They felt that the Commission had wasted money, particularly because there were many Robinson-Patman complaints to which it had not responded.

As with an increasing number of industries under FTC scrutiny, the funeral industry and the small business managers who wanted more Robinson-Patman enforcement had sought to restrain the agency through Congress. In both cases well-organized groups generated enthusiastic support in some quarters of Congress to apply extreme pressure on the Commission. Even though the Commission was forced to expend resources to defend itself,[19] little evidence suggests any constraint on the FTC's choice of what industries or activities to pursue, given the methods of congressional control that we have discussed thus far. Indeed, because Congress is unequipped and unmotivated to check the agency, and because the FTC has cultivated supporters in Congress for its activities, even its most controversial programs meet little resistance there. The Commission's efforts to regulate the funeral industry, children's advertising, and line-of-business reporting clearly demonstrate Congress's inability to deter FTC action, even when considerable congressional pressures are exerted.[20]

At times, however, congressional opposition may effectively constrain the Commission. Until late 1977, the political environment facing the FTC decreased the likelihood of congressional control over the FTC via new legislation – the most effective constraint available to Congress. By late 1977 and early 1978, the political support for the Commission had significantly diminished. By late 1979, new legislation limiting the FTC's power appeared likely, and the FTC was responding to this change in the political environment. It is, however, the threat of new legislation, not the oversight function itself (with its attendant "grilling" of the agency staff and occasional unfavorable publicity), that appears to constrain the Commission.

D. Legislative authority

Legislation is the most powerful tool available to Congress. Through legislation, industries can be exempted from FTC rules, new programs can be stopped, or general rule-making power can be removed from the agency. Its usefulness in constraining FTC decision makers is generally limited, however. Legislative control is most severely restricted by a political environment "favorable" to the Commission. Even when many Congress members strongly oppose FTC actions, the environment will still be favorable as long as enough either support or merely accept the

Commission to prevent an effective constraint. In an unfavorable political environment, however, Congress has two major devices to constrain the FTC effectively: massive budget cuts and legislation reducing or eliminating FTC powers (either in general, such as rule-making power, or authority over particular industries). The environment must be so unfavorable, however, that legislation will pass both houses and be signed by the president. The more likely the legislation is to constrain the Commission, the less likely it is to pass (all else being equal), given the Commission's ability to manipulate the political environment.[21] Thus, the FTC does not require extensive influence or support in Congress before congressional controls over the agency become, as a practical matter, ineffective.

As 1979 ended, the political environment did appear to be unfavorable, and new legislation constraining the FTC was likely.[22] The possibility of new legislation affects the FTC in at least two major ways. First, it may influence the career incentives of FTC officials, as discussed in Chapter 15. Second, and related, the staff may act to reduce the threats of new legislation. For example, in late 1979, the Commission was seriously considering modifying its unpopular funeral and used-car trade rules.[23]

Even in a hostile political environment, the FTC retains considerable freedom in the absence of the new legislation. Most controversial FTC programs continue unabated, and the Commission's budget continues to grow.[24] Moreover, an unfavorable environment is not likely to be a continuous and pervasive constraint. Based on past FTC history, a highly unfavorable environment will probably be of short duration. Further, serious informational problems remain, limiting the Congress's ability to constrain the Commission, except for a few highly visible programs.

Finally, the nature of the legislative process itself limits the ability of Congress to impose constraints on the FTC, even with new legislation. Explicit legislative authority or prohibitions may harm all parties involved, because the final approved legislation may be the product of compromise resulting in provisions that no single member of the Commission or Congress desired in the aggregate. For example, in 1977, Congress defeated proposed amendments to the FTC Act that were designed to increase FTC power by giving the Commission additional procedural rights and permitting private enforcement of FTC trade regulation rules in cease and desist orders.[25] Over the FTC's opposition, the amendments also would have included a one-house veto power. The House and the Senate disagreed over various sections of the bill, and it never became law.[26]

II. Congressional incentives and control of the FTC

Thus, despite the increased time Congress has spent in monitoring the FTC, in the absence of an "unfavorable" political environment, Congress has had little impact on directing or redirecting resources within the Commission since 1970. This lack of influence is largely the product of the structure of Congress itself.

First, most of the work of Congress is organized in committees.[27] Because appointments to committees dealing with the Federal Trade Commission are not those most sought out by members of either the House or the Senate,[28] committee members often come from the ranks of lower seniority, including newly elected Congress members. The lower status of committees monitoring the FTC and the lower level of experience of Congress members on those committees reduce the effectiveness of congressional control of the Commission.

Second, a large number of competing interest groups makes demands on Congress.[29] For our purposes, these groups can be generally classified as bureaucrats, businesses, consumers, and taxpayers. Interest groups affect Congress in two important ways. The very nature of an interest group dictates that its lobbying and other political resource activities will focus on options that benefit its members as opposed to the population as a whole. In addition, incentives of members of Congress are similar to those of the interest groups. Constituents who receive aid will often credit their representative for being at least instrumental in delivering the benefits. In return, politicians receive rewards in the form of electoral support and campaign contributions.[30]

The existence of interest groups has important consequences for the incentives and ability of Congress to control the Federal Trade Commission. Different interest groups will seek different benefits, and interest-group objectives will often conflict, resulting in a variant of the "voters' paradox." For example, a coalition of interest groups may prefer policy A over policy B, another B over C, and a third C over A.[31] Thus if no single position commands a majority and interest groups have similar strength, Congress members will have considerable freedom in choosing among alternative policies, because a majority may be formed by combining any two coalitions to support any of the three policies.

A further implication of interest-group politics is that the information and complaints that Congress and the Commission receive seldom are representative of the population as a whole. In an empirical investigation of consumer participation in Federal Trade Commission proceedings, LaBarbera found that consumers who actually communicated with the Commission came from groups that contained more older, better educated, and relatively affluent whites than the public at large. Furthermore, these consumers were also more negative toward the marketplace than the public at large was and correspondingly favored more government regulation to "protect" the consumer.[32] Thus, treating these individuals as speaking for consumers as a class, as the Commission sometimes does, is a mistake.

A third significant aspect of the relationship between the structure of Congress and control over the FTC is that the incentive of individual Congress members to monitor the FTC is less than for many other agencies. The FTC's budget is relatively small, and it does not hand out subsidies, resource rights, or other direct benefits that individual groups seek. Of course, FTC decisions do have harmful or beneficial effects on producing and consuming groups, some of which provide major political support to members of Congress. Given that Congress has not narrowed the FTC's range of actions, however, it will be harder to turn these impacts into a form of political subsidy than to similarly use direct monetary subsidies. This conclusion also follows because the Commission may reprogram its resources to take from one program and give to another one.

Fourth, the general inability of Congress to monitor individual FTC programs implies that Congress will neither seek complete information nor engage in excessive questioning during FTC hearings. Although it is impossible for us to formulate a specific test to reject or accept this implication, an examination of appropriation hearings from fiscal years 1970 through 1979 generally confirms our prediction. The official records suggest that Congress members use incomplete information in reviewing the proposed budget. For example, an examination of hearings during the entire 1970s reveals that beyond the brief FTC budget summaries, information about FTC programs was rarely provided to either the Senate or the House, presumably because it was not requested.[33]

Even more revealing are the number and types of questions asked the Commission during the hearings. Our own reading of the congressional questions for each of the hearings from fiscal years 1970 through 1979 suggests a definite pattern.[34] As Table 3.3 reveals, there are not only few questions, but the questions merely seek general information, such as the amount allocated for enforcement of the textiles and fur acts or the number of cases instituted under Section 7 of the Clayton Act. The Commission was also asked to explain certain processes, such as rule making and case selection, or to provide status reports for particular programs. While the Congress may use its power to influence the Commission agenda, such monitoring places few, if any, constraints on the agency.

Finally, our examination of FTC hearings during the 1970s reveals that they are occasionally used by Congress to "duck" issues rather than to monitor the Commission. For example, in 1974 the FTC, at congressional urging, spent a number of person-years investigating the "shortage" of canning lids.[35] This investigation, which produced no cases, was finally stopped after public pressure subsided, permitting the Commission to redirect its resources to other tasks. The canning-lids episode does illustrate the Congress's ability to "convince" the Federal Trade Commission to investigate a particular practice. Although the Congress may use its

Table 3.3. *FTC Congressional Oversight and Appropriations Hearings: budgets, documents, and major questions: fiscal years 1970–9*

Budget and documents	Major questions on:
FY 1970	
House (complete budget with no additional documents)	1. Method of choosing cases 2. General counsel's record for appeals 3. Merger increases 4. Fair packaging and labeling 5. Truth in lending, Washington, D.C., consumer protection program
Senate (summary budget with no additional documents)	1. Complaint procedure 2. Truth in Lending Act 3. Conglomerate mergers, FTC merger guidelines 4. Textiles and furs
FY 1971	
House (complete budget and statistical analysis of Robinson-Patman enforcement, 1934–date)	1. ABA and Nader reports 2. Activities of field office attorneys 3. Low number of pending cases
Senate (no budget and no additional documents)	1. ABA Report 2. Truth in lending 3. Effect of House budget cuts 4. Power to issue cease and desist orders
FY 1972	
House (complete budget and no additional documents)	1. Functional areas of the FTC 2. Transfer of 21 investigators out of textiles and furs 3. Shift in Commission priorities 4. Nader and ABA reports 5. Need for additional field office positions 6. Close down of cases
Senate (complete budget and letter charging lack of oversight)	1. Sufficiency of budget 2. Deemphasis of Bureau of Economics 3. Role of regional offices 4. Structure of various industries
FY 1973	
House (complete budget and FTC response to Appropriations Committee report on the FTC)	1. Policy planning after the ABA and Nader reports 2. Use of injunctive powers 3. Low productivity of hearing examiners 4. 1970 reorganization 5. Electrical, pharmaceutical, and auto industry studies
Senate (summary budget and no additional documents)	1. Natural gas reporting 2. Reduction in truth in lending and textile activities 3. Effects of OMB budget cuts 4. ABA Report—policy planning and ex parte communications 5. FTC flexibility as compared to courts

Table 3.3. (*Cont.*)

Budget and documents	Major questions on:
FY 1974	
House (complete budget and no additional documents)	1. FTC response to energy crisis 2. Number of cases heard by administrative law judges 3. Impact of policy planning task force 4. Drop in FTC cases in 1972 5. Effectiveness of compliance vs. enforcement 6. Reprogramming of funds
Supplementals (FTC requests for additional funds)	1. Review of Federal Energy Administration allocation regulations 2. Food industry study 3. Unauthorized furniture expenses
Senate Oversight	1. Increased autonomy of regional offices 2. Activities in children's advertising 3. Ex parte communication 4. Need for more cost/benefit analysis 5. Rule-making procedures
FY 1975	
House (complete budget and no additional documents)	1. Line-of-business program 2. New emphasis on office of executive director 3. Posner FTC advertising study 4. Administrative law judge workload and case backlog 5. Energy and food industry studies, cigarette warnings
Senate (summary budget and no additional documents)	1. Exxon case and children's advertising 2. Turnover rate in legal staff
FY 1976	
House (complete budget and House Appropriations Committee staff report)	1. Equipment expenditures and increased travel costs 2. Follow-up procedures to criticism of FTC 3. Dropping of condominium study 4. Resources devoted to various programs
Senate (no budget, FTC food chain report, FTC line-of-business supporting statement, journal articles on patents and market structure and concentration)	1. Line-of-business program 2. Magnuson-Moss–FTC Improvements Act
Oversight	1. Delays in promulgating rules and guides 2. Failure to respond to outside group requests for rules 3. Lack of new management information system effectiveness of unfair and deceptive advertising efforts
FY 1977	
House (complete budget and no additional documents)	No questions
Senate (complete budget and no additional documents)	No questions

Table 3.3. (*Cont.*)

Budget and documents	Major questions on:
FY 1978	
House (complete budget and no additional documents)	1. Original FTC budget requests to OMB 2. Energy, transportation, cigarette, and condominium programs 3. Rent and travel expense increases 4. Increase in mergers and joint ventures 5. Cost breakdown for various programs
Senate (complete budget and no additional documents)	1. Program contracts 2. Cost/benefit for line-of-business program 3. Function of Bureau of Economics
FY 1979	
House (complete budget and Pertschuk speech before New England Antitrust Conference)	1. Criticism of regional office setup 2. Food and children's advertising studies 3. Auto industry investigation 4. Antitrust policy effectiveness
Senate (complete budget and no additional documents)	No questions

Source: Congressional Oversight and Appropriations Hearings, 1969–78.

power to influence the Commission's agenda, starting an investigation does not make FTC law enforcement mandatory or even likely, particularly when the agency decides merely to study the problem and report its findings to Congress.

In sum, we conclude that in addition to Congress's limited powers to control individual programs of the Commission, individual members, facing numerous competing interests, will lack the incentive to control most FTC activities. Thus, unless their interests can be combined as they probably were in 1969 and 1970 (see Chapter 15), or unless some interest groups have influence greatly in excess of others, as producer groups appeared to have in late 1979, Congress will not exercise extensive control over the Commission.

III. Modifying congressional control: the legislative veto

In recent years, Congress has sought more effective control over the independent and executive agencies, including the FTC. Congress has considered and sometimes used explicit prohibitions, directives, and refusals to appropriate expenditures.[36] It has also proposed important legislation. For example, in May 1978 the House Appropriations Committee adopted an amendment to the FTC appropriation expressing concern with the First Amendment ramifications of banning certain television advertising. In the same month, the House refused to appropriate funds for the FTC without passage of the authorization bill, which amended the FTC Act to provide a legislative veto.[37]

The legislative veto, a device by which Congress (or one house thereof in some proposals) may stop proposed regulations or actions of independent or executive agencies, has recently gained popularity in Congress and elsewhere,[38] with the measure pending in Congress at the time of this writing. Some find the legislative veto a promising form of congressional control:

While a legislative veto requires routine submission of rules to Congress for review, in its absence oversight committee hearings occur sporadically and thus do not provide a regular opportunity to negotiate the substance of rules with agency personnel. . . . In contrast with these traditional oversight techniques, review under a legislative veto scheme is specifically and narrowly focused on the substance of proposed rules. Thus, the veto, unlike any of the traditional oversight techniques, permits regular and systematic examination of the substantive details of an agency's program.[39]

Others find that the veto would invite "political review" of the Commission, giving lobbyists and members of interest groups additional leverage in influencing agency behavior.

Resort to the legislative veto does indicate that other methods of controlling the FTC have not been effective. The FTC has become increasingly unpopular with many Congress members, who apparently realize that their effective control over the agency is minimal. Although the veto would increase the constraining power of Congress – particularly when an interest group is much more powerful than its competitors – not even this measure would effectively constrain the Commission. First, the veto would only occasionally be an effective tool. The volume of rules that the Commission passes will likely be so great, the information necessary to evaluate them so vast, and the political pressures surrounding rules so diverse that continuous, close scrutiny of the agency remains unlikely. Although a few Commission rules might be politically sensitive, Congress, even with its large support staff, is unlikely to muster the capacity or interest to comprehend the dozens of rule provisions that the FTC is likely to pass.

Second, because the legislative veto would place more direct responsibility on the Congress, it would increase the difficulty of "solving" ("ducking"?) problems by referring them to an agency. It is not clear that Congress members desire to exercise such controversial responsibility. Third, the necessity in Congress for compromise may well dilute the effectiveness of the legislative veto as a constraint. Finally, given congressional procedures, each regulation would probably be treated in combination with other measures by means of "logrolling." Some Congress members will find a veto less attractive when it is linked with a proposal they favor.[40]

For these reasons, direct control of the Commission's behavior by the legislative veto does not have a high probability of success. In other words, the legislative veto is unlikely to provide consistent and direct control over Commission resource allocation.

IV. Conclusions

The ability of Congress to monitor individual FTC activities effectively is limited. Its most effective tools are budget cutting and legislation. Yet these tools are most difficult to employ regularly and require an intense political climate that is historically rare and of brief duration. Even with its most effective tools, Congress can redirect resources into or away from specific programs only after detailed analysis at a level beyond the institutional competence of Congress except on an, at most, occasional project. Producer and consumer groups often exert pressure through Congress and occasionally force hearings or even investigations. They are usually unsuccessful, however, in redirecting FTC resources without widespread political support. Oversight and ad hoc monitoring seldom influence Commission activities, although they do cause the Commission to expend valuable resources in responding to them.

4   Judicial constraints

TIMOTHY J. MURIS

This chapter considers the limits that courts place on the Commission's substantive powers.[1] Our principal concern is whether the Commission or the courts determine the standard for legality when the agency challenges a business practice. Or, put in a form perhaps more comfortable to lawyers: Assuming no dispute over facts, will the courts routinely allow the FTC to decide whether those facts constitute illegality?[2] For example, when the Commission finds an advertisement to be unfair or deceptive within Section 5 of the FTC Act, to what extent will the reviewing courts allow the agency to define what is lawful?

We focus primarily on Section 5 of the FTC Act, which allows the Commission to prohibit "unfair methods of competition" and "unfair or deceptive acts and practices." The cases we discuss are from the Courts of Appeals and the Supreme Court, the only two levels of the federal court system that regularly review FTC substantive decisions. Because Commission substantive orders are appealable directly to the circuit courts, the district courts render few substantive decisions. From the circuit courts, the cases can be appealed to the Supreme Court. Finally, because decisions prior to 1970 not only have influenced, but to a major extent have determined, the current attitude of the courts toward the Commission, we will necessarily consider many cases decided before 1970.

We begin with early decisions indicating that the courts would constrain the Commission's prerogative to act in the way it chose (i.e., by limiting the agency's ability to define illegality). Next, Section II explains the shift toward great deference to the FTC, giving it, at least as to Section 5, almost limitless discretion in defining what commercial practices are illegal. Section III then explores the scope of judicial deference in more detail by considering the cases in the 1970s. Finally, Section IV discusses whether some of the most recent FTC and other administrative law cases indicate that the courts are becoming less reluctant to curtail the FTC's discretion.

35

I. Early decisions: judicial attempts to limit Commission discretion

During the Commission's first 16 years, three Supreme Court cases indicated judicial reluctance to grant the Commission wide discretion. In the 1920 *Gratz* decision,[3] the Commission alleged that the respondent engaged in what was in effect a tying arrangement illegal under Section 3 of the Clayton Act and Section 5 of the FTC Act. When the Commission argued that the practices were unfair because they hurt other firms, the Second Circuit Court of Appeals reversed, asserting that the practices "must be at least such as are unfair to the public generally."[4] On appeal, the Supreme Court considered whether the courts or the Commission would determine what methods of competition are unfair, deciding that: "It is for the courts, not the commission, ultimately to determine as matter of law what they [unfair methods] include."[5] In what eventually became the majority position of the Court, Justice Brandeis dissented, arguing basically that the FTC should decide what is unfair.[6]

In *Klesner*, decided nine years later, the respondent appeared to be, in effect, telling consumers that his products were those of another proprietor. The Supreme Court found that the filing of the complaint was not in the public interest, in part because whatever confusion the alleged deception may have caused had largely been dissipated by the time the Commission acted.[7] Addressing the matter of FTC power, the Court stated that "the mere fact that it is to the interest of the community that private rights shall be respected is not enough to support a finding of public interest. To justify filing a complaint the public interest must be specific and substantial."[8]

Finally, in 1931, the Court decided *Raladam*.[9] The Commission had charged that the respondent misled consumers in representing an obesity remedy. In considering whether the challenged practices were "methods of competition" proscribed by Section 5, the Court again denied the FTC the power to define legality:

It is obvious that the word "competition" imports the existence of present or potential competitors, and the unfair methods must be such as injuriously affect or tend thus to affect the business of these competitors – that is to say the trader whose methods are assailed as unfair must have present or potential rivals in trade whose business will be, or is likely to be, lessened or otherwise injured. It is that condition of affairs which the Commission is given power to correct, and it is against that condition of affairs, and not some other, that the Commission is authorized to protect the public.[10]

With this trio of decisions, court review of the FTC was not limited to asking if the facts indicated that the alleged practices took place; instead, the courts, not the Commission, determined important policy issues such as whether a practice was unfair or its prohibition in the public interest.

II. The courts shift: the ceding of discretion to the Commission

In analyzing the shift of judicial attitude towards the FTC, Section II.A discusses three crucial 1930s decisions signifying the shift. Then, Sections II.B and II.C consider the extent of the shift by analyzing court review of FTC findings of illegality in consumer protection and antitrust cases. Next, Section II.D analyzes the important 1972 Supreme Court decision, *S&H*. Section II.E considers court review of Commission orders and, finally, Section II.F summarizes the consequences of the changed judicial attitude toward the FTC.

A. *The Supreme Court in the 1930s*

First, in the 1934 decision of *Algoma Lumber Co.*,[11] the respondent sold what it called "California white pine," in actuality a form of yellow pine. Finding that white pine was superior to yellow, the Commission held that the representation was unfair. The circuit court disagreed, arguing that the facts did not show that yellow was inferior.[12] The Supreme Court reversed the circuit court, strongly admonishing the lower court for paying only "lip service" to the statutory requirement that Commission findings of fact are conclusive if supported by testimony. More important in terms of the development of the relationship of the courts to the FTC, the Court implied that the FTC had broad discretion in deciding which practices were illegal, asserting even that "[i]f the equivalence [between genuine white and California white] existed, the practice would still be wrong."[13] Further, the Court implied that whether or not consumers were harmed, the FTC was correct to consider the practice to be corrupting and injurious. In other words, the Commission may not have to show consumer injury. This deference to the Commission, together with the admonishment that the circuit courts should pay more attention to the Commission's findings of facts, apparently had an immediate effect on the lower courts.[14]

The same year, in *Keppel,* the Court brushed aside *Raladam* and read *Gratz* narrowly.[15] When the respondent introduced the element of chance in the sale of candy, with some pieces containing the purchase price within the wrapper, the Commission found that this form of lottery was unfair, especially harming children. Because the sales tactic diverted trade, thereby harming competitors, the Supreme Court agreed with the Commission rather than with the circuit court's finding that the practice was legal under *Raladam* as long as competitors could adopt the same technique. As to *Gratz,* the Court noted that the Commission was created to be a body of experts and that, "While this Court has declared that it is for the courts to determine what practices or methods of competition are to be deemed unfair . . . in passing on that question the determination of the Commission is of weight."[16]

Three years later the Court decided *Standard Education Society*.[17] The respondent sold encyclopedias, telling consumers (among other things) that the initial set of encyclopedias was free and that they had only to pay for a loose-leaf supplement, received annually for 10 years and known as an extension service. Speaking for the Court of Appeals, Learned Hand affirmed parts of the Commission order, but found that the Commission went too far in finding deception in the representation that the initial set of encyclopedias was given away:

The Commission . . . [should] bring trade into harmony with fair dealing . . . . To the discharge of that duty it should not, however, bring a pedantic scrupulosity; too solicitous a censorship is worse than any evils it may correct, and a community which sells for profit must not be ridden on so short a rein that it can only move at a walk. We cannot take seriously the suggestion that a man who is buying a set of books and a ten years' "extension service" will be fatuous enough to be misled by the mere statement that the first are given away and that he is paying only for the second. Nor can we conceive how he could be damaged were he to suppose that that was true. Such trivial niceties are too impalpable for practical affairs, they are will-o'-the-wisps, which divert attention from substantial evils.[18]

A unanimous Supreme Court disagreed. Responding to Hand's statement, Justice Black argued:

The fact that a false statement may be obviously false to those who are trained and experienced does not change its character, nor take away its power to deceive others less experienced. There is no duty resting upon a citizen to suspect the honesty of those with whom he transacts business. Laws are made to protect the trusting as well as the suspicious. The best element of business has long since decided that honesty should govern competitive enterprises, and that the rule of *caveat emptor* should not be relied upon to reward fraud and deception.[19]

Further, Black rejected the notion that the FTC must confine itself to weightier matters: "To fail to prohibit such evil practices would be to elevate deception in business and to give it the standing and dignity of truth."[20] Thus, the Supreme Court blessed, indeed encouraged, Commission inquiry into trivia.

B. Commission consumer protection cases[21]

Taking an extremely dim view of consumers' intelligence the Commission, with judicial support, brought case after case aimed at practices as apparently innocuous as those in *Standard Education*. Moreover:

General stupidity is not the only attribute of the beneficiary of FTC policy. He also has a short attention span; he does not read all that is to be read but snatches general impressions. He signs things he has not read, has marginal eyesight, and is frightened by dunning letters when he has not paid bills. Most of all, though, he is thoroughly avaricious. Fortunately, while he is always around in substantial numbers, in his worst condition he does not represent the major portion of the consuming public.[22]

No matter how stupid the FTC assumed that some consumers were, the courts refused to curtail the agency. For example, in 1965 the Supreme Court upheld a Commission finding that the continual offering of paint on a "buy one, get one free" basis was deceptive because the second can was not actually "free," although the practice apparently benefited consumers by encouraging price competition.[23] Further, when an advertiser claimed that a hair application could "color hair permanently," the Commission ruled that the claim was illegal because some people might believe the product would color hair that had not yet grown out of the scalp. The Second Circuit, constrained by the Supreme Court's command to defer to the FTC, affirmed.[24]

As to the standard of deception, the courts eased the FTC's burdens considerably by concluding that actual deception was unnecessary; instead, the FTC need only show a "tendency or capacity to deceive."[25] Coupled with the standard for judicial review of Commission actions – a Commission finding would be affirmed if supported by substantial evidence on the record – this test for deception made it virtually impossible to reverse Commission findings of deception.

If this were not enough to show the freedom of the Commission in the area of deception, the courts also stated that the meaning of an ad is a matter committed to the discretion of the FTC.[26] As one author stated, "this modest sounding rule is a principal reason that the Commission has managed to prevail in the appellate courts in the overwhelming majority of its [advertising] decisions that have been appealed."[27] Moreover, the Commission can determine how consumers understand an advertisement without even sampling public opinion.[28]

C. Antitrust

As explained in Chapter 2, the Commission can enforce the Clayton Act, an antitrust statute, as well as use Section 5 to bring what otherwise would be cases under the Sherman Act, another antitrust statute. When the Commission brings a case under either a Sherman or Clayton Act theory, the courts have not felt themselves bound to defer completely to the Commission in defining illegality. Instead, the Commission is held to the court-made principles of antitrust law when bringing its cases under those principles. Nevertheless, when reviewing the Commission's antitrust work, the circuit courts in effect treat FTC findings of fact like those of a trial court. If the Commission when sitting as a judge gives its prosecuting staff more favorable treatment than the federal district courts give private plaintiffs or the Antitrust Division of the Department of Justice, then the

Commission has an advantage in the circuit courts that private plaintiffs and the Antitrust Division do not enjoy.

In its "pure" antitrust cases, the FTC has had mixed success. With the Robinson-Patman Act (Section 2 of the Clayton Act), the agency has lost several cases because the courts have often been hostile to that statute.[29] Indeed, four of the nine cases that the FTC has (at least partially) lost in the Supreme Court since 1934 involved the Robinson-Patman Act.[30] With the other sections of the antitrust laws, however, the courts, particularly the Supreme Court, have until recently been much more favorable to the government. For example, until the mid-1970s, the rule of merger cases seemed to be that "the Government always wins."[31] Because the Court exhibited the same degree of approval for Department of Justice antitrust enforcement, this trend suggested no special deference to the FTC.

The Commission, however, need not proceed as if it were the Antitrust Division, bringing the case under only a Sherman or Clayton Act theory. If the Commission brings an antitrust case that would not necessarily be won under an antitrust statute, the agency may claim that the practice nevertheless violates Section 5. Both legislative history and the Supreme Court give the FTC at least some power to so act. As to the legislative history, both the FTC and Clayton acts reach practices not violative of the Sherman Act.[32] As to the Court, its decisions support FTC antitrust activity outside the parameters of antitrust laws.

For example, in *Brown Shoe* the Court considered "whether the Federal Trade Commission can declare it to be an unfair practice for Brown . . . to pay a valuable consideration to hundreds of retail shoe purchasers in order to secure a contractual promise from them that they will deal primarily with Brown and will not purchase conflicting lines of shoes from Brown's competitors."[33] Relying upon *Gratz*,[34] the circuit court had answered no. The Supreme Court replied that the *Gratz* majority had been rejected and that, as Brandeis had said in dissent in *Gratz,* the FTC has broad powers to declare trade practices unfair. The Court argued that Brown's "program obviously conflicts with the central policy of both Section 1 of the Sherman Act and Section 3 of the Clayton Act against contracts which take away freedom of purchasers to buy in an open market." Further:

Brown nevertheless contends that the Commission had no power to declare the franchise program unfair without proof [of in effect a Clayton Act violation]. . . . Our cases hold that the Commission has power under Section 5 to arrest trade restraints in their incipiency without proof that they amount to an outright violation of Section 3 of the Clayton Act or other provisions of the antitrust laws.[35]

At least two major problems arise concerning this passage as authority upon which to rest expanded FTC antitrust in the 1980s. First, the Supreme Court in a 1977 decision appeared to disagree that the central policy of the antitrust laws deals with freedom, either of competitors or purchasers.[36] Instead, the Court implied that economic analysis, under which some practices that limit freedom could be justified, should be the foundation of antitrust. Second, because the Clayton Act was intended to deal with incipient Sherman Act violations, an "incipient" Clayton Act violation is a peculiar concept. The meaning of "incipient incipiency" is unclear.

Despite these questions, FTC powers undoubtedly extend beyond the antitrust laws. In the *S&H* decision of 1972, the Court asserted this point in its most recent, and potentially most far-reaching, pronouncement on the relation of Section 5 to the antitrust laws and on the power of the FTC to determine standards for illegality. We now turn to that decision.

D. *S&H*

S&H, the owners of Green Stamps, attempted to prevent commercial exchangers and redeemers who, among other things, offered discounts in return for stamps without S&H approval. When the Commission argued that S&H's practices restrained trade under the principles of antitrust law, the Court of Appeals for the Fifth Circuit disagreed, holding that the practices did not violate either the letter or the spirit of the antitrust laws.[37] Only when it came before the Supreme Court, nine years after the proceeding began, did the Commission apparently shift its attention from antitrust considerations to focus on a new theory: S&H had committed an unfair act or practice. To the Court, whether the FTC could attack S&H's practices as unfair turned on (1) whether Section 5 empowered the Commission to proscribe practices as "unfair" that did not violate either the letter or spirit of the antitrust laws, and (2) whether Section 5 empowered the Commission to proscribe practices as "unfair" because of their effect upon consumers regardless of their nature or quality as competitive practices or their effect upon competition. The Court found that the Commission has these powers:

Legislative and judicial authorities alike convince us that the Federal Trade Commission does not arrogate excessive power to itself if, in measuring a practice against the elusive, but congressionally mandated standard of fairness, it, like a court of equity, considers public values beyond simply those enshrined in the letter or encompassed in the spirit of the antitrust laws.[38]

In terms of the relationship between the Commission and the courts, this decision has at least three notable characteristics. First, and probably least important, the case demonstrates one form of judicial check upon the FTC: A reviewing court will not affirm the agency on a theory that was not raised in the FTC hearings on the matter. *S&H* is in a very narrow sense a defeat for the FTC. The case was remanded to the Commission because the agency had tried it on an antitrust theory, the Court of

Appeals had held that the practices did not violate either the letter or spirit of the antitrust laws, and in the Supreme Court, the Commission had not attacked this conclusion of the Court of Appeals. Second, in stating that the Commission considers public values beyond those in the antitrust laws, the Court has arguably moved beyond *Brown Shoe*. It is one thing to say that the Commission can stop incipient Sherman Act (or even Clayton Act) practices before they become antitrust violations, but an entirely different point to permit the Commission to go beyond the policies of the antitrust laws. Finally, the court may have given the Commission nearly limitless discretion in defining "unfairness." *S&H* may free the Commission to find "public values" where it will, subject to minimal court review. Because the Commission has only started to test the powers of *S&H* (see, e.g., the FTC proposal to rewrite credit contracts discussed in Chapter 13), however, it is too early to tell.

E. Enforcement of FTC orders

Having left to the Commission the question of what commercial practices violated Section 5, the courts still could have curtailed the FTC's freedom by carefully limiting the agency's orders. The Supreme Court, however, has mostly resisted attempts to so restrict the agency. The 1946 *Siegel* decision revealed the Court's position. The Commission had found that Siegel's use of a trade name was misleading, and the court discussed the propriety of the order provision forbidding the use of the trademark: "The Commission is the expert body to determine what remedy is necessary to eliminate the unfair or deceptive trade practices which have been disclosed. It has wide latitude for judgment and the courts will not interfere except where the remedy selected has no reasonable relation to the unlawful practices found to exist."[39]

Although this often repeated test has given the Commission wide discretion in framing orders, unlike the question of legality under Section 5, the courts have not completely committed the question of what order is appropriate to the discretion of the agency. The courts have somewhat constrained the Commission in drafting orders by occasionally overturning an order or, more frequently, part of an order.[40] Courts give several reasons for reversing or remanding order provisions. For example, the order may be too vague, cover a practice or theory not part of the agency's case, or be too broad in the sense of covering a limitless set of activities.

An important distinction exists between judicial questioning of FTC orders and questioning of the FTC's determination of legality. Most of the reasons for setting aside an order provision involve poor lawyering by the agency, a defect that can be corrected. For example, once an order is remanded or overturned because the FTC sought on review to justify it by a theory not argued before the Commission (as happened in *S&H*), the Commission can avoid this problem in the future concerning identical business practices. On the other hand, if the courts found a certain practice legal under Section 5, the Commission would be powerless to prevent that practice in the future. Given the agency's freedom as to what commercial acts violate Section 5, court review of Commission orders thus serves more to caution the Commission to be careful than to limit the substantive areas that the agency can regulate.

F. Summary

The courts place almost no restraint upon what commercial practices the FTC can proscribe,[41] as even some high-level FTC staff members candidly admit. For example, when Robert Pitofsky was asked whether Section 5 constrained the Bureau of Consumer Protection, of which he was then director, he responded:

Never! Section 5 is the most marvelously flexible instrument of consumer protection that I could imagine. I have often said that if it were any vaguer it would probably be unconstitutional. It cuts across the whole area of industrial and marketing practices. Furthermore, courts have been extraordinarily generous with the Commission in terms of interpretation of the statute. We have the capacity in this agency to review virtually every consumer protection problem that's going to come up. . . . We can, in effect, get into anything.[42]

Besides such evidence concerning the freedom of the FTC, some additional evidence can be gleaned from the Commission's record in the Supreme Court on substantive cases. Before 1934, the agency won only four of 12 cases; from 1934 until 1958, it won 12 of 21, and since 1958 has won each of the 17 cases before the Court.[43] Further, of the nine (at least partial) losses since 1934, four involved the Robinson-Patman Act, a traditional area of judicial hostility. None of the others held that a practice was within the reach of Section 5, yet still lawful; instead, the Commission lost on grounds such as lack of jurisdiction because the practice was not in interstate commerce or because the practice was exempt from FTC scrutiny due to another statute.[44]

We do not assert that the Commission will always find that the practice before it violates the law. For a variety of reasons, respondents do win in the FTC. For example, the staff may be unable to prove the facts as alleged in the complaint or a majority of the commissioners, often not members when the complaint was approved, believe that the facts as proven should not constitute a violation. Our point is not that companies charged with violating Section 5 always lose, but that the courts have little influence as to the substantive grounds determining victory or defeat.

It is time to return to the 1970s. We next consider whether the defer-

Table 4.1. *Substantive FTC court of appeals cases: 1970–8*

Year	Won	Partially won	Lost
1970	4	2	1
1971	3	1	2
1972	3	1	0
1973	5	1	0
1974	3	2	1
1975	4	1	0
1976	1	4	0
1977	2	4	1
1978	3	1	0
Total	28	17	5

Source: The list of cases before 1977 was obtained from FTC Statutes and Decisions, 1977 cases from the agency's budget justification to Congress for fiscal 1979, and cases for 1978 from the CCH Trade Regulation Reports.

ence of the courts to the FTC has continued in the last decade. Although we shall see in Section IV that the attitudes of the courts may be shifting, most 1970s cases reaffirmed the enormous freedom of the FTC.

III. The FTC and the courts: the 1970s

Table 4.1 summarizes the FTC's record on substantive cases in the circuit courts of appeal during the 1970s. If only part of the order was upheld, the case is listed as a partial victory, even if the part reversed was insignificant.

Although a partial defeat in 44 percent of the cases might seem to indicate a shift from wide judicial deference to more careful scrutiny, a closer look at the cases belies that impression. First, the Commission did not lose (even partially) a single case because the practice under question was not an unfair method of competition or an unfair or deceptive act or practice within Section 5. Further, the courts affirmed important expansions of Commission authority, such as corrective advertising and advertising substantiation.[45] Third, the courts continued to affirm antitrust cases under a Section 5 theory when it was not clear that the Commission would win under a pure antitrust theory.[46] Finally, prohibition of a merchandising claim that probably few, if any, consumers would misunderstand was upheld in 1974 despite a strong attack by a dissenting circuit court judge and a dissenting commissioner that the problem was too trivial for FTC concern and that there was no proof of public injury.[47]

Analysis of at least three of the five defeats also reveals business as usual. Two of the three involve strictly procedural matters. In one, the

Commission lost when it did not follow its own rules and when Commissioner Dixon prejudged the matter.[48] In the other, involving a game of chance, the court held that the Commission's action was arbitrary because the FTC only regulated the practice in some industries while in this case the agency totally banned it.[49] The third Commission order was reversed because the Commission had found a violation based upon a theory neither in the complaint nor before the hearing examiner.[50]

The other two defeats may reveal a different judicial posture. The fourth defeat occurred because the court held that the Commission lacked the power to order restitution.[51] This issue is now of diminished importance, however, because Congress subsequently allowed the Commission to pursue such a remedy. Finally, the fifth defeat involved only the Clayton Act.[52] It may, therefore, represent a different attitude of the courts toward antitrust, a topic discussed in the next section.

Of the 17 cases that the Commission lost in part, four involved Commission failure to try the case on the theory apparently underlying the challenged provisions of the order.[53] Three concerned various sections of the Clayton Act under which the courts do not totally defer to the Commission regarding the determination of legality.[54] Three other cases also typify the deference discussed in Section II. In one, an order provision was overturned as too broad when the Commission gave almost no justification for the provision; in another, part of the order was too vague; and in a third, among the Commission's errors was its attempt to remedy wrongs that the agency specifically found were not committed.[55] The seven remaining cases, however, indicate a potential for a new, more careful judicial scrutiny of the Commission.

IV. The courts and the Commission in the 1980s: will the Commission's discretion be constrained?

Recent first amendment, administrative law, and antitrust decisions indicate some shift in the courts' attitude. We will discuss each in turn.

A. The First Amendment

As Supreme Court decisions have given commercial speech some First Amendment protection,[56] advertisers have argued that the Constitution curtails the FTC. Thus far, the main constraint has been upon FTC orders. From 1970 through 1978, parts of four Commission orders were struck down because they infringed First Amendment rights. An important example is *Beneficial Corporation*.[57] Finding deception in part of a marketing scheme in which Beneficial implied that it made loans to consumers who anticipated tax refunds, the Commission prohibited the words "instant tax refund." Although it affirmed the agency as to deception, the Third Circuit nevertheless struck down the prohibition of the challenged phrase:

[W]e are dealing in this case with the government regulation of a form of speech. The first amendment requires, we believe, an examination of the Commission's action that is more searching than in other contexts. . . . [T]he remedy for the perceived violation can go no further in imposing a prior restraint on protected commercial speech than is reasonably necessary to accomplish the remedial objective of preventing the violation.[58]

An unresolved issue under the First Amendment concerns whether the Commission can regulate nondeceptive advertising merely on the grounds of unfairness. Because the Supreme Court has focused on preventing deception to justify regulating commercial speech, perhaps promoting fairness cannot justify an FTC order. For example, the Commission's advertising substantiation program, making it illegal to advertise a claim without prior substantiation of its veracity, may not be allowed to apply to claims that, when challenged, can be demonstrated as truthful.[59]

The Supreme Court has stated that deceptive commercial speech can still be regulated, a proposition that the circuit courts have already reaffirmed in specific FTC contexts.[60] Nevertheless, it is unclear how the First Amendment will affect, if at all, the FTC's ability to find deception when only a small number of individuals would consider the advertisement misleading. Further, will the Commission be able to rely on its own reading of the advertisement, even if the overwhelming majority of consumers understand the ad in a different, and nondeceptive, manner? These issues have yet to be resolved.

B. Are courts changing their attitude toward agencies?

Until about 1960, what has come to be known as the "traditional" view of administrative law reigned supreme. Still reflected in many opinions today, this view was mainly concerned with limiting an agency to actions authorized by its statutes and with guaranteeing "fairness" in agency application of its mandate.[61] Underlying the traditional view was confidence in the competence of the administrative state to perform its assigned tasks without extensive court supervision. The long-standing judicial deference toward the FTC appears at least partially a product of this traditional view. This view, however, cannot reconcile the resulting enormous power and discretion of agencies with the idea that intrusions into the rights of individuals can be allowed, if at all, only by the legislature. Consequently, the traditional view is losing some of its force.

Recently, courts have placed more stringent requirements upon agencies, particularly in their rule-making activities. Many of these cases closely scrutinize the decisions of agencies to see precisely what empirical data and analytical resources the agencies use in making those decisions.[62] Although much of the traditional concern of administrative law is for "fairness," these new cases may also be arguing for "competence."

What does all of this mean for the FTC? Although many precedents support broad agency discretion, including the 1972 *S&H* decision, the Commission is not necessarily immune from changing judicial attitudes toward the administrative state. Indeed, two factors suggest that the Commission will be affected. First, the Commission is no longer involved with trivia. As noted in Chapter 1 and shown in more detail in Part II, many current Commission activities have enormous potential impact upon consumers. Second, although it is too early for them to indicate a trend, four recent cases seem to place more stringent requirements upon Commission orders than those of previous cases.

Ger-Ro-Mar,[63] decided in 1975, is the first of these decisions. The Commission attacked a scheme to merchandise lingerie and similar items through what appeared to be a pyramid selling system. Using a mathematical formula, the FTC argued that the number of people attempting to sell the goods would very quickly reach a level at which there would not be enough customers available. The court found that, although the agency's abstract principle was correct, it had not considered the realities of the marketplace. More important for us, the court stated that the courts, not the Commission, are to decide what unfair competition is, a distinct throwback to the era of the 1920s. Although the Commission offered no evidence of harm to consumers other than its formula, the court's deference appears less than traditional. The court simply refused to rely upon the Commission's judgment without stronger factual support.

Next, in the 1977 *Chrysler Corporation* case,[64] Chrysler claimed that *Popular Science* magazine tests showed that its small cars realized better fuel economy than did the Chevrolet Nova. Although the court affirmed the Commission's finding that this claim was deceptive, the court struck out two paragraphs of the FTC order as too broad. One paragraph prohibited representing the results of tests unless the "representation fully and accurately reflects the test results and unless the tests themselves were so devised and conducted as to completely substantiate each representation concerning any characteristic tested." The court said that this was potentially limitless and found that another provision, prohibiting petitioners from "misleading in any manner . . . the purpose, context or conclusion of any text . . . ," was limitless. Because the FTC conceded that the violations were unintentional, not continuing, and confined to only two of 14 advertisements, the court found no rational justification for the sweeping provisions. Thus, the court applied its own standard rather than leaving entirely to the Commission's discretion the establishment of criteria for the remedial order provisions.

In the other two cases, the violation was also unintentional. In both, the court struck out part of FTC orders as too broad, citing the lack of bad faith.[65] Further, one of the cases, *Standard Oil of California*, decided in 1978, appeared to question the agency's freedom to determine the standard for deception. The Commission had found that advertisements for a gasoline additive, F-310, were deceptive, in part because they allegedly implied that the additive would completely reduce pollutants. The court disagreed, stating that it did "not think that any television viewer would have a level of credulity so primitive that he could expect . . . [complete reduction]."[66] Finding that the record did support "the Commission's interpretation of the meaning the commercial would have to the average viewer," the court affirmed the agency as to other theories of why the ads were deceptive. Nevertheless, an average viewer standard is a far cry from affirming FTC orders designed to protect only fools.

C. A change in antitrust?

As discussed above, when the FTC brings an antitrust case under what is essentially a Sherman or Clayton Act theory, a court may apply a tougher standard of review by not deferring to the FTC determination of the standards for legality. This standard had traditionally affected only Robinson-Patman Act cases, about which the courts were never as enthusiastic as the FTC. Under the leadership of the Supreme Court, the courts routinely allowed the government to win cases under other antitrust statutes, preventing the potential tougher review for non-Robinson-Patman cases from becoming a reality. In the past few years, however, the Supreme Court has taken a new tack in antitrust. The government has lost merger cases, and the *Schwinn* doctrine, long a staple of private plaintiffs and to some extent of the FTC, was repealed.[67] Thus, a very real possibility exists that the FTC will no longer be so successful under Sherman or Clayton Act theories.

Through 1978, the 1977 *BOC International* decision is the only example of this possibility.[68] The FTC essentially argued that an acquisition of a large firm in an oligopolistic market violates Section 7 if the acquiring company would at some future date enter either de novo or through acquisition of a firm lacking a significant market share. The Supreme Court has refused to rule whether such circumstances violate Section 7.[69] When the Commission stated that a finding of reasonable probability of *eventual* entry was sufficient to find illegality, the Second Circuit reversed the Commission, stating that the FTC must show that the acquiring firm would have entered the market in the *"near"* future. The court was *not* saying that no substantial evidence existed to support the Commission's finding. Instead, the court concluded that the Commission applied the wrong legal standard.

As earlier discussions of *Brown Shoe* and *S&H* indicate, however, the Commission can proceed beyond the antitrust laws. The Commission has used this power in Section 5 as a "gap filler." In other words, when a practice that would violate one of the antitrust laws could not be reached for some jurisdictional reason, the Commission would use Section 5. For example, the FTC has successfully used Section 5 to reach buyer conduct that violated the policy of the Robinson-Patman Act but was not directly proscribed by the Act's prohibitions on sellers.[70]

Cases like *BOC International,* however, raise another possible use for Section 5: Can the FTC find an act to be illegal under Section 5 that is within the reach of the Sherman and Clayton acts and legal? Although there is language in many cases to the affirmative, the scope of this power is in doubt.[71] It also raises numerous problems. For example, what are the appropriate legal standards, given that application of antitrust standards does not result in a violation? Will the Commission be forced to articulate some theory of illegality that will inform businesses of the scope of legal conduct, or will the courts grant the Commission wide discretion in defining unfairness on a case-by-case basis? Further, when a Clayton Act type of case is involved, the problem that we have already mentioned arises – defining "incipient incipiency."

V. Conclusions

This chapter has asked whether, and to what extent, the courts limit the Commission's freedom to pursue whatever substantive policies it chooses. Since the mid-1930s, the courts have deferred to the agency as long as the case uses a Section 5 theory. Only regarding the orders that the FTC can draft is court review somewhat of a constraint, but more to require the agency to be careful in building its case than to prevent the FTC from pursuing a particular policy. Thus, the claim often made within the FTC that the Commission is merely a "law enforcement agency" cannot be sustained.[72] The FTC is an administrative agency. As such, it does not merely bring cases under statutes whose boundaries and standards are judicially determined. Within very broad limits, the agency determines what shall be legal. Indeed, the agency has been "lawless" in the sense that it has traditionally been beyond judicial control.

But we have noted that the FTC's relationship with the judiciary may be changing. It is too soon to conclude that a trend exists. Whether such a trend *should* exist is the subject of much of the rest of this book.

5 Executive constraints

KENNETH W. CLARKSON

This chapter considers constraints that arise from the White House, the Office of Management and Budget, the Civil Service Commission,[1] the Justice Department, the General Services Administration, and other executive agencies. Like the congressional and judicial constraints, we consider those that arise from the executive branch as external to the Commission, although Commission employees may occasionally help shape these constraints.

I. The White House

White House involvement with the Federal Trade Commission consists largely of appointments, agency reorganization, scrutiny of major issues, and the budget process.

A. Appointments

Today, the appointment of the commissioners is an important constraint on the Commission. The power to appoint the chairman is particularly significant because of the influence he or she has within the Commission, as discussed in Chapter 15. From the mid-1930s until at least 1970, however, the Federal Trade Commission had the reputation as an agency "steeped in political patronage,"[2] and as a "political dumping ground" where "positions were openly given because of personal connections and political patronage, with Southern Democrats receiving the lion's share."[3] Thus, presidents used their appointive power more to grant favors than to influence FTC activities. Beginning with Weinberger (see Chapter 1), this has changed. Congress also influences the appointments process, although more substantially when the president and the majority of the Congress come from different political parties. Thus, a White House advisor during

50

the Nixon administration commented that "there were a number of instances where we did have to yield" in appointments.[4]

Once appointed, the Commission independently selects its own staff. During Kirkpatrick's tenure, for example, Robert Pitofsky (Director of the Bureau of Consumer Protection) and Michael Mann (Director of the Bureau of Economics) were "card-carrying activist Democrats" whose political affiliations were well known by the Nixon administration. Even though high-level appointments customarily required White House review, such review was more of "a formality and act of courtesy" than an exercise of a veto.[5] In short, once appointments of commissioners and chairmen are made, White House involvement is sporadic at best.

B. Reorganizations

By its very nature, major restructuring of the Commission occurs less frequently than appointments, but permits more White House involvement. If so motivated, the president can effect a reorganization by appointing a chairman committed to his own views on restructuring the Commission. As the White House wanted major changes in the FTC, President Nixon's appointment of Caspar Weinberger in 1970 illustrates this power.

In 1977, the Senate Committee on Government Operations reported that four critical elements would produce a successful reorganization. First, the White House and top advisors must make a substantial commitment to agency reorganization. Second, the White House must select an agency head who shares that commitment and possesses the qualities necessary to implement it. Third, a detailed analysis and evaluation of existing agency structure and personnel must be made. Fourth, the new agency head must have the cooperation and support of the White House because it can sometimes influence the outcome of the reorganization.[6] These requirements are illuminating. Not only must the incentives of the FTC decision makers be taken into consideration, but there must also be cooperation among the interested parties.

C. Budget Process

The most potent White House constraint, other than designation of the chairman, involves the budget. In practice, however, presidential involvement in the budget process does not appear to bind the Commission to any large extent despite the fact that a president who does not like what the Commission is doing can reduce the budget. Although the White House·could conceivably recommend to Congress a large shift in the FTC budget, it has not been so inclined. Rather, the White House prefers to leave the budget issue to the Office of Management and Budget (OMB).

Once the budget has cleared the initial OMB review, the White House exercises little control over any individual FTC program. On rare occasions, however, the White House will become involved in major issues. Like other agencies, however, White House resources are scarce and, given its relatively small budget and the hundreds of Commission activities, the White House can monitor, let alone direct, only a tiny percentage of them.[7]

II. Office of Management and Budget

A. Budget process

The formal budget review process begins early in each calendar year when OMB sends the FTC an "allowance letter," specifying budget ceilings and discussing various issues confronting the agency. Next, there is a spring review, which may include a meeting between FTC and OMB officials to pinpoint major issues for the following budget season. Such meetings between FTC and OMB officials occur only two or three times annually. After the spring review, OMB sends a planning allowance letter, which again may discuss major issues. For example, the budget for the Exxon case was discussed at the spring review, with OMB's thoughts on that issue transmitted in the planning allowance letter.[8]

The next major interaction between the two agencies occurs in September, when the FTC submits its appropriations requests to OMB with supporting documents. During the following few months, an OMB examiner extensively reviews the requests, spending approximately half of this time analyzing major issues confronting the agency and the rest acquiring background information.[9] Following the examiner's review, the director of OMB normally spends one morning reviewing the FTC and several other regulatory agencies. The director concentrates on changes in appropriations within the agency. Following that session, approximately one hour of the president's time has traditionally been spent reviewing several agencies, including the FTC.

The OMB's recommended FTC budget submission to Congress,[10] called the OMB "mark," emerges from this OMB review. OMB traditionally reduces the Commission's request, with the difference generally arising over the resources needed to accomplish the Commission's missions. In former years the Commission has requested that OMB maintain a balance between consumer protection and antitrust in arriving at its mark,[11] resulting in a relative increase from the previous allocations for antitrust activities. Because both the Commission and the executive branch favored this reallocation, it cannot be classified as an executive branch constraint.

Since the advent of zero base budgeting in the late 1970s, OMB's instructions to the Commission have become more detailed. The list of program priorities that OMB receives from the Commission runs program by program to a minimum budget, a current budget, and an expanded budget. After arriving at a total dollar amount that it wishes to budget for the FTC, OMB examines the programs that would not be funded with the chosen budget level. OMB therefore may now be making some indirect determination about marginal programs, the margin being defined by the total budget that OMB recommends (OMB, however, has made little effort to rerank the Commission's programs). During the late 1970s, the OMB allowance exceeded the current budget, but fell below the expanded budget. After it receives the OMB mark, the Commission usually opposes in writing some of the OMB's proposed budget cuts. These analyses may result in restoration of some of the funds cut initially.[12]

The OMB budget review process is most effective on the FTC budget as a whole. Specifying the allocation between the two major bureaus is less effective because the Commission retains considerable flexibility in specifying its activities. For example, the Commission has attacked restrictions on advertising through both the Bureau of Competition (BC) and the Bureau of Consumer Protection (BCP). Thus, a reduction, for example, in total BCP funds would not necessarily cut back activities that the Commission desires to undertake. In addition, OMB faces problems similar to those of Congress in gathering current, complete information about the FTC.

Although OMB's ultimate authority and the repeated contact between OMB and FTC officials would seem to make administration scrutiny of the Commission a potentially significant constraint on Commission behavior, the results of the process suggest that no significant OMB constraint exists. Table 5.1 shows the impact of OMB decisions on the FTC budget requests for fiscal years 1971 to 1979. Despite the potential for an OMB constraint, the Commission has not curtailed or eliminated any ongoing major projects or activities and has received increased resources.[13] OMB has consistently increased FTC budget authority from year to year, except for government-wide personnel freezes.[14] Perhaps more important, throughout the 1970s the administration has viewed the FTC favorably. Because the president appoints the chairman, an attack on the agency would be an implicit criticism of the president's judgment, and thus the favorable environment between the administration and the agency is probably the norm.

B. Informal contacts

In addition to the formal budget process, informal contacts between OMB and FTC officials occur throughout the year. The OMB examiner receives

Table 5.1. *Impact of OMB decisions on FTC, fiscal years 1971–9*

Fiscal year	Funding		Number of positions	
	FTC request to OMB[a] (thousands of dollars)	OMB allowance[a] (thousands of dollars)	FTC request	OMB allowance
1971	$29,982	$23,615	1,922	1,477
1972	25,996	25,189	1,494	1,462
1973	30,428	26,854	1,625	1,417
1974	37,080	32,236	1,748	1,570
1975	56,374	39,479	1,859	1,631
1976	53,907	47,443	1,780	1,682
1976 (T)[b]	13,829	12,543	1,780	1,682
1977	62,334	55,053	1,849	1,692
1978	69,496	62,611	1,874	1,694
1979	70,927	66,485	1,869	1,760

[a] Includes all supplemental requests.
[b] Transition quarter.

monthly staffing reports, various budget information, and the FTC News Summary. OMB personnel generally make a few informal visits to the FTC each year, and occasionally representatives of the two agencies meet informally at OMB.[15]

C. Additional constraints

The Office of Management and Budget can also affect the FTC by other methods. For example, OMB issues a number of guidelines or circulars designed to constrain agencies in their research allocation activities.[16] Although little evidence exists about the impact of these regulations, they do not appear to play an important role in the Commission's day-to-day decision making.[17] The Commission itself, in formal documents submitted to the Congress, has totally ignored some of the circulars that were intended to guide FTC decisions.[18] Further, OMB usually comments on FTC-suggested legislation and other congressional proposals. During the early 1970s, however, the agency's power increased dramatically, and OMB did not oppose any of the Commission's requests for expansion of its statutory authority.[19]

D. Overall effect

Despite its potential influence on the Commission's total budget, OMB has not had much influence on the allocation of particular resources within the Commission. Consequently, OMB and the White House affect the overall size of the agency, but not the directions of FTC policy. During the 1970s, however, even the ability to limit the overall budget could hardly be called a constraint on the FTC because its budget more than tripled. We turn, therefore, from budgetary to personnel control as a potential constraint.

III. The Civil Service Commission

The FTC faces a wide variety of policies in appointment, retention, and promotion of employees, with many of these policies stemming from laws and regulations administered by the Civil Service Commission. FTC positions may be either competitive or noncompetitive. Competitive positions are subject to rigorous Civil Service Commission requirements as to hiring, promotion, and firing, leaving the Commission with less flexibility in dealing with such employees than with noncompetitive positions. Competitive positions at the FTC include the administrative law judges, economists, consumer protection specialists, administrative personnel, secretaries, typists, and certain other nonattorney positions. Noncompetitive positions at the FTC include attorneys, who comprise approximately 75 percent of Commission professional employees.[20] Traditionally top staff positions, such as the Secretary, General Counsel, Assistant to the Chairman, the Director of Office of Policy Planning, and the Director of the Bureau of Economics,[21] were also noncompetitive and thus exempt from Civil Service regulations. Recent reforms, however, may give top staff who qualify for Civil Service positions additional protection. The potential constraining effect of this increased protection is uncertain at this time.[22]

Termination procedures for Commission employees depend upon whether the employee is (1) in the competitive service; (2) a preference-eligible individual, such as a veteran, or (3) in the exceptive service. Individuals in the competitive service or with an eligible preference and one year or more of tenure are guaranteed specific procedural rights before termination. Civil Service Rules pertaining to hiring, promotion, pay increases, and firing specify how these employees must be treated. Although the Civil Service constraint may be important for the employees covered, it has no significant effect on most FTC professionals, because they are exempt from Civil Service requirements.[23] The major restriction on discharge of those employees is that the employee not be discharged for unconstitutional reasons, such as exercising the right of free speech.[24] This greater flexibility allows for the use of more discretion with regard to hiring and firing of noncompetitive employees. This discretion was demonstrated in the 1970 reorganization discussed in Chapter 1. During that reorganization, Chairmen Weinberger and Kirkpatrick replaced at will many FTC attorneys without having to answer to the Civil Service Commission.

Although the Commission has more flexibility in dealing with its attorneys and with many upper-level positions, it is still somewhat constrained by the government pay scale. Initial compensation for attorneys and other key employees in the lower and medium levels is competitive with comparable positions outside the FTC. The maximum level for salary growth, however, is limited, and is usually quickly reached, causing the turnover rate of FTC attorneys to nearly double that of private law firms.[25]

The Civil Service Commission further constrains the FTC with its authority to disapprove any supergrade (GS-16 or above) positions. Such approval is often denied, causing the Commission to lose qualified people whom it is unable to promote or cannot hire from the outside at the position and salary it desires.[26]

To summarize, even though the Civil Service Commission does have a significant influence on some FTC personnel matters, its overall impact on the Commission's policy and choice of activities has been minimal.

IV. Department of Justice

Prior to the Magnuson-Moss Warranty and Federal Trade Commission Improvements Acts of 1975, the Justice Department could constrain the FTC through its authority to approve FTC cases brought in the courts. In practice, however, the constraining effect of this approval power appeared to be minimal.[27] In any event, the Magnuson-Moss Act decreased the FTC's dependence on the Justice Department by allowing the FTC to represent itself in cases concerning injunctions, consumer redress, review of substantive rules or adjudicative orders, and enforcement of compulsory process. Further, the act allowed the Commission to seek certiorari on adverse circuit court decisions merely by informing the attorney general of the exercise of its authority in the specific case before proceeding on its own.

The Commission must still refer possible criminal violations (primarily certain forms of price fixing) to the Justice Department for prosecution. Further, when the Commission seeks civil penalties, when a party sues to enjoin the Commission, or when a party seeks documents under the Freedom of Information Act, the Justice Department must act within 45 days, or the Commission may proceed on its own. Of course, if the Justice Department does handle a case, Commission lawyers generally have substantial input in its preparation. The Justice Department's right of first refusal on certain FTC actions usually does not represent a major constraint on the Commission (unless the department takes the rare step of announcing its intention to oppose the FTC openly in court). It does, however, represent enough of an impediment for the Commission to desire the authority to represent itself in all civil cases involving its regulatory functions. The FTC complains that the current procedure causes confusion and wastes time because Commission attorneys must educate Justice Department lawyers on the facts as well as on Commission practice and procedure.[28]

The Department of Justice's and FTC's joint enforcement of the antitrust laws lends itself to a close working relationship between the two agencies. Pursuant to a 1948 agreement, whenever one agency initiates a new investigation, it sends to the other a card disclosing the nature of the investigation. If the other agency has no similar matter pending, then the submitting agency proceeds without any further liaison. If the other agency is active in that area, liaison occurs before the new investigation continues.[29] Although the relationship between the FTC and the Antitrust Division is generally harmonious (perhaps because each agency has carved out its own principal litigation areas), this liaison can lead to tension. Potential problems include one agency advising private parties on matters under common jurisdiction and both wanting the same case (e.g., an important merger).[30]

V. Other administrative constraints

A number of other agencies interact with the FTC in varying degrees. The General Services Administration, for example, effectively controls office space for the Commission. Further, formal and informal relationships with several executive agencies require coordination of certain acitivities in areas of overlapping jurisdiction. Included are the Department of Agriculture, the Federal Energy Administration, the General Accounting Office, the Department of Transportation, the Environmental Protection Agency, the Consumer Product Safety Commission, the Department of Health and Human Services, the Veterans Administration, the Federal Reserve Board, the Department of Housing and Urban Development, the Securities Exchange Commission, the Postal Service, and the Federal Communications Commission.

Potential conflicts exist between the FTC and these other agencies. If the Commission, for example, aggressively pursues a matter that another agency feels is within its own jurisdiction, that agency might directly attempt to dissuade that Commission activity or may attempt to put pressure on the Commission through OMB. There is no evidence that these other agencies significantly constrain Commission substantive activities.

VI. Conclusions

Only a few meaningful executive constraints affect the substance of FTC action. First, the White House can change the direction of FTC policy by its appointment of commissioners, particularly the chairmen, who share

White House goals. The significance of the appointment power, however, can be more limited when the president and Congress are of different parties. Second, OMB has an impact through its power to trim and, less dramatically, shape the FTC budget before it reaches Congress. Although this power is potentially significant, its use in the past decade has at most postponed action. Third, the salary scale contributes to rapid turnover, which in turn has consequences for FTC behavior that are discussed in Chapter 15. Finally, the Justice Department Antitrust Division occasionally constrains particular FTC investigations or cases.

Part II

Nature and consequence of FTC actions

Introduction

In this part, several scholars analyze major FTC cases and rules, considering their impact upon consumers. To evaluate whether the Commission has improved since 1969, this is *the* crucial issue. At that time, the Commission was condemned for ignoring or even harming consumers; the Commission's improved reputation stems from its perceived role as a staunch consumer protector.[1] Thus, this reputation stands or falls based upon the real impact of FTC actions upon consumers. To determine that impact, the authors employ economic analysis. Economic analysis is necessary to assess FTC performance even when the Commission's goal is not to help all consumers. For example, if the FTC is attempting to help the poor at the expense of other consumers or to help businesses at the expense of consumers, economic analysis can determine whether the Commission has accomplished its goal.

We divide our inquiry along the two major substantive bureaus of the agency, competition and consumer protection, and use activities selected on the basis of two criteria. First, we cover the major components of the work of the two bureaus, making our analysis comprehensive. Second, some matters are important in themselves, not merely because they represent a class of FTC actions. To choose these matters, we relied both on our evaluation of what was major and on Commission statements made in response to congressional inquiries in 1976 and 1978. For example, in early 1976, Senator Moss asked the Commission to compile the "twenty-five most significant steps" that the agency took during the previous 10 years to improve consumer welfare. A similar request was made in 1978. As indicated below, most of the projects analyzed are from these two lists.

I. Bureau of Competition

The Commission's antitrust work in the 1970s has received extensive praise in Congress, within the Commission, and in many quarters of the academic community.[2] Despite varying opinions of whether current FTC antitrust enforcement is praiseworthy, a general consensus exists that the Commission has moved, in significant part, from the trivial to the substantial. This consensus undoubtedly reflects widespread knowledge of the fewer Robinson-Patman cases, the nearly quadrupling of FTC antitrust funding from 1970 through 1979, the Commission's major suits to restructure the oil and cereal industries, its consent agreement with Xerox, and its current major investigations of the automobile industry and of various parts of the chemical industry. With Chairman Pertschuk's appointment by President Carter in early 1977, Commission antitrust activities promised to take an even more expansive and important role. Particularly in the first year of their tenure, Pertschuk and other top FTC officials contended that antitrust enforcement should not be narrowly tied to economic considerations, but should instead consider broad social objectives such as corporate responsibility, the alleged political power of large corporations, and possible noneconomic benefits of a diversified economy.[3]

Wesley J. Liebeler, professor of law at the University of California, Los Angeles, and former director of the Federal Trade Commission's Office of Policy Planning and Evaluation, begins the specific evaluation of competition activities with a detailed overview of FTC antitrust since 1970. He provides a comprehensive analysis of the various subcategories into which FTC competition activities fall. In the process, Liebeler addresses several major substantive issues, including whether FTC antitrust has indeed changed in the 1970s, whether the cases enhance the welfare of consumers, and whether the antitrust activities of the Commission have followed generally accepted economic principles or whether, and to what extent, they are based on alternative theories.

The remaining three chapters each involve an individual project that the Commission has listed in its 25 most important recent activities. First, Kenneth Elzinga and William Breit, industrial organization and antitrust specialists from the Department of Economics at the University of Virginia, analyze the Commission's line-of-business program. Under this program, large manufacturing companies must report certain financial data, including costs, sales, and profits, by individual product lines. Although the Bureau of Economics is primarily responsible for this program, we include it in our discussion of antitrust enforcement because the Commission apparently intends to use it in part to pursue one of its major antitrust projects, namely its inquiry into the legality and economic necessity of the current structure of the American economy.

Next, Charles Goetz, an economist from the University of Virginia School of Law, and Warren Schwartz, a lawyer from the Georgetown University Law School, evaluate the Commission's Xerox consent order. In *Xerox,* the Commission negotiated a consent agreement to improve competition by lowering what it felt was the "patent barrier" that Xerox had erected. The case is significant both because of the importance of the industry and because the Commission considers it to be the one outstanding success in its major effort to improve the competitive condition of concentrated industries.

Finally, together with Donald L. Martin, an economist at the Law and Economics Center of the University of Miami, we evaluate the Commission's prohibition of certain restrictive covenants in shopping center leases. These cases represent numerous actions in which the Commission seeks to improve competition by attacking practices that are said to be exclusionary.

II. Bureau of Consumer Protection

As with antitrust, the FTC's consumer protection work, severely criticized prior to 1970, has undergone significant change. A recent consensus among observers of the Commission is that the current consumer protection activities – for which the budget in 1979 was nearly three times larger than the budget in 1970 – now focus on matters of great importance to American consumers. Controversy exists, however, about whether the benefits of the actions exceed the costs. This controversy grows as the Pertschuk Administration moves into more detailed regulation of an increasing number of activities, such as its recent proposal to prohibit certain advertising aimed at children.

Because the diversity of the Bureau's work makes unmanageable a single paper such as Liebeler's competition overview, the next few paragraphs provide some summary remarks concerning BCP's projects and the specific impact evaluations that follow. For pedagogical convenience we divide the work into three main topics, rule making under Section 5 of the FTC Act, advertising, and special statutes. These categories overlap because at least some of the FTC's advertising matters involve Section 5 rule making and because some work under special statutes involves rule making, although it is often under procedures of the special statute in question. Activities within these three categories have resulted in Commission efforts to regulate the substantive terms of contracts, to require mandatory disclosure of information, to require businesses to make restitution to consumers either in dollars or in goods or services, to regulate advertising so that certain claims cannot be made until other stringent requirements are met, and to institute rules designed to eliminate government restraints upon competition. The following chapters consider all these activities.

Probably the major change in the Bureau since 1969 is its increased reliance upon rule making, particularly since the FTC Improvements Act became law in early 1975. At least half the BCP is now engaged in rule making,[4] under which the agency is reshaping the rules of conduct for entire industries. The power that rule making allows the FTC is potentially enormous, leading to the description of the agency "as the second mos powerful legislature in America."[5] Three chapters evaluate the FTC's use of this rule-making power. We begin with an overview of the FTC's rule making efforts by Dorsey Ellis of the University of Iowa College of Law Two additional chapters deal with specific FTC rules: one, by Louis De Alessi of the University of Miami School of Law, and Law and Economic. Center, considers the proposed mobile homes rule; the other, by Richard Peterson of the Credit Research Center at the Krannert Graduate School of Business at Purdue University, evaluates the proposed creditors' reme-dies rule.

Besides evaluating in detail Commission handling of proposed rules the De Alessi and Peterson chapters serve two vital functions. Probably most significantly, the projects studied represent an important trend within the Commission, namely, increased regulation – either through rule making or adjudication – of the practices of entire industries. The Com-mission has proposed detailed rules regulating the pre- and postpurchase relationships between consumers and producers. Of the many FTC activi-ties that involve such regulation, we have chosen the creditors' remedies and mobile home rules as specific examples.[6] Further, these chapters, particularly Peterson's, allow us to examine carefully the Commission's use of its broad power to attack "unfair" practices under the *S&H* case discussed in Chapter 4.

Of the non-rule-making activities, perhaps the most controversial, most influential, and best known is its regulation of advertising. This area con-sumes roughly 25 percent of the BCP's budget. Indeed, particularly in the early 1970s, new and stricter regulation of advertising was the centerpiece of the "revitalized" FTC. The agency's support for and claims about the effectiveness of its advertising cases continue today. Mark F. Grady, now a professor at the University of Iowa College of Law, and formerly acting director of the Office of Policy Planning and Evaluation and attor-ney advisor to Commissioner Calvin J. Collier, analyzes FTC advertising cases.

Finally, we consider the FTC's consumer protection work under stat-utes other than Section 5 of the FTC Act. Although, as explained in Chap-ter 2, this work is of much less importance today than it was prior to 1970, the Magnuson-Moss Warranty Act of 1975 has large potential impact. This Act interposes significant federal influence on the relationship be-tween buyers and sellers regarding warranties attending the sale of con-sumer products. Further, it delegates authority to the Commission to pre-scribe rules and regulations for the content of warranties and contract remedies. George Priest of the University of California, Los Angeles, School of Law analyzes this major statute.

6 Bureau of Competition: antitrust enforcement activities

WESLEY J. LIEBELER

Almost a decade has passed since Miles Kirkpatrick became chairman of the Federal Trade Commission and set about to rejuvenate its antitrust enforcement program. That is time enough to provide a basis on which to evaluate that effort. It is appropriate to ask whether the Commission's performance has significantly improved, as much public comment and its vastly increased budget would seem to suggest.

To answer that question I examine the antitrust decisions and settlements made and complaints issued by the Commission from January 1, 1970, to December 31, 1977 (hereafter "the period"). I have classified them as shown in Table 6.1.

I evaluate these cases by the standard of maximizing consumer welfare, a goal reached when society's resources are allocated so that the costs of any reallocation would exceed its benefits.[1] I proceed on the assumption that the Commission is not bound blindly to follow existing law in the antitrust and trade regulation field. As discussed more fully below, this assumption is based on the Commission's wide discretion as to which cases to bring or not to bring and on the proposition that its presumed economic expertise should put it in the position of a leader in the application of economic analysis to antitrust theory. I discuss first the FTC's "industry-wide program," its major innovation in antitrust enforcement since 1970. I divide consideration of the remainder of its antitrust enforcement work into horizontal and vertical categories.

I. The industry-wide cases

In recent years the FTC has budgeted upwards of 40 percent of its total antitrust enforcement resources to various industry-wide cases scattered in several categories of its program budget.[2] These matters include the petroleum industry litigation and an investigation of the automobile industry, both separate programs in the budget, and the breakfast cereal case,

65

Table 6.1. *FTC antitrust cases, 1970–7*

Type of cases	Number of cases	Percentage of total
Vertical		
Resale price maintenance	42	16.5
Other vertical restraints	38	15
Vertical mergers	18	7
Robinson-Patman Act cases	52	20.5
Industry-wide cases	2	1
Total vertical matters	152	60
Horizontal		
Horizontal mergers	51	21
Horizontal contract restraints	28	11
Industry-wide cases	6	2
Total horizontal matters	85	34
Section 8 Clayton Act matters	15	6
Total matters	254	100

included in the food program. The industry-wide program itself has included investigations of the household detergent industry and the household appliance industry as well as litigation in such diverse industries as office copiers, automobile crash parts, title insurance, and automobile rentals. None of these cases has yet reached a final trial decision, and of the major cases only the office copiers matter (Xerox) has been settled. As that case is discussed in Chapter 8, I will confine my discussion primarily to the development of the Commission's industry-wide cases and to the economic theory that underlies them.

A. *The attempt to apply cost/benefit analysis*

The Commission's industry-wide approach to antitrust enforcement was largely a response to its critics of the late 1960s, who found it to be "imperative" that the Commission establish goals, priorities, and effective planning controls. The principal response was an effort to apply cost/benefit analysis to the Commission's antitrust activities. This effort peaked in the early part of 1972, when 100 industries were ranked in terms of the potential gains to society claimed to be available in them from "shared monopoly" and from antimerger cases. This ranking was done under a model developed primarily in connection with proposals to mount a general attack on concentrated industries. These proposals led to the Commission's industry-wide approach to antitrust enforcement.[3]

The model on which this ranking was based was the only attempt the Commission staff made systematically to apply cost/benefit analysis to the antitrust case-selection process. But the model was never accepted by the Commission itself, and no serious, sustained effort seems to have been made by the staff to use it in the case-selection process.

Although there appear to have been many reasons why the proposed cost/benefit model failed to win acceptance within the Commission, the eventual reason given was that the model could not operate effectively on available data. Even though its proponents had initially claimed that the model could operate on existing data, they had also recognized that line-of-business data were desirable. The problem was that profit rates, on which the model depended so heavily, were available only on a company-wide basis, and most larger companies operated in more than one industry. There were no pure "industry" profit rate figures available. The proposed model's need for more disaggregated data led directly to the FTC's controversial line-of-business (LB) reporting program, which is discussed in Chapter 7. Although some supported the LB program for other reasons, one of the major reasons for its creation was the need to obtain figures to make the proposed cost/benefit model work. There is some irony in the fact that although the cost/benefit model has been abandoned by the Commission, the LB program continues. The Commission's eventual public position was, in effect, that LB had been substituted for the previously proposed cost/benefit model.[4] But an information-gathering program is not a case-selection process. Without a coherent theory or model with which it can be used, the information produced by LB will be largely without meaning.

Just as numbers cannot have meaning without some theory, some theories cannot work even with perfect numbers. I believe this to be the case with the cost/benefit model originally proposed. Its underlying theory was mistaken. Although this had nothing to do with its rejection by the Commission, it does relate to the question of whether the FTC has made, or is able to make, the changes in its case-selection process that its critics urged. The fact that one (perhaps the principal) purpose of LB was to produce information for a deficient model raises additional questions, both as to the structure of LB and as to the uses to which the information that it produces will eventually be put. But first we must consider the deficiencies of the cost/benefit model that the staff originally proposed to use in selecting cases in its industry-wide program.

B. The market-concentration doctrine

The theory underlying the original cost/benefit model, which theory appears to continue to guide the case-selection process in the industry-wide program, assumed a direct relationship between high industry concentration and deficient competition; it also ignored the possibility that antitrust action could increase production and marketing costs.[5] The first assumption is based on the so-called market-concentration doctrine, which predicts a positive relationship between high industry concentration and high profit rates on the hypothesis that collusion is more likely to occur as concentration rises and that higher profit rates are generally associated with collusion. The important thing to note is that this doctrine relies on collusion, either tacit or explicit, to make the link between high concentration and deficient competition. The assumption of a direct relationship between those two conditions points attention away from collusion as the appropriate subject of inquiry. It also forecloses other possible explanations of a correlation between high concentration and high profit rates, most notably superior efficiency.

Consider an industry in which one firm has about half the market and a return on equity of about 20 percent and in which two other firms have market shares of 25 and 15 percent with returns on equity of 13 and 12 percent, respectively. Smaller firms with an average return of 10 percent make up the rest of the industry. Suppose also a relatively high advertising/sales ratio and significant product differentiation. If the industry had appreciable sales, the FTC staff would almost certainly undertake further investigation. But high concentration, coupled with high profit rates, does not support an inference of tacit or explicit collusion. The high *industry* profit rates are explained by the superiority of one firm, the large market share of which raises the average industry profit rate above the average. If one firm in an industry is more profitable than its rivals, it must have lower costs or produce more highly valued products. If so, at least some of the time, the theory underlying the FTC's current industry-wide efforts would prompt further investigation of efficient, noncollusive industries.

This would be inefficient even if collusion and competitive superiority explained an equal number of correlations between high concentration and high profit rates. Even if the FTC dropped all cases of competitive superiority after a preliminary investigation, waste would result about half the time. But the problem is worse; recent research shows that competitive superiority is more likely to explain high profit rates in concentrated industries than is collusion.[6] If so, any case-selection process based on the theory underlying the FTC's original attempt to apply cost/benefit analysis to antitrust cases seems likely to produce perverse results.

Competitive superiority in an industry is suggested by an uneven distribution of profit rates among its constituent firms, which suggests differential efficiency (again, either in terms of lower costs or in producing superior products). Although a dispersion of profit rates does not rule out collusion, a dispersion like the one in the hypothetical industry discussed above, where the higher profit rates of one firm raise the industry average above the norm, certainly negates any inference of collusion that might be drawn from high industry profit rates alone. This suggests that if antitrust cases are to be selected on the basis of profit rates, the emphasis should be on the differences in *firm* profit rates within the industry, particularly on the difference in profit rates between larger and smaller firms. The presence of such differences should raise a presumption against antitrust enforcement action.

Besides assuming a direct link between high concentration and deficient competition, and thereby suppressing the issue of whether collusion or competitive superiority explains any association between high concentration and high profit rates, the FTC's theory also ignores the possibility that deconcentration could adversely affect productive and marketing efficiency. The theory suggests that a decrease in profit margins caused by deconcentration would lead directly to a decline in market price. This overlooks the fact that industry-average profit margins can be decreased in at least two different ways. They can be cut, as the theory assumes, by reducing market price with costs remaining the same. They can also be reduced, however, by increasing the costs of one or more firms in the industry or by shifting production to less efficient firms with prices remaining the same or even rising.

Consider deconcentrating the hypothetical industry discussed above by creating two new firms with 15 percent of the market each and leaving the dominant firm with only a 20 percent share. If the sources of the dominant firm's superior profit performance could not be divided and transferred to the new firms, we would not expect their costs to be lower than those of the preexisting smaller firms. Thus, costs would rise for 30 percent of the industry's production, and, if economies of scale at least in part explained the low costs of the old dominant firm, the new, smaller dominant firm's costs will rise as well. The industry-average profit margin would decline, but price could drop only if the old smaller firms had been colluding *and* if adding two more firms would prevent such collusion in the future. If neither of these were the case, deconcentration would produce an unambiguous net social loss. Costs would rise to produce social losses, and prices would not decline to produce offsetting benefits.

Suppose, however, that collusion is present and some of the efficiency-producing assets of the dominant firm are divisible and, therefore, transferable to its artificial offspring without total loss of their efficiency-producing characteristics. Then deconcentration could lower price without totally destroying the advantages of lower costs or superior products associated with the competitive superiority of the dominant firm. Those price declines would not, however, necessarily produce net social gains; they may be offset by cost increases also occasioned by the deconcentration. Such increases will be present unless the factors responsible for the superior profitability of the dominant firm are completely divisible and transferable without any loss in efficiency to the new firms created by the dissolution.

Because the Commission's theory assumes that the costs of all firms in an industry are approximately the same both before and after deconcentration, the Commission staff did not address the question of the extent to which the sources of competitive superiority might be divisible. As a result, no real showing has even been attempted, let alone made, that the sources of competitive superiority are divisible and, therefore, transferable in a deconcentration proceeding in such a way that will not increase production and/or marketing costs. I offer no definitive estimate here of the extent to which this may be the case. I venture the speculation, however, that divisibility would not often be likely, if for no other reason than that the rivals of the firm(s) holding assets on which competitive superiority is based have not been able to bid them away from the dominant firm(s) or otherwise to replicate them. Although this would not necessarily suggest indivisibility if the asset were something like the most advantageously located source of high-grade ore, it certainly would suggest indivisibility if no asset like that appeared to be involved.

In the absence of complete divisibility, however, dissolution of a competitively superior firm will increase costs to some degree. If those increased costs exceed the welfare gains from any price decline that might result from deconcentration, the "remedy" would produce net social losses. Any true cost/benefit analysis of shared monopoly cases must take both factors into account: productive efficiency losses must be traded against allocative efficiency gains. The FTC has not attempted to do this in connection with its current industry-wide cases. This is a significant failure, particularly as to the effect of its shared monopoly cases. For the price declines that may result from deconcentration are not exchangeable against resulting cost increases on an equal basis. This is so in part because the efficiency effects of such a price decline relate only to the increased output that it prompts, whereas the efficiency effects of cost increases relate to the total output that must be produced at higher costs because of the dissolution of a competitively superior firm.[7] Under quite plausible assumptions about real-world conditions, this makes the positive value of such price declines worth much less than the negative value of such cost increases. Although it may strain credulity, at least of noneconomists, some idea of what is involved may be gained from the fact that under such assumptions it can be shown that the gains from a 4 percent decline in the price of domestically produced automobiles, for example, would be wiped out by an increase of less than *0.16 percent* (0.0016) in General Motors' costs alone. With relative values like this involved, it is hard to excuse the FTC's failure to take seriously the possibility that deconcentration could increase production and/or marketing costs.

C. Barriers to entry

Competitive superiority, based either on lower costs or on the production of goods regarded as superior by consumers, is, of course, the most effective and perhaps the only effective barrier to the entry of new firms and/or the expansion of existing rivals in response to the above-average profit rates usually associated with effective collusion. Recognizing at least implicitly the inappropriateness of attacking entry barriers such as these, the Commission has often sought to find the needed barriers by focusing on advertising and on so-called exclusionary practices. I will discuss by way of example one genre that has appeared in several of the industry-wide cases in which the Commission has already become involved.

In its first litigated industry-wide case, alleging shared monopoly in the ready-to-eat breakfast cereals industry, the Commission claimed that heavy advertising, product and package-size proliferation, and a shelf allocation plan were the principal barriers to entry.

Consumer ignorance is claimed to be created by "artificial" product differentiation when consumers purchase fairly durable goods that are complex in design or composition.[8] The idea is that consumers have little experience in buying such products, because they are durable and purchased relatively infrequently. It is argued that the cost of obtaining the information needed to make an informed purchase is "high" because the product is complex. Sensible consumers will, nevertheless, invest more in information as the purchase price and the expected variance in price and performance characteristics between different products rises.

It is hard to see, however, what that has to do with industries such as breakfast cereals or household detergents, in both of which the Commission has used this view of advertising and product differentiation as a barrier to entry. The products of these industries are relatively low-priced, purchased frequently, and their performance or other characteristics can easily be ascertained by buyers on the basis of experience after purchase. Given this, it is hard to imagine that consumers of breakfast cereal, for example, are more influenced by advertising than they are by the taste, texture, price, and similar characteristics of the cereal itself. "Consumer ignorance" simply cannot exist as to products the salient characteristics of which can be so readily determined by consumers themselves.

Another argument the FTC staff makes in these cases is that the number of products and package sizes has been "proliferated" to create entry barriers. The Bureau of Competition has voiced its suspicion that the large number of different brands of cereals or detergents offered for sale in so many different-size boxes may be designed to preempt valuable shelf space rather than to fulfill a legitimate consumer need. A firm might, of course, try to fill supermarket shelves with many different brands that consumers did not want, but this would be an expensive strategy because the firm would have to pay resellers to take space away from products that consumers did want. Instead of incurring the expense of producing different brands, the firm could, of course, produce only one or a few brands and pay the dealers to leave empty the shelf space that other brands now occupy (or much the same, fill that space with the one or a few brands that it actually produces). Or it might use these funds to exclude its rivals by cutting prices, perhaps below cost.

So used, product, package size, or model proliferation can be recognized as predatory behavior in the same sense as below-cost pricing might be so viewed. If that is not what the FTC staff has in mind, and I doubt that it is, I know of no plausible "theory" of how such proliferation can be used as an exclusionary device, except that existing firms are attempting to identify and to meet all segments of consumer demand. In any market situation there will be an optimal number of brands, package sizes, or models, depending on the extent of demand for various specialized product characteristics and the cost of delivering them. If existing firms effectively identify and respond to different classes of consumers who demand different product characteristics, which they will tend to do in the absence of collusion to restrict innovation, there will be little or no room for new firms to enter with distinctive products of their own. In the absence of predation, which is another issue entirely, the lack of such room for entry seems to be more consistent with effective competition than with collusion. It is hard to see, therefore, how the FTC can legitimately use this notion of proliferation to support cases against concentrated industries that are supposedly more collusive than others.

D. The costs and benefits of the industry-wide cases

I do not mean merely to second-guess the FTC's judgment in the cereals and similar cases or to show that the purported justifications offered for them are ephemeral. These cases are typical of the Commission's industry-wide cases. Although the form of the "barrier to entry" and other details of the argument may vary from case to case, at bottom none have more economic validity than the cases I have discussed above. I am able to state without equivocation, on the basis of almost two years as director of its policy planning office, that the FTC lacks the theory, the data, and the incentive to conduct cost/benefit estimates of its industry-wide cases.[9]

In addition, or perhaps because of this, most industry-wide matters have been instituted and pursued without any clear articulation of a theory of how successful prosecution of the case will improve economic welfare. In many cases, the FTC will have failed to articulate a theory, even to itself, of what the case is about. That symptom will be readily recognized in the petroleum industry litigation, for example, where the staff proposed to issue almost unlimited subpoenas and the question of their proper scope had not been resolved more than five years after the complaint was issued.[10] This situation becomes comprehensible only when it is remembered that the relevance of a subpoena cannot be determined unless the issues involved in the proceeding have been specified.

The absence of cost/benefit analysis, or articulation of economic theory on which such analysis might be based, and the failure even to specify the issues in many proceedings are accompanied by the use of highly questionable economic analyses, which in many cases are little more than ad hoc responses to the particular facts of individual cases. This leads to a situation, familiar to most FTC respondents and their counsel, in which the "theory" of the case changes (or simply disappears) as the facts are developed. These new "theories," which usually provide a pejorative explanation of things that are perfectly consistent with competition, are ordinarily designed to avoid the admission that the case never had a sound theoretical basis or, if it did, that the developed facts did not comport with it.

In short, the FTC has not shown that its industry-wide cases will improve consumer welfare. Primarily because of defective policy planning and case-selection standards, its failure to focus on collusion as the essential link between high concentration and deficient competition, its refusal to consider the possibility that its own remedies may increase production and marketing costs, and its search for entry barriers in activities more properly viewed as healthy competition, it is unlikely that the agency could make such a showing. The FTC has failed to heed its critics' injunction to establish sensible priorities and a workable case-selection process. It has instead involved itself in a number of sizable and costly industry-wide proceedings unlikely to produce benefits and which, wholly apart from the often considerable costs of the proceedings themselves, will most probably inflict economic losses on the community as a whole.

II. Vertical matters

Although there is a specific vertical category in the FTC's Program Budget, vertical cases are also scattered among several other budget categories, including the petroleum industry litigation, the largest individual case in current FTC budgets. Following a general overview of the FTC's vertical cases, I examine its approach to vertical contract arrangements, to vertical mergers, and to the petroleum industry litigation. I conclude this section with an evaluation of the FTC's general performance in the vertical area.

A. Overview of the FTC's vertical matters

The FTC acted in 77 vertical contract matters during the period. Forty-two of these were resale-price-maintenance cases, 33 of which were settled on the consent-order docket. Two opinions were written in the nine remaining cases; both involved strictly legal issues relating to the extraterritorial application of state fair-trade laws. These issues have been mooted by repeal of the federal enabling legislation authorizing the states to adopt fair-trade laws governing transactions in interstate commerce.

Most of the resale-price-maintenance cases involved products that appear to require the production of at least some information on the local level to aid consumers in making informed judgments about them. Examples include eight high-fidelity sound equipment cases, four hearing-aid cases, and three cases each involving ski bindings, firearms, and cookware or kitchen gadgets. Manufacturers of such products appear to have used resale price maintenance to create for their resellers property rights in the information that such resellers produce on the local level. Such property rights enable resellers to obtain a return on their investment in producing information about the manufacturer's product, thereby providing an incentive for the resellers to produce the optimum amount of local sales information.[11] Without interbrand cartelization of either the dealer or reseller level, there is nothing anticonsumer about this use of resale price maintenance.[12] The principal effect of FTC orders in these cases would be to force manufacturers to use less efficient means of providing for the production of local sales information, thus tending to increase costs and/or reduce the amount of such information produced.

The Commission acted in 30 miscellaneous vertical contract matters other than those involving resale price maintenance, the cases being evenly split between the consent and the regular dockets. The settlements include an industry-wide matter that had previously been described as an attempt to break Gallo's alleged near-monopoly hold on the domestic wine market. Four involved reciprocity; there is a smattering of tying arrangements, territorial and customer restrictions, exclusive dealing, and requirement contract cases. Eight separate cases have been joined in the soft drink bottling cases, involving territorial restrictions on various franchised bottling companies. Three opinions were written during the period in the 15 matters on the regular docket and will be considered in greater detail below.

There were 18 vertical merger cases, 14 of which appear on the regular docket; four opinions were written in them during the period. In two of these, the Commission dismissed complaints challenging acquisitions by General Mills of a frozen fish stick company[13] and by United Brands of a number of lettuce farms in Arizona and California.[14] In two others, cement companies were ordered to divest ready-mixed concrete operations.[15]

The Commission acted in 52 price discrimination cases during the period, almost all of which involved enforcement of the Robinson-Patman Act. These price discrimination cases constituted 21 percent of all cases in which the Commission acted during the period, more than any other single type of case. Twenty of these cases were reported in Volumes 77 and 78 of the *FTC Reports*, which cover the very early part of the period. Since then, there has been a striking decrease in the number of these actions. If the progress of the FTC could be measured by the decline in its Robinson-Patman Act cases, it would be clear that matters had improved since 1970. The problem is not that simple, however; it requires a more detailed analysis of the vertical cases, to which I now turn.

B. Vertical contract arrangements

The Commission wrote opinions in three vertical contract cases during the period.[16] Although the questioned arrangements in each case were quite different, the policy issues involved are quite similar and can readily be covered in a discussion of only two of these cases.

1. Great Lakes Carbon (GLC)

The FTC attacked a series of requirements contracts under which GLC had agreed to purchase petroleum coke from various refineries. The initial terms of those contracts varied from 7 to 20 years; extensions were for minimum periods of 5 years. Petroleum coke is a by-product of the refining process, although it is not produced by all refineries. The refining process yields more valuable "light" products, such as gasolines, and less valuable "heavier" products, ranging down to residual oil. With a machine known as a coker, a refinery can process this residual oil again, producing more light products and petroleum coke, a solid black mass resembling coal. Prior to 1932, when GLC developed an economical way to calcine this raw coke into a useful product, the few refineries with cokers had no economical way of disposing of the mountains of valueless coke they produced; the accumulated stockpiles ran into the millions of tons.

At the time of the FTC proceeding, the coke-processing industry was concentrated and considerably integrated vertically by ownership. GLC had started the industry in 1932, but entry had reduced its share of petroleum coke purchases to about 39 percent by 1969. Sixteen firms had entered since 1945.[17] Four of them were oil companies disposing of their own raw coke directly to end users; six were end users, primarily aluminum companies, which the FTC said were "not engaged . . . in active and continuing competition with Great Lakes in the day-to-day selling of petroleum coke."[18] There were only four significant firms in the nonintegrated coke market; GLC had two-thirds of the total sales of those firms. "It is here," the FTC said, "that we find the true measure of its power to influence price and exclude competitors."[19]

To the FTC, this power was based on the long-term contracts, which in its view excluded or foreclosed others from the processing market. GLC and the refiners, however, defended the contracts on the grounds of "business justification," arguing that their limitation would prompt an increase in ownership vertical integration. Of interest is both the way in which the FTC concluded that the contracts had unlawfully suppressed competition and the way in which it handled the business justification defense.

The Commission addressed the question of suppressing competition in the context of a rather extensive analysis of vertical integration, which emphasized as probable efficiency-creating explanations the alternatives of (1) achieving greater technical efficiencies and (2) avoiding the exercise of market power by one or more firms in the distributive chain. The Commission concluded that vertical integration in this industry did not produce any technical efficiencies resembling those involved in its paradigm, which was "the merging of ingot casting and component shaping into a continuous operation in the steel industry, thus saving the cost of having to reheat the steel at the subsequent state." As it had considered only two possible explanations for such integration, the rejection of the first necessitated the acceptance of the second, i.e., that GLC was exercising market power. This market power existed "largely as a result of the long-term exclusive contracts at issue in this matter." The FTC concluded that reducing the length of these contracts would reduce GLC's market power.

The "business justification" defense of GLC and the refiners was based on the argument that the contracts should be upheld "as a necessary protection from an unacceptable degree of 'risk' in their industry," that is, the risk "involved in the construction of new plants at two stages of the production process here, coking and processing (calcining, etc.)." The FTC admitted that prudence would not justify investing in either cokers or calciners unless satisfactory arrangements were previously made so that the refinery could dispose of its coke and the calciner could obtain a constant supply of that product. It concluded, however, that the costs of building either of these facilities could be recovered within a period of five years and that efficient operations could be maintained after that under three-year contracts.

GLC argued that it needed contract coverage not only during the period of cost recovery but also during the subsequent period, when it was recovering a reasonable profit on its investment. Rejecting this, the Commission said:

A five year old plant does not suddenly vanish at the end of that period and does not cease to be profitable merely because its owner has been required to start competing with others at that point for sales and supplies in the open market. The notion that new plants will not be built in an allegedly competitive industry unless the builders are allowed to shield those plants from competition not only long enough to get back their full costs but what they consider an adequate profit as well is one that is alien to the antitrust laws.[20]

Although one might have thought that it was also alien to the antitrust laws to permit plants to be shielded from competition even long enough to get back their full costs, the Commission was willing to limit contracts relating to new calcining kilns or new cokers to five-year terms. All other requirements contracts were limited to a three-year period.

There are two basic weaknesses to the FTC's approach. The first becomes apparent when we ask how 16 firms could have entered the coke-processing industry from 1945 to 1969 if these requirements contracts were so effective at barring entry. Although much of this entry occurred through the vertical integration of end users, if the requirements contracts did not bar that entry, there is no reason to believe that they would bar others who might wish to produce solely for the "unintegrated market." The fact that entry reduced GLC's share of the market from almost 100 percent in 1945 to less than 39 percent in 1969 belies the formidable nature of those contracts as barriers to entry.

A much more fundamental weakness – and one that exists in all its vertical cases – lies in the Commission's theory of vertical integration. The two reasons it gave for the occurrence of such integration, although correct as far as they go, are only examples of a much broader class of ways in which vertical integration can contribute to efficiency. We can describe that class in general terms by defining vertical integration as the substitution of administrative processes for those of the market, and by positing that such integration will occur whenever transactions may be accomplished less expensively by using administrative means than by using market exchanges.[21]

One situation in which administrative processes will be less costly than market transactions arises when there is an opportunity for the parties to a transaction to take advantage of each other in circumstances in which the other's next best alternatives are significantly less advantageous. For example, building specialized assets without previously agreeing on the split of the cost savings moves the parties from a competitive to a small-numbers bargaining environment. In the absence of previous agreement (which will involve vertical integration in some form), both parties are open to the opportunistic behavior of the other, that is, activities designed to obtain, at the expense of the other, as much of the cost savings as possible. In such situations vertical integration, occurring before the assets are specialized to each other, will be commonly observed. Indeed, without it the specialization that produces the "technical" efficiencies favored by the FTC is quite unlikely to occur.

Although this integration may be by ownership or by contract, for our purposes the form is not important. The important thing is that the integration may be expected to occur in one form or another whenever specialized assets are made subject to opportunistic behavior, as they were in the FTC's steel plant paradigm. Such integration will occur to avoid the costs of detecting and preventing subsequent opportunistic behavior by the parties to the transaction.

Once this is understood, the reason for the long-term contracts between coke processors and refinery suppliers becomes clear. The cokers in the refineries and calciners in which that coke was processed were highly specialized to each other. Although some calciners were fed by more than one refinery, in most cases the calciners were built right next to the refinery that was to be the principal source of coke.[22] One reason for this was that calcining reduces the weight of the raw coke by 15 to 30 percent by removing moisture.[23] The savings in transport costs alone from placing cokers and calciners close together thus would appear to have been significant, as would the incentives and the possible returns from opportunistic behavior in the absence of the vertical integration provided by the requirements contract. Such behavior would take the form of attempts to alter the price at which coke was transferred from refiners to calciners. That problem was alleviated by tying such transfer price to the price of some commodity whose price was set outside the environment of a "small numbers bargaining" situation. In this case that product was usually crude oil.

When viewed this way, one can see that the requirements contracts created transactional efficiencies of precisely the same type as those involved in the FTC's ingot-casting/component-shaping paradigm. Its focus on technical efficiency, to the exclusion of transactional efficiency, led the Commission to an overly restrictive view of the efficiency-creating potential of vertical integration. In this case the FTC based its inference of market power on three factors: (1) GLC's share of a gerrymandered market, (2) the existence of the requirements contracts, and (3) the fact that a number of end users had integrated backward into coke processing. It used the latter two factors to support its inference of market power because, consistent with the observed tendency of many economists and most antitrust enforcement officials to seek monopoly explanations for unfamiliar business arrangements, it was not able or willing to articulate a theory that could relate those two factors to the creation of efficiency.[24] If it had done that, it would have seen that both the requirements contracts and the vertical integration by end users were perfectly consistent with competition and with the achievement of transactional efficiencies. Monopoly did not need to be hypothesized to explain their existence. Much the same was true in the *Coors* case, to which I now turn.

2. *Coors*[25]

Here the Commission objected principally to territorial restrictions on Coors' distributors, to Coors' alleged attempt to fix both the wholesale and retail prices of its beer, and to a provision in the distribution contracts giving Coors the right upon breach to terminate the distributor on five days' notice. Without attempting to analyze why Coors had adopted the questioned arrangements, the Commission unanimously reversed an administrative law judge's dismissal of the complaint. Although it recognized that territorial restrictions might be desirable under some circumstances, it held the ones in this case to be illegal per se because they were associated with price fixing. The short-notice termination provisions were held unlawful on the theory that they could be used to coerce compliance with the other "anticompetitive" policies described above. Before we can fully evaluate the Commission's performance in this case, we must develop a more complete understanding of what Coors was trying to accomplish with these restrictions. I am indebted to Professor Benjamin Klein of the UCLA Department of Economics for the basic analysis of the Coors distribution system set forth below.

The distinctive nature of the Coors distribution system relates to the fact that unlike other beers, Coors is not pasteurized. It is at its highest quality right off the packaging line; deterioration sets in immediately. As a result, the beer is best moved to the consumer quickly, and it must always be kept refrigerated. These facts, which dictate a high degree of quality control, suggest that the questioned arrangements were designed to make the Coors distribution system as close a substitute as economically feasible for one in which Coors performed the distribution and retailing functions itself, which it did not do, presumably, because it was cheaper to have distributors and retailers do those jobs for it. The restrictions were designed to create incentives for those parties to handle Coors beer in much the same way that Coors would handle it if it were doing their jobs itself.

Although Coors would want to achieve rapid distribution under refrigerated conditions, distributors and retailers would not necessarily share that interest. To understand this, suppose that Coors permitted several distributors to sell its beer in any given area. Because effective inventory control, rotation of product, and constant refrigeration cost money, why would it not be in the interest of one or more of these distributors to cut costs by reducing these services and still sell the unserviced beer at the same or a slightly lower price than the others? Consumers could not tell before buying whether the services had been provided. And few, if any of them would be able to tell after they tasted the beer whether Coors, the distributor, or the retailer was responsible for its unhappy condition.

The appearance of some bad-tasting Coors would, of course, tend to reduce its consumption. The harm from that decline, however, would not be visited only upon the one who caused it; it would be shared by the other distributors and by Coors itself. The opportunistic behavior of the cheating distributor enables him to take a "free ride" on the efforts of fellow distributors and the supplier to provide consumers with a high-quality product and *thereby reduces their incentive to produce that product*. The injury from this opportunistic behavior, therefore, will fall on consumers who desire to purchase high-quality Coors beer as well as on Coors and on noncheating distributors.

This ability to free-ride will be reduced by Coors' efforts to police the performance of its resellers. But as policing is not free, it will not be conducted in unlimited amounts; there will always be room for some cheating. Because policing costs would no doubt rise with the number of distributors in any given area, we could expect the room for cheating to do the same.

Exclusive territories could greatly alleviate this problem. Because no one else could sell Coors beer in his territory, the authorized distributor would in effect have a property right to all future sales of Coors in the area. Because the distributor would make all future sales that would occur due to the high quality of the product, his incentives to provide the optimal type and level of services to ensure that quality should be more like those Coors itself would have if it were integrated directly into distribution. In addition, the cost of any policing by Coors would be reduced.

But the exclusive territories create another problem, which Coors apparently solved by "suggesting" distributor resale prices. Although both the complaint and the Commission opinion give the impression that Coors was trying to maintain *minimum* prices at the distribution level, it is clear that Coors was primarily concerned with establishing *maximum* prices, a not uncommon concern when a supplier of a differentiated product grants exclusive territories to its resellers. Once the exclusively franchised reseller is protected from intrabrand competition by the exclusion of other dealers in the same product from his territory, the reseller will tend to increase his resale prices, perhaps above the level the supplier desires.[26] The supplier can solve this problem in part by setting maximum prices, but that will still leave room for the resellers to increase prices indirectly by reducing the quality of the product, for example, by cheating on providing services to it.[27]

Once it set distributors' maximum resale prices, Coors would be able to control the distributors' margins by varying the prices it charged them for beer. Coors could change those margins from a perfectly competitive level to one in which all of the gains available from its specialized or differentiated position in the market went to the distributors. If Coors did the latter and if the distributors had the same view of demand for Coors beer as Coors did, the maximum price limitations on distributors would no longer be needed. The distributors would be in a profit-maximizing position and would not have any incentive to increase prices directly. Nor would they have any incentive to increase price indirectly by cheating on services; the need for policing would also be eliminated. Coors could well believe, however, that this was a more expensive way to stop cheating than setting the distributors' margins at some level between the high and low points described above and doing some policing. There would presumably be an optimum trade-off between the level of distributors' margins and the level of policing by Coors, which would depend in large part on the costs of policing and the potential gains from cheating.

A putative cheater would also want to weigh the gains from that activity against the expected sanctions if caught. This seems to explain the short-notice termination provisions in the distributor contracts. Coors could terminate on five days' notice if the distributor were caught cheating. The distributor's enthusiasm for honesty would vary directly with the probability that Coors would actually terminate and with the extent to which quick termination would reduce the value of his investment in the distributorship. The probability that Coors would actually terminate would probably increase with distributor recidivism. The value lost by sudden termination would be considerable because refrigerated facilities were not needed for the distribution of other brands of beer.

Viewed in this way, the short-period termination provision is a highly useful device to keep distributors from cheating on the provision of the services required to deliver high-quality beer to consumers. As an inducement to distributor honesty, it should not have concerned the Federal Trade Commission. The greater the distributors' commitment to honesty, the fewer resources Coors would have to spend on policing, and the lower it could keep the distributors' margins. The first result is efficient; the second is proof that honesty is its own reward.

Coors did attempt to set minimum resale prices at the retail level, but these minimum prices seem to have been designed to accomplish much the same purpose as the maximum prices at the distributor level. Maximum prices were not needed at the retail level because competition among retailers would prevent the price from rising above a competitive level. But price cutting by cheating retailers (those with lower costs as a result of not providing refrigeration, etc.) could drive returns to non-cheaters below a competitive level. In addition, Coors may have wished to allow the retailers a return somewhat above that level for the same reasons it appeared to have done so on the distributor level: to reduce the incentive to cheat and thereby to achieve the optimum trade-off between resellers' margins and policing as discussed above regarding distributors. This follows from the fact that retailers would have incentives to cheat on services similar (and most likely greater because of the absence of exclusive territories for retailers) to those of the distributors. As with the distributors, the most efficient way to limit retailer cheating on services is to couple a particular margin with a particular level of policing. Thus, the two price-setting programs ultimately shared common goals, even though they had opposite effects on a superficial level. The distributor program kept prices from rising; the retail program kept them from falling, particularly as a result of price cuts by those retailers who might shave costs by not properly caring for the beer. Yet both programs shared the ultimate purpose of permitting Coors to control distributor and retailer margins in such a way as to economize on its quality-control costs.

When we view the territorial restrictions, maximum and minimum price setting, and the short-notice termination provision in the way just described, we can see that they all fit together to form a consistent and integrated structure by which Coors was trying to obtain more quality control and market penetration for a lower expenditure of resources. It was a structure designed to create efficiency. There is no plausible way that this distribution system standing by itself could have contributed to anything about which the antitrust laws or the agencies that enforce them should legitimately be concerned.

Perhaps the Coors's distribution system attracted antitrust attention because it was different from those used by other brewers. Whereas its principal competitors were spending more than $4 per barrel on advertising each year, Coors was spending less than $1.[28] It would appear that at least part of Coors' savings on advertising went to produce a more expensive and presumably higher-quality beer and to achieve an extremely high level of quality control during distribution. The amounts that the Coors system saved in advertising appear to be analogous to the cost savings realized by locating ingot casting and component shaping operations in close proximity in the steel example discussed above. *Coors* and the steel hypothetical are analogous also in that the vertical integration that characterized both of them was present for the same reason: to solve the problem of allocating those cost savings among the parties whose joint investment and effort produced them. The Coors distribution system, with its refrigerated warehouses and delivery trucks (not useful in distributing other brands of beer, which did not require refrigeration during distribution) and the Coors brewery, producing the only beer that needed constant refrigeration, are specialized to each other in the same *economic* (not physical) way as the ingot casting and component-shaping operations in the *Great Lakes Carbon* example. The same problem of allocating the cost savings achieved by the joint operations of these specialized assets could be expected to arise in both cases. The problem is, in fact, worse in *Coors* because the resellers can secretly affect the allocation of these cost savings by cheating on services. In the steel industry example, any reallocation of the jointly produced cost savings would involve a confrontation on the issue; at least the party from whom those cost savings were being reallocated would have some notice of what was happening. Since the FTC properly thought that vertical integration was desirable in its steel industry example, it should have thought the same in *Coors*. The only difference between the two cases is in the form of the vertical integration and in the fact that one product had to be kept hot and the other cold.

Perhaps most disturbing is that no one connected with this case even attempted to construct a coherent statement of the purposes and effects of these arrangements. Coors or its counsel presumably could have made the kind of analysis that I sketched above, or hired someone to do it for them, but they did not. The administrative law judge did not construct such an analysis on his own; the Commission contented itself with applying a rigid *per se* rule. Clearly not happy about affirming the FTC, the Court of Appeals produced the feeble suggestion that the Supreme Court was responsible for the sad state of affairs and that it might wish to set things straight by doing something about the *Schwinn* case,[29] which both the Court of Appeals and the FTC followed blindly to reach the *Coors* result.

No doubt the Supreme Court does bear a heavy responsibility for the unfortunate condition of most of the law of antitrust. But the Commission cannot be absolved in *Coors* simply because *Schwinn* was the "controlling" law at the time. This is so for at least two reasons, the first of which is that the Commission has wide discretion in deciding which cases to initiate in the first place. The existence of the *Schwinn* rule did not require the FTC to proceed against Coors. It is noteworthy that the Antitrust Division has brought few, if any, vertical cases of this type after its "victory" in *Schwinn*, although the Commission has devoted a significant amount of resources in this area. In short, if the Commission had a solid understanding of the economics of vertical relationships, it would, in the exercise of its "prosecutorial" discretion, never have initiated *Coors* in the first place.

The second reason for not excusing the Commission's performance in *Coors* on the ground that it was merely following the Supreme Court's mandate in *Schwinn* raises a more fundamental question of the role of the FTC. If it is simply to follow the lead of the Supreme Court, it is hard to distinguish it from any United States district court. But the Commission was created to constitute a body of experts in matters of antitrust and trade regulation; it was supposed to develop an expertise in these areas supposedly not within the reach of the district courts. The Commission has not hesitated to claim such expertise and to attempt to change the law as laid down by the Supreme Court whenever such changes expand the powers of the FTC.[30] Its reluctance to apply that "expertise" in a case like *Coors* is difficult to understand. It may, however, be related to the fact that the development and application of a coherent rule of reason to vertical arrangements such as those involved in *Coors* would most probably reduce the number of cases brought by the Commission and, as well, reduce the number of cases it could win once they were brought. *Schwinn* was finally reversed, but this resulted primarily from the efforts of academics and the refusal of the Ninth Circuit Court of Appeals to act as both the FTC and the Tenth Circuit did in *Coors*.[31]

The history of the law on vertical territorial and customer restrictions following *Schwinn*, developed almost entirely in the context of private litigation, is highlighted by the tortuous ingenuity of the federal courts to avoid applying that case to destroy arrangements that they sensed to be efficiency-creating in nature. Their performance, although leaving much to be desired, has been consistently better than that of the FTC, the agency originally created to apply economic expertise to these problems. The FTC's performance in *Coors* is almost identical to what it was a decade earlier when it struck down efficiency-creating vertical arrangements in *Snap-on-Tools*[32] and in *Sandura*.[33] The main difference is that then the Courts of Appeal set aside the Commission's orders. This history seems to be repeating itself in the aftermath of *GTE Sylvania*,[34] the case in which the Supreme Court reversed *Schwinn*. Just as it did in *Snap-on-Tools* and in *Sandura*, the FTC appears to have struck down efficiency-creating arrangements in its *Coca-Cola* decision.[35]

There does not appear to have been any noticeable improvement in the Commission's understanding and treatment of vertical arrangements during the last 10 years, notwithstanding the widely heralded changes made in response to the Commission's critics of the late 1960s.

C. Vertical mergers

The FTC's approach to vertical mergers and, more important, its view of the value of efficiency and hard-nosed competition, is nicely shown by comparing the administrative law judge's opinion with the Commission opinion in *Ash Grove Cement*,[36] involving a cement company's acquisition of two ready-mixed concrete firms and the assets of an aggregate-producing firm in the Kansas City metropolitan area. After defining the relevant product and geographic markets, the Commission disposed of this case in slightly more than three pages. It observed that vertical mergers foreclose competitors of either party from a segment of the market otherwise open to them, acting as a "clog on competition" which deprived "rivals of a fair opportunity to compete." After noting the share of the market foreclosed by these acquisitions, it said:

Foreclosure manifests a particularly anticompetitive character when it occurs as part of a trend toward forward integration in a concentrated market. For example, in such a situation, barriers to entry, often already high, are raised in the supply market. As the percentage of foreclosed transactions grows, less of an open market remains to attract potential competitors of the integrated suppliers. The would-be entrant is thus faced with the choice of: (i) entering at the supply level to compete for a continually shrinking market dominated by oligopolists; (ii) entering at both the supply and customer levels, facing the significantly increased costs integrated entry implies; or (iii) abandoning all thoughts of entering the market. To create this series of options for a potential entrant is clearly to impede entry.[37]

Adverse effects would not be limited to the supply market; by narrowing the margin between open-market cement prices and the ready-mixed concrete price, these integrated oligopolists could exercise "leverage" over nonintegrated ready-mix firms. The result: "The net effect would be to keep any of the independents from competing too aggressively, to maintain prices above competitive levels, to keep out new entrants – in short to permit the ready-mixed market to function as a highly concentrated oligopoly."[38]

We can surely find no fault with the theory that inefficiency results if firms collude to raise prices, particularly if they can bar entry in some way not related to their own lower costs. The Commission's opinion reflects concern that these acquisitions would facilitate tacit or explicit collusion. The danger in these acquisitions, as seen by the Commission, lay in their propensity to increase prices. The Commission justified finding them illegal in the now-familiar language of oligopoly theory. The question of efficiency was never mentioned.

A completely different view, however, appears from the administrative law judge's findings, which reflect concern that the acquisitions would reduce costs and intensify the competitive pressures on other firms. He found, for example, that:

In addition to Lee's Summit's [one of the acquired ready mixed concrete firms] ability to obtain the costliest raw material, portland cement, at less than prevailing market prices, it has the double advantage of obtaining its aggregates from its parent also at a reduced price. The vertically integrated Lee's Summit, therefore, has decisive cost advantages over its nonintegrated competitors, which if passed on in the form of lower concrete prices, could result in prices lower than competitors' costs and force those competitors out of business.[39]

The administrative law judge thought that the actual effects of vertical integration in the Kansas City area were demonstrated by the history of Fordyce Concrete, another of the acquired firms. Fordyce had entered the market in 1961, borrowing substantial sums to build up its operations.

By 1965, shortly before it was acquired by Ash Grove, it "was backed against the wall." The interesting thing is what happened after Ash Grove took over:

In the two years subsequent to its acquisitions of Fordyce and Lee's Summit, Ash Grove furnished additional financial aid. Lee's Summit was acquired on Jan. 4, 1966, for $1,250,000 and by Feb. 28, 1966, had been advanced $39,000. Fordyce received advances from Ash Grove in 1967, totalling $1,057,226, which increased in 1968 to $1,654,444.98. Also in 1968, Fordyce increased the KCMA ready mixed capacity by purchasing 39 new mixer trucks.[40]

Because of this and other increases in capacity made by the larger concrete sellers, price competition in the Kansas City area was severe. Some of the smaller firms operated at a loss and others, because they "were not vertically integrated and consequently did not have the advantages which respondent was able to give to Fordyce and Lee's Summit, but were forced to leave the cement business when they ran out of operating capital."[41]

On the question of entry, the administrative law judge also saw things somewhat differently than did the Commission. To him, "without adequate financing, entry would be very difficult since costs were high and prices and profits were low. Any new entrant would have to take business from its competitors by cutting prices." This would be doubly difficult because of "the fact that the cement suppliers were under pressure to utilize their production capacities at a high level."[42]

The Commission did not consider whether these findings that vertical integration provided "decisive cost advantages," that "prices and profits were low," that integrated firms had increased concrete capacity, and that the cement firms were under pressure to keep their output *up* were erroneous or not supported by the record. It simply ignored them. The Commission ordered divestiture on the stated grounds that the merger would tend to raise prices, whereas the record and the opinion of the ALJ showed just the opposite. One would not suspect from the face of the Commission's opinion that this decision was aimed at the protection of competitors from competition rather than at the preservation of the competitive process. Closer examination, however, shows this to be the case. Once again, there does not appear to have been much improvement in the Commission's performance since 1969.

D. The petroleum industry litigation

This is by far the largest single litigated matter now pending before the FTC. Budget reports show that from fiscal years 1975 through 1978 the FTC itself has expended or allocated 227.5 person-years and about $16.8 million on this case. The fiscal 1977 and 1978 budgets each allocate to this case approximately 30 percent of all resources available to the FTC for antitrust enforcement programs. The resources expended by the eight respondents are undoubtedly much greater. The complaint was issued on July 18, 1973; five years later the respondents had not turned over a single document pursuant to FTC subpoenas. In April of 1978, Exxon, apparently correctly, stated: "After almost five years of adjudicative proceedings, complaint counsel have neither specified the central legal and factual issues they intend to pursue, nor identified the unlawful acts and practices in which Exxon is alleged to have engaged."[43]

Although it is clear that the FTC seeks respondents' vertical dismemberment as a remedy, neither the purposes to be achieved by this nor the theory underlying the FTC case is clear. Although it appears that vertical arrangements can be used in some circumstances to facilitate the policing of horizontal collusion, those circumstances do not appear to exist in the oil industry, and the FTC does not appear to base its case on this theory.[44] Although there are other theories of how vertical integration may injure consumer welfare,[45] these theories are based on notions of firm behavior that I and a large number of economists find to be implausible. I have discussed these points at length elsewhere and will not review them here.[46]

To determine whether *Exxon* is likely to increase consumer welfare, we must make some attempt to determine the Commission's purpose for bringing the case or to state some plausible theory under which successful prosecution of the case would be likely to increase economic welfare. Although the FTC has never articulated such a theory, it has claimed that the case is designed to remedy problems in the industry that it had been unable to solve effectively in the past, using a case-by-case approach, because the oil companies would simply change their way of doing business to accomplish the same results indirectly.[47] If this is so, it may be possible to obtain some insight into the FTC's purposes by examining its past proceedings against members of the oil industry.

To do this, I will briefly review all FTC antitrust cases directly involving oil companies brought during the 27-year period from January 1, 1950, through December 31, 1977, discussing in turn those brought after January 1, 1970, and those brought during the two preceding 10-year periods. If, as the FTC claims, *Exxon* is designed to solve the problems which those cases attempted to solve but did not because of strategic responses by the oil companies, an examination of their purposes should tell us something about the purposes of *Exxon*.

Besides *Exxon*, the FTC was involved in eight other oil company cases during the period.[48] Two consent-order cases alleged reciprocal dealing,[49] two charged oil companies with permitting new-car dealers to accept charges on oil company credit cards if the dealers bought substantially all of their requirements of petroleum products from the oil companies involved,[50] and two others involved acquisitions – one of certain crude oil reserves and one of a crude oil pipeline – neither of which could conceivably have affected consumer prices.[51] There were also two regular docket cases alleging coercion of dealers by major oil companies,[52] something the FTC has seen as a problem in many of its oil company and other cases. This coercion is usually thought to be exercised at least in part by the use of short-term leases. Phil Neal has described cases such as this as having a "bondage" strain: "An increasing number of businessmen are seen as victims, for whom the antitrust laws should provide relief against ill-advised bargains or superior economic force."[53] Robert Bork adds:

The "bondage" concept, exemplified by any number of cases that attempt to ensure the position of smaller firms in chains of distribution, and thus to reorganize at least a part of society on the basis of status rather than contract, has no ascertainable intellectual content. Manufacturers cannot engage in a policy of systematically binding their dealers to unfair arrangements. They must allow dealers at least a competitive rate of return or they will gradually lose their dealer organizations. Given that fact, it requires an extraordinarily unsophisticated sentimentality to perceive the dealer as so oppressed that the federal courts ought to rewrite his contract for him. Of course, the dealer wants more; everybody does. But that is what bargaining, rather than antitrust litigation, should be about.[54]

Not only is there no justification for using the antitrust laws to attempt to enrich dealers at the expense of their suppliers by changing certain provisions of the contracts between them, such attempts cannot succeed over time because suppliers are free to alter other terms of such contracts. Nor is there any way in which such redistributive attempts can increase consumer welfare. Quite the contrary, there are straightforward efficiency reasons for the existence of these short-term leases. Those reasons appear to be the same in the oil industry as they were in *Coors*. The refiners have placed a highly specialized asset – their reputations and the reputation of their products as exemplified in their trademarks and other similar rights – in a position in which those assets are subject to depreciation by the opportunistic behavior of their dealers. The suppliers will expend real resources to prevent such depreciation, and it is in the interests of consumers, who value the information conveyed by the suppliers' reputations, that they should do so. Just as in *Coors*, the short-notice termination provisions and similar arrangements reduce the cost of this policing and thereby enhance efficiency. It is noteworthy that the FTC has never explained how *consumers* are likely to be injured because a lease between a refiner and a dealer contains a provision permitting termination on short notice.

From January 1, 1960, through December 31, 1969, there were only three oil company cases on the FTC consent-order docket; one involved a joint venture into the plastics industry, another a merger into the fertilizer industry, and the third alleged the use of restrictive licensing practices in the production and sale of polypropylene.[55] There were four cases on the regular docket, three of which were dismissed by the Commission itself and one of which was vacated by the Court of Appeals.[56] Three of these were Robinson-Patman Act cases, and the fourth involved a charge against Crown Central for selling below cost.

A total of 15 complaints were issued from January 1, 1950, through December 31, 1959. Four were Robinson-Patman act cases; three were dismissed by the FTC and the fourth was settled.[57] Three involved charges of exclusive dealing; the Commission dismissed two of them.[58] Three concerned attempted resale price maintenance in the context of price wars; the Commission dismissed one of them.[59] One merger case was settled by consent order.[60] One complaint charged price discrimination in connection with the purchase and sale of tires by Atlas.[61] Finally, three others attacked the sales-commission method of distributing tires, batteries, and accessories (TBA).[62]

This is a surprisingly dismal record; complaint counsel lost fully one-half of the 20 cases litigated to disposition over this 27-year period. Most striking is the fact that 90 percent of these losses were administered by the Commission itself. Three cases were settled and seven were won in litigation. Those seven consist of the three TBA cases: two resale-price-maintenance cases and one case each involving price discrimination and exclusive dealing. Adding the settlements, the Commission entered a total of 19 antitrust orders against oil companies during the 27-year period. As five of these were proscribed mergers or joint ventures, *Exxon* is presumably not needed to further their goals. Nor do the two Robinson-Patman orders, two reciprocity orders, and the order relating to polypropylene production appear to need such additional aid. The nine remaining orders are split evenly among TBA sales, exclusive dealing, and resale price maintenance/dealer coercion. The exclusive-dealing cases are without serious significance, two of them involving settlements of cases attacking the use of oil company credit cards at new-car dealerships. Even if this were a serious problem, it is hard to see why vertical dismemberment of an entire industry is required to solve it, or even how that draconian remedy would help to solve it.

On the basis of the cases that the FTC has brought against oil companies in the past, it would appear that the idea that dealers are being coerced into unfair contracts is more responsible for *Exxon* than is any other issue, leaving aside the possibility that the case is simply a political response to the "energy crisis." Persistent attempts to shift wealth from major oil companies to their dealers, by attempting to control the terms of the contracts between them, would probably involve the eventual extinction of the dealers. As the cost of operating through independent dealers or lessees rose, the majors would shift to distribution through their own retail outlets.

If the majors could be prevented from operating at the retail level directly, as they have in Maryland,[63] the opportunities for shifting wealth to independent dealers would be much improved. Increasing the returns to independent gasoline retailers, however, will not increase consumer welfare. It will, indeed, have exactly the opposite effect. Until the FTC comes forward with a coherent statement of its theory of the *Exxon* case, together with at least a minimal analysis tending to show that the benefits of this case are likely to exceed its costs, it appears that even the mildly skeptical would be justified in doubting that the net result of this proceeding will be an increase in economic welfare.

E. Summary

Economists' and lawyers' understanding of the economics of vertical arrangements has developed significantly over the last 20 years. Most economists and many lawyers knowledgeable in antitrust matters would now agree that such arrangements do not ordinarily injure consumer welfare and that they can create significant transactional efficiencies.[64] This change in thinking has culminated in a Supreme Court decision that has the potential of revolutionizing the law governing vertical arrangements.[65] Most of this appears to have been lost on the FTC. It has clung and appears determined to continue to cling tenaciously to outmoded and erroneous concepts of the economics of vertical arrangements that could not command the agreement of more than a handful of populist-minded American economists. Rather than leading or even contributing to the movement toward better economic understanding of antitrust law, which it was presumably intended to do as the repository of economic ''expertise'' in this area of the law, the FTC has hindered and continues to hinder understanding and progress toward an antitrust enforcement program and structure of law that seems likely to contribute to increases in consumer welfare.[66]

Its record in terms of attempting to accommodate the harshness implicit in any *per se* rule to the needs of economic efficiency is inferior to that of the federal courts, whose supposed inadequacies in the admittedly complex field of antitrust law led (in part) to the creation of the FTC in the first place. There had been widespread if not general agreement on the FTC's deficiencies up to the time of its supposed reform after the barrage of criticism leveled against it nearly a decade ago. As far as vertical arrangements – the largest single area of the FTC's antitrust enforcement activity – are concerned, however, that reform has simply not occurred.

III. Horizontal matters

The FTC acted in 28 horizontal contract cases during the period. In eight it attacked shopping center leases that gave principal tenants a veto over other tenants proposed by the developer. These cases and their ramifications for consumer welfare are discussed in Chapter 9. There were five trade association cases: two charged attempts to fix prices and other terms of trade, and three alleged attempts to limit the access of non-members to the association's trade shows or to limit the rights of members to attend the shows of others. Eight cases, none of which has yet resulted in a Commission opinion, attacked relative value schedules used in pricing various kinds of medical services and other "professional" restrictions on advertising and price competition. These seem to be among the few FTC antitrust cases that have the potential to improve consumer welfare. Three cases attacked bid depository arrangements requiring members or users to make and receive all their bids through the depositories. Three cases attacked basing point or delivered pricing in the plywood industry; one case charged a lettuce producers' cooperative with price fixing.

There were 51 horizontal merger cases during the period, including all mergers between direct competitors as well as those which alleged that the parties were significant potential competitors.[67] Fourteen were on the consent order docket. By December 31, 1977, the Commission had written opinions in 18 of the remaining 37 cases, 7 cases brought during the period had not yet been resolved at the Commission level, and the remaining 12 had been either settled or dropped after the merger had been abandoned. The Commission prevailed in whole or in part in all 27 cases that were either settled or dropped after the merger was abandoned. Only 3 of the 18 cases litigated to disposition at the Commission level were dismissed by the Commission.[68] In one case the FTC changed its mind, first finding that Litton's acquisition of a German typewriter maker violated Section 7 of the Clayton Act but then reversing its divestiture order.[69] I take up the merger cases in greater detail after discussing the cases involving horizontal contract arrangements.

A. Horizontal contract arrangements

Horizontal contract arrangements, of course, include price fixing, a subject that takes up considerable resources at the Antitrust Division, as it should. Although Lewis Engman made a considerable effort during his term as chairman to shift more resources into horizontal matters, including price fixing, that movement flagged with the end of his tenure and subsided even more after Calvin Collier left the chair.[70] It does not appear to have produced any straightforward price-fixing cases. The closest thing to real horizontal collusion cases are the *California Lettuce Cooperative* case,[71] which the Commission dismissed on the ground that the coop was exempt from the antitrust laws, cases against professional groups for restricting advertising and competitive pricing, and plywood-delivered pric-

ing cases. As I have said, the attack on restrictive practices by professional groups appears to have more promise of contributing to an
improvement in consumer welfare than any of the FTC's other antitrust
cases.

The failure to pursue Engman's initiative to increase resources allocated to horizontal matters is unfortunate. Now that mergers to a monopoly position are no longer a serious threat, horizontal conspiracy appears
to be the most serious remaining problem for antitrust. The Antitrust Division of the Department of Justice has recognized this to a significant degree, spending a large proportion of its resources attacking price fixing
and government regulation that facilitates noncompetitive horizontal behavior. During the period, however, the FTC spent only a small fraction
of its antitrust resources in this area;[72] two of its most successful horizontal cases – *Bakers of Washington* and *Tetracycline* – were completed before 1970. The Commission is not presently involved in any cases that
seem even remotely capable of increasing consumer welfare to the extent
that those two cases appear to have done, although, as noted above, the
Commission has recently increased antitrust activities aimed at government caused and sanctioned restraints, particularly those dealing with
regulated industries and with health care.

B. Horizontal mergers

To evaluate a horizontal merger enforcement program, we must keep
clearly in mind that such mergers can either injure or improve consumer
welfare, understand how they may accomplish those two opposed ends,
and be able to tell whether the enforcer had some reasonably effective
way of distinguishing those mergers that are likely to injure consumer
welfare from those that would probably improve it. Generally speaking,
there are three categories of possible effects that a horizontal merger can
have on consumer welfare. Such a merger will injure consumer welfare if
it facilitates horizontal collusion without increasing productive and/or
marketing efficiency. It will increase consumer welfare if it increases efficiency without facilitating horizontal collusion. A horizontal merger that
both facilitates horizontal collusion and increases efficiency will injure or
improve consumer welfare depending on the relative magnitude of those
two effects.

It is, of course, much easier to state this theoretical framework than it is
to make the trade-off required in the third possible case or even to estimate reasonably well what effect any given merger will have in terms of
facilitating collusion or creating efficiency. Thankfully, however, it is
much easier in many cases to make these estimates as to the efficiency-
creating or collusion-facilitating effects of a merger than it is to make a

trade-off between them. With this theoretical framework in mind, I examine briefly the 18 horizontal merger cases litigated to disposition at the Commission level during the period.

Two cases were not primarily merger cases at all, but instead involved alleged attempts to monopolize the dubiously important markets for bananas in Los Angeles and spaghetti in the Pacific Northwest.[74] In three other cases the Commission dismissed the complaints, in two of them unanimously.[75] The third case, dismissed by a 3 to 2 vote, raises the question of the effect to be given to efficiency creation, an issue that runs implicitly through all the horizontal merger cases and through most of the FTC's other antitrust work as well. I discuss this case because, even though it appears to have been correctly decided by the Commission, it treats the efficiency issue more directly than do other cases. The case involved the acquisition of Gindy Manufacturing Corporation, the fourth largest firm– with about 6 percent of the market – in the truck trailer market, by Budd Co., the 250th largest industrial corporation in the nation in 1965.[76] Although there were other issues, most notably definition of the relevant product market, I focus only on the treatment of efficiencies.

In finding that the merger "entrenched" Gindy, the ALJ made a number of findings that Budd significantly increased Gindy's efficiency, which, because similar issues arise in other cases, are worth close examination. He found that:

1. Budd advanced $12 million to establish a finance company for Gindy, a very important factor in this industry because so many trailers were sold on credit.
2. Budd enlarged and redesigned one of Gindy's plants, resulting in a 40 percent capacity increase. The ALJ said: "Such alterations made Gindy by 1971 a more efficient van trailer producer than it was at the time of its acquisition by Budd."
3. Budd had plans to build two new plants, which would not only expand capacity but would give Gindy the advantage of having plants located throughout the country, which was regarded as important in the industry.
4. It was advantageous for a van-trailer maker to be integrated into the manufacture of the components used in assembling trailers. After the merger, Budd increased the extent of that integration.
5. Budd opened new branches (as opposed to independent dealers) for Gindy; branches were considered in the industry to be more efficient than independent dealers.
6. "Subsequent to the acquisition, Budd has improved the quality of the Gindy van trailer" and "has broadened the types of van trailers which it offers by adding" other types to its line.

7. "Subsequent to the acquisition, Budd has increased substantially the amount of advertising done for Gindy's van trailers, compared to the amount of advertising done by Gindy prior to its acquisition."[77]

The important fact about all these findings is that, because they made it more difficult for smaller firms in the industry to compete, the ALJ regarded them as reasons to hold the merger to be illegal.

Writing for the Commission majority, Chairman Engman focused specifically on Gindy's improved ability to finance its own trailer sales and its greater ability to deal with trade-ins, which resulted from the increase in the number of branches. He noted that respondent had argued that these were not such great efficiencies that they increased barriers to entry to the point where the acquisition should be struck down. Noting that, nonetheless, the large leasing companies and common carrier companies preferred to deal with "manufacturers who can accept trade-ins on a large scale and extend favorable financing terms," Engman wrote:

Lest there be any misunderstanding, we do not suggest, as does the initial decision, that the superior ability of the larger trailer manufacturers to offer services and financing is an "unfair" advantage that is somehow anticompetitive. The advantages are ones that basically arise out of firm size and, although in part may be caused by imperfections in the capital market, are nevertheless beneficial to the customers who are served thereby. They should therefore, be viewed as providing real, and not simply "pecuniary," economies.[78]

Including *Budd*, arguments that efficiencies created by the merger should be counted *against its legality* or that the apparent absence of such efficiency creation should be counted *for its legality* appear in one form or another, either on the Commission of ALJ level, in 8 of the 18 cases litigated to disposition at the Commission level.[79] Not one of these 18 cases even considered the possibility that increased efficiency should count in favor of the merger's legality, the closest approach to that position being Engman's opinions in *Budd* and in *Beatrice Foods Co.*[80] The strongest proposition that Engman's language in those two cases will bear, however, is that efficiency creation should not be counted against the legality of a merger. In another case it appeared that the merger would both create efficiencies and would probably increase market power as well. That merger was struck down without any discussion of the possibility that the efficiencies should count in its favor or that a trade-off between efficiency creation and increased market power should be made.[81] In another case, the opinion suggested the existence of efficiency creation; there was little or no reason to believe that the merger would facilitate collusion. This merger, too, was struck down without any direct discussion of the effi-

:iencies point.[82] The efficiency issue did not figure directly in any of the remaining six cases.[83]

As in almost half of the 18 cases either the Commission or the ALJ regarded efficiency creation as *weighing against* the merger's legality, we need not inquire further into the FTC's understanding of how horizontal mergers can increase consumer welfare or how well it balances increases in efficiency against possible increases in market power occurring by means of an increased facility to collude. The FTC has never attempted such a balancing process or even suggested that it might be worthwhile to try to do so. It never gets to that question, because, with the exception of Engman's two modest attempts to the contrary, it has counted efficiency creation against the legality of mergers. If both efficiency creation and facilitation of collusion are regarded as detrimental, the wonder is that respondents can ever win a merger case before the FTC. It is not surprising that most of them seem to believe that they must convince the Commission that the merger involves no possibility of increased efficiency to have even a chance to preserve the merger. This condition is scandalous.

The FTC's handling of the collusion issue is not much better. The opinions in these merger cases are made up largely of charts and tables comparing the concentration ratios in the case at hand with those that were present in *Philadelphia National Bank*[84] or in other FTC cases holding other mergers to be outside the pale. Insurmountable barriers to entry are found in the most modest capital requirements or in the fact that new firms will have to advertise their products before they can expect consumers to buy them. If no barrier to entry, no matter how implausible or discordant with economic theory, can be found, it is just as likely as not that the merger will be struck down anyway, as it was in *Jim Walter Corp.*, on the basis of some language from a previous FTC case and without any attempt to analyze the underlying economic issues involved.[85]

The FTC is so enmeshed in concentration ratios and fictitious barriers to entry that it has completely lost sight of the fact that the problem in these horizontal merger cases is collusion, not concentration ratios. I have not found a single merger case decided during the period in which any of the many factors other than concentration ratios and barriers to entry that bear on the ability of firms in an industry to collude successfully were even mentioned, let alone seriously analyzed. If the FTC, with its presumed economic expertise, is content to deal with these merger cases largely on the basis of concentration ratios, to the exclusion of the many other factors that are relevant to the collusion issue, and to hold them to be illegal *because* they create efficiencies, there is no reason why those cases should not be handled by the United States district courts. Although their performance also leaves much to be desired, they at least do not exhibit as much of this peculiar distaste for efficiency creation and on the whole seem to be doing a better job.

IV. Conclusions

The most prominent of the Commission's late 1960s critics, the ABA Committee, expressed the sanguine hope that it would be the last of a long line of critics of the FTC. In its view, if the Commission did not improve there would be no substantial purpose to be served by its continued existence.[86] The FTC has attempted to change, and there can be no doubt that those who directed those attempts believed that they were headed in the right direction. But when all the dust has cleared, as far as antitrust enforcement is concerned, the principal change has been the substitution of *Exxon* and a number of other industry-wide cases and investigations – without the benefit of any real attempt at cost/benefit analysis of those proceedings – for a large number of counterproductive Robinson-Patman Act cases. From the point of view of academic criticism this is an important change. It is hard to find an academic in the country today who supports the Robinson-Patman Act. There are, however, still those who believe that *Exxon* and the other cases in the FTC's new industry-wide program are capable of producing economic benefits for society as a whole, even though this belief is based on their adherence to an increasingly discredited structural analysis of concentrated industries.

This shift from Robinson-Patman Act enforcement to a series of cases and investigations against major concentrated industries has other political benefits that augur well for the continued existence of the FTC. This has nothing to do with economic analysis, but rather lies in the fact that it is so easy, for example, to rail against domestic oil companies when the Arabs raise the price of oil, or to malign Safeway when food prices rise because the rain fails to fall on the plains of Asia. The fact that blame is cheaper than analysis bodes well for the waxing of the FTC. The Commission's new attack on oligopoly and "shared monopoly" is a return to the fundamental root of the FTC's creation, which lay in the broadsides of the old Corporation Commission's attacks on the "old" oil trust, the steel combine, and the like. In that sense the "new" FTC is not new at all. It is more like a malformed phoenix arising, through metamorphosis as it were, from the decline, if not the death, of the blue eagle of its NRA-inspired interlude of Robinson-Patman Act enforcement.

I have argued that the FTC's industry-wide program, based on deficient theory and plagued with procedural delays, cannot improve economic welfare. The same is true with most of its other antitrust enforcement efforts – the only possible exception being its recent moves against guildism in the "learned" professions. Most egregious, perhaps, is its horizonal merger program – the flip side of its industry-wide cases – in which it often perversely uses efficiency creation as a basis of illegality.

It seems to me that the FTC can be understood only in political terms. Although its creation was supported by the views of many economists at the time, the role and effect of government regulation have come to be viewed quite differently since then. It could be argued that the FTC continues to exist, in spite of all the criticism of its performance, in large part because Congressmembers need it as a place to refer complaints from constituents about all the tedious ills of life that can possibly be blamed on the business community. In this view, the Commission's principal function is to take the blame off the Congressmembers when, as is inevitable in the vast majority of cases, they are unable to produce satisfaction in response to constituents' complaints.

An FTC performing this function might produce little economic harm and some political good as long as its limited purpose is understood, as it now is not by most. But it should be able to do this with far fewer resources and much less fanfare than that to which the present Commission has grown accustomed. Should this be taken as cynicism at its worst, I invite the reader to try his or her hand at making economic sense of the Commission and its antitrust works.

7 Information for antitrust and business activity: line-of-business reporting

WILLIAM BREIT AND KENNETH G. ELZINGA

Among the items on the agenda of the "new" Federal Trade Commission, the agency's line-of-business program must rank as one of the most controversial. Line-of-business has prompted lawsuits by literally dozens of the nation's largest corporations, raised fundamental questions about the relationship between economic analysis and accounting and stirred controversy within branches of the federal government. It bears the potential for changing the direction of antitrust enforcement.

The dispute over the line-of-business program (hereafter LB) may seem at first glance surprising. After all, the gathering of information and its dissemination has long been one of the chief justifications for the existence of the Federal Trade Commission (hereafter FTC or Commission). Woodrow Wilson, in his recommendation for the creation of the FTC, saw the new commission "as an indispensable instrument of information and publicity, as a clearing house for the facts by which both the public mind and the managers of great business undertakings should be guided."[1] What the Commission seeks to gather is information on the financial performance of the nation's largest corporations by separate product lines or subdivisions. Some 274 lines of business have been delineated for monitoring. According to the FTC, the figures on sales, assets, costs, and profits submitted to it will be aggregated by individual lines of business and published in such a way that the financial statistics from any one company will be obscured. The stimulus for LB is the diversified nature of many large corporations. Because in most cases these corporations publish their financial statistics in a highly aggregated fashion, an observer generally cannot determine the relative profitability of particular divisions within a company.

LB purportedly would change this situation. Proponents of the program have argued that segmented data would: highlight industries in the economy where profits are high (or low or negative); guide the FTC in the allocation of its antitrust enforcement efforts; permit more rational behavior on the part of investors; and as a nod to the academy, generate better data for testing hypotheses about the structure and performance of industries.[2] Thus, the program would seem to offer advantages to businesses (which could make better entry and exit decisions), consumers (who more likely would be buying in competitive markets), and investors (who could scrutinize more closely the earnings record of a diversified company). All this, the FTC promises, would be done at rather nominal costs to the corporations which must submit the data.

This analysis of LB first outlines for the uninitiated the backdrop of the program itself by discussing its origins and development. The remainder of the chapter then addresses the major issues in determining whether LB is in the public interest. Section II considers whether the data are reliable and Section III whether the costs of gathering and using the data are significant. Some concluding remarks are presented in Section IV.

I. Origins and development of LB

Before addressing whether LB is in the public interest, a description of the essential background concerning the program will assist the reader in understanding LB. In this section, we address the mechanics of LB, compare LB with other reporting requirements, and consider the legal and policy issues as they have been debated in the various branches of government.

A. *The FTC's line-of-business program*

The concept of LB has been discussed within the Commission staff for many years. In 1970, the first LB form was published by the Bureau of Economics; in August 1974, the LB program was formally introduced when 345 companies were ordered to file data for their fiscal year 1973. The initial program, however, became submerged in difficulties soon apparent to the FTC, and the original orders were withdrawn. The original LB form of August 1974 had delineated 357 manufacturing and 97 nonmanufacturing categories; this then shrank to a less burdensome 219 manufacturing and 9 nonmanufacturing lines by December 1974. The current form contains 261 different categories in manufacturing and 14 nonmanufacturing categories. This current form was revealed in mid-1975, when information was sought from over 400 corporations on their operations for the fiscal year ending June 30, 1974. The companies were to submit a listing of their subsidiaries, a brief description of the business endeavors of each, and the sales, assets, costs, and profits for certain specified lines of business. In addition, each respondent was to reconcile the LB data it submitted with the company's published financial statistics and certify the accuracy of the figures.

A corporation completing the LB form is required to distribute its costs and revenues among the designated lines of business. The corporations, however, have some discretion in selecting methods by which they will report the costs of production for given lines of business; the FTC does not specify how costs and assets common to more than one product are to be allocated among the different business lines engaged in by the same corporation. Moreover, the FTC will accept in one LB business activity that actually belongs in another if the "outside" activity is no more than 15 percent of the aggregate and if it would be costly for the reporting company to segregate the figures.

B. How does LB differ from other financial reporting done by corporations?

Large corporations already spend millions of dollars in the production of financial reports, providing information not only to shareholders and government but to potential rivals and investors as well. As LB would be unnecessary if it merely duplicated other sources, it is instructive to see if these other sources differ in kind or in principle from the LB program.

1. Annual reports

The annual reports of large U.S. corporations constitute the most widely disseminated picture of their financial performance. These reports inform shareholders, investors, and other firms of the overall financial performance of the corporation and its total asset and debt structure. In addition to the financial statistics, the reports are often lavishly fabricated and ingeniously composed to portray the corporation's interest in minority groups, the environment, and technical progress. Most of the recent reports of large corporations reflect an abiding concern on the part of the company with the conservation of energy. But from the standpoint of data by line of business, annual reports offer humble returns.

Let us inspect, for two recent and typical years, the annual reports of two corporations, each a *bête noire* of business critics and both notorious for past antitrust difficulties: GE and ITT. In GE's 1971 report, in addition to the corporation's aggregate sales and profits, the public was informed of "substantial growth" in power generation, rail transportation, medical systems, engineering plastics, and commercial jet engines. There were "decreased sales and orders" in military aircraft engines and space projects. Two product lines were publicly eliminated: integrated circuits and vacuum cleaners. GE does proffer sales and earnings data by five "major categories": industrial components and systems, consumer, industrial power equipment, aerospace, and international.

A customer or potential entrant into, say, electric pump motors could not determine GE's performance in this sector from the annual report, the information being hopelessly concealed among GE's business in transit cars, machine tool controls, plastics, locomotives, telecommunication systems, medical equipment, computer services, and elsewhere. In its industrial power equipment breakdown, where pump motors would fall, all one can infer is that GE's entry into the delivery of turnkey nuclear plants was an expensive mistake. The disaggregated sales and income figures—still too broad to provide information on GE's performance in any one market – are further muddied because no explanation is given of the allocation among categories of such expenses as top management, research and development, interest, and income taxes. To further complicate matters, GE's international sales in 1971, approximately 14 percent of its total, cut *across* the other four major categories.

The quantity of information in the 1975 annual report of GE contained the same sectoral breakdown. In the text of the report, one could learn of markets within these sectors where sales had flagged, and of others that had remained strong. Somewhat more detail is given in 1975 on the performance of various products, but the indicators are usually descriptive, not quantitative.

The 1971 annual report of ITT provides a more extensive performance breakdown by product groups. ITT offers sales and income for four categories within its manufacturing group and five (including Hartford Fire) within its consumer and business services grouping. Notwithstanding the number of categories, each is broad, encompassing more than one economic market. In the text one can learn about ITT's performance in some relevant markets: for example, 1971 was a bad year for Sheraton Hotels; things did not go well for the Chile Telephone Company; and in Europe the manufacture of telephones and central office telephone switching equipment prospered. Although the report claims that ITT was one of the first multinational corporations "to adopt the principle of local management of local operations" and that "ITT's divisions and subsidiaries are established as separate profit centers," the data behind these statements are not revealed.

By 1975, the ITT report, although continuing with nine principal product groups, depicts a restructuring of their composition that prevents a close comparison of sectoral performance with earlier years, even for categories as broad as these. There is in 1975 only one telecommunications product group (in 1971, there were two involving telecommunications).

Yet the figure given in the 1975 report for "telecommunications" is not the sum of the categories "telecommunication equipment" and "telecommunication operations" from the 1971 annual report. Further, the group "natural resources" had sales of $313 million in the 1971 annual report; in the 1975 version, 1971 sales for the "natural resources" are listed as $382 million. "Food processing and services," a principal product group in 1971 with $961 million in sales, gains an additional $10 million in 1971 sales when relisted as "food products" in the 1975 version. Curiously, even the aggregate sales for the whole company for 1971 differ in the two volumes.[3] The text of the report, like GE's, just cited, and others of this genre, contains many examples of new product lines, plant expansions, the reception of new contracts, and the citing of particular sectors where sales have lagged.

From these reports, two conclusions are warranted. First, LB data are not offered; the principal product categories embrace too many economic markets and are themselves subject to regrouping by the companies over time. On the other hand, for some of the purposes LB data are to serve, annual reports are of value. In the case of ITT, for example, investors, rivals, or potential entrants may find useful the information that ITT has added capacity in fluff pulp (used to make disposable diapers), that Sears, Roebuck has contracted to feature ITT's Scott Turf Builder grass seed exclusively, or that Morton's frozen doughnut was one of the most successful new frozen food products of the year.[4]

2. Submissions to the Securities and Exchange Commission

In addition to their annual reports, corporations submit financial data on their operations to the Securities and Exchange Commission (SEC). Indeed, the SEC receives annually over 2 million pages of information from corporate respondents. As these data are available for public surveillance and thus might serve the intended purposes of LB, it will be useful to inspect how they differ from the requirements of the FTC's LB program. The SEC currently requires the deconsolidation of some financial data by diversified corporations in reports to the agency. Since 1969, the SEC has required limited statistics on segmented performance to be included in the registration statements of new securities. The SEC "10-K rule" of 1970 directed corporations under SEC regulation to file information annually on the sales, costs, and profits of their lines of business. This rule, however, allows the corporations great leeway in selecting the product groupings by which they would report. In January 1971, the SEC required, on its 10-K forms, sales and profits from each line of business accounting for more than 10 percent of sales and profits, but still permitted the corporation to determine the lines of business that it would report. Thus, the SEC has no prefabricated LB categories.

In general, the SEC regulations permit companies to report sectoral financial performance in a fashion consistent with their normal public accounting data. A comparison of the annual 10-K reports submitted by GE to the SEC with the company's annual reports to its stockholders shows a virtually identical financial breakdown of operations in terms of lines of business. The 10-K forms, however, generally provide a more detailed itemizing of the different products made by the respondent than revealed in its annual report. Nevertheless, although the SEC data may provide an investor with some knowledge of the performance of a corporation's subsidiary, it would not likely provide information regarding what an economist refers to as an "industry," nor would the composition of that segment necessarily be kept constant over time, nor could the profit or loss figures be confidently summed with those submitted by other corporations to obtain an industry profit or loss figure. Further, 10-K forms do not divulge the methods by which respondents allocate common costs or handle the costing of intracompany transfers. For these reasons, F. M. Scherer, one of the architects of the FTC's LB program, concluded: "It is impossible to escape the conclusion that if one seeks to make inter-firm comparisons or analyze performance in specific industries, the SEC-mandated segmented reporting system is of little use."[5]

Currently, the SEC requirements are being revised in accord with the proposals of the Financial Accounting Standards Board (FASB).[6] The *Federal Register* for May 1977 contains the SEC's proposed Rule on Industry and Homogeneous Geographic Segment Reporting, which now requires a form of LB reporting.[7] According to the SEC, the breakdown "must depend to a considerable extent on the registrant's management" and may entail disaggregation by existing profit centers. However, in forming LB segments, the corporation is to assemble products that are substitutable in consumption and have high cross-elasticity of supply or flow through common marketing channels. One indicator of the broad reach of acceptable LB segments is the SEC's contention that probably no more than 10 will be delineated for most corporations.

Impetus for this revision has not come from the SEC but from the FASB, which now requires segmented reporting by corporations before audits can be certified as meeting generally accepted accounting standards. Although the SEC requirements are still in flux, they represent only a modest movement toward the data desired by the FTC. The SEC and FASB programs lack the prior delineation of lines of business. Further, neither specifies rules for handling common costs and intersegment transfers, thereby precluding the aggregation of corporate profits by business lines. Moreover, the SEC classifications will still allow groupings broader than meaningful economic industries or markets.

II. Will the data be reliable?

Before one can support LB, the need to determine the reliability of the data is paramount. The data need not be perfect, but they must not be so imperfect as to be useless or even misleading. Our discussion of the reliability issue covers two major topics. First, we consider the controversy over costs, including the problem of whether accounting numbers are good proxies for the necessary economic ones, the problem of joint and common costs, and the problem of intracompany transfers. Second, since LB data will be reliable only if LB categories conform to economic markets, we consider whether that conformance exists.

A. The controversy over costs

1. Accounting versus economic profit

As a guide to public policy, the relevance of published profits of the aggregative sort that the FTC intends to use hinges upon the economic content of the accounting data base. Unfortunately for supporters of LB, the use of accounting profit data as a proxy for economic profit presumes a coherence between accounting numbers and economic value that does not exist. As Kenneth E. Boulding once put it, accounting profits and economic profits are "uncongenial twins."[8] Several reasons explain the distinction:[9]

a. Owing to inflation, accounting data of the sort that the FTC will use to report profits will understate the values of assets, because assets are typically valued at their original cost. This means that profit rates as a percentage of assets will appear higher than would be the case if the assets were valued at reproduction cost.

b. Accounting data for diversified firms will involve arbitrary and differing treatments of joint and common costs and therefore will not be comparable from firm to firm and industry to industry, a point that will be discussed at length below.

c. Accounting figures do not always reflect the highest valued foregone alternative of the resources used (opportunity costs) by the firm, and therefore economic rents are not always capitalized into costs. This means, for example, that an individual monopolist making high profits (as reported by an accountant) could sell the business and the new owner's accountant would report only normal profits. Yet nothing has changed but ownership.

d. Accounting figures would give a different sum for profits for two identical firms if one owns an input that it uses and the second rents or leases it. To the economist, both firms would have identical profits. Similarly, accounting sums would give a different figure for profits for two firms identical in every way in terms of all other receipts and expenditures if one firm was financed by issuing common stock, another by issuing bonds. But the accidental financial structure of an enterprise does not affect profit in the economist's sense.

e. Accountants charge to current expense items that produce future income and thereby create economic assets. Expenditures on advertising, recruiting, research and development, and training personnel, among others, produce intangible assets. As accountants normally do not record them as assets, however, accounting profit as a percentage of assets usually overstates the true economic profit. This causes a distortion of the asset position of companies because some industries have outlays on intangibles that are high relative to other industries.[10] It thus seems clear that a tally of accounting data will not dovetail nicely with economic profits.

2. Joint and common costs

On the first page of his seminal study of overhead costs, J. M. Clark described such costs as those ". . . that cannot be traced home and attributed to particular units of business in the same direct and obvious way in which, for example, leather can be traced to the shoes that are made from it."[11] The relevance of allocating "overhead cost" to the success of LB is apparent: even assuming that accounting numbers cohere with economic costs, a further condition necessary for the success of LB would be the ability of diversified companies to allocate properly their costs as among the FTC's designated lines of business. If a rational division of its total costs cannot be made, a company's segmented profit and loss reports will be suspect. Moreover, if diversified companies do not follow a common method in allocating their costs, the aggregated line-of-business statistics will not be authentic.

Cost allocation is not, of course, a problem for the totally nondiversified corporation. In calculating its income statement, all of its costs are subtracted from all of its revenues. At the other extreme would be a debt-free company, paying no taxes, that is diversified into industries in such a way that all production, marketing, research, and management functions are distinct. Only common stock certificates link the divisions under a corporate umbrella. In such a peculiar case, profit and loss figures for the different business segments could be unambiguously gathered. Unfortunately for LB, the allocation problem that Clark cited arises in the case of costs that are joint or common to two (or more) lines of business, a problem confronted by every respondent to the FTC's data demands.

Joint costs and common costs occur when multiple products, whether facilities or services, of a corporation draw upon the same inputs and the use of the inputs cannot be associated with any particular product. Economists distinguish between joint and common costs, a bifurcation not as clearly drawn by accountants. With joint costs, no attribution of costs as between lines of business can be made that is not both arbitrary and meaningless because the lines of business are produced in fixed proportions from (at least some of) the same inputs. An illustration would be an airline company selling passenger fares and freight service on the same planes. Clearly, two different products are involved. But there is no scientific way that one can allocate, say, the cost of the pilot's services between freight and passenger business. Consequently, although the profitability of the whole corporation can be ascertained, no attempt to assign precise figures to represent the performance of its freight and passenger business is possible.

Common costs involve the far more usual case in which inputs are used by different lines of business in variable proportions. For example, if product lines X and Y share the services provided by a centralized personnel office, legal staff, billing service, sales force, warehouse space, top management, research and development effort, or even production plant facilities, the use of more of one of these inputs by product X will mean that less is available for Y; therefore, the cost of X should include a portion of the common costs if the inputs could have been used in the production of Y. For this reason, common costs, as A. E. Kahn put it, have "objective reality."[12]

Fortunately for LB proponents, truly joint costs are generally located in the public utility sector of the U.S. economy and therefore involve product lines not now found in the FTC's LB list. Common costs – often referred to by accountants as overhead costs – are, however, incurred by every LB respondent. But the fact that these costs have "objective reality" does not mean that they are readily calculable. To allocate common costs among business segments, most accountants suggest some readily applicable rule of thumb. The most obvious are proportional allocation of common costs based either on the segment's sales or on the size of the variable expenses directly attributable to it. Neither of these is wholly satisfactory. As J. M. Clark explained: "Most of the real problems involve one . . . fact; namely, that an increase or decrease in output does not involve a proportionate increase or decrease in [common] cost."[13] Top management may spend the majority of its time on the smaller line of business in hopes of improving its stature; the legal department may find the modestly sized division more litigious than the others; warehousing expenses may be more a function of product bulk than of dollar sales; the smaller subsidiary (in sales or expenses) may be unionized or less capital intensive and therefore place greater demands upon the personnel office; billing is usually more related to the number of transactions than to a subsidiary's sales or variable costs. In each case, more precise rules of thumb could be formulated. But unless they can both be refined and uniformly adopted by all firms reporting in a given line of business, the resulting profit and loss aggregates could be grossly misstated.

Proponents of LB have argued that common costs are not a major portion of total costs, implying that any efforts in allocation or lack of uniformity across respondents would be small or cancel out. But one must be cautious about such inferences because, in matters of economics, tails often do wag dogs. A change in the allocation of a common cost, which may be only a minor part of the corporation's overall cost structure, can have significant effects on the performance of a line of business. The standard source documenting this point is a study by R. K. Mautz and K. Fred Skousen.[14] They examined data submitted by conglomerate corporations from which one could infer the approximate proportion of a firm's common costs to its total profits. The firms' noninventoriable common costs (the authors excluded federal income tax as a common cost) generally were found significant compared with their net incomes. The magnitude of the allocable common costs thus provides the potential for considerable play in line-of-business statistics. Companies could, through innocence or dissembling, proffer misleading figures on profits and losses.

Mautz and Skousen found this potential to be realized in practice. The 306 responding corporations used a variety of methods to allocate common costs. Some corporations used proportional rules of thumb of various sorts; in other cases, the managements of the subsidiaries negotiated the division among themselves. The study also showed that "many companies use more than one basis for allocating such costs."[15] The crucial conclusion of the Mautz–Skousen research was that the choice of methods commonly used could readily alter the income figures and, occasionally, the rank order of rate of return on investment by lines of business. Not surprisingly, the authors found the measurement problem to be more severe when the firm's product segments were of relatively equal size and its common costs were large relative to the total income of the corporation.

To illustrate the potential scope of the problem, consider a hypothetical conglomerate firm with only two divisions, X and Y, each with sales of $350 million and total profits for the enterprise of $50 million. Assume that

X is more capital intensive, with 65 percent of the corporation's $500 million in assets ($325 million); Y has 70 percent of the production employees. Assume also, following Mautz and Skousen, that only 8 percent of the firm's costs are common ($52 million) and that direct, attributable costs are identical for each division ($299 million). If common costs are allocated by an asset benchmark, X will show profits of $17.2 million (a 5.3 percent return on assets) and Y will show profits of $32.8 million (an 18.7 percent return on its assets). Now if the same costs are apportioned by employees, 30 percent of the $52 million goes to X ($15.6 million) and 70 percent to Y ($36.4 million), leaving X with segmented profits of $35.4 million (*more than double* its performance under the former method and a rate of return on assets of 10.9 percent), whereas Y earns profits of $14.6 million (an 8.3 percent return on assets).

The figures in this example are illustrative of the tail-wags-dog phenomenon. Although the numbers are hypothetical, they do not portray a situation beyond the pale of ranges generated by Mautz and Skousen in their application of various allocation methods to the six actual conglomerate firms they studied in detail.[16] Their work vindicates the assertion of one executive in response to their survey:

In many cases the method used to allocate costs . . . can have an extremely important effect on the income reported for each of the units involved. High profits and rates of return on one unit . . . can be reversed in many cases merely by changing the method of cost allocation. . . . In light of this it would be possible for a company to manipulate the results to create the impression that they wish to convey. On the other hand, a management sincerely trying to be objective could be accused of manipulating results simply because another party could use different accounting methods to arrive at significantly different results. Based on a wide variety of methods being used today (most of which have support in accounting literature) either of the above mentioned results could occur to the disadvantage of those companies doing their best to be informative.[17]

Oddly, the FTC has moved in the direction of noncomparability on common-cost allocation. In its original submission of the proposed LB form to OMB in August 1973, the Commission required standardized procedures for common-cost allocation. At that time, the FTC recognized that even a relatively small common-costs element could shift profit figures, depending upon its allocation. Yet to reduce the cost of compliance, the current forms leave the allocation standards to the respondent's discretion, although the companies must state the criteria used to allocate nontraceable items. The FTC then will apply different rules to the submitted data on operating profits to test their sensitivity to these alternatives; if the results dictate, the FTC may shift back to a standardized procedure at a later date.[18] This is an example of being pennywise and pound foolish. Given the incentives for corporate dissembling and the fact that even conscientiously developed allocation procedures would certainly differ among companies, the value of any business or government decisions based on essentially unaggregatable data would be questionable. No matter what other objections might be raised to LB and its intended use, the program is enfeebled if common costs are not rationally and uniformly defined and allocated.

3. Intracompany transfers

The problems here are in part similar to those of common costs. A hypothetical example will illustrate the potential for the debasement of LB data in the case of vertically integrated firms. Consider a corporation producing X and Y, X being an input in the production of Y. If the enterprise earned $25 million last year, by a simple shift of accounts the $25 million can be made to show up as profit for X (using a very high transfer price) or as $25 million in profits for division Y (by adopting a low transfer price). There are millions of dollar-profit combinations in between.

Ideally, in calculating Y's profitability, the cost of X would be its opportunity cost, with the open-market price being a proxy for such a cost. If the firm is engaged in dual distribution, such a figure should be available from subsidiary X's own invoice records. If no outside sales are made, an estimate must be determined involving rule-of-thumb allocations, adopting either prices of other firms who do sell a product comparable to X in an open market or some negotiating arrangement between X and Y. As was the case with the allocation of common costs, corporations use a variety of means in selecting shadow prices, with most of them not using an open-market price.[19] Interestingly, most companies surveyed by Mautz used more than one method of cost calculation, some as many as four and five.[20] The study on intracompany transfers by the National Association of Cost Accountants concluded that in the majority of firms, shadow prices are developed not to portray profits but to "implement such managerial objectives as decentralizing management, minimizing taxes, and controlling return on invested capital."[21]

The original LB program of the FTC, no doubt reflecting its Bureau of Economics. origins, called for all transfers between lines of business within a company to be done at market prices. The statement of purpose read: "Given the needs of the FTC, it appears that the use of market prices is appropriate. The use of any alternative procedure would distort the measurement of relative profitability."[22] This assessment is correct. Nonmarket transfer prices make the profit figures useless from any outsider's standpoint. Yet the FTC now has retracted this requirement and would allow respondents to use (in the interests of lowering compliance costs) whatever current system the corporation uses, even if involving standard cost measures or negotiated shadow prices. The Commission's LB categories combine activities that involve large numbers of intracompany transfers. Since, for the first 224 companies submitting LB reports on 1973 business, intracompany transfers averaged 7 percent of total sales and at least 15 percent of sales for 24 of the respondents, the reliability of the data is reduced. A further weakness is that the FTC permits respondents to combine vertical lines of business whenever the firm uses more than half the output of the intermediate product as an input in a later stage of production.

As with common costs, the Commission is caught, intractably, upon the horns of a dilemma. Only shadow prices "at market" will provide conceptually meaningful LB data, just as uniform common-cost allocation rules are taxonomically required. Yet it is only with detailed regulation of the corporations that such uniformity could be obtained. With vertically integrated firms, there is great variety in the divisional levels at which firms, producing the same end product, transfer their inputs, as well as significant diversity in the nature of the input sold on the market and the input transferred internally. Even within a nonvertically integrated corporation, there will be different real costs in the transfer of inputs to divisions in different markets. Often newly developed products are used only internally, with no open-market proxy available until an external market develops. Unless the FTC would be prepared to iron out (or preclude) all these dissimilarities, integrated firms with operations beyond one LB are unlikely to be able to provide profit and loss figures for a particular LB that are either accurate or comparable with the data of other firms.

The conceptual difficulty of ascertaining an appropriate cost is not the only obstacle in costing intracompany transfers. For a wholly different reason, the FTC's inquiry into LB profits by vertical level is questionable. The economic theory of the firm posits its form as being a product of economic forces. A firm arises because of the costs of using the price mechanism, notably the costs of learning about prices and the expense of entering detailed contracts for each use of inputs. As R. H. Coase has put it:

It is true that contracts are not eliminated where there is a firm but they are greatly reduced. A factor of production (or the owner thereof) does not have to make a series of contracts with the factors with whom he is co-operating within the firm, as would be necessary, of course, if this co-operation were as a direct result of the working of the price mechanism. For this series of contracts is substituted one.[23]

Thus, there is a certain arbitrariness in selecting any point in the production process and examining it, in effect, as a legal transaction in the price mechanism – when the whole purpose of the integration in the first place was to avoid the economic costs of using the price mechanism.

B. Definition of the LB market

Another problem with the reliability of LB data is the disparity between LB categories and economically meaningful markets. The use of LB for antitrust and for investment decisions rests on the economic theory of markets. A market in economics encompasses products that customers find substitutable (within the range of prevailing prices), and the market's boundaries should encompass all the primary demand and supply forces that determine prices in the market. Profit data of firms aggregated by lines of business can be made to square with the teachings of economic theory only if the line of business corresponds to an actual market. The profitability of a line of business comprising "shoes, ships, and sealing wax" would be a reliable guide neither to antitrust authorities nor to anyone in the business world. Therefore, in critiquing the FTC's LB program, one must evaluate whether the currently delineated LB's correspond to real-world markets. In addition, there is the question of data correspondence: Does the FTC program gather profit data truly attributable to the segment in which it is reported?

The current LB lineup for manufacturing comprises 98 three-digit Standard Industrial Classification (SIC) categories, 84 four-digit categories, and the rest made up of three-digit categories from which four-digit SIC industries have been subtracted.[24] Therefore, the question of relative correspondence of FTC-designated segments to actual markets is itself a question of the correspondence of the four-digit and three-digit codes to real markets – one of the more debated topics in the economics of industrial organization. Critics of the FTC program have argued that there is little coherence, citing the agency that compiles the SIC data in support of their position.[25] The economists at the FTC obviously hold a contrary view.

The problem is not so much that the truth lies somewhere in between but that the correspondence of some LB segments to actual industries is closer than others. It is possible to select horror stories of incongruence as well as to select segments that seem reasonable matches. The FTC has not yet endeavored to offer an analysis of overall correspondence, and one cannot predict how discerning the users of the data will be in separating the wheat markets from the chaff segments. The skepticism that critics of LB have toward the current LB boundaries is perhaps understandable given the track record, in some instances, of the FTC in selecting relevant markets in antimerger cases.[26]

The original LB version of August 1973 called for data on a "market" basis, emphasizing the attribute of substitutability in consumption – in the FTC's words, groupings of products "perceived by buyers as close

substitutes for each other." The final version of March 1974 broadened
the scope of the categories (they were now called "industries") and lessened the correspondence to economic markets. To the extent that the new
categories encompass substitutability, it will more likely be on the supply
side. For example, substitutability for consumers among the products encompassed by "power-driven hand tools" is low, but may be rather high
for suppliers of such tools. Most of the LB categories are far broader than
those put forth by the FTC (and the Antitrust Division) in the prosecution
of merger cases. As it happens, the selection of LB segments is oriented
to sectors of the economy with relatively high four-firm concentration
ratios.

Perhaps more serious than the correspondence problem is what has
come to be called the contamination problem: data tallied into one LB
that belong in another. Disagreements in opinion about the correspondence of particular LB segments to an economic market would, after all,
be in the open. The extent of contamination in the data is more opaque. In
complying with the August 1974 LB program, a respondent could allocate
the sales, costs, profits, and assets of a given *establishment* (generally, a
plant at a single location) wholly to that line of business accounting for the
largest proportion of the plant's sales. If the plant were devoted to the
business of only one LB, all data would pertain to that segment. But if the
plant were multicategory, all data could then be tallied for the modal LB
and the results for that LB would be overstated (whereas the economic
contribution of the secondary activity would disappear). The first version
of LB (August 1973) did not permit a firm to assign financial data for a
specific line of business to a wholly different LB category simply on the
grounds that the product represented less than 50 percent of the output
from a particular establishment.

Betty Bock conducted a study of the potential for data contamination
under the establishment-base rule. She revealed the significant potential
for abuse of this methodology, particularly where multicategory establishments make products in different stages of their life-cycle.[27] By the use of
census data, she estimated the severity of the contamination problem with
regard to sales, revealing that one-fourth of the FTC's LB categories
would be overstated by at least 11 percent, and over one-fourth would be
understated by 11 percent or more.[28] FTC tabulations based on the 1973
LB reports place the weighted average level of sales contamination at
slightly less than 6 percent.[29]

Attempting to lessen the contamination problem, the FTC, in its latest
LB version, has recanted the establishment-based rule and now calls for
LB figures to be built up from what it calls "basic components."[30] These
lines of business can be establishments or organizational units (e.g.,

"profit centers" or current product lines), provided that products foreign to the LB (i.e., secondary products) are not more than 15 percent of the LB total.[31] This does not mean, however, that data contamination on sales cannot exceed 15 percent. It easily can for firms vertically integrated across more than one potential LB.

The FTC claims that in spite of the variations permitted in tabulating data, the aggregated information it will publish will be reasonably accurate, indeed more so than the figures of an individual respondent because the law of large numbers cancels out errors. This is, however, a curious invoking of that statistical principle. The law of large numbers tells us about the stabilization of a measure of central tendency, such as a simple average, in the case of many observations. But with the bias of LB definitions toward high-concentration segments, and the limited number of respondents, only a few firms will dominate most lines of business – hardly the large number needed for reliance on the law of large numbers. Moreover, any data contamination based on sales is not transferable to the contamination of costs and profits unless these factors are directly proportional to sales for all respondents in the particular line of business. Both advocates and critics of LB are in the dark as to whether they are.

Obviously, whenever a given LB encompasses more than one real market, the resulting LB financial statistics are debased, both for purposes of economic analysis and business action.[32] The fact that the data under current LB reporting requirements might be significantly contaminated further enfeebles their usefulness. Even if the aforementioned problems were not present, economic analysis also suggests that another caveat must be attached to the figures: LB data in almost every instance will not include all the supply units in that line of business. If only successful firms are designated as respondents (or the sample is biased toward them), even "accurate" data from these firms would bias upward the profit figures of the line of business and not portray the true returns being made by suppliers as a whole. Thus, an industry could be in long-run equilibrium making on the whole only normal returns, but a (nonrandom) selection of the most successful firms might seemingly portray above-average returns, thereby erroneously attracting the attention of the antitrust authorities and new investors.

Thus, the reliability of the data of LB is in considerable doubt. Problems of the imprecise nature of accounting costs, of common costs, of intracompany transfers, and of the deviation between LB and economic markets cause one to seriously question the reliability of LB data. Even if the data were reliable, however, this still would not justify the LB program. For, as the next section demonstrates, the usefulness of LB data would remain in doubt.

III. Is LB useful?

A. Does LB affect entry?

There appears to be confusion in the theory of entry as presented in the standard economics textbook. This arises because of the ambiguity in the meaning of profits as a "signal" to enter an industry and the technical role of profit in the economic theory of the firm. The confusion permeates the Commission's discussion of the role of profit and thereby the FTC's arguments that LB data will help improve the allocation of resources by facilitating new entry.

A typical treatment of the role of profit in a market is given by Lipsey and Steiner in their widely used textbook:

Profits in some industry are the signal that resources can profitably be moved into that industry. Losses are the signal that the resources can profitably be moved elsewhere. Profits and losses thus play a crucial signaling role in the workings of a free-market system. Only if there are zero profits is there no incentive for resources to move in or out of an industry.[33]

This statement, implicitly or explicitly, is representative of the reasoning that underlies much of the discussion of the need for LB reporting. For example, the staff of the Federal Trade Commission supported LB reporting on the grounds that the absence of profit and cost information on a segmented basis destroys the signals necessary to move resources into areas where they are most needed. Indeed, they called this "the most serious problem posed by the absence of detailed data."[34] The real gravamen of their case for LB is that the absence of such reporting creates barriers to entry. In the words of an FTC staff report: "If above-normal profits arise in the production and sale of a product (if revenues exceed the sum of all economic cost), then new firms will enter an industry in the absence of appreciable barriers to entry. In this way entry, or the threat of entry, will lower prices and reduce profits to more competitive levels. . . . In this fashion rates-of-return between industries will tend to be equalized."[35] They conclude: "Above-normal profits and any attendant resource misallocation can continue for a longer period of time if such information is hidden within conglomerate corporations. Above-normal or monopoly profits may not act as a trigger to new entry if their presence is unknown."[36]

The textbook treatment of profits as signals may be useful to facilitate thought, but the treatment is misleading when taken to describe how decisions are actually made to enter a market. For that analysis one must look to the theory of the firm. The FTC arguments for LB as a "trigger to new entry" are based on this misconception of what data firms use in making entry decisions. As shown below, at the firm level, industry accounting profits do not play the role of "signal" for the potential entrant in the same way that economic profits do at the market level for reallocating resources.

Perhaps this confusion over the treatment of profits arises because economists often think of profits as the price of management, whereas in fact they are no such thing. Profits are a residual. They do not attach to the price of any particular factor of production. Instead of profits, the force that motivates an individual's decision to enter an industry is the expected revenue relative to *anticipated* costs.

Consider the individual making a decision whether or not to enter an industry, a choice made under conditions of uncertainty. The individual has imperfect knowledge of his own capabilities and of various objective costs: raw materials, labor, interest, advertising, and the cost of hiring skilled managers. Further, the potential entrant firm cannot directly observe the true total costs of its competitors because it cannot get information on the returns to entrepreneurial capacity that may be accruing to established firms, and may not know the proportions in which existing firms combine inputs in producing their product. Although the potential entrant firm observes a plethora of data in the form of prices for the product, factor costs that would have to be paid, and, in the case of undiversified firms, data on the accounting profits of established firms, such information is not all of the same importance to it. Moreover, the firm realizes that its potentialities as an assembler of inputs are not necessarily revealed in the accounting figures of others. Since the potential entrant firm's management knows that it will have to use some factors of production on a contractual basis, guaranteeing a return, any information on wages, interest, and rents is relevant to its decision making.

More important, the prospective entrant firm also knows that it will receive an uncertain return, a residual; the decision to enter an industry is based on the *anticipations* about the probability distribution of costs and receipts (which form the residual) expected from alternative courses of action on its part. The course of action that is expected to yield the highest expected return to the resources used is the course that is chosen. The market prices of other resources give the entrant information on what its opportunity cost is in forming a firm rather than hiring out its own resources to other firms. For its management realizes that there may be a difference between the productivity of its resources when hired out to others and their productivity when used by the firm itself. To the economist, this difference is called "entrepreneurial capacity."[37]

In economic theory the decision to form a firm and enter an industry is essentially, then, a decision to become a residual income recipient, deriving one's return from uncertainty and counting on one's ability as an entrepreneur. The quantity and quality of such entrepreneurial capacity is highly subjective, varying from firm to firm within an industry. One person may expect to have greater entrepreneurial capacity than another, but there is no way of comparing, *ex ante,* that person's entrepreneurial capacity with anyone else's based solely on LB data.

As with an individual, a firm's return is the difference between total receipts (sales) and total contractual costs. But the firm in advance cannot determine its total return, which, by its nature, can only be known ex post. What motivates the firm is not the unanticipated return arising from uncertainty (what economists call "profit") but rather its *expected* return accruing to entrepreneurial capacity. This is what the firm attempts to maximize.

If potential entrants do not have the scarce entrepreneurial capacity possessed by the profit-realizing firm, returns of this nature cannot be taken away. This capacity is called a rent in economics.[38] The fact that some firms receive this rent does not mean that entry by others will be forthcoming. In the absence of barriers to entry, in long-run equilibrium, rents are due only to the existence of entrepreneurial capacity. Clearly, the publication of accounting data partially reflecting these returns would not and should not induce new entry. Further, in the short run, economic profit, the unanticipated residual of the firm, may also be included in accounting data. These accounting data may be affected by accidental occurrences, random events, or simply mistakes on the part of the firm. This information, too, would not and should not induce new entry.

Thus, in many cases where LB data reveal high profit, entry should not occur. To the extent that LB induces entry in such cases, it will misallocate resources. In any event, the correlation between high LB profits and the desirability of entry is much weaker than the Commission claims that it is.

Further, the FTC's argument that high accounting profits should attract entry is no more plausible than the argument that low profits discourage entry. A low rate of return in an industry, or received by certain firms within an industry, might convey the signal that entrepreneurial skills are very limited among existing firms. Just as *low* profits (not relatively high profits) attract takeover bids by aggressive entrepreneurs who believe that their skills can make the firm efficient, thereby realizing rents to their entrepreneurial capacity, so might a firm be inclined to enter a low-profit industry de novo because it sees potential for returns to its particular and unique entrepreneurial capacities, potentials that existing firms have not exploited, as signaled or revealed by the low profits. But accounting data might be just as misleading a signal to enter in this instance as they are when profits are high.

This analysis leads ineluctably to what may seem to be a surprising result. Profits are likely to be poor signals for entry. The appearance of industry profits (in the accounting sense) is not, itself, an inducement to entry. A prospective entrant will want to compare projected sales in the market and its own expected contractual costs, and not rely on profit figures. This result is surprising only because it has become habitual to think of firms as maximizing profit, which is incorrect. They maximize returns to entrepreneurial capacity. Demand conditions in the industry are highly useful data to the potential entrant, but not published profit figures, which may, after all, include rents to the capacity of other entrepreneurs in the industry, risk premiums to successful firms, quasi-rents to temporarily fixed factors, market power, or the results of chance and random occurrences. These are purely ex post considerations for the potential entrant and cannot influence its decision at the margin, which always involves anticipations of its own future, not the bygones of others' pasts.

B. Does LB aid antitrust enforcement?

A primary use to which the FTC plans to put LB data is in antitrust enforcement. Presumably, industries and firms with high profits, as recorded by the LB program, would be more likely candidates for antitrust investigation, and defendants with high reported profits would be more vulnerable than those with a more modest showing. As explained in another chapter, the Commission considers the attack upon high-concentration industries that perform poorly (as is allegedly revealed by high profits) as one of the most important uses of LB.

The problems in relying on LB data as a guide to antitrust enforcement require little elaboration. As mentioned earlier in the discussion of accounting versus economic costs, in building the LB program upon accounting data, there is little guarantee of a good fit between the data for an LB segment and true economic profits for a meaningful industry. And that is not all. Even assuming that LB data could be made reliable and be made to dovetail with an economic market, knowing the economic profits of an industry is not the same as learning whether there is economic power in the industry. Before that can be ascertained, one must separate "profits" attributable to superior skill, changes in tastes, risk differentials, random occurrences, and quasi-rents from those attributable to market power.[39] LB data themselves could *never* be conclusive, in that the statistics might be influenced by other factors not associated with antitrust problems. Thus, any attempt to use LB as a tool in a campaign to deconcentrate American industry – an apparent reason for the creation of LB – could be seriously misguided. At most, LB data might serve as a prelude to further investigation of the profit statistics themselves, or to see if any anticompetitive elements are involved. But the further investigation of the profit data would involve the very difficult task of distinguishing the various components of economic profits before any precise conclusions about market power could be drawn from the data.

Indirectly, LB data have been suggested for use to further test the question as to whether industry concentration, or a firm's market share, is correlated with (accounting) profit.[40] This question has already generated a sizable literature.[41] The issue, of course, merits more than casual interest only if accounting profit is highly correlated with economic profit. It should be noted that the current LB program would not allow a resolution of the question of a correlation between industry profits (economic or accounting) and concentration, because profitability data from all firms in an industry, including the small- and medium-size members, are not included.

C. Does LB aid investors?

The preceding analysis of entry has direct bearing on the question of whether LB data would be useful information to investors. If our discussion of the role of entrepreneurial capacity in explaining long-run persistent rents to the firm is valid, LB data would have less relevance for investors than might otherwise seem to be the case. The importance of entrepreneurial capacity has been recognized by at least one investment analyst: "In my firm's work of developing investment research material for professional investors, we become more impressed each day with the importance of considering each company as a unique entity. Down through the fundamentals of products, markets and especially in the key qualitative area of management prowess, fewer and fewer companies have close comparisons."[42]

Moreover, a potential investor examining LB data published by the FTC could not identify individual companies as candidates for investment decisions, because to protect the confidentiality of the respondents, profits are reported as aggregates and averages of the information provided. In addition, any usefulness of the data, in this sense, presumes that the rate of return is not already embedded in the share price at the time the FTC data are revealed. Yet recent studies on the efficiency of the stock market indicate that LB data are not necessary or meaningful to investors and do not affect investors' expectations. George J. Benston has reviewed studies of the effect of the publication of corporate financial data on investment behavior and found that most studies conclude that such information is either known (by a sufficient number of investors to make it irrelevant to others) or anticipated before publication.[43]

Moreover, a recent study by Horwitz and Kolodny supports Benston's findings. They tested for the effect on security prices of companies that reported segmented financial data to the SEC with those of a sample of companies that did not, and concluded that there was no evidence to support the contention that such data furnished potential investors with valuable information.[44] On the other hand, Daniel W. Collins, in two related studies, has found that segmented data can permit a more accurate prediction of a corporation's future success than models based on consolidated data.[45] His research, however, indicates the relative value of segmented revenue figures, not profits, in predicting the future performance of a diversified firm.

This does not mean to imply that an investor would reject all information on the various industries in which a diversified company is involved. Such data could be helpful in analyzing a company's potential. But LB profit data will not provide such information.[46] If they did, there is a circumstance in which reliable firm-specific LB data might be of assistance to investors. A current stockholder might find such profit data useful because he or she could reduce the ability of management to engage in what Oliver Williamson has called discretionary behavior. For example, a diversified firm would be less able to pay the top management of a losing division exorbitant salaries in the face of the publication of these losses. This would mean that any problem associated with the separation of ownership and control in the modern corporation would be less likely to occur should individual shareholders be willing to incur the costs of disciplining such managements through complaint or litigation.

IV. The costs of LB

From the very outset, the FTC LB requirement stimulated controversy over the compliance costs of the program. The old adage that "more is better than less" is unequivocally true only at zero cost. Since the gathering of data can be expensive, however, the economist wants to ascertain whether the costs of any proposed program exceed the benefits. For that reason, knowledge of the probable cost of LB is essential in making a confident judgment regarding its efficacy.

Not surprisingly, the FTC's initial estimates of cost were much lower than those made by the corporations that were affected by the LB program. Moreover, the estimates of costs vary over time as the FTC has changed the information required.[47] Many of the companies affected by LB claimed that it would impose an undue compliance burden on them. Thirty-one companies provided cost estimates for the 1973 and/or 1974 LB form reporting requirements. Of the 11 companies that estimated the costs to them of complying with the 1973 form, the range was from $6,000 to $400,000, with a median value of $40,000. Of 25 companies estimating the costs of complying with the 1974 form, the range was from $5,000 to $1.8 million, with a median value of $56,000. The highest cost estimate was that of DuPont, which has 21 reportable lines of business. DuPont argued that its accounting records are geared toward product lines rather than establishment reporting and that as a consequence its first-time reporting costs would range from $1.2 to $1.8 million, followed by annual costs of several hundred thousand dollars. This estimate should be lower with the FTC's shift to product-line reporting.

Although other companies reported high estimates, the Commission claimed that its estimate of compliance costs for all companies in the 1974 LB survey averaged $24,000 per company (and ranged from under $10,000 to $100,000). This estimate was much larger than an earlier one made to OMB of an average of $800 per company.

So far, all of the evidence is not in on this issue. However, to the economist, the direct costs of compliance with LB reporting are only the tip of the iceberg. The real costs also involve the possibility of misinformation being generated by faulty data which, to the extent that firms attempt to use it, could lead managers to make inefficient entry or exit decisions, causing a misallocation of resources.

V. Conclusions

Obviously, LB data will always be imperfect. But that alone does not vitiate the case for LB. Less than perfect data can be useful, but at some point data are so much less than perfect that they are useless or, worse, misleading. LB data would seem to be on the dangerous side of the separation between useful and useless data.

Quite aside from the question of the meaningfulness of LB data is the more fundamental question of whether such data on profits, even if not marred by the kinds of "noise" mentioned above, would be relevant to the decision of a potential competitor to enter an industry. Since the past profits of other firms are not a reliable guide to the future, nor wholly informative about a potential entrant's own prospects, the publication of such information is not likely to stimulate new competition. Since the facilitation of entry is one of the main justifications of the FTC's LB program, the analysis of this paper weakens a major pillar of its support.

Further, although estimates vary as to the precise amount of those costs, the immediate effect of the FTC's order has been to increase costs both to those business firms affected by the program and to the Commission itself in carrying out its regulations.

The final conclusions that can be drawn from this paper are few, and experience with the program over the next few years will be necessary before much can be stated with certainty. But at present it can be asserted that the LB program will not bring about the myriad of benefits claimed for it by its proponents. On the contrary, because the costs of compliance (although in dispute) are assuredly greater than zero, it can be confidently predicted that the net harvest from the FTC's line-of-business innovation will not be bountiful.

Acknowledgments

We wish to thank Betty Bock, Salem Katsh, and J. Fred Weston for helpful comments on an earlier draft.

8   Industry structure investigations: Xerox's multiple patents and competition

CHARLES J. GOETZ AND WARREN F. SCHWARTZ

This chapter evaluates the FTC's proceeding against Xerox Corporation, the firm that revolutionized the copying industry and continues as its most important member.[1] We focus on charges that Xerox, through various means, accumulated patents covering the technology for office copying (or at least its plain-paper submarket) that were so extensive, complex, and obscure in their overall scope that effective competition in the industry was eliminated.[2] The proceeding was terminated by a consent order imposing extensive requirements on Xerox, including a mandate to license any three patents without charge and all patents on terms specified in the order.[3]

Although the FTC's complaint does contain other allegations about the marketing practices of Xerox and its territorial divisions with foreign affiliates,[4] the contention that lends unique importance to this proceeding is that of domination of the industry by control of the essential patented technology. The desirability of the FTC's leveling this charge and resolving it through this consent order can be assessed only by making difficult and far-reaching judgments concerning the proper reconciliation of the ends underlying the patent laws with those served by the antitrust laws.

The basic conflict between these laws has long been well understood. To encourage invention, the patent laws confer a monopoly and therefore the power to choose a price–quantity combination as any monopolist would, with the attendant undesirable allocative and distributional consequences. The central aim of the antitrust laws is to avoid these very consequences. What has often been troublesome is deciding "how far" the patent monopoly goes, given its consequent displacement of the competitive goals of antitrust. What is unique about the Xerox proceeding is the context in which this conflict is presented. Xerox undoubtedly achieved a revolutionary breakthrough that has created enormous social benefits in improved means for assembling, storing, and disseminating information. It accomplished this by detecting the commercial possibilities of theoreti-

121

cal inventions made by others, by improving and perfecting these basic processes, and by incorporating them in products of great practical usefulness.[5] Thus, Xerox has, presumably in response to the incentives created by the patent laws, produced in very large measure just those social benefits that patent rights are designed to create.

At the same time, Xerox did not simply have a single patent to exploit. It first acquired the basic patents for the process known as xerography and then over time added to its control patents for improvements on the basic process.[6] In analyzing the acquisition of subsequent improvement patents, it is important to note that the patent laws confer advantages with respect to future development for a firm holding the basic patents. Improvement patents developed by others cannot be practiced without the consent of the holder of the basic patents. The holder of the basic patents can time the introduction of the improvements that it develops to serve its own ends in terms of the cost and revenue effects both on existing products and on the improved versions that it is capable of manufacturing.[7]

Xerox earned monopoly profits,[8] attributable partially to its innovative contribution, but perhaps also partially to its utilization of strategic opportunities resulting from ownership of many related patents. The central issue in evaluating the Xerox case is what limits the antitrust laws should impose on the exploitation of any special opportunities that may be available to a firm holding a series of related patents.[9] How should the patent laws and antitrust laws be reconciled when the property rights conferred by multiple patents also create incentives for monopolistic conduct? This basic substantive issue also poses a series of subordinate issues with respect to remedy and institutional competence. The relief available in an FTC proceeding, although designated as a cease and desist order, has both (1) remedial effect on competition in the industry directly involved and (2) deterrent effect throughout the economy, because in choosing the behavior in which they will engage, firms must now balance the cost of complying with the legal rules underlying the order (including the avoidance of lawful conduct that might erroneously be held a violation) against the potential cost of sanctions imposed against them under a similar order.

We will assess the consent order from both perspectives. From the remedial point of view, the question involves comparing the state of competition at the time the proceeding began (or the consent order was entered) with the improvements or anticompetitive effects that the order provided. The deterrence issue is more complex in principle, more difficult as a matter of empirical measurement, and undoubtedly more significant as a matter of social policy. The deterrent effects of the order depend crucially on the interpretation placed upon it by decision makers whose conduct might in subsequent proceedings be proscribed and sanctioned on grounds similar to those underlying the charges against Xerox. The deterrent effects may be either negative or positive from a social point of view. The desired positive effects presumably derive from wider dissemination of new technology *once it is invented,* as well as from greater competition, with the consequent reduction in the social loss imposed by monopoly pricing. At the same time, undesired effects, such as "too little" investment in invention, may result because the returns from invention are reduced by risk of exposure to prosecution for antitrust violations.

The analysis of the deterrent effect of the order proceeds in several stages. In Section I, we look to the language of the complaint in a preliminary attempt to identify the objectionable elements of Xerox's conduct. Because the complaint does not sufficiently identify the objectionable conduct, Sections II.A and II.B endeavor to articulate a more precise legal rationale that would be consistent with the pattern of facts cited by the FTC. Premised on this legal basis, the final part of Section II addresses the issue of an appropriate rule to regulate the conduct in question. Section III takes up the effect of the FTC's actual order in the copying industry itself, both in the short and long terms. Finally, Section IV discusses the wider implications of the order for future business conduct in the general economy. One strong conclusion is that the considerable residual uncertainty about the underlying legal basis of the FTC proceeding – even after careful analysis of the complaint and the consent order– will impose significant social costs in the future. This uncertainty extends both to the definition of illegal conduct and the determination of the magnitude and character of the sanction imposed.

I. The complaint

The legal grounds of the FTC charges with respect to Xerox obtaining dominance by "monopolizing . . . patents applicable to office copiers"[10] are obscure. A series of acts are alleged with respect to (1) the securing of patents on inventions developed by Xerox or a research laboratory doing research under contract with Xerox,[11] (2) obtaining access to technology developed by competitors,[12] and (3) restricting the use to which licensees under Xerox patents could put the licensed technology.[13] The complaint, however, does not allege that any one of these acts constitutes a violation of law. Moreover, there is no allegation that the aggregate of acts with respect to patents would constitute a violation. Rather, at the end of the entire complaint it is asserted with respect to all of the conduct alleged that "the aforesaid acts, practices, and methods of competition in commerce are unfair and constitute violations of Section 5 (a) of the Federal Trade Commission Act."[14]

Thus, one possible basis for the complaint is that an aggregation of acts, many and perhaps all of which would individually be lawful, together constitute a proscribed course of conduct. But this apparent explanation is at odds with the specific allegations, which in some instances use terms suggesting the wrongfulness of the individual act alleged. Moreover, even in such instances, there is no explanation of why the act is regarded as objectionable. This difficulty of interpretation is particularly acute with respect to the allegations concerning patents.

For example, Xerox is charged with "maintaining a patent barrier to competition by attempting to re-create a patent structure which would be equivalent in scope to expired patents"[15] and "developing and maintaining a patent structure of great size, complexity and obscurity of boundaries."[16] This implies that the choices made by Xerox in its allocation of resources to various types of research and development were somehow improper, even though the research and development effort yielded inventions that qualified for exclusive protection under the patent laws and the methods utilized by Xerox to restrict competition were limited to those expressly afforded by the patent laws. It also suggests that Xerox strategically arrayed its inventions within its total patent holdings so as to confuse rivals regarding the extent of the patent protection it enjoyed. Here, too, the charge is apparently made on the assumption that each of the patents was validly issued. The respects in which the behavior of Xerox, either in selecting the research and development it would pursue or securing patent protection for its inventions, was improper are nowhere specified.

Similar difficulties exist with respect to the remaining allegations concerning patents. With respect to securing technology from competitors, Xerox is charged with "using its patent position to obtain access to technology owned by actual or potential competitors"[17] and "entering into cross-license arrangements with actual or potential competitors."[18] Cross-licensing of related technology is a common, indeed an inevitable, consequence of the patent laws. For example, the introduction of an improvement on existing technology requires the assent of the owners of both the original patent and the patent covering the improvement. Here the complaint does not even use pejoratives to suggest the underlying theory of illegality.

A brief description of the office or "convenience copier" industry is necessary to understand the final set of allegations.[19] The convenience or office copier industry involves decentralized copying on machines that are simple to operate and do not have the size, noise, and mess of offset presses, printing presses, or other large-scale methods of producing multiple copies. In this market, Xerox is the largest seller of machines using what is known as plain-paper copying. A competing method is coated-paper copying, in which a specially treated paper represents a large portion of the cost. Xerox controlled basic technology utilizable for both plain- and coated-paper copying. It chose to manufacture only plain-paper copiers and to license no one else to make plain-paper copiers.[20]

The remaining allegations with respect to patents concern limitations on patent licenses imposed in accordance with this basic decision. The limitations consisted in some instances of restricting the licenses to use in making coated-paper copiers, in others of limiting them to use of low-speed copiers, and in still others of restricting them to making office copiers.[21] The position taken by the complaint is therefore presumably that Xerox, if it wished to license its technology, could not restrict the uses to which its technology could be put, could not restrict the grant to alternative types of copying machines, and could not restrict the grant to markets other than office copying. Why Xerox was under such an obligation is not, however, made clear.

II. The rationale of the charges

A. The FTC and existing law

As we have indicated, the legal position underlying the complaint is obscure. In addition to the complaint, the Commission staff also produced a document designated "Complaint Counsel's Tentative Outline of the Type of Facts to Be Proven in Support of the Complaint," to which we will refer for additional details of the Commission case. It too, however, lacks a reasoned statement of the Commission's theory of illegality.

Nor do the reported cases, most of them arising under Section 2 of the Sherman Act, provide a rationale for determining the legality of conduct such as that alleged in the complaint.[22] These cases, dealing with a single firm possessing "market power" (the ability to choose price or quantity within significant limits without constraint from competition), make it plain that the market power must have resulted from acts that were in some respect wrongful. The basis, however, for characterizing acts as "predatory," "exclusionary," or "coercive," rather than as acts representing superior skill in satisfying consumer demand, is very poorly articulated. In particular, the scattering of cases dealing with the use of strategic opportunities afforded by ownership of related patents offers no rationale for deciding when utilization of these opportunities will be held to violate the antitrust laws.[23] Dictum asserts that the "mere accumulation of patents" is not a violation,[24] but there is great uncertainty as to what is required for "mere" accumulation to become "predatory," and therefore unlawful.

B. A proposed rationale

Although neither the complaint, the supporting documents, nor prior law identify the respects in which conduct such as that engaged in by Xerox might be objectionable, the facts of the case do suggest a plausible rationale for concern.[25] Because the proceeding itself was not focused on the issues that we believe should be controlling and was terminated through a consent order, it is difficult to determine whether and to what extent Xerox really engaged in the type of conduct we shall cite as possibly justifying proscription. It does appear, however, that the following analysis might provide a conceptual basis for prosecution.

Xerox, through its control of the basic patents on xerography, could block anyone else from making plain-paper copiers unless they "invented around" the Xerox patents. Xerox refused any license requests for use in plain-paper copying. Plain-paper copying is superior enough to similarly priced alternatives to offer substantial opportunities for monopoly pricing. Within the general category of plain-paper copying, many variations in features are possible. Different machines embodying various combinations of features are substitutes; that is, the demand for one machine will be affected by the price of another.

Because of the effect that a change in price of one substitute has on the demand for the other, a monopolist who controls both substitutes can enjoy greater monopoly profits than can be earned if each substitute is monopolized but separately owned. (We shall call the practice followed when two substitutes are monopolized "joint profit maximization."[26]) A simple way to understand this is to consider the profit-maximizing calculation of a monopoly. A monopoly sells up to that point at which marginal revenue equals marginal cost. Essentially, what a monopoly is able to do is consider not only the increase in revenue from additional units sold as the price is lowered, but also the decrease in revenue from the lowered price on the units it could have sold at the higher price. As the monopoly expands production, its marginal revenue is the net of the increase attributable to new sales and the decrease due to lower price on the old sales volume. It is this net revenue that the monopoly compares with the associated cost, and it stops supplying units when additional revenue no longer exceeds additional cost. Because this "net" marginal revenue is always less than price, the monopoly will supply a suboptimal quantity of goods because it ceases furnishing additional goods even when price – the value of the good to consumers – exceeds the cost of producing the good. The excess of price over marginal cost measures the social loss.

A monopoly controlling two substitutes can do even better for itself and visit more harm on society. When it makes the marginal revenue calculation, it will still include as an offset to the revenue generated by price reductions the drop in price on the quantity of the same product that it could sell at the higher price. However, it will now include an *additional* offset resulting from the decrease in revenue from the substitute good it also controls. Thus, the "marginal revenue" in this extended sense will fall short of price by an amount even greater than in the case of a single-good monopoly. Consequently, an even more suboptimal quantity of the total of both goods will be supplied and greater monopoly profit earned when a single monopoly controls two or more substitutes.[27]

It should be cautioned that we focus herein on the situation where the dominant economic relationship among the controlled patents is assumed to be one of substitutability rather than complementarity. If, instead, complementarity dominates, the effect is the mirror image of that outlined above; sales of one complement will increase with a reduction in the price of the other, thus mitigating the usual tendency for a monopolized product to be overpriced and underproduced. Hence, asserting a "special problem" depends not just on the mere existence of interrelated patents, but also on an empirical inquiry into the precise form of the interrelationship.

Xerox may have been in a position to utilize the opportunities thus available to a firm having a monopoly on two or more substitutes.[28] These opportunities, if utilized, would have given Xerox systematically greater incentives than its rivals to engage in research and development or acquire from others technology that would yield substitute copying machines within the plain-paper market it controlled. This factual situation is a provocative starting point for contemplating legal action. What the appropriate response to the phenomenon should be, however, is a difficult question.

C. The rationale applied: the appropriate legal rule

1. The scope of the rule

The first issue to be decided is the class of cases to which the joint-profit-maximization objection applies. The result with respect to one type of case seems straightforward. If a firm, or several firms, control patents providing independent ways to produce substitutes, joint profit maximization should not be permitted. Without employing the joint-maximization strategy, full monopoly returns can nonetheless be gained on each patent for the superiority it enjoys over alternatives. There will, moreover, be undesirable effects both in the short term and the long term if the practice is followed. In the short term, joint profit maximization leads to greater underutilization of the patented substitutes and the enjoyment of greater monopoly profits than if patents on the substitutes were separately owned. At this point, we should make explicit a fundamental premise of the succeeding analysis: that the monopoly profits earned if each patent were separately owned are an appropriate legislatively determined bench-mark of the "right" return to invention. On this assumption, a key long-term implication of joint profit maximization is that too many resources will be committed to groups of inventions for which the joint strategy is efficacious in raising the expected rate of return to an abnormally high level not contemplated in the grant of patent rights.

A major problem, however, is how to deal with a firm such as Xerox, which owns basic patents that can be utilized in a variety of ways, as well as improvement patents. Combining these patents could yield a great variety of copying machines that are substitutes for each other. The question is whether Xerox was under an obligation, with respect to each possible substitute that it could produce, to ignore all opportunities it had to practice joint profit maximization and consider only the separate demand curve for each machine containing a unique combination of features.

Although the result seems harsh and far-reaching, there is a compelling logical argument for the conclusion that in principle Xerox should have been obliged to consider only the demand curve for each particular copying machine in exploiting its patent monopolies. One important reason for this conclusion is that to hold otherwise gives the holder of basic patented technology a systematic advantage over its rivals with respect to improvements of the process, provided that interfirm arrangements that permit joint profit maximization are proscribed. Although the law in regard to interfirm agreements is somewhat unclear, it does pose obstacles to arrangements among firms that might seek to realize the same joint-profit-maximizing opportunities that seem to have been available internally to Xerox. We shall briefly outline the basis for arguing that intrafirm joint maximization should be treated analogously to the interfirm equivalent.

Cross-licensing agreements with the type of price-fixing clauses that are necessary to enforce joint profit maximization among two or more firms are plainly illegal per se.[29] Further, the acquisition of a competing patent that can be used without infringing the patent of the acquiring company has been held to violate Section 7 of the Clayton Act.[30] There is some uncertainty concerning these arrangements when an improvement patent cannot be used without infringing a basic patent. If the holder of the basic patent and the inventor of the improvement both wish to manufacture the product embodying the improvement, a price-fixing agreement between the two firms as to the price of the improved product is necessary to avoid having them compete away the monopoly value of the improvement patent. The accomplishment of this purpose would not require an agreement as to the price of the original product covered by the basic patent. Conceivably, a price-fixing agreement limited to the purpose of securing the monopoly return on the improvement patent might be excepted from the general ban on price fixing accompanying cross licensing. However, the language of the cases indicates that the ban is all-inclusive. This result may not be unreasonable given the possibility that such agreements with respect to improvement patents can provide "cover" for (1) price fixing of the improved product when in reality one or both of the patents is invalid or the improvement patent can be practiced without infringing the basic patent, or (2) joint-profit-maximizing pricing, taking into account the effect of the price of the improved product on the demand for the product covered by the original product. In any event, even if a price-fixing agreement that allowed the realization of the legitimate monopoly return on the improvement were permitted, the use of such an agreement to practice joint profit maximization might still be held illegal.

One case indicates that the acquisition of a patent that cannot be practiced without infringing a patent held by the acquiring company does not violate Section 7 of the Clayton Act on the grounds that, because the patent could not have otherwise been practiced, competition has not been impaired.[31] The Court did not, however, consider the possibility of joint profit maximization that might result from the ownership of both patents. Whether proof of such a possibility could lead to the merger being held unlawful under Section 7, or the subsequent practice of joint profit maximization held to constitute unlawful monopolization under Section 2 of the Sherman Act, is unclear.[32]

If the legal impediments to the practicing of joint profit maximization by separate firms remain while equivalent conduct is allowed within a firm, the adverse effects of a single firm gaining control of basic technology are intensified. Outside firms can, of course, devise improvements that cannot be practiced without infringing the basic patents and sell those improvements to the holder of the basic patents. As noted above, however, if exclusive rights are conveyed that permit the practice of joint profit maximization, there are doubts as to the legality of the transaction. Moreover, if the firm that devises the improvement wishes itself to make a machine embodying the improvement, there are real difficulties even in fashioning a lawful arrangement with the holder of the basic patents that preserves the monopoly value of the improvement patent. Any coordination of their price or output of the machine embodying the improvement would raise serious questions of illegality under the antitrust law. Joint profit maximization would in any event almost certainly be ruled out.

As a result of the legal restriction on the practice of joint profit maximization by more than one firm, a company such as Xerox, which can realize these opportunities internally, has systematically greater incentives to innovate improvements on the basic process than does its rivals. Thus, its dominance within the plain-paper-copying industry will steadily grow because its rewards at each stage are greater than those of its competitors. The biased incentive situation persists until competitors eventually do "invent around" sufficiently to produce substitutes. At this point, impacts on substitutes begin to be regarded by the original dominant firm as largely external "spillover" effects and the joint-maximization motivation wanes.

One factor in the copier industry does suggest that something can be said for giving Xerox a greater return than its competitors. Xerox was a pioneer in an industry where there was a great need to acquaint users with the advantages of decentralized "convenience" copying. If there had been more competition at the early stages, more of the benefits of establishing the usefulness of the technology would have "spilled over" to other firms. Under the familiar "free-rider" analysis, investments yielding benefits that would have to be shared with others would be suboptimal. Of course, allowing internal joint profit maximization does constitute a crude device for increasing the overall incentives in an "infant" industry.

Given (1) the social costs imposed by joint profit maximization and (2) the explicit legal prohibitions of the practice if engaged in by agreements among firms, we conclude on balance that the practice by a single firm should *in principle* be proscribed.

2. Administrative difficulties

Joint profit maximization involves an interplay of cost and demand interdependencies. Although not necessarily determinable with great precision, production costs can frequently be estimated with reference to an objectively defined reality. The basic problem in identifying joint-profit-maximizing pricing is therefore that of determining the demand conditions for the various actual and potential substitutes. This is extremely difficult to do, particularly with respect to products that are never introduced because of their effect on the demand for substitutes. Unfortunately, the latter case is perhaps the most serious instance of the "suppression" that can result from joint profit maximization.

Application of the rule would, moreover, raise questions as to the intent of the firm in its pricing decisions. Even if the true or objective demand for various substitutes could be ascertained, the possibility that the firm's behavior was based on a mistaken conception of one demand curve rather than an illicit consideration of demand-curve interdependencies would also have to be eliminated. Mistakes as to demand are very easy to make. Ascertainment of the considerations that really motivated a firm might, therefore, be extremely difficult.

We are very uncertain about the ultimate costs and benefits of a rule directly proscribing joint profit maximization of substitutes subject to the protection of the patent laws. The administrative costs and risks of error of such a rule seem substantial. The magnitude of the harm created by the practice is extremely difficult to assess. We are content to urge here that these were the pragmatic questions that the FTC should have addressed in deciding whether to bring this action and the manner of its actual prosecution. It is, of course, conceivable that in deciding whether to bring the proceeding, an analysis such as the one we advance was actually conducted by the Commission. We are not privy to its internal documents evidencing these deliberations. But even if this were done, the analysis should have been manifested in the complaint so that Xerox could have responded to a carefully framed objection to its behavior.

We emphasize that we have independently devised a rationale that might justify this proceeding. The complaint and related Commission documents are filled with such language as "obscure" patent boundaries,[33] "trivial" patents secured by Xerox,[34] and "extensive surveillance of product and technological developments in the office copier market."[35] A literal reading of the complaint leads to the conclusion that the real objection to the behavior of Xerox is that it successfully used the opportunities afforded it by the patent system. Even if the Commission analysis had been more sophisticated than is manifested in the public documents, the failure to articulate it deprives the litigants and persons affected by the rule in the future, as well as scholars and participants in the political process, of an opportunity to ascertain and refute the premises upon which it chose to proceed.

Had issues we have raised been considered, it is also possible that alternative rules that reduce the administrative costs and likelihood of error of a rule directly proscribing joint profit maximization could have been devised. For example, if a firm had patents on alternative technology that it neither used nor would agree to license, a prima facie case of joint profit maximization might be considered to be established. There may be reasons other than the desire to practice joint profit maximization that explain the willingness of a firm to forego revenues from patents it is not using. But the likelihood that the desire to practice joint profit maximization is the real explanation seems great enough at least to place a burden of justification on the firm refusing to license technology that it is not itself employing.

It is impossible confidently to recommend any of these alternatives. We are, however, convinced that the facts in the Xerox case may provide an occasion for action under the antitrust laws. Unfortunately, the FTC response never focused on the significant issues. Moreover, as we now demonstrate, the relief secured in the consent order is of doubtful value both in providing guidance for the future and in improving competition in the copier industry.

III. Impact of the order on the copying industry

The final consent order in the Xerox proceeding was issued on July 29, 1975. Although the order is complex, its salient features may be summarized briefly. Paragraph IV is the key section dealing with patent licensing. It compels Xerox to license any three patents, as designated by the licensee, on a royalty-free basis. In addition, any number of additional patent licenses may be acquired, subject both to a specified royalty level and a one-to-one cross-licensing of the licensee's patents to Xerox and other firms. Except for IBM, the patents of Xerox's competitors are partially insulated from the cross-licensing requirement by a four-year lag provision following the order or the commercial availability of the patent, whichever is later. Paragraph VII requires Xerox to supply its licensees with the complementary "know-how" applicable to office copier products. Paragraph III prohibits suits against licensees for alleged preorder infringements of Xerox patents.

In assessing the effect of this order within the copying industry itself, it is convenient to separate the short-term and possible longer-term impacts. Hence, we deal first with the results actually observed in the industry during the initial three years under the order. Then we speculate on some of the possible developments over the longer term.

A. Short-term condition of copier industry

During the entire decade of the 1960s, Xerox's early patents provided it with an unchallenged position as the sole producer of plain-paper copiers. Competition from producers of coated-paper copiers was handicapped by low consumer acceptance of the necessity to use a special paper, one that is both heavier and of a different texture from the ordinary bond paper usable in xerographic copying. Hence, although coated-paper copying did represent a partial technological alternative to Xerox products, the practical degree of substitutability and rivalry in the marketplace was apparently not very great.

As the decade of the 1970s opened, the competitive situation was ripe for a change.[36] First, some of Xerox's basic patents acquired in the early 1950s were beginning to expire, thus making key elements of the Xerox technology accessible to potential competitors. Second, perhaps inspired by hopes of lucrative profits from the dramatically expanding plain-paper-copier market, serious attempts were under way to "invent around" many of Xerox's remaining basic patents. In combination, these factors led to the capture by IBM and several other firms of a combined 14 percent share of the worldwide plain-paper-copying market in 1973, about 24 percent in 1974, and slightly over 30 percent by 1975, the year the FTC's final order was issued. In February 1973, an authoritative copier industry source reported that it had identified at least 32 new models of plain-paper copiers either already introduced or in the final stages of development by Xerox's competitors in the United States, Japan, and Europe. In addition, it alluded to substantial activity in all three areas of the world by other companies whose development efforts had not yet become known.

Hence, although Xerox was completely insulated from competition in 1969 when the FTC's inquiry first began, there is evidence of substantial and rapidly increasing competitive pressure by mid-1975, when the proceeding drew to a close. These already-emergent competitive forces make it difficult to attribute subsequent market events to the FTC order. For instance, the order was almost immediately (in September 1975) followed by major Xerox marketing changes, which appear to have had little to do with the order itself. Xerox's approximately 8.5 percent average price cut to its commercial customers at that time was almost certainly motivated by preexisting direct competition with IBM, both with respect to pricing and to technology on Xerox's aging and obsolescent 813/7000 line. Indeed, it is difficult to identify any salient characteristic of the postorder market that could not be plausibly attributed to forces already in motion in mid-1975.

In any event, Xerox's dominant position continues to erode, although at a declining rate, with the non-Xerox share of the market projected at about 46 percent in 1980. As suggested above, substantial competition would have occurred quite independently of the order, but one might argue that the recent accessibility of Xerox's technology and know-how may nonetheless have strengthened Xerox's market rivals. Because the patent-licensing provisions of the FTC order were visualized as an important technological conduit to the rest of the industry, the way in which competitors have responded to the licensing opportunities is a possible method of testing this argument.

Under the order, a licensee may receive three patents without any cost or obligation, plus any number of additional Xerox patents subject to a royalty fee and cross-licensing requirement. We have examined all licenses issued through May 1978. The 34 companies actually licensed are, with a few exceptions, little-known companies that are not now, nor are expected to be, significant factors in the copying market. Conversely, many of the major companies have not sought licenses at all. Only 13 licensees have exceeded the three "free" patents available to each company. Although 134 different patents were specifically designated by the licensees, only 32 of these were taken by more than a single company. The most frequently chosen patent was designated by just 12 companies. In seeking to identify "key" patents, one might have expected that the most important patents (1) would show up as almost universal picks and (2) would almost invariably be chosen as one of the three royalty-free licenses. Yet not only was there little evidence of consensus on choices, but the leading selections on a frequency basis were seldom chosen as royalty-free.

The record of licensing under the FTC order therefore provides surprisingly little evidence in mid-1978 for the existence of key, entry-preventing Xerox patents. One plausible explanation of the surprisingly faint interest in Xerox's patent portfolio is that, although the patents originally caused Xerox to achieve its dominant position, the technological barriers to successful entry had already been substantially surmounted by the time of the FTC order.

Xerox's period of unchallenged dominance did allow it to achieve certain nonpatent marketing advantages, including financial resources, an enormous installed machine base, and a large pool of skilled personnel. However, insulation from competition may have been in certain respects a double-edged blade, contributing to various inefficiencies in Xerox's later operations. Xerox's early technological dominance of an explosively expanding market doubtless made it difficult for the company to evaluate its own internal operations – to discriminate between real managerial efficiency and success due to mere coattailing on Xerox's original market position. On this approach, Xerox's failure to stay lean during years of boom has adversely affected its more recent marketing performance. Still, this argument at best suggests some mitigation of the residual advantages otherwise attendant to Xerox's period of entrenchment. The FTC did not, however, incorporate in its final order any of the dissolution remedies that it apparently had earlier contemplated against Xerox.[37]

Much of the attempted competition with Xerox in the 1970s has come from corporate giants, which are themselves operating from extraordinary resource bases (e.g., IBM, Eastman Kodak, SCM, and 3M). Nevertheless, the "Ricoh Consortium," consisting of Ricoh, Kalle, Savin, Nashua, and Infotec, exemplifies a highly successful muticompany cooperative venture that has achieved significant market penetration. Hence, Xerox's alleged resource advantage has not prevented entry by a variety of companies, even if the marketing and manufacturing commitments involved are admittedly formidable.

Is there, then, any notable difference between the present market situation and that which would exist in the absence of the FTC proceeding? Persuasive evidence for such a difference is not apparent, and claims that the FTC order is responsible for significantly heightening competition therefore appear to be poorly founded.

B. Longer-term effect on the copying industry

Although the short-term effects of the FTC order on the plain-paper-copying market do not seem to be significant, interesting questions do exist about the longer-term impact. These questions arise to a considerable extent from the potential effect of the licensing provisions upon both competition and the rate of technological progress in the industry.

As noted earlier, Paragraph IV-C of the order exposes a Xerox licensee of more than three patents to the risk of mandatory cross-licensing of its own patents on a one-for-one basis as Xerox may designate. In turn, Paragraph IV-C(9) provides that, once Xerox has been licensed, any other competitor must also be granted a license on reasonable terms and conditions. The possibility exists that this cross-licensing provision will ultimately have anticompetitive overtones, but this possibility depends on several key factual assertions about the role of technology in the industry.

One major premise is that, owing to the technical complexity of copying equipment, the three "free" Xerox patents do not constitute adequate access to xerographic technology.[38] From this it follows that meaningful benefit from the Xerox patent portfolio inevitably exposes a company's own innovations to loss of market exclusivity, as cross-licensing to competitors is called for. The truncated four-year exclusive period of market exploitation is, in turn, alleged to be too short to recoup adequately the investment in sophisticated research and development efforts; the flow of "reasonable royalties" will tend to be less than the profits from market exploitation of the legalized monopoly rights.

If its empirical premises are accepted, the reasoning just outlined suggests a decline in the rate of technical innovation for several reasons. On the one hand, the rate of return on new invention is clearly reduced for Xerox, whose entire patent portfolio is vulnerable to the mandatory licensing through July 29, 1981. At the same time, the cross-licenses to Xerox act, over time, as a pooling mechanism for innovations produced by competitors. The net result is that the return from any company's research and development tends to be reduced, and the cost of access to the technology of others is also reduced. Both effects, of course, militate against investment in new technology.

From the standpoint of consumer benefit, any dampening of the incentives to innovate would presumably be adverse. Evaluated for its competitive effect, however, an artificially accelerated dissemination of technology among the competing companies is arguably anticompetitive even if the rate of innovation were itself unchanged. This hypothesis is grounded on the premise that, at the present stage of the industry's life-cycle, technical aspects of products have become less and less important relative to marketing capability. In turn, marketing advantages are most likely to lie with the large, established firms, such as Xerox itself. Hence, it may be argued, the technological leveling effect of the sublicensing pool would prevent a smaller firm from redressing an initial marketing disadvantage by developing technically superior products. Carried to the extreme, this process could culminate in domination of the industry by a few very large firms possessing overwhelming marketing capabilities, thus creating the potential for interdependent behavior or even collusion.

The scenario just described is an intriguing one, but it does depend on unproven factual premises. In particular, for the process to function, vulnerability of a firm's own patents is the "price" that firms must be willing to pay to tap Xerox's technology. However, if the cost is regarded as too high – or the benefits too low – no competitor will "buy in" to the Xerox patent portfolios. In fact, the evidence cited above about the incidence of licensing under the order indicates that there has been no stampede to buy in beyond the three free patents. On the other hand, the possible consequences of the cross-licensing effect do suggest an explanation of why the major companies would be particularly reluctant to expose themselves: the cost of the cross-licensing requirement is directly proportional to a firm's assessment of its own success at future technological innovation. Thus, a firm with no intention of major R&D effort has nothing to lose by tapping Xerox's technology, but major competitors may wish to guard the opportunity of preserving the fruits of their own future developmental research.

A plausible alternative scenario, then, is that the marketing of advanced state-of-the-art copiers would be confined to a restricted number of major firms, none of which are entangled via the cross-licensing provisions of the FTC order. At another level of the market, it might nonetheless be quite possible for less sophisticated copiers to be marketed by firms who license from Xerox on a large scale.

Ironically, the real impact of the cross-licensing provision of the FTC order may be to deter the licensing of Xerox patents to other major competitors, as compared to the quantity of such licensing that would have occurred in the order's absence. Our argument in an earlier section suggests that, as Xerox's plain-paper copier dominance broke down, the attractiveness of voluntary licensing of competitors would have increased. Under the order, however, Xerox may now license only when it imposes upon the licensee what the licensee will be likely to regard as an additional and potentially very onerous cross-licensing exposure. Moreover, the Xerox licensee will generally not even be able to identify which of its own patents is thus exposed. By imposing what is likely to be in many cases a contractual term desired by neither party, the FTC order can generate inefficiencies by obstructing what otherwise would represent socially advantageous dissemination of technology on terms that are also mutually beneficial to the direct parties.

In sum, the particular mode of cross-licensing required by the FTC order injects peculiar considerations into the decisions of firms with respect to technology acquisition. At one extreme the effect could be both anticompetitive and innovation-deterring. More likely, however, the cross-licensing exposure will simply impede technology exchange between Xerox and the other major competitors, an inefficient scenario to be sure, although probably not as harmful as the alternative.

IV. Implications of the order for future conduct

The final issue to be addressed here concerns the implications of the order for the behavior of firms in other industries as these firms contemplate the possibility of a similar order in their own industry. Such implications, which were termed in our introduction as the "deterrent effect" of the order, are a consequence of the way in which the order is perceived as altering the benefits and costs of different types of market behavior. In turn, perceptions of the order's implications relate to questions of both liability and sanction.

A. The liability rule

Much of the foregoing discussion has been an attempt to read into the FTC complaint a coherent theory of liability that explains an otherwise obscure set of factual allegations. Although the joint-profit-maximization hypothesis does, we believe, supply a tenable conceptual rationale for the key patent-abuse allegations, there is no direct evidence that the FTC itself viewed its case in the same light. Indeed, the final order in no way addresses the joint-profit-maximization phenomenon.

Assuming that our joint-profit-maximization hypothesis is relevant, the liability rule implied by the case does militate against behavior that is genuinely socially undesirable; joint profit maximization has both adverse distributional effects, through its increase of profits at the expense of consumers, and involves additional social loss by inducing inefficient allocation of resources to innovation and exacerbating the tendency of monopolists to choose allocatively suboptimal outputs. A more pessimistic view of the Xerox case would be that the FTC moved against the company merely because of "excessive" market success. Although this is surely a much more naive theory of liability, one cannot reject the hypothesis that a regulatory agency might find it appropriate simply to redistribute (among consumers and competitors) what would otherwise be a company's massive returns from a perfectly legitimate use of a strong patent portfolio. This position also resurfaces quite bluntly the inherent tension between the rights accorded under the patent statutes and the traditional goals of antitrust policy.

On economic policy grounds, a disinterested observer might prefer one liability rule over another. The "mere success" rule would, for instance, arguably sacrifice future gains from innovation and efficient performance for short-run distributional motives. Regardless of one's policy preferences, however, the plain fact is that the Commission's rule of the Xerox case is a matter of pure speculation.

This uncertainty about the liability rule seems to us to constitute grounds for strong criticism of the FTC. In the first place, uncertainty as to the case's proper interpretation imposes excessive costs on normally risk-averse firms as they choose their conduct in future market situations. Second, it may be argued that the entire proceeding made little sense unless it articulated some rule for future behavior in other industries. If, as we have suggested above, the remedial effects of the order were minor, and even possibly perverse, its justification presumably should be sought in the enunciation of a policy.

A third and final criticism relates to accountability. If the FTC was setting policy at all in the Xerox case, the needless obscurity of that policy handicaps criticism and commentary as much as it does behavioral reaction. As we concede in this chapter, the rationale of the case cannot be analyzed except in a hypothetical or inferential sense. This fact frustrates a socially desirable process of debate over agency activities.

B. The sanction imposed

Even in the event that the liability rule were quite clear (i.e., firms knew what conduct would provoke an FTC action), the expected magnitude of the sanction imposed remains a key determinant of how firms will modify their future behavior. In choosing their alternative commercial strategies, firms must weigh the costs (forgone profits) of "obeying the rules" against the penalties associated with the proscribed behavior. Hence, the expected magnitude of the sanction is a prime determinant of prospective behavior based on firms' interpretations of a proceeding such as that of the FTC against Xerox. In addition to this purely predictive interest, however, there is a further societal interest in seeing that the sanction is appropriately calibrated: that it neither overdeters nor underdeters firms.

Unfortunately, the evidence in the Xerox case as to likely sanctions in analogous future cases is, once again, frustratingly muddy. The actual provisions of the final order are, of course, known and we have suggested that their effect was probably not very great. The cost of these sanctions to Xerox would nonetheless have been very substantially higher had the proceeding been advanced in time by even a few years. Perhaps more important, the provisions of the FTC's original Notice of Contemplated Relief were much more sweeping and onerous than those incorporated in the final order. With respect to the patents, for instance, the FTC apparently contemplated unlimited royalty-free licensing of all Xerox patents, including those obtained for a period stretching 20 years after the date of the order.

Once the possibility of very costly sanctions is conceded, the vagueness of the liability rule is reemphasized in several respects. First, the prospect of very weighty potential costs would induce firms to exercise extreme caution in risking exposure to liability. Since the class of conduct producing potential liability cannot be confidently narrowed by reference to a clear rule, the scope of behavior deterred will be overbroad and will probably include socially desirable conduct as well as that conduct which, in principle, should really be targeted by the FTC. For instance, all research on "related" patents might be inefficiently chilled by fear of antitrust exposure.

Second, the absence of any clear articulation of the liability theory makes it impossible to deal sensibly with the issue of proper sanction calibration. Sanctions are, after all, designed to alter the incentive structure by raising or lowering the payoffs to certain activities. Unless one can state the goals of a legal policy, it is virtually impossible to discuss whether a particular set of incentives has been altered by too much or too little. The question of appropriate incentives extends to the "quasideterrent" implications of the order for competitors of the party against whom a potential future order might be issued. In other words, there are implications for the behavior of the "victims" of the alleged improper behavior as well as for the "perpetrator" of the behavior.

One way of posing this issue is to ask what implications the Xerox case would have for Xerox's competitors if, with full precedential knowledge of the case, the history of the copier industry since 1960 were to be rerun. Would IBM and others have invested to the same extent in "inventing around" the Xerox patents if the prospect of FTC-mandated licensing were viewed as being highly probable? If not, what effect on society's position would occur from balancing investments in essentially duplicative technology against gains from genuine improvements on Xerox's processes? Finally, if "inventing around" had not reached an advanced stage, would the remedial measures not have been more extreme?

The issue here is what signals society wants to send to future competitors in a Xerox type of situation. The signals depend on one's resolution of the ambiguities in the present case. One reading of the case, however, is that reliance on FTC intervention to guarantee patent access would be more profitable than investment in bypass technology. Society would then lose valuable innovation.

V. Conclusions

The Xerox case was meant to be one of the FTC's pathbreaking policy initiatives of the past decade. Nevertheless, in most important respects the results have been a bizarre mix of anticlimax and frustrating insubstantiality. Resolution of the issues we have raised above is in many cases very difficult. Still, our basic criticism of the FTC is its failure even to confront explicitly those questions which, in our own attempt to evaluate the proceeding, appeared to be absolutely fundamental. This criticism is, moreover, a basic conceptual one, because it abstracts entirely from the many additional complexities of a factual nature that would have had to be addressed in a full adjudication of the Xerox case. Hence, we conclude that the proceeding does not represent a jewel in the FTC's crown.

9 Exclusionary practices: shopping center restrictive covenants

KENNETH W. CLARKSON, TIMOTHY J. MURIS, AND
DONALD L. MARTIN

> If an economist finds something – a business practice of one sort or another – that he does not understand he looks for a monopoly explanation.[1]
> Officials charged with enforcing antitrust laws are even more inclined [than economists] to find monopoly purposes lurking in unfamiliar or unconventional business practices.[2]

During the past three decades, shopping centers have become the dominant form of organization for retail sales. Although centers differ in such important characteristics as size and the type of goods provided, they share a common form of business organization. In particular, a shopping center comprises "a group of commercial establishments, planned, developed, owned and managed as a *unit,* related in location, size and type of shops to the trade area that the unit serves; it provides on-site parking and definite relationships to the types and sizes of stores."[3]

The lease details the relationship between the shopping center developer (an entity usually separate from the individual merchants) and the stores within the center. These leases often contain conditions, restrictions, covenants, and (or) easements that control signs, remodeling, parking, cleanliness, trash removal, and other activities that may contribute to the overall success of the center. Further, at least as recently as the early 1970s, the leases often constrained merchants as to the type of store (e.g., discount stores were often prohibited), goods offered, or other market activities. In addition, most leases require membership in a merchants' association to provide a forum for determining cooperative behavior, hours of business, advertising, and other matters common to all merchants. Thus, unlike most traditional shopping locations (i.e., the "downtown" of most cities), the participants in the shopping center *directly* control lighting, security, parking, landscaping, and other environmental elements, as well as at least some of the terms of competition.

In the last decade, the Federal Trade Commission has expressed con-

141

siderable interest in whether certain lease clauses in large shopping centers (more than 200,000 square feet) violate the antitrust laws. In the "new" FTC of the early 1970s, shopping center cases were considered of "fundamental importance."[4] These cases primarily involved three types of lease clauses that influence activities within the shopping center. First, *approval* clauses give a tenant the right to approve or disapprove the leasing of space to prospective tenants.[5] Next, *use* clauses generally restrict use of leased space, for example, limiting use to provision of certain products or to products of a certain quality or price line. Finally, *exclusive* clauses give a tenant the sole right to operate a certain kind or class of business within the center.[6]

This chapter examines the logic and the effect of the FTC attack on restrictive clauses in shopping center leases. Section I discusses the premier FTC decision and devotes special attention to the appropriateness of a *per se* rule of illegality to the restrictive clauses. To understand the economic function of these clauses, Section II presents a theory of the shopping center firm from which are derived testable implications that have particular relevance to the economic rationale of lease restrictions in shopping centers. To test these implications, we use survey data that we developed, together with data from industry sources. Section III matches our theory and its implications against predictions of the FTC concerning the consequences of banning restrictive clauses from shopping center leases. Data for these comparisons were also taken from our surveys and from industry sources.

I. FTC cases

Except for *Tysons Corner,*[7] all FTC complaints attacking allegedly anticompetitive leases between tenants and developers[8] have resulted in consent decrees. Since *Tysons Corner* reveals FTC attitudes toward the antitrust implications of shopping center leases and is the case upon which subsequent investigations and orders have relied, we discuss it in some detail.

A. Per se *or rule of reason*

On May 8, 1972, the Commission charged that certain practices at the Tysons Corner Regional Shopping Center, located in Washington, D.C.'s northern Virginia suburbs, violated Section 5. Basically, the complaint alleged that certain lease clauses, in particular the clause granting major tenants the right to disapprove the entry of other tenants, in effect established a price-fixing arrangement that excluded discount stores.

The Commission and antitrust courts had little experience with such lease clauses. When facing such inexperience, courts must determine whether to apply a *per se* or a rule-of-reason approach. Generally, antitrust law distinguishes between naked restraints (or agreements), whose sole purpose and effect is to restrain competition, and other restraints that accompany some valid purpose, usually involving an integration of the productive facilities or efforts of the parties to the agreement. Naked restraints are *per se* illegal. The plaintiff must merely show the existence of the restraint; if the restraint exists, justification evidence will not be heard. Other restraints are judged by the rule of reason. Any practice that is "manifestly anti-competitive" is illegal and may even be found to be *per se* illegal if the court, after a full hearing on the purpose of the restraint, cannot envision circumstances that could justify it.[9] If, however, the restraint is "merely ancillary" to the valid purpose of the arrangement, it is legal. Deciding whether or not the restraint is manifestly anti-competitive or merely ancillary apparently requires a factual determination of whether the challenged practice benefits consumers.[10]

As an example of whether to apply rule-of-reason or *per se* analysis, consider horizontal mergers. These mergers completely eliminate competition between the merging companies, yet may not violate the antitrust laws. Accordingly, whether or not the merger is illegal turns upon the particular circumstances at hand. In other words, such mergers are judged under a rule of reason. What is true for complete integration is also true for partial integration, such as joint selling agencies and joint ventures: *Per se* illegality is inappropriate.

If anything is obvious about shopping centers, it is that they involve partial integration. When a shopping center is built, the members of the center exert a substantial common effort. In essence, a new firm is created, a point that we explore in detail in Section II. An agreement among the three principal department stores in Tysons Corner simply to limit price competition in all their stores would not involve integration of the productive facilities and skills of the parties and hence would be *per se* illegal. The actual agreement under which the developer and the three principal tenants joined to form a new center was, however, a different matter. Given the integration of efforts involved in forming and running the center, the legality of the restraints depends upon their purpose and effect. As the antitrust bench was unfamiliar with the purpose and effect of the lease clauses, rule-of-reason analysis was appropriate.

Nevertheless, the Bureau of Competition (BC) argued for a *per se* standard, contending that the acts and practices amounted to price fixing, a boycott, and unfair methods of competition. To the BC, it was apparently sufficient that "discounters are not in regional shopping centers . . . in part [because of] major tenants acting to exclude discounters . . . [since] the discounters provide pricing competition for the major tenants."[11] As Administrative Law Judge Needelman argued, however, the BC argument was fatally flawed: "The thing that bothers me about this is can't you say . . . practically any business practice amounts to a price fix or boycott that has the effect on a price, or if it means that competitors are excluded from the market?"[12] Only its failure to recognize the difference between naked and ancillary restraints could have caused the BC's argument to have missed such a telling point.

B. The FTC opinions

After the others signed a consent order, the remaining defendant, City Stores (a major tenant), argued that *per se* treatment was inappropriate. The argument, however, was very narrow. Because it neither sought nor used the challenged lease provisions, it could not be found to have violated Section 5.[13]

In his opinion regarding City Stores, Judge Needelman rejected *per se* illegality both as to the price-fixing and boycott arguments. Nevertheless, he found against City Stores primarily because of probable anticompetitive effects, the importance of the practices involved, and the lack of a justification. Although one can question the finding of probable anticompetitive effect, it is perhaps not surprising, given the lack of a justification and the proclivity of antitrust enforcers to find monopoly explanations in unusual (to the enforcer) arrangements.

City Stores appealed, again making the narrow arguments that it had made before the administrative law judge. The BC did not appeal, but suggested to the Commission that it could affirm on alternative grounds, in particular *per se* illegality. Its *per se* argument was, however, more tempered than previously. Although continuing to assert a *per se* approach, the complaint counsel admitted at oral argument that some limited approval clauses could be justified, stating, "we started out in this case arguing *per se* and were persuaded [that] Respondent was entitled to offer evidence to justify some sort of restriction upon entry. . . ."[14] This concession, that limited approval clauses may be necessary, recognizes that some approval clauses are reasonable. It also raises the issue of how to distinguish between reasonable and unreasonable. Any distinction must (at least implicitly) be based on some theory of how shopping centers operate and on the relation of the clauses to that operation. Thus, this concession – one that the Commission has in effect endorsed by allowing tenants a limited veto power in certain consent orders[15] – is nothing less than a statement that approval clauses cannot be properly evaluated without an inquiry into how shopping centers work. The ultimate test of the validity of the findings of that inquiry will be factual – a foundation identical to that of the rule of reason. Certainly in the context of litigation, that process should not take place without the benefit of a full record.

In its opinion, although applying a rule-of-reason approach to one of the challenged clauses (floor-space limits), the Commission found the approval clauses to be *per se* illegal as (in effect) price fixing and a group boycott. Thus, the Commission failed to recognize the valid nature of shopping center arrangements and the possible ancillarity of the clauses to those arrangements. A further weakness in the Commission's rationale is its rejection of City Stores's argument that agreements between a supplier and a distributor are akin to exclusive distributorships, which are not *per se* illegal. The Commission responded: "While the line between the two is far from clear, it is apparent that by its terms an approval clause is not an exclusive dealing agreement, but merely a grant to the tenant to exclude at random those competitors it may choose."[16] This is hardly persuasive. At the most, an approval clause can allow a tenant to have exclusive rights in the center, making the Commission's line drawing meaningless. At the least, an approval clause is less restrictive than an exclusive clause, and the Commission would then be saying that because approval clauses are *less* restrictive than exclusive dealing arrangements, the law should treat them *more* harshly.

C. Conclusion as to FTC cases

In determining whether a practice that is not clearly a naked restraint and with which the courts are unfamiliar violates the antitrust laws, rule-of-reason analysis is appropriate. Such a practice can be condemned as *per se* illegal only after à full hearing. One can hardly imagine a poorer record upon which to find *per se* illegality than that involving City Stores. Because the complaint counsel, despite considerable waffling, basically argued for a *per se* rule, it presented few facts. The respondent not only failed to provide facts, it argued irrelevancies. In these circumstances, one should not, indeed one can not, condemn broad approval rights as *per se* illegal. Of all the participants involved, only Judge Needelman seems to have grasped this essential point.[17]

Because a correct application of the rule of reason requires knowledge of the operation of shopping centers and of the purpose and effect of the restrictive clauses, we turn next to developing that knowledge.

II. The shopping center industry

This section develops a theory of the shopping center to discuss the benefits of shopping centers and the desirability of restrictive clauses. We also test several implications (or hypotheses) that we derive from the theory.

A. A theory of the shopping center firm

To consumers, shopping centers are a convenient collection of retailers organized to sell goods and services. To economists, shopping centers are noteworthy because their innovative form of market organization is a substitute for certain market exchanges. That is, the shopping center, as a firm, provides benefits, both to retailer–tenants and to consumers, that would not otherwise arise from the unattenuated incentives of retailers located in proximity to, but acting independently of, each other. The benefits in locating complementary economic activities centrally, sometimes called economies of agglomeration, arise from many sources, including:

1. Savings in direct and indirect transportation costs to consumers and wholesalers.[18]
2. Benefits to retailers from greater sales per dollar of selling expense by optimally combining retail establishments, type of goods, and environmental amenities offered to the public.
3. Benefits to consumers from lower indirect search costs and more environmental amenities.[19]
4. Savings to retailers from lower costs in product packaging, advertising, and promotion.
5. Savings to retailers from group insurance plans and police security measures.
6. Economies associated with large-scale investment financing.

These economies, however, are subject to certain "shirking" problems. Because a part of each retailer's earnings is attributable to the *collective* benefits of agglomeration and because the cooperating retailers *jointly* produce these benefits, there is some incentive for each participant to shirk in its productive efforts. For example, individual store owners will probably not provide the optimal level of promotional activity because adjacent stores will also gain from the additional customers attracted by the special promotion. Each store owner thus has an incentive to "shirk" and to rely on the efforts of other owners. Thus, fewer economies of agglomeration than are potentially available may be generated, yielding fewer net benefits to both retailers and consumers. The costs of monitoring fellow participants to discourage shirking can be high (compared to potential benefits) for any given retailer because monitoring sacrifices resources that may be more efficiently used in selling to the public.[20] Moreover, if the number of potential participating retailers is large enough, transaction costs of contracting among them to capture the benefits of agglomeration may be prohibitive. Although these problems are not insurmountable, they are sufficient to make alternative arrangements attractive.

It is our hypothesis that the shopping center firm is just such an alternative arrangement. Instead of independent market transactions between retailers, the center employs nonmarket constraints on cooperating retailers, thereby producing benefits that are not available to individual retailers acting independently. That is, the profit-maximizing shopping center firm, as owner and landlord, produces and sells to retailer–lessees net benefits that they could not otherwise easily produce for themselves because of shirking or undesirable incentives that yield externalities.

To simplify the analysis without sacrificing its operational content, we have compressed the six benefits of agglomeration listed above into two. The first we define as the time savings to all consumers in their search for goods and services. It includes both the time used in transport to and from the point of purchase and the time spent in locating and purchasing a specified good. The second benefit is the resource savings to retailers that arises from all other sources of agglomeration, including those environmental amenities that would otherwise be too costly to produce in the absence of an internalizing agent such as a center. For example, the center can provide pleasant surroundings, special exhibits, and other amenities that attract potential customers but are too costly for an individual store to offer.

Because of the shirking problem, retailers can acquire the full value of these two benefits only when they lease space in the center. Moreover, to the extent that the shopping center firm has a comparative advantage in producing the benefits of agglomeration, it can further enhance the profit opportunities of the retailers in its center. Because the shopping center firm is also the landlord, it can capture some of these benefits as ordinary rent through its leasing arrangements with retailers, with the size of its profits depending in part upon the extent of competition between (actual and prospective) landlords.

The shopping center lease helps produce these benefits for shopping center retailers (and ultimately for consumers), just as labor and capital help produce the benefits that retailers and consumers obtain from the physical environment of the shopping center. For example, the lease plays an important role in prohibiting behavior that would jeopardize the profits of all parties concerned. To monitor and police behavior that would threaten profits, shopping center firms enter into leases with retailers that specify and penalize various forms of potential shirking or undesirable external effects. For example, practices that one retailer uses to enhance profit may attract customers that have preferences inconsistent with those of the consumers of the other retailer–lessees in the center. Thus, potential sales are lost for other shopping center members because of the "inappropriate" selling strategy of the unconstrained retailer. This may be a problem, for example, if discount stores are allowed to lease space in shopping centers containing retailers appealing to consumers with relatively high values associated with their time. To maintain low prices the discounter may keep maintenance costs low, or provide inferior service. Although this may be profitable to the discounter, other tenants whose selling strategy is to provide an ambiance of cleanliness, quality service and dependability *throughout the center* could be harmed. Thus, consumers would lose the opportunity to shop at a center providing a uniform group of stores and services.

Thus, it may be desirable to exclude some tenants from certain centers. Because not all shirking behavior may be economically regulated by specifying permissible conduct through leasing arrangements, the developer may choose to exclude particular tenants rather than attempt to regulate their conduct in detail. Further, it may be efficient for the developer to delegate the exclusion decision to existing tenants via approval clauses. If errors in screening potential lessees are disproportionately costly to particular tenants, shopping center firms may find it economical to allow those incumbents to perform the screening function themselves. In this sense, screening rights held by major tenants are a substitute for developers' screening and for greater, but more costly, detail in leases specifying permissible and nonpermissible activities.

B. Implications and tests

The theory of the shopping center developed above yields several testable implications (or hypotheses). Much of the preliminary evidence discussed is from surveys that we conducted comparing shopping centers to conventional shopping areas usually located in downtowns.[21]

Implication 1. Relative to conventional shopping areas, the physical characteristics at shopping centers will be organized to reduce the transaction, transportation, and search costs of consumers.

If owners and developers of shopping centers reduce search costs, including transaction and transportation costs, centers will be relatively more attractive, permitting the center either to increase sales volume or to raise prices, depending upon market conditions in the locality. Owners and developers may use a limited but important array of methods to lower search costs. For example, individual stores in the center may be laid out in a manner to reduce the distance and time spent in moving from one store to another. Thus, 47.1 percent of the consumers surveyed at shopping centers indicated that the most enjoyable aspect of the center was the close proximity of stores, compared to 37.6 percent of consumers surveyed in conventional shopping areas. Further, consumers spend less time at shopping centers but find more goods that they like (measured by total expenditures) than do their counterparts in conventional shopping areas.[22] Finally, shopping centers are able to reduce search costs by providing more adequate parking to potential consumers. Because owners and developers can strategically locate shopping centers, they can avoid the free-rider problem of competing stores using parking facilities for which they do not pay. Consequently, it is in the center's interest to provide a sufficiently large number of parking spaces to potential consumers. Not surprisingly, four times as many consumers at conventional shopping areas listed adequate parking as the attribute they "liked" the most.

Next, shopping centers will differ in the general type of goods and services offered consumers:

Implication 2. Owners of shopping centers will choose stores that sell goods with relatively higher search costs as a percentage of transaction prices than will landlords in conventional shopping areas.

This follows from at least two facts. First, the expected gains from additional search for items with high relative search costs are relatively low by definition. Thus, a buyer who finds a 30 percent discount on a $20 item will obtain only $6 in savings, while a buyer of a $1,000 item would save $300. Second, and more important, shopping center developers will find that stores offering goods that are (relatively) frequently purchased will generate more total savings to consumers. Therefore, the gains to stores will be greatest for those commodities that contain a relatively high amount of search costs, including transportation costs, relative to the value (measured by the transaction price) of the item. For example, finding the ideal dress or suit usually involves high search costs (measured by time spent at various stores) relative to the retail price paid per item, and clothing stores will consequently be found more frequently in centers. For the same reason, commodities such as major appliances, furniture, carpeting, and other goods with relatively low search costs as a percentage of transaction prices will be found less frequently in shopping centers. Thus, rather than focus only on the total search cost to explain the type of goods in shopping centers, one must look at the relative costs of search compared to the transaction prices.

Although our preliminary evidence is not overwhelming, it is consistent with this implication. Four of the five shopping centers studied offer relatively more clothing and shoe stores than conventional shopping areas, despite the fact that 55.8 percent of the consumers in shopping centers and 54.8 percent of the consumers in conventional shopping areas indicate that they most often purchase clothing and shoes. Further, conventional shopping areas contain more furniture stores than centers do.[23]

Third, shopping centers will also differ from conventional shopping areas in the number and quality of competing products:

Implication 3. Shopping centers will offer a wider range of competing products (both in number and quality) of the type of goods they carry than will conventional shopping areas.

Table 9.1. *Price ranges and competing products in shopping centers and conventional shopping areas, June 1978*

Price range, number of competing products, and date of shopping center opening[a]	Conventional shopping area less than shopping center (percent)	Conventional shopping area equal to shopping center (percent)	Conventional shopping area greater than shopping center (percent)
Price range of competing products			
Pre-1972	64.4	0.0	35.6
Post-1972[b]	66.7	5.5	27.8
All	65.1	1.6	33.3
Average number of higher-priced substitutes			
Pre-1972	57.8	11.1	31.1
Post-1972	41.2	11.8	47.0
All	53.2	11.3	35.5
Average number of lower-priced substitutes			
Pre-1972	42.2	20.0	37.8
Post-1972	41.2	29.4	29.4
All	41.9	22.6	35.5

[a] Includes all items that were simultaneously present in the shopping center and conventional shopping area of each surveyed city.
[b] In 1972, the Commission's position against restrictive covenants first became clear.
Source: Calculated from price survey data developed by authors.

Shopping centers can lower search costs to potential customers by offering both a larger number of choices of similar items and a wider selection of different qualities of these items for the type of goods they carry. When consumers are offered a wider range of competing qualities and a larger number of options, their search costs are reduced. Thus, whereas centers are more homogeneous as to the general types of goods offered, they provide a wider choice within the classes of goods that they do offer.

Table 9.1 provides some preliminary evidence supporting this implication. Shopping centers provide a wider range of quality (measured by differences in average prices) 65.1 percent of the time compared to conventional shopping areas which provide a wider range of quality 33.3 percent of the time. In addition, shopping centers provided both a higher average number of more expensive substitutes and a higher average number of less expensive substitutes than their conventional counterparts. For example, shopping centers were found to provide a larger number of more expensive substitutes in 53.2 percent of the cases studied, compared to 35.5 percent for conventional shopping areas.

Fourth, shopping center owners and developers have an added interest in maintaining sufficient inventories of offered products:

Implication 4. The average inventory in shopping centers will be equal to or higher than the average inventory in conventional shopping areas.

To meet expected consumer demands, shopping centers will hold inventories equal to or greater than average inventories in downtowns, thereby lowering search costs. We found that shopping centers have larger average inventories more often (57.5 percent) than do their counterparts in downtown shopping areas (35.6 percent). As an indirect proxy for the average inventory of "personnel," we also measured the average waiting time for customers in shoe stores and conventional shopping areas. We found, however, no appreciable difference (3 seconds) in the average waiting time between shopping centers and conventional shopping areas.

Fifth, if owner–developers combine physical activities, types of stores, and other factors that contribute to lower search costs, shopping centers would have a relatively narrow dispersion of consumer opportunity costs:

Implication 5. Consumers in shopping centers will have lower variation in their opportunity costs than will consumers who purchase in conventional shopping areas.

Implication 2 indicates that centers specialize in the type of stores within them. With this specialization, certain types of stores will not be provided. Consequently, our model predicts that not all individuals will be attracted to a particular shopping center if that shopping center specializes. Shopping centers will design physical locations, choose types of stores, and engage in policies that will attract individuals with a particular opportunity cost of time. Like the specialization of stores, this follows because lowering the search costs for all types of consumers is difficult. On the average, shopping centers therefore tend to focus on lowering the search costs of a particular group of consumers. We expect shopping centers to attract mostly high-, middle-, or low-income individuals, but not roughly equal parts of any two of the three (or of all three) groups.

Our research tends to verify this implication. For example, the shopping center in Louisville, Kentucky, seeks to attract individuals with relatively higher incomes than those found among consumers who shop in the conventional shopping areas, whereas the center in Kalamazoo, Michigan, attracts consumers whose average income is lower than their counterparts in the conventional shopping areas. In four of the five shopping centers visited, the coefficient of variation,[24] which measures relative dis-

Table 9.2. *Average purchase costs, search costs, and full prices in shopping centers and conventional shopping areas, June 1978*

Shopping area	Average total purchases	Average search costs[a]	Search costs as a percentage of total purchases
Charlottesville, Va.			
Shopping areas	$18.76	$17.51	93.3
Shopping center	22.65	15.07	66.5
Kalamazoo, Mich.			
Shopping areas	18.77	10.55	56.2
Shopping center	20.71	13.69	66.1
Long Beach, Calif.			
Shopping areas	19.53	11.80	60.4
Shopping center	19.71	10.64	54.0
Louisville, Ky.			
Shopping areas	19.24	17.21	89.4
Shopping center	27.49	19.01	69.2
Miami, Fla.			
Shopping areas	27.36	14.67	53.6
Shopping center	41.96	21.93	52.3
Average			
Shopping areas	20.50	14.28	69.7
Shopping center	26.28	16.03	61.0

[a] Search costs are calculated by multiplying the average time traveling to and spent in shopping area or center times average hourly wage.
Source: Calculated from consumer survey data developed by the authors.

person, was lower in the shopping center than in its conventional counterpart.[25]

Sixth, shopping centers will provide lower search costs than will conventional shopping areas:

Implication 6. The search costs of goods and services (per dollar expenditure) in shopping centers will be equal to or lower than search costs in conventional shopping areas.

The full price of a good includes not only its transaction price, but the costs of search, including transportation to and from the center, in locating the goods and services that are desired. Table 9.2 presents preliminary evidence of the relationship of transaction prices to search costs of goods and services in shopping centers compared to conventional shopping areas. Although this evidence is not conclusive, it supports the implication that shopping centers are effective in lowering search costs per dollar expended on goods and services, despite the fact that shopping centers specialize in the provision of goods with relatively higher search costs. The average search costs in shopping centers were equal to or lower than those in conventional shopping centers in four of the five cases studied.[26] For example, the average search costs in the conventional shopping area of downtown Miami were 1.3 percent higher than that in the shopping center a few blocks away. Overall, the search costs in shopping centers were 61.0 percent of average total purchases, or 8.7 percent lower than the search costs in the conventional shopping areas.[27]

Finally, we return to our model for an implication concerning actual transaction prices in shopping centers relative to those in conventional shopping areas.

Observation. Transaction prices will not necessarily differ between conventional shopping areas and shopping centers.

Our theory does not provide an unambiguous prediction concerning relative transaction prices. On one hand, although the search costs to consumers may be lowered, individual firms within the shopping center may attempt to increase transaction prices. On the other hand, greater competition from other stores within the center and from other centers may decrease transaction prices relative to those found in conventional shopping areas. With lower costs to consumers of going to alternative stores in the center, one would expect to find more consumers searching for prices as well as quality, thereby adding to the competitive pressure within the center. Consequently, no a priori implication concerning transaction prices can be derived from our theory. Preliminary evidence indicates that the competitive nature of shopping centers is a slightly more influential factor than lower search and transportation costs in determining prices.[28] Thus, we find that 41.1 percent of the transaction prices found in conventional shopping areas are greater than their counterparts in shopping centers, whereas only 35.6 percent of all transaction prices are lower in conventional shopping areas relative to shopping centers.

To summarize, incorporating search costs, including transportation, in the price that consumers pay is a reasonably good predictor of behavior in shopping centers relative to behavior in conventional shopping areas. With this explanation of the organization and function of shopping centers, we may understand more fully what the theory tells us about the effect of Federal Trade Commission orders on the shopping center industry.

III. Impact of FTC cases

According to FTC and shopping center industry sources, the FTC cases have resulted in the elimination of approval and other lease clauses that arguably restrict price competition.[29] In Section III.A, we contrast the effects that the Commission would predict to follow from this change with those that our theory implies. For each of the predictions, we present some preliminary, occasionally crude, evidence. In addition, Section

III.B uses our theory to derive and test in a similar manner other implications concerning the FTC orders.

A. Commission propositions contrasted with the model of Section II

First, elimination of approval clauses and of use clauses dealing with pricing practices should lead to:

FTC Proposition A. The number of discounters in major shopping centers will increase.

If the restrictive covenants are the sole barrier to discounter entry in major shopping centers, the Commission's proposition would be confirmed. On the other hand, our theory implies the existence of procompetitive benefits from the exclusion of certain stores from some shopping centers:

Implication 7. With the elimination of restrictive clauses, the number of discounters in major shopping centers will not necessarily increase.

According to the Commission's view of shopping centers, major tenants coerce the developers to exclude discounters. Thus, the Commission apparently sought to leave the decision of tenant mix solely to the developer's discretion. As Tony Joseph, one of the lead FTC attorneys in *Tysons Corner,* remarked: "I think department stores are going to have to trust the major developers. And they're going to have to be able to find out from the major developer what kind of center he intends to run. Talk to him, find out what he's done and what he intends to do, and rest on that – not on their subsequent control of what he does." Further, Joseph stated, "The developer cannot agree with a tenant that the tenant cannot be a discounter in the center. The developer, in my opinion, has absolute discretion as to whom he will let in the center."[30]

As contrasted with the Commission's opinion, our theory indicates that developers may exclude discounters even without pressure from major tenants.[31] In most leases, the developer's rental fee is directly related to the revenues of his tenants. The total revenues of the center may decline while the discounter's revenues increase if the discounter shirks or relies on other tenants' actions. This decrease would directly injure the developer by lowering overall rental fees. Consequently, the developer has a strong, independent incentive to exclude such a discounter. Thus, we would not expect a rush toward discounter tenancy in major shopping centers.

Another economic phenomenon occurs that may lead many discounters to avoid regional and other large shopping centers. As we argued in Section II, shopping centers reduce the search and transportation cost components of the full price of a commodity. The cost of reducing search and

Table 9.3. *Number of discount stores in Florida and Ohio shopping centers*

State	Shopping centers opened prior to 1972		Shopping centers opened post-1973	
	Neighborhood[a]	Others[b]	Neighborhood[a]	Others[b]
Florida				
Number	88	31	17	4
Percent	73.9	26.1	81.0	19.0
Ohio				
Number	40	25	21	5
Percent	61.5	38.5	80.8	19.2
Total				
Number	128	56	38	9
Percent	69.6	30.4	80.9	19.1

[a] Centers of less than 100,000 square feet, usually 10 to 15 stores.
[b] All other centers in excess of 100,000 square feet, including community, regional, and superregional shopping centers.
Source: Calculated from data in National Research Bureau, *Directory of Shopping Centers in the United States,* 1978.

transportation costs is reflected in the transaction price of the goods. Many discounters, on the other hand, obtain their comparative advantage by maintaining low transaction prices, in part by avoiding expenses that may reduce consumers' search costs. For example, discounters may provide less extensive service to customers. Many consumers with lower opportunity costs of time probably prefer higher search and transportation costs over a higher transaction price. Because consumers have different opportunity costs, our theory predicts that shopping centers and discounters will attract different consumers. According to this formulation of discount consumer demands, discounters find it less profitable to move to major regional shopping centers because their major advantage, lower transaction prices, would be reduced or offset by the higher rental fees that developers charge to cover the expenses of reducing search costs to consumers. In effect, the discount stores would then be less attractive to their normal consumer constituency.

Thus, the independent interests of both developers and discounters indicate that the number of discounters in major shopping centers should not rise significantly. Table 9.3 presents evidence consistent with our theory and rejects the Commission's proposition that the relative number of discounters in the major shopping areas would increase. Prior to 1972, approximately 30 percent of the discount stores in Florida and Ohio opened in community, regional, or superregional shopping centers. If the Commission had been correct, the percentage should have increased following its cases, which began to bear fruit in 1972. Precisely the opposite oc-curred, however, a fact that weakens the Commission's case against re-strictive lease clauses.

Second, because of the anticipated entry of discounters and the elimi-nation of clauses limiting the pricing freedom of other tenants, the Com-mission theory implies:

FTC Proposition B. Transaction prices in shopping centers with restrictive clauses will be higher than those in shopping areas, and these prices will fall in new centers without the restrictive clauses.

On the other hand, our analysis indicates that transaction prices may rise or fall depending on factors independent of the restrictive clauses. We found that prices are usually lower in shopping centers relative to shop-ping areas. (See the foregoing Observation). Further, in the one center tested that was constructed and opened after the FTC's cases, the trans-action prices were *higher* than in an equivalent conventional shopping area. Again, the available evidence does not support the FTC proposi-tion.

B. Implications of the effects of FTC orders

To begin with, elimination of the lease clauses increases the risks that major tenants face, because the clauses afford protection against shirking. Accordingly:

Implication 8: To compensate for the loss of the restrictive clauses, major tenants will receive other concessions in the leases.

As rough evidence to support this implication, major tenants in shop-ping centers have been able to obtain more favorable rental rates relative to minor tenants in the period since the first Commission orders. Depart-ment stores in regional shopping centers pay only 27.8 percent of the me-dian rent paid by ladies-wear stores (chosen as a typical minor tenant) in 1978. In 1972, that comparative amount was 36.4 percent. Moreover, ad-justments for inflation reveal that, in constant dollars, department stores in major shopping centers pay 31.4 percent less, but minor tenants have not enjoyed as large a decline (e.g., only 9.9 percent for ladies wear). On the other hand, neighborhood shopping centers, which have not been sub-ject to the Commission's orders, have had little change in the relative rates paid between variety stores relative to ladies-wear stores (which are approximately one-tenth the size of variety stores). Finally, the decreases in rental rates in constant-dollar terms for variety and ladies wear stores in community centers were more similar than the differences found in re-gional shopping centers.[32]

In addition to concessions, major tenants may attempt to respond to the

Table 9.4. *Local and national developers of superregional shopping centers*

Item	Year opened	
	1960–71	1974–80
Number of centers developed	48	48
Average square feet (1,000s)	1,238	1,173
Percentage local developers[a]	69	29
Percentage national developers[a]	31	71

[a] National developers were treated as local developers for centers developed in their home states.
[b] Six out-of-state developers with no other centers listed were treated as national developers.
Source: Calculated from a random sample of superregional shopping centers from data in National Research Bureau, *Directory of Shopping Centers in the United States,* 1978.

FTC orders by seeking more established developers, owners, and tenants:

Implication 9. Developers without established reputations will face increased entry costs after the Commission's orders.

As we established in Section II.A, restrictive clauses can be used to guard against the undesirable behavior of both developers and tenants. With the removal of the clauses, the major tenants may more carefully choose the developers with whom they associate. In fact, as the foregoing quotes from Tony Joseph indicate,[33] the Commission staff has in effect encouraged this development. Consequently, major tenants can reduce their increased risk by choosing developers with established reputations. Thus, it is not surprising to find that in Table 9.4 national firms (which would tend to have more established reputations than local firms) developed 71 percent of the superregional shopping centers that opened after the FTC's position became clear. Local firms had developed 69 percent of the superregional centers that opened during the 12-year period prior to the announcement of the FTC's position on the lease clauses. Of course, as with other evidence in this section, we have not tested whether alternative factors have contributed to the observed change.

The Commission itself may have caused additional problems. Besides making it more costly for smaller (i.e., local and less well-known) developers to compete, the FTC orders may have made it more difficult for local tenants to locate in large shopping centers:

Implication 10. Shopping center developers will tend to choose tenants with more established reputations than previously.

This argument follows because, without the restrictive clauses, developers would be less able to control the activities of their tenants. They avoid this risk to some degree, however, by choosing tenants whose practices are well known. Thus, national chains, which tend to have more established reputations, may receive an advantage relative to local stores. As evidence is not available for new shopping centers, our data include centers where this advantage will not have been a factor. Yet since 1972 a trend has emerged showing the location of larger numbers of national chain stores in regional shopping centers. In 1972, national chains owned approximately 63 percent of the stores in regional shopping centers; by 1978 that figure was 68 percent.[34] On the other hand, occupancy of national chain stores in neighborhood shopping centers declined from 44 percent in 1972 to 42 percent in 1978. The Commission has not sought to have this kind of impact.[35]

A final set of potential effects of the orders concerns the costs of forming and running shopping centers. Because the parties choose restrictive covenants to obtain the benefits discussed in Section II, alternative arrangements are presumably only as efficient and, in fact, may be less efficient for this purpose.

Implication 11. If the Commission eliminates restrictive covenants, the overall costs of developing and operating shopping centers will rise.

We would expect to find administrative overhead to rise both prior to opening and during operation of centers if restrictive covenants are forbidden. More important, leasing costs and other legal fees would rise. Finally, to the extent that outside financing companies believe that the alternatives to the restrictive covenants are not as efficient (i.e., are more risky) in obtaining desired outcomes, interest and financing costs would rise. An inspection of Table 9.5 is consistent with the hypothesis that the Commission's cases have caused developers and tenants to choose alternative and more costly methods of achieving their desired outcomes. Total overhead and development costs as a percentage of capital costs have risen for those shopping centers opened since the Commission's position became clear. For centers in excess of 200,000 square feet (i.e., those centers about which the Commission has expressed concern), these costs have risen from 7.9 percent of overall capital costs (before the FTC activity) to 16.4 percent of overall capital costs (after the changes in leasing practices). On the other hand, total overhead and development costs as a percent of capital costs have not risen substantially for those shopping centers that are not subject to the Commission's concern. These costs have risen only from 9.0 percent (1968–70 opening dates) to 9.7 percent (1976–7 opening dates).

Once the center is in operation, the model predicts that shopping centers will also continue to have higher operating costs, because the restric-

Table 9.5. *Overhead and development costs as a percentage of total capital costs (dollars per square foot of gross leasable area)*

Overhead and development costs as a percentage of capital costs	Median for shopping centers opening in:	
	1968–70	1976–7
Regional shopping centers		
Gross leasable area (ft²)	543,000	413,000[a]
Interest and financing (%)	3.2	7.2
Administrative overhead (%)	1.4	3.4
Leasing costs and legal fees (%)	1.2	3.6
Other overhead prior to opening (%)	2.1	2.2
Total (%)	7.9	16.4
Community shopping centers		
Gross leasable area (ft²)	166,000	144,000
Interest and financing (%)	2.3	4.6
Administrative overhead (%)	2.1	1.5
Leasing costs and legal fees (%)	0.6	1.8
Other overhead prior to opening (%)	4.0	1.8
Total (%)	9.0	9.7

[a] Includes superregional shopping centers (median of 418,000 square feet) and regional shopping centers (median of 409,000 square feet).
Source: Urban Land Institute, *The Dollars and Cents of Shopping Centers,* 1972 (p. 190) and 1978 (p. 254).

tive covenants were designed to eliminate certain undesirable behavior. The overall operating costs of the building, mall, and surrounding areas will rise if the Commission prohibits restrictive covenants designed to lower the costs of this behavior. In 1972, building, mall, and parking lot costs expressed as a percentage of total operating costs were roughly 25 percent for both new centers (ages one to three years) and older centers (seven to nine years). By 1978, maintenance costs as a percentage of total operating costs had risen substantially both for newer and older centers. However, maintenance costs for newer centers (i.e., those presumably influenced by the Commission's orders) had increased approximately 24 percentage points. Older shopping centers had experienced an increase of approximately 6 percentage points.[36] Although this evidence is hardly conclusive, it is consistent with the view that the Commission's position has caused shopping center developers and tenants to use more expensive methods of obtaining the benefits of the shopping center.

IV. Conclusions

As Section I argues, because the antitrust courts have no experience with the lease clauses and because those practices are not traditional *per se*

violations, they should be judged under a rule-of-reason standard. Fur
ther, primarily because the respondent did not attempt to justify the leas
clauses, the one case that was actually litigated (*City Stores*) presented a
completely inappropriate record upon which to find *per se* illegality.

Under a rule-of-reason analysis, the lease clauses can indeed be justi
fied. Section II develops a theory of shopping center firm behavior base
on consumer demands. This theory accurately describes both develope
and tenant behavior by focusing on the full cost of consumer purchase
and the combination of inputs that developers and tenants use to mee
consumer demands. A main function of the shopping center is to lowe
the costs of transportation and search that consumers face. *Restrictive
covenants are actually useful in lowering these costs, thus lowering the
relative search costs to consumers shopping in the centers relative to the
full prices found in downtown shopping areas.*

The Commission sought to improve price competition by, *inter alia,* fa
cilitating the entry (and thus increasing the number) of discounters into
shopping centers and by eliminating clauses that allegedly hindered the
pricing flexibility of some tenants who did enter. On the other hand, we
predict that the number of discounters will not necessarily increase and
that the lease clauses do not reduce consumer welfare by facilitating price
fixing. As detailed in Sections II and III, evidence exists to *refute* the
Commission's predictions and to *support* our theory. The number of discounters in new centers has not increased, nor does the evidence available to us, albeit preliminary in development, indicate that the existence
of lease clauses permitted higher prices in shopping centers.

Instead of benefiting consumers, the cases seem to have had detrimental effects. The orders appear to have made it more costly for new developers to compete with established developers and for local merchants to
compete with national chains. Further, the orders may have raised the
costs of developing and maintaining new shopping centers. Instead of
benefiting consumers, the FTC's shopping center cases appear to illustrate Commission actions that have raised costs to consumers.

10 Legislative powers: FTC rule making

DORSEY D. ELLIS, JR.

The Federal Trade Commission Improvement Act of 1975 (FTCIA)[1] expressly authorizes the FTC to promulgate rules that "define with specificity acts or practices which are unfair or deceptive,"[2] the knowing violation of which may result in a "civil penalty" of $10,000. The FTC has thus become a powerful consumer protection agency. Whether consumer welfare will thereby be enhanced depends on the manner in which this rulemaking authority is implemented by the FTC, particularly the care with which the Commission constructs its Trade Regulation Rules (TRRs) to comport with the economic realities of the marketplace. As the more detailed analysis of specific TRRs in succeeding chapters confirms, the experience to date is disquieting.

This chapter addresses in a general way the question of whether the FTC is implementing its rule-making power in a manner that will effectively improve consumer welfare. Particular rules are analyzed in depth in the chapters that follow. This chapter provides an overview of some of the recurring problems in the FTC's approach to rule making, and draws for the most part upon rules that are not the subjects of intensive particularized analysis in later chapters. It begins with a brief description of the origin and framework of the Commission's rule-making authority and summarizes the types of rules adopted or proposed. Because the statute authorizes rules that proscribe practices found to be "unfair or deceptive," the Commission's efforts to provide some content to those vague concepts are then analyzed. This is followed by an analysis of the explicit and implicit conceptual bases underlying the Commission's rule-making activities in the areas of restriction on the functioning of the market, mandated disclosures, rewriting contracts, and other miscellaneous requirements. Finally, this chapter presents a brief assessment of the nature and quality of the evidence relied upon by the Commission and its staff in support of the rules adopted and proposed.

161

I. The FTC's rule-making authority

Prior to the adoption of the FTCIA, the FTC's authority to proceed by rule making rather than by adjudication was doubted by many, including at least some members of the Commission itself.[3] The Commission's first significant effort to exercise a substantive rule-making power, its   Trade Regulation Rule for the Prevention of Unfair or Deceptive Acts or Practices in the Sale of Cigarettes,[4]   had been mooted by passage of the Cigarette Labeling and Advertising Act of 1965,[5] which preempted the FTC's rule. The next major rulemaking effort came in 1971, when the FTC issued TRRs requiring care labels to be affixed to clothing, and octane ratings to be posted on gasoline pumps.[6] Although the validity of the octane-rating rule was successfully challenged in the District Court for the District of Columbia, the Court of Appeals reversed that decision,[7] thereby providing the first judicial recognition of the FTC's asserted rule-making authority. After the district court decision struck down the octane-rating rule and held that the FTC lacked authority to issue TRRs, Congress began an inquiry into whether the FTC should be given substantive rule-making power. Congressional consideration of that question continued after the court of appeals upheld the FTC's power to promulgate TRRs, and culminated in the adoption of the FTCIA.

The FTCIA imposed a number of procedural requirements on the FTC. In addition to following the "notice and comment" procedures required by the Administrative Procedure Act (APA),[8] the FTC is also required to

(1) publish a notice of proposed rule making stating with particularity the reason for the proposed rule; (2) allow interested persons to submit written data, views, and arguments, and make all such submissions publicly available; (3) provide an opportunity for an informal hearing . . . ; and (4) promulgate, if appropriate, a final rule based on the matter in the rulemaking record . . . together with a statement of basis and purpose.[9]

The Statement of Basis and Purpose must include

(A) a statement as to the prevalence of the acts or practices treated by the rule; (B) a statement as to the manner and context in which such acts or practices are unfair or deceptive; and (C) a statement as to the economic effect of the rule, taking into account the effect on small business and consumers.[10]

In going substantially beyond the APA's requirement of "a concise general statement of . . . basis and purpose,"[11] and imposing specific content requirements on a statement of basis and purpose underlying rules promulgated by the FTC, Congress specified the factors to which the Commission must give particular weight in deciding whether to issue a rule. Congress evidently intended that the FTC, in exercising its rule-making capacity, must explain and justify its action, and consider and explain both the manner in which a proscribed practice is "unfair" and the "economic effect" of any rule that it promulgates. As a final check against the issuance of ill-considered rules, the FTCIA expressly provides for immediate judicial review of any rule promulgated, on the initiative of any interested party.[12]

Since the FTCIA became effective, the Commission has promulgated three TRRs. The first, *Advertising of Ophthalmic Goods and Services*[13] (the Eyeglasses Rule), was issued in July 1978. It was followed by *Franchising Business Opportunity Ventures*[14] (the Franchise Rule) and *Proprietary Vocational and Home Study Schools*[15] (the Vocational Schools Rule), both of which were issued in December 1978. In addition, the FTC has under consideration 17 proposed TRRs, as well as proposed amendments to three other rules that were adopted prior to the FTCIA becoming effective.[16] Two of the rules already adopted and 13 of the 17 proposed rules deal with single industries. Two of the promulgated rules and seven of the proposed single industry rules are targeted at the retail sales level, which contains large numbers of small firms.

The adopted and proposed rules take various forms. Some preempt state laws and regulations and other institutional barriers to competition. Others require the collection and disclosure of information by sellers (often in a particularized form specified in the rule); prohibit certain statements by sellers, including some "true" statements or expressions of opinion; require specified disclaimers in advertising; restrict the freedom of parties to contract; and specify in detail the form of contracts. The FTC has not articulated a consistent theory justifying this variety of approaches, nor can one be discerned from an analysis of the rules. Indeed, the explicit or implicit theories underlying at least some of the rules are directly in conflict.

II. The development of a concept of "unfairness"

A. The concept of "unfairness" prior to the enactment of the FTCIA

The rule-making power granted to the FTC by the enactment of the FTCIA extends to acts and practices that are "unfair" or "deceptive." These characterizations, especially "unfair," are hopelessly vague on their face and thus require explication and refinement before they can provide any standard against which to gauge the Commission's rule-making activity. The Commission's own efforts at refining the concept of "unfair" for rule-making purposes predate the passage of the FTCIA. In the opinion accompanying its 1964 Cigarette Rule, the agency listed three criteria for deciding if particular conduct is unfair:

whether the practice, without necessarily having been previously considered unlawful, offends public policy as it has been established by statutes, the common law, or otherwise – whether, in other words, it is within at least the penumbra of some common law, statutory, or other established concept of unfairness; (2) whether it is immoral, unethical, oppressive, or unscrupulous; (3) whether it causes substantial injury to consumers (or competitors or other businessmen).[17]

This language has been referred to by the FTC and its staff in subsequent rule-making proceedings, and the Supreme Court has quoted it with approval.[18] Nevertheless, it is of only limited usefulness as a standard against which any proposed rule can be measured. For example, the FTC has invoked the first criterion when existing law or its penumbra supports a proposed rule[19] and rejected it when a proposed rule conflicts with existing law.[20] The second criterion is hardly less amorphous than the notion of "unfair" practice that it seeks to define. The terms "immoral," "unethical," and "unscrupulous," if they are not precisely synonymous, are at most slight variations on the theme of "wrong" or "bad." ("Oppressive" in this context seems to denote "unfairly burdensome," which brings us back full circle to "unfair.") Without more explanation, the second criterion provides no guidance either to the Commission or to a reviewing court. Even apparently simple distinctions between "good" and "bad" or "right" and "wrong," such as that between telling the truth and lying, turn out to be quite complex and to provoke disagreements among those – mainly theologians and moral philosophers – who specialize in such matters.[21] The FTC does not explicitly indicate the sources of its notions of "immoral," "unethical," or "unscrupulous" when it decides that a practice falls within this criterion, which suggests that the explicit or implicit value preferences of its members are determinative.

The third criterion, whether a practice imposes "substantial injury" on consumers or other firms, is potentially a more meaningful standard, depending upon the content of "injury." If what is meant is that a practice is "unfair" when its elimination would result in lower costs (the consumption of fewer resources) without reducing consumer satisfaction, then eliminating the practice would result in a real savings in resources and a corresponding increase in welfare (providing, of course, that the costs avoided exceed those incurred in the process). For example, requiring sellers to disclose specified information to buyers might result in a reduction in the search costs of buyers by an amount greater than the sum of the additional costs incurred by sellers in providing the information plus the costs of enforcing the requirement. But "injury" may also refer to a judgment about the propriety of a transfer payment between two parties that does not result in any decrease in resources consumed. If that is what is meant, then this third criterion must either refer back to one of the first two or to some other set of value preferences by which the propriety of the transfer payment is to be judged.

Thus, despite the Commission's effort in the Cigarette Rule opinion to make it more precise, the notion of "unfair" acts or practices remained vague when the FTCIA was enacted.

B. The concept of unfairness under the FTCIA

The first attempt by the Commission to explicate and apply the concept of unfairness guiding its rule-making activities under the FTCIA came in the Statement of Basis and Purpose accompanying the first TRR issued pursuant to that act: *Advertising of Ophthalmic Goods and Services* (the Eyeglasses Rule). Relying in part on the reference to "public values" in the Supreme Court's opinion in the *S&H* case (discussed in Chapter 4), the Commission concluded that "the intent of Congress was to protect consumers from unwarranted injury in the marketplace." Thus, "the Commission has increasingly concentrated on the examination of whether particular acts or practices are in fact causing injury."[22] Other public policies are to be brought into the analysis only as aids in determining whether there are other justifications or compensatory benefits supporting the challenged act or practices. The Commission concluded, therefore, that the test of unfairness requires two inquiries: "(1) Whether the acts or practices result in substantial harm to consumers. In making this determination both the economic and social benefits and losses flowing from the challenged conduct must be assessed, and (2) Whether the challenged conduct offends public policy."[23] This statement of the issues at least discards the Cigarette Rule's emphasis on "immoral, unethical, oppressive or unscrupulous" conduct and the amorphous "public values" language of the *S&H* opinion. But it lacks definitions of "substantial harm to consumers" and of "economic and social benefits and losses," and provides no guidance as to the sources of "public policy."

III. Application of the FTC's concept of unfairness

Ultimately, the FTC's understanding of the concept of unfairness, its conception of "harm to consumers" and of "economic and social benefits and losses," as well as its notions of appropriate sources of "public policy," can only be inferred from the rules that it adopts or that the Bureau of Consumer Protection (BCP) proposes, and the explicit and implicit justifications offered for them. Accordingly, this section undertakes an analysis of illustrative rules, adopted or proposed, dealing with market restraints, disclosure requirements, rewriting contracts, and other miscellaneous regulatory provisions.

A. Market restraints

The Eyeglasses Rule, the first TRR adopted under the FTCIA, preempts state laws restricting price advertising of eyeglasses and eye examinations. It also proscribes advertising bans adopted by professional and trade associations. Thus, the principal purpose of the rule is to remove institutional barriers to the dissemination of information in the marketplace. The theory of consumer injury underlying the rule is that these barriers impose higher search costs on consumers than would a free market and that these higher search costs permit sellers to charge higher-than-competitive prices. Fewer units of goods and services (eyeglasses and eye examinations) are being produced than would occur under free-market conditions because some consumers who would purchase them at the market price will substitute other goods and services, perhaps by merely forgoing or delaying eye examinations and glasses. Because the substitute is by definition less satisfactory at the free market price, there is a real loss of consumer welfare (i.e., "harm to consumers"). This conclusion is demonstrable by conventional economic analysis irrespective of any separate calculus of "social benefits and losses."

The Commission's reliance on the market mechanism is quite explicitly set forth in the Eyeglasses Rule opinion, both as a basis for concluding that advertising restraints have caused "harm to consumers" and as support for the conclusion that the restraints "offend public policy," the second issue considered in determining whether conduct is "unfair." Thus, rejecting the argument that the advertising ban provides health and safety benefits to consumers, the Commission observed that

the public policy of this country favors the existence of free markets to the maximum extent possible. While the complexity of the modern economy often necessitates a departure from free market organization, as a general proposition a market-perfecting solution to a perceived problem is preferable. There should be a heavy burden of proof on those who would opt for a different form of economic organization; that burden has not been met here.[24]

The Eyeglasses Rule and its accompanying Statement of Basis and Purpose suggested that the FTC had begun to recognize the importance of the market in furthering consumer interests, and demonstrated the FTC's considerable potential as a means of freeing the market from excessive regulation, at least at the state level.[25] But the eyeglasses opinion itself confuses the effect of institutional barriers to the dissemination of information with the effect of mere failure to disseminate information.[26] This emphasis on result rather than process is both critical and unfortunate. Because the FTC failed to distinguish market processes from market results, the Eyeglasses Rule did not simply remove real impediments to the efficient functioning of the market but attempted to dictate market results.

The Commission's investigation of the funeral industry provided another opportunity to promote consumer welfare by freeing the market from excessive regulation. The report of the presiding officer in that proceeding documented the extent to which state regulation of the funeral industry had served to insulate firms from competition.[27] State regulatory boards are usually composed of active or retired funeral directors.[28] Typical of a state-enforced cartel, these boards use their power to inhibit competition from potential new entrants offering less costly forms of service.[29] State laws require unnecessary embalming facilities, thereby increasing costs and erecting a further barrier to alternative forms of competition. In the presiding officer's opinion, state laws requiring the embalming of bodies that are not to be interred within a specified number of days probably cannot be justified on health grounds, and the annoyance from the odor of a decomposing body can be avoided in other, less costly, ways.[30] Moreover, some states have imposed trust-fund requirements on the sale of "pre-need" funeral arrangements that far exceed actuarially sound requirements, thereby restricting the ability of sellers of such services to compete with the established sellers of "at-need" services. Finally, states have progressively increased the educational requirements for licensure, thereby further limiting entry, especially by persons who propose to offer alternative services (e.g., immediate disposal services) that compete with traditional funeral homes. The presiding officer concluded that if "this market were free to operate competitively," many of the problems he found might be corrected.[31] The final staff report on funeral industry practices substantially agreed with and reinforced the presiding officer's findings, but except for a prohibition of private restraints on the advertising of alternative services,[32] did not even consider that removing the regulatory and other institutional barriers to competition would effectively eliminate the real injury to consumers. Instead, as discussed below, the staff proposed the addition of yet another layer of detailed regulation.

Thus, in the Eyeglasses Rule, the FTC demonstrated that its rule-making authority was capable of becoming a powerful force for improving consumer welfare through deregulation. The Commission recognized that consumers are harmed when state-imposed restraints on the market inhibit competition, and it took decisive action to preempt state laws prohibiting advertising, thus allowing competition to function more effectively in the eyeglasses market. This approach to the concept of "unfairness" possessed considerable potential for improving consumer welfare, especially if applied to restraints more subtle, but not necessarily less effective in impeding competition, than advertising restrictions, especially those restraints that erect barriers to entry. The Funeral Industry Rule provided the FTC with an opportunity to enhance the consumer welfare by preempting a congeries of state laws and regulations that shelter the industry from effective competition and inhibit the entry of innovative and lower-cost methods of delivering services. Although the effects of state regulation in allowing cartel-like conditions to exist in the funeral industry were recognized by both the presiding officer and the staff, a deregulatory approach was not undertaken or even seriously considered. Instead, another layer of regulation was proposed.

B. Disclosure requirements

A number of the adopted and proposed TRRs mandate disclosure of information, often in a form precisely specified in the rule. Yet the Commission has not articulated a consistent theory to justify such requirements. Whitford has posited three models applicable to disclosure requirements in credit transactions[33] that seem equally applicable to the disclosure requirements in the TRRs. The predictive model states that specified information provided to consumers will affect their buying decisions. The normative model "describes the manner in which somebody – usually the formulator of the model – believes people should behave."[34] According to this model, a disclosure requirement may reflect an implicit effort to persuade consumers to act in a manner consistent with the value choices of the regulator. Finally, there is the political model, which posits that proponents of disclosure requirements know that disclosure will have little effect upon buying decisions but are reacting to the transitory political demand for consumer-oriented legislation. Disclosure requirements satisfy "the political demand for consumer legislation because it appears and is represented to be proconsumer and because the ordinary citizen simply has neither the sophistication nor the information needed to realize that the legislation will have little impact."[35] Although it is frequently not possible to distinguish between the normative and political hypotheses as explaining any given disclosure requirement, a close analysis of the TRRs mandating disclosure indicates that a number of them can be explained only by one or the other hypothesis.

Because the predictive model posits that additional information will bring about a change in consumer behavior, it implies that the information is of value to the consumer. But in that case, the market will normally produce the information, because it will be to sellers' advantage to inform consumers of the desirable qualities their products possess and of the undesirable properties they lack. The production and distribution of information is not costless, however. Where the cost to a seller of producing the information exceeds the value of the expected gain in custom from disclosing it, the seller will not voluntarily produce it, and to require it to do so would be inefficient. But even where a single seller does not produce specific information, it may be efficient for other agents to do so.

Thus, supermarkets, department stores, credit rating bureaus, trade associations, unions, the press, consumer organizations, and government agencies may provide information about goods or services that would be too costly for a single seller to provide or for individual buyers to search out. Alternatively, surrogates for specific information in the form of seller reputation or warranties may serve the same purposes as detailed information.[36]

Where the cost of disclosure is small relative to the price of the product, the fact that particular information is not being disclosed strongly implies either that it will affect few purchasing decisions, or that some barrier – such as monopoly, collusion, or regulation – prevents the market from functioning effectively. There are several reasons why specific information may not affect buying decisions. An obvious one is that the buyer may be relatively indifferent to that factor compared to some other properties of the good in question. In some cases the cost to the buyer of "consuming" the information may be high relative to its usefulness.

The Vocational Schools TRR requires the costly collection[37] and disclosure of information under circumstances suggesting that the information is unlikely to affect purchasing decisions. Schools covered by the rule must collect and disclose, in a form specified in the rule, detailed information regarding graduation rates and, if any reference to jobs or earnings is made in any promotional material, the placement and salary records of their graduates. But some students enroll in a vocational course for avocational reasons or to obtain associated products (color TVs, etc.), thereby converting their VA educational entitlements into something of greater value to them. They will be indifferent to information regarding job placement and earnings, and their purchasing decisions are unlikely to be affected by receiving it. More important, the BCP has argued that "the 'typical' vocational school student is an individual who is unusually vulnerable to deceptive and misleading advertising and unfair sales and enrollment techniques."[38] Such students, according to the BCP, are young, inexperienced, likely to have dropped out of other postsecondary education, and "impulsive and motivated by extrinsive standards as opposed to being inner-directed and careful in their decisions." Many are high school dropouts or "inner-city blacks."[39] In short, the BCP portrays the "typical" student as lacking the capability of evaluating the information that the TRR requires to be disclosed. Thus, there is little reason to believe that the disclosure is likely to have a significant impact on the buying decisions of the group whom the FTC is most concerned to protect.

The Funeral Industry Practice Rule, as proposed in the final staff report of July 1978, would require disclosure of (1) a detailed casket price list prior to discussion of casket selection; (2) a detailed price list of outer burial containers (vaults or grave liners) before discussion or showing of outer containers; and (3) a general price list, detailing prices for a minimum of 11 categories of services and products before discussion or selection. Both the presiding officer and the final staff report portray the grief-stricken survivor as disoriented, guilt-ridden, status-conscious, dependent on and susceptible to suggestions from the funeral director, ignorant of details about funeral arrangements (owing both to inexperience and to society's "attitude of death denial"), and under severe time pressure.[40] Again the portrayal is of a person for whom the consumption of the kind of detailed information that the rule would require is difficult. Hence, the probability that such disclosures will materially affect purchasing decisions is low. The presiding officer expressly noted the "paradox":

> If the consumer is disoriented and he or she is the one who is making the arrangement or the decisions relative thereto, then will a series of written disclosures be meaningful? How much written (or for that matter, oral) information can be absorbed, given the short time available and the necessity to deal with emotional consequences of death such as guilt?
>
> On the other hand, if the arrangements and decisions are being made by someone not in deep grief, a friend of the family or a distant relative, are extraordinary measures, such as some of those contemplated by this proposed rule, justified?[41]

The staff argued that the bereaved would nevertheless "benefit" from the disclosure, emphasizing that the survivor is often accompanied by an advisor who might help make use of the information disclosed.[42] But both the presiding officer and the final staff report indicate a disagreement with value preferences that equate status with the elaborateness of a funeral, or respect for the deceased with such things as the quality of a casket or the duration of protection from seepage provided by a vault – values that funeral directors are seen as "exploiting."[43] The evidence of such attitudes suggests that Whitford's "normative model" substantially explains the proposed disclosure requirements.

The funeral industry TRR produced a schism within the BCP, with the result that substantial modifications to the rule as proposed in the final staff report have been recommended by a group of staff members assigned to the funeral rule proceeding subsequent to the report (the "new staff").[44] The modifications are supported by the director of the BCP[45] but opposed by those staff members who drafted the final staff report (the "original staff").[46] These disagreements about the propriety of various provisions of the proposed rule stem in part from differences in attitudes regarding the appropriateness of regulation and in part from differences in the levels of understanding of the way in which a competitive market functions. A hearing has been held by the Commission,[47] but as of this writing the disagreements among the staff have not been finally resolved and the position that the FTC will ultimately take is unknown. Hence, the following discussion analyzes the disclosure aspects of the funeral industry TRR both as proposed in the final staff report and as proposed to be modified.

The disclosure of detailed price lists and the requirement that funeral homes display lower-priced caskets, as proposed in the final staff report, were premised on the assumption that funeral directors are able to charge higher than competitive prices by quoting package prices and by inducing survivors to purchase higher-priced caskets. Since under competitive conditions such prices could not be extracted by manipulating the form of the transaction, regardless of what sellers of funeral services may believe, the BCP must therefore assume that competitive conditions do not prevail. In fact, as indicated above, there is substantial evidence in both the presiding officer's report and the final staff report that cartel conditions enforced by state regulatory agencies are common in the funeral industry. If that is the case, then requiring that nominal prices be stated in different forms or that specified grades of merchandise be available will not eliminate either the cartel or the higher prices that result. The promulgation of the proposed regulations might produce some instability in the prices of caskets or funeral services in the short run while sellers seek new profit-maximizing price relationships, but there is no reason to assume that prices will be lower after that period than they were before the adoption of the rule. It is at least equally plausible that they will be higher. This would be so under either of two conditions that might prevail in these circumstances: (1) where members of the industry incur additional costs in adjusting to the rule to minimize its impact on profits, resulting in a higher profit-maximizing price; or (2) where the required disclosures make it more difficult for members of the cartel to cheat by offering disguised reductions from the cartel's joint profit-maximizing price (e.g., through package prices).

The proposed modifications to the rule would retain the requirement that a detailed price list be disclosed, but would allow the offering of a package price lower than the sum of its components (in order to allow the realization of possible economies in package transactions) and would eliminate the requirement that low-priced caskets be displayed (because it "is simply not clear that [this requirement] will have the intended effect"[48]). The original staff opposes both changes. It argues that allowing package prices would allow funeral directors to "set the itemized component prices high and thereby push consumers into selecting the package" and asserts that "there are not any substantial economies which could be realized by packaging funeral items."[49] The incentive that funeral directors would have to induce package purchases by setting artificially high component prices is not specified nor does any come to mind, and the asserted lack of economies in package transactions is neither supported by evidence nor intuitively obvious. The original staff's opposition to the elimination of the display requirement is based solely upon its stated conviction that it "will have a beneficial effect on funeral consumers."[50]

The proposed Used Car Rule would require each dealer to carry out a prescribed inspection of each car offered for sale and post the results on the window of the car. In contrast with the BCP's reports on funeral homes and vocational schools, its report on used cars does contain an explicit theory of market failure that is explicated in some detail to justify the proposed rule. The only difficulty is that the theory is incoherent.

The BCP argues – and cites much testimony to the effect[51] – that consumers desire information about the mechanical condition of used cars at the point of sale. Under competitive conditions, the market will usually provide the desired amount of information at the point of sale, and any regulatory requirement to provide more will therefore result in the production of an excessive amount.[52] The utility of the incremental information produced will be less than the cost of producing it. However, the BCP argues that the asserted inadequacy of information provided at the point of sale of used cars is an example of market failure. It argues that the market does not produce the desired amount of information about the mechanical condition of used cars, and that the utility of additional information will exceed the cost of generating it.

The BCP's theory hypothesizes that used-car dealers have a disincentive to disclose defects in their cars because purchasers prefer the risk of buying a car with unknown qualities to buying one with known defects. Purchasers will therefore avoid dealers who inspect their cars and disclose mechanical defects, preferring dealers who falsely pass off their cars as defect-free. This substitution effect is compounded by purchasers' being misled into equating good appearance with good mechanical condition. Buyers may appear to prefer good appearance to good mechanical condition, but this is misleading because they are in fact treating appearance as a surrogate for mechanical condition. This leads to dealers' overinvesting in appearance restoration. This, in turn, produces the "lemons" effect that Ackerloff identified.[53] Because buyers cannot effectively distinguish mechanically good cars from bad, the former will be undervalued, which will result in too few of them coming on the market. Finally, because "private sellers have been shown to be substantially more forthcoming about serious mechanical problems than dealers,"[54] buyers substitute away from dealers to private sellers. In the staff's view, this explains the observed long-term trend toward an increase in private sales relative to dealer sales of used cars.

It is at this point that the incoherency in the theory becomes apparent. The BCP does not explain how the "glib misrepresentations" of dishonest dealers simultaneously "draw business from honest dealers and drive consumers to the private market."[55] A single consumer cannot simultaneously prefer "glib misrepresentations" over disclosed defects and disclosed defects over "glib misrepresentations" regarding the same product. It is implausible that consumers' tastes change from preferring appearance or uncertainty in the dealer market to preferring disclosure of defects or more certainty when they go to the private segment, and no reason in theory or fact is suggested to support such a phenomenon.

This incoherency is compounded by the BCP's prediction of the effects of adopting the proposed rule. In the BCP's view, "dealers who now gain from warranty misrepresentations would suffer under this rule, as consumers would be cautioned against relying on oral promises," and "consumers who currently buy privately may be induced to purchase in the dealer market once risk has been recognized."[56] Finally, the BCP asserts, the "lemons" effect will be "cured" by the increased amount of information required by the rule, with the result that higher-quality cars will enter the market in larger numbers because they will no longer be undervalued. In other words, as a result of the rule, consumers' tastes will change from preferring cars whose mechanical state is unknown to preferring those with known levels of defect; they will shift from risk preference to risk avoidance. Again, no explanation is offered for this transformation.

A coherent theory would posit that consumers have varying preferences for information about mechanical condition and appearance and are subject to varying budget constraints. Because some consumers will give greater weight to knowledge about mechanical condition, dealers who have a comparative advantage in obtaining that information (e.g., dealers who service as well as sell cars) will provide it (or a substitute for it in the form of warranties or superior postsale service) and thereby gain trade. Other things being equal, the prices of the cars they sell will be higher. Obtaining and providing that information involves costs. Moreover, they will tend to deal only in cars without material defects, because there will be a substantial congruence between those customers who prefer information about mechanical defects and those who prefer defect-free cars. Cars with fewer defects will carry a higher price tag, reflecting either a higher purchase price paid by the dealer or costs incurred by the dealer in remedying defects. Other consumers will express a preference for appearance, and some firms will specialize in selling cars with superior appearance. Other things remaining constant, including the defect profile, the prices of the cars they sell will also be higher, reflecting the higher prices they must bid for "clean" cars and the costs incurred in restoring appearance. Still other dealers will bid for the patronage of consumers who have a comparative advantage in making repairs or who value quality less, and will offer cars that lack both information regarding mechanical condition and aesthetic qualities. Varying combinations of preferences and income constraints will be expressed by consumers' buying decisions. For example, some consumers will express their preference for appearance and their lower income by purchasing a car with appealing appearance but will not pay the added cost involved in obtaining information by either purchasing from a dealer who provides that information or by having the car independently inspected.[57] In effect, they are betting that the risk of undisclosed defects is less than the cost of obtaining the information. Of course, if it turns out that they bet wrong, they may blame the dealer for not providing the information for which they were unwilling to pay at the time of purchase.

Under competitive conditions, the price differential between cars with and those without mechanical information will reflect differences in cost and nothing more. But the BCP argues that dishonest dealers inspect used cars before purchasing them and then, rather than disclosing the information learned from that inspection, pass the cars off to consumers as defect-free. Because consumers, unlike dealers, cannot distinguish between levels of defects, the dealers are thereby able to sell cars with high levels of defects at prices usually associated with cars that have few defects. But that argument overlooks the fact that other dealers who have purchased cars with high levels of defects will gain customers by offering them for lower prices. Consequently, competition will result in the retail price of used cars reflecting the level of defects.

Disclosure requirements account for a substantial number, perhaps the majority, of the FTC's adopted and proposed regulations. Yet no consistent theory explains or justifies the Commission's decisions in this area. The very evidence offered to support the need for mandated disclosure often demonstrates why the disclosure is unlikely to affect significantly consumers' buying decisions, either because the recipient is unable to absorb and act upon this information (owing to bereavement in the funeral context, or lack of sophistication on the part of potential vocational school students) or because many consumers prefer some value other than that which is the subject of the disclosure (status or protection of the corpse from the elements by relatives of the deceased; avocational education or stereos by vocational school students; appearance by used-car buyers). These factors go far toward explaining why the market does not produce information in the quantity that the FTC believes appropriate. They also suggest that the imposition of the rules is explained by the normative model (reflecting a disagreement by the FTC with the value preferences expressed by consumers) or the political model (reflecting the agency's need to be seen to be doing something for the consumer). The modification recommendations in the funeral rule proceeding provide a partial exception to this conclusion, in that they reflect greater concern that a rule have some prospect of affecting consumer's purchasing decisions.

The proposed Used Car Rule does purport to be based upon a theory of consumer behavior and market failure that attempts to explain why information desired by consumers is not provided by the market. But the theory is incoherent in that it assumes that a single consumer simultaneously expresses conflicting value preferences. Once again the normative model seems to represent the fundamental explanation for the rule: In the FTC's view, consumers ought to prefer information about mechanical condition over appearance.

C. Rewriting contracts and other miscellaneous regulations

Chapters 11 and 12 analyze the FTC's proclivity for rewriting contracts and imposing other miscellaneous regulations in considerable detail in the context of the Creditors' Remedies and the Mobile Home Rules. Accordingly, this chapter analyzes other rules, primarily those affecting the eyeglasses, vocational schools, and funeral industries.

Although it recognized in issuing its Eyeglasses Rule that consumer injury results from artificial barriers to competition and that there ought therefore to be a strong presumption against intervention in the market, the FTC ignored its own precept in that very rule. Section 7 of the Eyeglasses Rule, entitled "Separation of Examination and Dispensing," makes it an unfair act or practice for a refractionist to:

(a) [f]ail to give to the buyer a copy of the buyer's prescription immediately after the eye examination is completed . . . ;
(b) [c]ondition the availability of an eye examination to any person on a requirement that that person agree to purchase any ophthalmic goods from the refractionist;
(c) [c]harge the buyer any fee . . . as a condition to releasing the prescription to the buyer . . . ; or
(d) [p]lace on the prescription [or otherwise provide] . . . a . . . notice [to the buyer] . . . disclaiming the liability or responsibility of the refractionist for the accuracy of the eye examination or . . . ophthalmic goods or services dispensed by another seller.[58]

The Commission's rationalization for these provisions falls far short of the "heavy burden of proof" that it had earlier concluded must be met to justify intervening in the market.[59] It simply asserted that the prohibited practices injure consumers through the "lost opportunity" for comparison shopping for eyeglasses or through the payment of a separate fee for the prescription, and concluded that the practices are against public policy "in that they deny consumers the ability to effectively use available information and inhibit the functioning of the competitive market model."[60]

Implicit in the Commission's statement are two assumptions: (1) that there are no efficiencies to be gained from integrating the sale of eye examinations with the sale of glasses; and (2) that the sale of examinations and glasses as a single package therefore represents an effort to raise prices. But the Commission does not offer any explanation for such higher prices surviving competition once the barriers to information dissemination are removed. In the absence of barriers to price advertising, some firms would offer lower prices, inform consumers of them, and thereby gain customers. Thus, if package sales produce higher prices, they must be sheltered by advertising bans or other barriers that prevent consumers from locating lower-priced sellers. However, the tying of examinations and eyeglasses may reflect cost savings from integration and produce lower rather than higher prices. By minimizing the number of transactions (thereby reducing transactions costs) and spreading joint costs between examinations and the sale of eyeglasses, cost savings may be realized and reflected in a package price (whether nominally stated as a single price or separate prices) that is lower than the sum of the prices for examinations and eyeglasses sold separately.[61] If the Commission's rule frustrates the realization of such economies, the real cost of providing examinations and eyeglasses will necessarily increase and will result in higher prices to consumers.

In addition to the cost savings that may be directly realized from integrating eye examinations with the sale of glasses, there is at least one other economic explanation for practitioners' and consumers' desiring a single source for examination and dispensing. A consumer who receives an unsatisfactory product may not know whether the fault lies in the examination or the dispensing and hence may refuse to patronize either firm in the future. Competent practitioners therefore have an incentive to integrate the two functions to improve their control over the quality of the end product. The Eyeglasses Rule not only prevents the achievement of quality control through integration of examination and dispensing, but also prohibits the examiner from cautioning the purchaser that the examiner is not responsible for the accuracy of glasses dispensed by another practitioner.

Proscribing the tying of eye examinations to the sale of eyeglasses contrasts sharply with the BCP's attitude toward the tying of the inspection of used automobiles to their sale. Under the proposed TRR regulating the sale of used motor vehicles, dealers would be required to carry out an extensive inspection of each used motor vehicle offered for sale and to post the results of that inspection on the vehicle.[62] The BCP staff argues that it is more efficient to have dealers inspect automobiles than to let the consumer bear directly the cost of shopping for and obtaining an inspection.[63] The parallels between integrating examination (inspection) and sale of automobiles and integrating the examination of eyes and the sale of eyeglasses are imperfect, and the nature of the costs forgone in the two cases is different in some respects. But the point remains that the BCP relies upon efficiencies from integration to justify requiring a tie-in in the used car market, whereas the Commission did not even consider whether efficiencies were being realized from integration in the eyeglasses market before intervening to proscribe it.

The Vocational Schools Rule also contains significant limitations on parties' freedom to contract. In addition to requiring a "cooling-off" period of 14 days during which a student may cancel a contract and receive a full refund of any charges paid, the rule prevents students from contracting to make full or partial payment for a course once they have begun it, except on terms specified in the rule. Those terms require that a student who drops out of a course after the cooling-off period not be required to pay more than the registration fee (to a maximum of $25) plus a percentage of the contract price equal to the percentage of lessons completed or classes attended.

This provision would make economic sense only if all inputs were infinitely divisible and all costs were variable. But that is obviously not the case in education, at least for residence courses. The costs of classroom space, utilities, equipment, and teachers may be variable (e.g., through rental of space and equipment) prior to the beginning of a term (or course), but once the term has begun, those costs are fixed.[64] Under competitive conditions, the cancellation charges for which students contract would include an appropriate contribution to such continuing costs. But under the rule, students cannot contract to pay a share of the costs that continue after they drop out. Those costs must therefore be reflected in higher tuition charges, which will result in students who continue the course subsidizing those who drop out.

Ironically, this provision may also produce an effect opposite that which the FTC intends to bring about through the disclosure and cooling-off requirements – careful evaluation of the benefits and costs before contracting for a course. Because a student can cancel a course at any time, paying only the pro rata fees, prospective students who are uncertain about their qualifications or interest in a course will have a greater incentive to sample courses. Other things being unchanged, the initial enrollments in vocational courses will increase, but so will the dropout rate. The higher dropout rate will result not only from the increase in students' sampling courses, but also from the decreased incentive to continue the course, because of the absence of any cancellation penalty. If schools enlarge their capacity to handle the increased number of enrolled students, costs will rise and will have to be spread over a smaller number of continuing students, which will further increase the costs borne by the latter.

The Funeral Industry Practices Rule as proposed in the final staff report would also limit the rights of the parties to contract. The rule would require, among other things, that (1) agreements be in writing, particularize fees in a minimum of eight categories, and contain other formalities; (2) funeral homes not charge customers for the cost of advancing money to other persons providing goods or services (although the net amount advanced could be recovered as part of the fee); (3) any rebates, commissions, or discounts from other persons be passed on to customers; and (4) funeral homes make "alternative containers" available for cremation. These provisions implicitly assume that increasing the formal requirements of contracting and the form in which prices are quoted will result in lower prices to customers, that money tied up in prepayment of fees to third parties is costless, that funeral homes are necessarily the most efficient providers of certain information,[65] and that funeral homes will voluntarily impose costs upon themselves.

As discussed above in connection with the disclosure requirements of the proposed Funeral Industry Practices Rule, a funeral home can charge higher than competitive prices only if there is effective collusion in the industry. Under competitive conditions, charges by funeral homes will reflect costs. But if collusion prevails, merely changing the form in which prices are quoted will not necessarily reduce prices, even though adjustments in nominal prices may result.

Formalizing agreements increases transactions costs, some of which will be borne directly by the customer (in the form of time, travel, attention, etc.) and some by the seller. At least part of the seller's increased cost will ultimately be recovered from the customer through higher fees. Under competition, agreements will be formalized to the point where the marginal costs of additional formality exceed the marginal benefits. Therefore, requiring additional formality will increase costs without producing a corresponding gain in benefits to the parties. Similarly, competition will result in an appropriate amount of specificity regarding the prices of component goods and services making up the funeral. If customers desire the charge for use of a hearse to be computed separately rather than included in the package price quoted for the funeral, those funeral homes that separately quote it will gain customers at the expense of those that do not.

"Alternative containers" for cremation will also be provided in appropriate numbers under competition. If some funeral homes provide only caskets, rather than alternative containers for cremation, it is either because it is less costly to do so[66] or because customers prefer caskets to alternative containers. Otherwise, other firms would make the availability of alternative containers known to potential customers. Moreover, competing funeral homes are not the only firms that would potentially benefit from the sale of alternative containers and have the incentive to make their availability known. Container manufacturers and crematoria have similar incentives. It is therefore not apparent why all funeral homes should be required to incur the costs of making alternative containers available.

The requirement that funeral homes not charge for the service of advancing money to cemeteries, florists, musicians, newspapers, and so on, and strictly account to each customer for any rebates or commissions is particularly misguided. First, it ignores the reality that there is an opportunity cost for money tied up in advances to third parties.[67] (If the funeral home is a net borrower, the cost would equal the rate of interest it pays at the margin.) The presiding officer and the BCP[68] argue that the funeral home collects for its services in making arrangements with third parties (and presumably for the cost of the money advanced) through its ''professional services'' fee, and that collection of a separate fee for cash advances is double-charging. In effect, although the proposed rule would require detailed separate statements of other components of the funeral charges, it would prohibit the separate statement of fees for cash advances, requiring instead that such costs be buried in a general ''professional services'' category. Moreover, the proposed rule would require that any statement of cash advances reflect any commission or discount (including anticipated rebates based upon annual volume), necessitating additional record keeping and computational costs. All of this is once again based upon the fallacious assumption that gimmicks such as overstating the amounts of cash advances allow funeral homes to raise prices above what they would otherwise be. There is no reason to assume that, after the rule became effective, prices would not be effectively as high (not counting any increased costs imposed by the rule), through higher fees for ''professional services,'' hearse rental, or some other category.

The proposed modifications to the funeral rule would eliminate all of these requirements except the first (regarding contract formalities, etc.) but would substitute additional mandatory disclosure requirements.[69] The ''new staff'' has questioned the FTC's authority to mandate ''alternative containers'' and recognized that competition will result in adequate provision of such containers. It concluded that no valid purpose would be served by prohibiting the statement of separate charges for advancing funds, that the proposed requirement conflicted with the explicit disclosure provisions regarding other charges, and that to prohibit separate charges for this service would result in the costs being included in some other nominal price, with the likely result that it would be borne by customers who do not use the service as well as by those who do. The requirement that rebates, commissions, and discounts be passed on to customers is eliminated by the modification recommendations without comment.

In summary, the FTC has manifested a willingness to prescribe the form and content of contracts and to impose other miscellaneous regulations with little justification, unsupported by any clear and consistent concept of what constitutes harm to consumers. Indeed, the rules often prevent the realization of economies, as in the case of the Eyeglasses Rule's prohibition of integrating examination and dispensing, or compel one group of consumers to subsidize others, as in the case of the Vocational School Rule's prohibition of cancellation penalties.

The modification recommendation by the new staff evinces a more conservative approach to regulation, in that it argues for the deletion of regulations that deal with infrequent conduct, that are incapable of being enforced, that are otherwise unlikely to affect consumer behavior, or the effect of which will be brought about by increased competition predicted to result from other provisions of the rule. The original staff has indicated its opposition to this approach and it is not possible to predict which approach the Commission will adopt. Even the new staff, however, seeks to induce increased competition by additional regulation, thereby reducing the choices available to buyers and sellers and hence their ability to respond to the signals provided by the market, rather than by removing state-imposed restraints and increasing freedom of choice.

IV. The use and abuse of evidence

In contrast to the APA, the FTCIA provides that the reviewing court shall "hold unlawful and set aside" a TRR if it finds that "the Commission's action is not supported by substantial evidence in the rulemaking record . . . taken as a whole."[70] Chapters 11 and 12 include detailed analyses of the FTC's development, evaluation, and use of evidence in two proceedings. This section briefly appraises the quality of evidence relied upon by the Commission in other proceedings but draws upon the analysis of the Creditors' Remedies Rule for comparison.

The evidence relied upon by the Commission and its staff (including presiding officers at rule-making hearings and the BCP) varies greatly in regard to quantity, reliability, and relevancy. In developing the Eyeglasses Rule, for example, the Commission relied principally upon an objective scientific study comparing prices in states that banned or limited advertising with prices in states without such restrictions; the study found that prices were higher in states that restricted advertising.[71] The data provided by the study thus were consistent with the hypothesis that externally imposed restrictions on the freedom of sellers to disseminate information artificially increased search costs and hence prices.

In the Used Car rule-making proceeding, the BCP relied to a substantial extent on empirical studies, in particular a study of used-car prices in Wisconsin before and after the adoption of a mandatory inspection law (MVD 24) in that state.[72] But the BCP made selective use of the Wisconsin study, rejecting or ignoring its findings when they were inconsistent with the BCP's arguments. The Wisconsin study, which was commissioned by the FTC for the purposes of the rule-making proceeding, found that prices of used cars in Wisconsin were lower after MVD 24 went into effect than they were before. It also found that they were lower in Wisconsin than they were in Iowa (which required safety inspection only) and in Minnesota (which required no inspection). The BCP noted that the reliability of the data used in the Wisconsin study is questionable on several grounds. Most significantly, however, especially since the Wisconsin study data allow a cross-sectional comparison with other states for the postlaw period only, it does not exclude other explanations for the fall in prices.[73] Nevertheless, the BCP argued that the study supported its position that mandatory inspection and defect disclosure would cause the prices of used cars to decline (or at least would not cause prices to rise), at least in the short run. This is a surprising conclusion. Inspection and information communication involve added costs, which should be reflected in higher prices.

Where the results obtained in the Wisconsin study were inconsistent with the BCP's theory, they were either explained away or ignored. Thus, although the BCP argued that mandatory inspection should increase consumers' confidence in the quality of cars sold by dealers and therefore cause them to substitute away from private sellers, the Wisconsin study shows that the dealer market share has dropped since the enactment of MVD 24 (which applies only to dealers). This was brushed aside by the staff by speculating that the Wisconsin inspection rule had a "low visibility to consumers" or that it "could reflect a nation-wide trend rather than the effect" of the law.[74] An alternative explanation (not considered by the BCP) is that the increased costs associated with mandatory inspection caused some consumers to substitute away from dealers to private sellers. This is consistent with another finding of the study – a finding ignored by the BCP – that the price differential between private sellers and dealers narrowed after the act (from 11.6 percent to 9 percent),[75] which suggests that the volume increase in the private share of the market reflected an increase in demand rather than supply. Finally, the BCP argued that MVD 24 resulted in lower postsale repair costs, relying on findings in the study that postsale repair costs on dealer-sold cars dropped by 77.6 percent after the act and were lower than those in Iowa and Minnesota. However, postsale repairs on privately sold cars, which were not covered by the law, dropped 60.8 percent. The BCP passed this off by asserting that the private market "shows competitive behavior, roughly matching the dealers' quality increase."[76] The BCP did not explain how this "competitive behavior" would be consistent with the supposed "low visibility" of the act offered as an explanation for the increase in the private share of the market.

Of course, it is possible that the changes in used-car prices, market shares, repair records, and so on, found by the Wisconsin study were not caused by MVD 24 but by phenomena exogenous to the used-car market, such as diminished demand for large cars, resulting from public reactions to the OPEC oil embargo, or more generally, *high levels of unemployment, reductions in overtime, a high rate of inflation, and an increase in interest rates to lenders.* The possibility that factors such as these might have influenced the study's findings was belittled by the BCP.[77] This is remarkable because the italicized terms above come from the Report of the Presiding Officer on the Creditors' Remedies Rule and are cited by him as reasons for concluding that none of the three studies of the Wisconsin Consumer Act "provides an accurate or reasonably precise estimate of the effect of the Wisconsin Consumer Act upon creditors."[78]

The Wisconsin Consumer Act, like MVD 24, became effective in 1973, and in the absence of an explanation, general market conditions such as those cited as reasons for questioning the validity of the credit study should have applied equally to the used-car study. But the findings of the used-car study generally supported the BCP's position, whereas the studies of the Wisconsin Consumer Act contradicted the BCP's position that restricting creditor remedies would not affect either the cost or the availability of credit. The latter studies found that the Wisconsin Consumer Act had resulted in higher costs in providing credit and in a tightening of credit, especially to low-income borrowers. These findings were rejected in favor of the "subjective opinions of those having direct experience in the Wisconsin consumer credit market place" (mainly consumer advocates and enforcement officials), who testified, without benefit of systematic investigation, that "the dire predictions of creditors were not correct. Adequate amounts of credit are available in Wisconsin . . . without a significant increase in costs to either creditor or to consumers."[79] In striking contrast to the BCP's brushing aside of criticism of the studies buttressing its position on the Used Car Rule, most of the economic evidence offered in the Creditors' Remedies proceeding was dismissed or downgraded by the presiding officer. On the other hand, the subjective opinions of consumer advocates and enforcement officials were repeatedly accorded considerable weight.

Reliance upon subjective and ad hoc evidence appears to be the rule, not the exception. For example, the Final Staff Report on Funeral Industry Practices relies almost entirely on subjective and ad hoc evidence. Summarizing the evidence produced in the hearing, the presiding officer concluded: "Throughout this proceeding the paucity of data was apparent."[80] This did not deter the BCP from forcefully recommending the adoption of a comprehensive TRR regulating many facets of the industry, including some practices which the presiding officer found little or no evidence of having occurred. Furthermore, the BCP report discloses a number of ignored opportunities for systematically testing the validity of its hypotheses regarding the economic impact of various provisions of its proposed TRR. For example, it notes that five states have enacted laws prohibiting funeral homes from requiring a casket for cremation, a practice that the BCP argues increases the cost of funeral services. No time-series or cross-sectional study of the actual effect of such laws is cited. Similarly, at least two states require itemization of the prices of goods and services as proposed by the TRR. Again, no studies of the effects of such laws were made.

V. Conclusions

The FTC's rule-making power is a potentially powerful vehicle for promoting consumer welfare. However, its usefulness is hampered by the vagueness of the statutory standards of "unfair or deceptive" acts. The Commission's efforts to provide operative content to these terms have often resulted in merely a restatement in equally vague terms. The more recent emphasis upon "injury to consumers" as the principal consideration in determining whether a practice is "unfair" holds promise, provided that the notion of "injury" is itself adequately defined.

However, the Commission's application of the injury-to-consumers concept has been uneven. It has recognized that regulation purporting to be in the public interest can result in substantial harm to consumers by sheltering an industry from competition and has asserted the authority to preempt state regulation that has that effect. But that authority has been effectively used in only one instance. In other contexts the Commission has demonstrated a continuing predilection to impose additional layers of detailed regulation, at least some of which potentially increase the injury to consumers by preventing the realization of economies or by compelling one group of consumers to subsidize another. This apparent bias in favor of more regulation has also manifested itself in the FTC's evaluation of evidence, especially its choice between systematic analyses of data or ad hoc and anecdotal testimony by interested parties. There appears to be a pattern of giving deference to evidence that supports regulation and downgrading, explaining away or disregarding that which is inconsistent with the need for further regulation.

Acknowledgments

The author wishes to thank Tom Slaughter for his research assistance, while a law student at the University of Iowa, and Professors Malcolm Wheeler, Gary Fethke, Ken Clarkson, and Tim Muris for their valuable comments on earlier drafts.

11 Rewriting consumer contracts: creditors' remedies

RICHARD L. PETERSON

As Ellis has detailed in Chapter 10, in terms of its potential impact upon society, rule making is perhaps the most important activity that the Commission undertakes. Although Ellis addressed the overall Commission rule-making program, it is worthwhile to discuss in detail the Commission work on a particular rule. Thus, this chapter focuses on the Federal Trade Commission's (FTC) proposed Trade Regulation Rule (TRR) on Creditors' Remedies. Besides providing a look at Commission development of a rule, this chapter focuses on a major substantive part of the Commission's consumer protection program of recent years – rewriting consumer contracts.

The proposed TRR would prohibit consumers from waiving certain rights, such as the right to a hearing and rights under the state statutes that exempt certain property from attachment by creditors. Further, it would limit a creditor's security by, for example, eliminating cross-collateralization. Finally, in other relevant provisions, the TRR restricts creditors in taking assignments of debtors' wages, in obtaining deficiency judgments, and in collecting attorneys' fees.

Section I describes the philosophical viewpoint and empirical guidance that underlie the Bureau of Consumer Protection[1] (BCP) proposal to ban or restrict certain collection procedures and practices that creditors presently employ when a consumer defaults. Section II criticizes the BCP arguments. Next, because the empirical evidence presented by the BCP at the time that the rule was proposed was sketchy, Section III presents findings from the empirical studies presented at the FTC hearings on the proposed TRR. Section IV discusses how the official presiding over the rule-making proceedings used these studies. Finally, Section V assesses, given the evidence, the effect of the economic trade-offs that would occur if the rule were enacted.

I. Theoretical analysis and empirical support underlying the proposed creditors' remedy Trade Regulation Rule

A. *Theoretical analysis*

The basic viewpoint taken by the BCP in proposing its rule was that certain remedies were "unfair" to consumers and should therefore be banned. Much of the analysis was devoted to presenting theoretical arguments and supporting evidence that could be used to support the "unfairness" hypothesis. The BCP took the view that "unfair" practices resulted from "overreaching" by creditors. In the BCP's eyes, creditors were able to take advantage of their superior knowledge and market power to force consumers to accept uniform "contracts of adhesion" that provided creditors with every remedy permitted by law. In particular, the BCP felt that consumer credit markets were characterized by "enormous disparities in power, sophistication, knowledge, and need."[2] In the BCP's view, such disparities allowed creditors to overreach in their consumer credit transactions because of consumer ignorance and the "vast disparity in size and strength between the two parties."[3]

Because the BCP recognized that creditors' remedies did have a potential value to "commercial interests," it felt that commercial justification for a practice must be weighed against potential consumer injury from that practice before a practice should be restricted as unfair.[4] When a remedy was deemed to be unfair in the BCP's eyes, however, it felt that creditors could absorb any resulting increase in cost as part of the costs of doing business. In particular, the BCP Memorandum states that "creditors could minimize these costs and bear them as a cost of doing business."[5] Even if the deletion of remedies should raise costs of collecting delinquent or defaulted loans, the BCP states that: "Staff feels the bookkeeping, telephone calls, and reminders are clearly ordinary costs of doing business to be assumed by the businessman rather than the consumer."[6]

This line of argument, however, left the BCP open to several counterarguments: (1) business cost increases resulting from the proposed restrictions on creditors' remedies might be substantial, (2) some portion of the increase in business costs would be passed on to consumers, and (3) some consumers, particularly the riskier consumers from whom it would be harder to collect if certain remedies were abolished, might no longer be offered credit by businesses who desired to reduce their collection costs in the new credit environment.

In an attempt to defuse these counterarguments, the BCP first argued that business cost increases resulting from restrictions on the use of particular creditors' remedies need not be substantial, and might even be negative because creditors may not be operating their credit operations as efficiently as possible.[7] Second, even if all cost increases would not be fully absorbed, the BCP argued that the costs of remedy restriction can be viewed as a form of insurance premium payment. All borrowers are protected against the exercise of certain creditor remedies against them in the event of default and as a result, "where reform's increased cost translates into higher prices for credit rather than reduced supplies, the price increment may be seen as a form of compulsory insurance against default."[8] Third, to defuse the argument that riskier consumers will find it more difficult to obtain credit when creditors have fewer remedies available to collect on delinquent or defaulted debts, the BCP essentially argued that higher-risk customers would be better off if they did not use credit. This attitude is apparent in the Memorandum's discussion of deficiency judgments, where it states that "we believe that it is reasonable to eliminate them even if some high-risk debtors will have to acquire less expensive cars than they now do while others, at least for a time, will be able to purchase none."[9]

B. Empirical support

The primary source of empirical evidence used by the BCP consisted of data on over 6,000 customer accounts. Those accounts were drawn from branch offices of 13 major finance companies in 26 states. No data were obtained from small finance companies, commercial or mutual savings banks, credit unions, retailers, or other consumer creditors who would be affected either directly or indirectly by the proposed TRR. In addition to data obtained from consumer loan files, the BCP also collected consumer loan contracts and finance company policy manuals for major finance companies. The contracts were analyzed to determine if creditor remedy clauses were equivalent for each company, and the policy manuals were used to analyze the way that finance companies used different remedies in the collection of delinquent and defaulted debts.

The BCP cited additional evidence of an indirect nature, including the well-known studies of Caplovitz[10] and of the National Commission on Consumer finance. The Bureau's use of this evidence and of other evidence available to it was, however, highly questionable. This topic, together with the inadequacies of the Bureau's theoretical analysis, is discussed next.

II. Major deficiencies in the analysis-supporting proposals

There were major deficiencies in the BCP's initial arguments. Many of these arguments were not consistent with economic theory or extrapolated from selective, chosen, or limited evidence. The following critique of the BCP's argument relies heavily on Johnson.[11]

A. Unfairness, overreaching, and "contracts of adhesion"

The BCP concluded that many practices in the consumer credit markets were unfair because consumer finance companies take advantage of all remedies legally available and then offer only form contracts on a take-it-or-leave-it basis. However, the BCP sample was limited to finance companies in 26 states.[12] Further, the National Commission on Consumer Finance (NCCF) studies show that wide variety exists among credit grantors in the frequency of the inclusion of various creditors' remedies in their contracts.[13] In addition, there is no evidence that commercial banks and credit unions (which, between them, hold over 60 percent of all outstanding consumer credit) issued identical contracts. The wide variety of contract clauses discovered by NCCF investigators suggests that the BCP sample was not random in nature.[14] Thus, the BCP allegation that consumers have limited choice with regard to the potential collection remedies that they face is not well documented.

Further, even if consumer finance company contracts contained all permitted remedies, consumers were still not necessarily harmed. If a remedy is worth more to a creditor in terms of deterring credit losses than it is to consumers (who would discount any possible pain of loss by the knowledge that any default would occur in the future and that there is only a small probability that they might default), one would expect that remedy to be included in the credit contract because the creditor would be willing to give up more to retain the clause than the consumer would be willing to sacrifice not to have it. If consumers were to value the deletion of remedies more highly than creditors, they could induce creditors to delete those remedies by either (1) bargaining them away or, more likely, given the high transaction costs involved in bargaining, (2) avoiding creditors who offered contract terms that they found unsuitable.[15]

Moreover, it is easy to explain why consumers would concentrate their shopping efforts on contracts with low interest rates, low monthly payments, or longer maturities, even if this means more stringent remedies, because these nonremedial terms are usually of more importance to them than legal remedies that, once discounted by the expected time and probability of default, would have a relatively low value. Johnson has provided an example[16] showing that if a particular remedy would insure the consumer by $800, if the expected probability of default were 4 percent, and if the consumer were likely to default within six months, the present value to the consumer of deleting the remedy would be under $23. This would be of less consequence to the consumer than a 1 percent increase in the finance charge on a 36-month, $1,300 loan. Thus, the consumer might better spend his or her time searching for lower finance charges than for contracts with fewer remedies.

B. Lack of competition

The BCP Memorandum makes much of the fact that 21 major companies hold roughly three-fourths of total finance company consumer credit. This, they allege, gives the companies considerable market power.[17] This argument neglects the considerable competition between the 21 major finance companies, as well as competition between those finance companies and the more than 3,000 smaller finance companies that hold 20 to 30 percent of the total finance company market. In addition, it ignores evidence presented in the NCCF technical studies that significant competition apparently exists between finance companies and other consumer creditors. As there are 23,000 credit unions, 14,000 commercial banks, and hundreds of thousands of credit-offering retailers, such competition can be quite extensive. Further, other studies indicate that many borrowers can obtain credit from many types of consumer creditors.[18] Therefore, given the complete absence of any evidence that shows collusion between the major finance companies, the BCP allegation that major finance companies hold significant market power is totally unsupported.

C. Costs and effects of remedy restriction

The BCP argues that (1) through increased efficiency, creditors can and should bear the increased costs from regulation as "ordinary" costs of doing business; (2) any such costs that creditors pass on would represent an insurance premium for protection against remedies that all borrowers will pay equitably; and (3) any reduction in credit availability that occurs as a result of remedy reduction will be to consumers who should not use credit anyway. Each argument will be analyzed in turn.

1. The desire for profit ensures that if there were a more efficient way of conducting consumer loan operations, for example, through credit screening or more efficient collection procedures, creditors would use those techniques without having to be goaded into their use through legally imposed restrictions. The imposition of restrictions, by reducing the set of policy options available to creditors, would force them to adopt credit screening and collection policies that would be *at least as costly* to them, *if not more expensive,* than any policies that they would adopt if left to their own devices. In sum, the BCP argument that increased creditor costs from remedy restrictions could be offset by efficiency gains is vacu

ous. If such efficiency gains were feasible, profit-motivated business managers would already have taken advantage of them.

Further, it is a fallacy to think that these added costs of doing business would merely be "assumed by the businessman," as alleged in the Memorandum. Instead, as Johnson concluded:

Where permitted to do so, credit grantors will pass the higher costs on to consumers in the form of higher finance charges. Where rate ceilings prevent this approach, they must compensate for the higher costs by raising credit standards; i.e., by reducing availability. If neither of these actions are taken, the higher costs would be reflected in reduced profits, in which case capital will be withdrawn from the industry until a new equilibrium is reached such that an adequate rate of return is available from the remaining customers. In the real world a firm does not simply absorb added costs "as a cost of doing business." In one way or another it transfers those costs to consumers, either by raising the price of credit or by restricting its availability.[19]

2. Even assuming for the sake of argument that it is a proper government function to force "insurance" upon individuals for the sole purpose of protecting them against themselves, BCP's argument that any increased costs to consumers are a necessary form of "product liability insurance" fails to meet one of the bureau's principal goals, namely, helping the poor. For in the credit market, the cost of limiting creditors' remedies will fall most heavily on creditors who service the highest-risk customers.[20] Thus, their customers – the high-risk customers who are disproportionately poor – would bear the largest share of the "insurance" premiums. For this reason, and because lower-risk customers could switch more easily to different creditors who take lower risks, incur lower increases in collection costs, and raise finance rates less, lower-income consumers are ". . . likely to bear a larger share of any increase in finance charges than the more affluent."[21] Further, 93 to 95 percent of all credit customers do not have serious problems of default. Thus, one can question whether forced insurance is necessary for a problem that strikes so few.

3. Where creditor remedy restrictions increase creditor costs and where rate ceilings are binding, cash creditors will no longer find it profitable to service the highest-risk classes of customers. As a result, such customers will be forced (a) to obtain credit from merchants who increase the price of their goods to cover increased credit losses, (b) to obtain credit or cash from illegal sources, or (c) to go without goods or services they desire to purchase. As to individuals faced with these choices who, before the TRR, could have obtained credit, the Bureau concludes that they should not use credit. Yet what if a consumer must borrow to buy a used car so that he or she can get to a job? Is this consumer better off without credit? As Dunkelberg and Stephenson have shown, credit-financed expenditures on

durable goods often yield explicit rates of return to the buyer that may far exceed the rate of interest they must pay to borrow.[22]

D. Empirical evidence presented by the BCP

1. Personal loan file data

The BCP gathered original empirical evidence from 6,000 personal loan files of 13 finance companies in 26 states. Such data, however, may not provide appropriate insights into the typical nature of consumer – creditor transactions and collection procedures.[23] The contracts and collection procedures of major finance companies probably are not typical of contracts used by other creditors. The NCCF data compiled by Greer suggest that wide variety exists in contract terms and collection techniques for different types of creditors.[24] Commercial banks, credit unions, and retailers who hold their own consumer paper to some extent serve different clienteles and may rely on different types or combinations of creditors' remedies to collect on delinquent or defaulted loans.

The fact that the data collected by the BCP were not typical would be unimportant if the proposed TRR were addressed specifically to only finance companies. However, the proposed TRR would apply to all major consumer creditors, without exception. Even if the data could be taken as typical of finance companies in general, they are likely to be inappropriate for many creditors to whom the proposed TRR would apply.

2. The use of NCCF data

The second major data source of the BCP was the information supplied in the *Report of the National Commission on Consumer Finance and Its Technical Study,* Volume V. The major deficiency in the BCP use of the NCCF information was that the BCP generally cited only information that supported its conclusions and failed to report on findings that were not supportive. For example, the BCP did not report on the many NCCF econometric findings that suggested that various creditors' remedy restrictions might have an adverse effect on credit availability or finance rates. In particular, the econometric work presented in *NCCF Technical Study,* Volume V, suggested that (a) attorneys' fees prohibitions might significantly reduce the number of personal loans made by finance companies and (b) restrictions (but not outright prohibitions) on wage assignments might significantly reduce the number of personal loans made by credit unions as well as the volume of commercial bank and credit union installment credit extensions. Further, many findings of Volume V were supported by other econometric tests of the personal loan market.[25] Although some of these results were not uniformly statistically significant, or varied from equation to equation, others supported the hypothesis that restrictions on creditors' remedies may either affect the price or (especially in states with restrictive rate ceilings) the availability of consumer credit.

The econometric work provided evidence that suggested that certain restrictions on remedies were likely to reduce credit availability or raise loan rates. Yet the BCP did not cite these results in its presentation of the empirical evidence relating to its proposed restrictions on creditors' remedies.

3. The Caplovitz studies

The BCP made extensive use of data developed by David Caplovitz.[26] Those studies described in detail the types of consumers who were most likely to incur debt and the implications of default on their physical and economic state of health. Although the data provided in these studies generally supported the points the BCP was trying to make, it did not always do so. Further, the data presented in the Caplovitz studies provided insights that should have, but did not, lead the BCP to reconsider at least some of its proposals.

At least one important point about the Caplovitz data was inadequately reflected in the BCP Memorandum, namely, that the BCP may have erred in focusing on finance company borrowers. From the Caplovitz data it appears that major problems of credit overextension and subsequent creditor remedy use most frequently originate with retailers who specialize in selling goods on credit to low-income customers. In particular, 71 percent of the credit contracts involved in consumer defaults originated as conditional sale contracts, whereas only 20 percent originated from loan contracts and only 12 percent from loan contracts extended by small loan companies.

Thus, '' a high portion of the defaults and use of creditors' remedies arose in an environment where it is relatively easy for credit retailers to mark up the price of goods and services . . . in order to cover potential credit losses.''[27] And because retailers specializing in low-income credit markets can behave differently from other creditors (i.e., they can mark up prices of goods substantially and still sell on credit even if finance charges are restricted and credit collection costs go up), they may be less affected by the FTC's proposed changes in collection remedies than other creditors would be. If the FTC remedy restrictions would have little effect on such creditors while restricting credit availability to low-income customers from more responsible credit sources, the Trade Regulation Rule

might be counterproductive. Although a careful reading of the Caplovit;
studies suggests this problem, the FTC staff did not pursue it.

4. The repossession studies

The major remaining source of data used by the BCP was devel
oped by Schuchman, and Firmin and Simpson on resale prices of repos
sessed automobiles.[28] The BCP used those data to support the dual hy
potheses that (a) repossession often results in "deficiency judgments'
that compensate the creditor for any deficiencies remaining on the bor
rowers' debt once the good is repossessed and sold, and (b) repossessed
goods often sell for less than the average price of similar goods (mainly
they believe, because creditors do not have proper incentives to sell re
possessed goods at maximum possible prices). However, both the evi
dence presented in these studies and other statements[29] on repossession
cited by the BCP were either faulty or failed to support the BCP's conclu
sions.[30]

As to the frequency of deficiency judgments, Schuchman's claim tha
". . . our observations and inferences are consistent with the Federa
Trade Commission report that default followed by repossession, defi
ciency-judgment proceedings, and wage garnishment is accepted as nor
mal business routine"[31] is unfounded because his work studied *only* cases
where suits were filed for repossession. In contrast, a more general study
conducted for the National Commission on Consumer Finance showed
that deficiency suits followed only 22 percent of repossessions.[32]

As to the sale price of repossessed goods, the Firmin and Simpson
study that the BCP relied on has an important discrepancy. Although the
NCCF study provided the source materials upon which the Firmin–Simp
son study was based, the Crane study found that the sale of repossessed
automobiles was at 90.5 percent of the (National Automobile Dealers
Association) wholesale value, whereas Firmin and Simpson stated that
only 80.1 percent of NADA wholesale value was realized. The BCP made
no attempt to explain this discrepancy.

5. Conclusion

Overall, even if the BCP discussion had in fact been a fair and
objective survey of the universe of available evidence, the BCP Memorandum would have provided a very thin body of empirical data upon
which to propose such a major rule. However, the Bureau did not provide
an objective or complete view of the available evidence. First, the BCP
disregarded or failed to mention data, often drawn from the same source
documents that it cited, that either provided evidence contrary to the BCP

hypotheses or could be construed as being inimical to its proposals. Thus, although some of the NCCF findings were used to support its rule, NCCF evidence that indicated that the same creditors' remedies were not used by all lenders and that certain creditor remedy restrictions would raise the price or reduce the availability of credit were ignored. Also, Firmin and Simpson's repossession study was cited, whereas Crane's more comprehensive work, which was less supportive of this hypotheses, was not. Second, the Bureau did not mention possible deficiencies in the data or methodology of the studies that it did cite. Methodological deficiencies were particularly evident in Schuchman's work. Finally, the BCP did not attempt to evaluate evidence, particularly from Caplovitz, suggesting that to help poor consumers the TRR would need to be reshaped. That evidence implied, for instance, that many defaulting debtors experienced credit problems after borrowing from retail merchants that served low-income customers – but that class of creditor would be least affected by the rule.

III. Additional evidence

Evidence presented during testimony on the proposed TRR showed that it would be very costly. That evidence also suggested that the rule would reduce credit availability. Most of those studies were commissioned by the FTC. The Barth and Yezer studies were commissioned by the BCP; most of the remaining studies were commissioned by the FTC's Office of Policy Planning and Evaluation.

A. The Barth and Yezer studies[33]

The BCP had commissioned Barth and Yezer to study the potential impact of the TRR. Because they had been commissioned by the BCP, they had ready access to the finance company personal loan data file compiled by the BCP. Owing to time limitations and the incompleteness of many files, they analyzed only slightly over one-tenth of the BCP files. Because of the possible nonrandom nature of the files, and because data were used from only seven finance companies operating in 18 states, their data sample was perhaps not truly representative, although as to some of their findings it would be difficult to assess a priori the direction of bias in their results.

The study showed that loan rates on finance company personal loans were significantly higher in states that imposed restrictions on creditors' remedies. Specifically, they concluded that remedy restrictions of the type proposed by the FTC would likely generate 2.97 and 4.93 percentage point increases in the price of credit for the pure annual percentage rate (called APR1) and adjusted APR (APR2), respectively.[34] The roughly 3 percent increase in APR1 and the 5 percent increase in APR2 that they ascribed to FTC-related remedy restrictions were both increases *relative* to the existing level of state remedy restrictions in the states from which they obtained their loan data. Given differences in state remedies, it is a little hard to assess the probable impact of the FTC remedy restrictions on the nation as a whole. Further, because substantial creditor remedy restriction already exists, the Barth and Yezer estimates understate the total impact of the FTC restrictions vis-à-vis an unrestricted environment.[35]

When Barth and Yezer attempted to decompose the total increase in finance rates into a supply-induced increase (caused by a reduction in creditors' willingness to supply credit on the same terms when remedies were restricted) and a demand-induced increase (caused by an increase in consumer demand for loan contracts in states with lesser remedies), they calculated that more than half of the increase in loan rates could be ascribed to increases in credit demand.[36] However, they also noted, in a later caveat,[37] that their demand for credit estimates probably was biased upward. This was so because their sample of loans was drawn *only* from debtors with credit problems. Insofar as sample debtors anticipated their potential problems, their demand for credit would be higher (relative to credit demand by less-risky borrowers or borrowers in general) in states with more restrictions on creditors' remedies.

Overall, Barth and Yezer concluded that the structural *supply* curve estimates implied that APR1 would increase by almost 1 percentage point if existing remedies were changed as proposed by the FTC. APR2 would increase somewhat more. Those increases would be *in addition to* whatever rate increases resulted from a shift in credit demand due to greater remedy restrictions. Thus, they represent that portion of the cost of implementing the FTC restrictions in the present regulatory environment that *exceeds* consumers' willingness to pay for the incremental protection granted by the restrictions.[38]

B. *The Peterson and Ginsberg studies*

Michael Ginsberg and I conducted two studies on the determinants of commercial bank personal and auto loan rates. Those studies provide additional insight into the impact that restrictions on creditors' remedies have on consumer loan rates.

The first of the studies investigated the determinants of auto loan rates.[39] It suggested that banks located in states with the most highly restrictive creditors' remedies charged new auto direct loan rates approximately 0.4 percent higher than banks located in other states. Since bank direct-loan customers are typically low risk, we can assume that creditors' remedies restrictions would have little effect on bank customer demand for credit. Thus, most of the effect of creditor remedy restriction can be ascribed to shifts in the banks' willingness to supply credit in an environment characterized by highly restrictive creditors' remedies. In other words, most of the increase in price probably reflects higher costs rather than consumer willingness to pay higher rates for contracts with fewer remedies.

The second study[40] was of personal loans and was designed, in part, to determine the impact of restrictions on the abilities of creditors to collect attorneys' fees. The results showed that personal loan rates charged by banks located in states that did not prohibit attorneys' fees clauses were lower by 0.9 percent than personal loan rates charged by banks located in other states.[41] That the effect of attorneys' fees is this large is somewhat surprising because, as one lender put it, "if you can't collect the loan, you can't collect attorneys' fees." However, bank customers in general tend to be relatively low risk and may thus be more likely than other borrowers to have access to personal assets or nonbank sources of credit. Rather than default on a bank loan and face the payment of attorneys' fees, such customers might prefer to (and be able to) obtain funds elsewhere. If this line of reasoning is correct, attorneys' fees clauses may be highly useful in helping banks collect their outstanding loans.[42]

Finally, in an additional analysis, I attempted to put the findings of these two studies in perspective. That work used the model and coefficients generated in the earlier studies to estimate the total impact on consumer loan charges of nationwide creditor remedy restriction.[43] Given the assumption that banks and other creditors would respond similarly to remedy restriction, *annual* finance charges by banks on auto loans would rise by *at least* $215 million at commercial banks and $214 million at all lenders if creditors' remedies on automobiles were restricted to the level existing in the six most restrictive states.[44] In addition, nationwide restrictions on various personal loan remedies could lead to an *annual* increase of *as much as* $288 million on finance charges on personal loans. Because banks generally serve the lowest-risk borrowers, if anything, rate increases would be at least as large at other lenders as at banks. Thus, these estimates are conservative. In particular, one would expect that increases in personal loan rates at finance companies, owing to their generally riskier clientele, would exceed those at commercial banks. Indeed, the Barth and Yezer findings suggest that this would be the case.

Overall: Nationwide reductions in the amount of remedies available to consumer creditors might cause finance charges on consumer personal and auto loans to rise by as much as 500 million to 1 billion dollars per year. Some reductions in credit availability (particularly to riskier customers) probably would accompany these finance charge increases – particularly in states where creditors are already operating at or near applicable rate ceilings.[45]

C. The Peterson and Frew study

Here, we reestimated the personal loan rate and availability equations of the NCCF studies after allowing for the importance of competing creditors in the personal loan markets, something that the NCCF did not do. If creditor remedy restrictions had an impact on the credit market, creditors would tend (where rate ceilings were permissive) to raise loan rates unambiguously. Where rate ceilings were not permissive, they would unambiguously reduce credit availability. Further, if credit supply shifts resulting from remedy restrictions were to exceed credit demand shifts, such restrictions would also tend to reduce credit availability. Based on the results of those econometric tests, we concluded:

Overall, our studies and those by the NCCF were in substantial agreement. Both studies found, as would be theoretically expected, that restrictions (or prohibitions) on creditors' remedies significantly reduced credit availability and/or increased personal loan rates. We documented highly significant effects emanating from outright prohibitions against attorneys' fees clauses, confession of judgment clauses, and garnishment. In addition, we found that restrictions on wage assignments, garnishment and confession of judgment clauses also had statistically significant effects on the price and/or availability of consumer credit.[46]

D. The Wisconsin studies

The Credit Research Center at Purdue undertook three studies of creditor responses to enactment of the Wisconsin Consumer Act, one on automobile finance companies,[47] one on consumer finance companies,[48] and one on commercial banks.[49] Wisconsin creditors were selected for intensive study because the Wisconsin Consumer Act (WCA), enacted in 1973, parallels in many respects the proposed Trade Regulation Rule.[50] The results of each of the studies will be discussed in turn.

1. The automobile finance company study

The three major automobile finance companies (which hold almost all finance company automobile credit outstanding) were asked to complete a detailed questionnaire on the national and Wisconsin credit operations. For a control state, they provided data on their operations in the geographically contiguous and socioeconomically similar state of Minnesota. Data on their operations in several other states were also requested but, for one reason or another, had deficiencies that seriously limited their usefulness.

The major results of this study, for new-car loans, are summarized in Table 11.1. Based on the data shown in Table 11.1 and on additional information provided by the respondent companies, I concluded that although some possible indices of credit restraint, such as contract maturities and

Table 11.1. *Auto finance company operations*

Average values for 12 months ending Aug. 31, 1975	Level			As percent of national level	
	Wisc.	Minn.	Nation	Wisc.	Minn.

I. Repossession and delinquency rates, August 1975

Number of accounts outstanding	43,072	40,521	4,936,510	0.9	0.8
Repossessions per account outstanding (%)	8.36	3.92	7.63	109.6	51.5
Delinquency rate (30 days or more)	3.184	1.574	2.447	130.1	64.3

II. Characteristics of new-car credit contracts acquired, August 1975

	Wisc.	Minn.	Nation	Over (under) national average[a]	
				Wisc.	Minn.
Average loan to value ratio (%)	83.312	87.123	86.800	(3.488) p.p.	0.323 p.p.
Average contract maturity (months)	37.438	37.990	37.912	(0.474)	(0.078)
Application rejection rates (%)	27.378	9.550	18.227	9.151 p.p.	(8.677) p.p.
Number of contracts acquired and percent of U.S. total	853	1,160	121,070		
	0.70	0.96	100.00		

[a] p.p., percentage points.
Source: Richard L. Peterson, "The Impact of Restricted Creditors' Remedies on Automobile Finance Companies in Wisconsin," Working Paper No. 12 (W. Lafayette, Ind.: Credit Research Center, Purdue University, 1977), at 28 and 29.

finance rates, showed a mixed picture, passage of the WCA appeared to increase delinquencies and losses in Wisconsin for all three auto finance companies and to make at least two of them less willing to extend credit. Further, down-payment requirements were higher than would otherwise be the case. Contrasts of this sort were most marked when comparisons were made between Wisconsin and Minnesota, but they also tended to hold for comparison between Wisconsin and the nation as a whole. The elevated contract rejection rates and increased down payments suggested that automobile credit in Wisconsin became less available to marginal risk borrowers after passage of the WCA. Although it is difficult to know how many people were rationed out of the finance company auto credit market by increased down-payment requirements and/or increased credit standards after passage of the WCA, for low income applicants the rationing might have been quite severe. One company noted that it was now accepting only one-third as many "highest acceptable risk" applicants as it had prior to the WCA.[51]

2. The consumer finance company study

This study used data compiled from two surveys. One was a survey of major national finance companies that asked questions about their delinquencies, losses, use of credit insurance, credit volume, and credit standards in the nation as a whole and in various states, including Wisconsin and Minnesota. The second was a survey distributed by the National Consumer Finance Association to all finance companies operating in Wisconsin. That survey addressed a number of open-ended questions asking if the companies had altered their credit standards or loan policies in recent years, how they had done so, and why they had done so.

Based on the results of the questionnaires, the written explanations of the respondents, and the survey of national finance companies, I concluded that generally Wisconsin consumer finance companies experienced increased delinquencies and losses and reduced credit availability (particularly to marginal risk borrowers) after enactment of the WCA. Specifically:

1. Most companies operating in Wisconsin tightened credit availability after enactment of the Wisconsin Consumer Act, citing the WCA (either directly or indirectly) or increased losses (or inadequate returns) as the reason for their actions.
2. A number of companies indicated that they had changed their policies toward the type of personal loans that they favored – with larger loans and real estate secured loans gaining favor and small loans, loans secured with household goods, or loans purchased from others generally losing in favor. This tendency was reinforced by rate changes, made around the time of enactment of the WCA, that favored larger, longer maturity loans.
3. After the WCA, credit insurance was much more likely to be associated with personal loans made in Wisconsin than in the nation as a whole. This could have reduced the riskiness or increased the net yield of Wisconsin lending, but no systematic pattern was found that credit insurance use either systematically increased finance company profits in Wisconsin or was associated with severe creditor remedy restrictions in other parts of the nation.
4. Although delinquency rates and losses were lower in Wisconsin than in the nation as a whole (possibly because low rate ceilings kept finance companies from taking substantial risks in their Wisconsin lending), Wis-

consin delinquencies and losses increased after enactment of the WCA. In addition, a higher proportion of Wisconsin delinquencies were long-term than in the nation as a whole, and gross losses were higher relative to delinquencies. This suggests that it was more difficult for the national finance companies to cure or collect on delinquent debts in Wisconsin during the early stages of delinquency. Nonetheless, somewhat unexpectedly, recoveries on charged-off Wisconsin debts were somewhat higher (proportionately) than in the nation as a whole.[52]

3. The commercial bank study

This study was conducted by Dunkelberg, who used a questionnaire almost identical to that used in the survey of consumer finance companies. He concluded that:

[f]orty-six percent of the respondents said they had changed their lending policies during the period, 61 percent tightened their credit standards, and 88 percent reported higher rates.

When asked to report the three most important specific policy changes, 42 percent reported tighter lending standards, six percent a reduction in "marginal loans," 11 percent eliminated loans on household goods, 13 percent required higher down-payments, three percent shortened maturities, nine percent reduced small loan activity, three percent switched loans to open-end types of credit, and 21 percent said they raised their rates. Some changes in the opposite direction were also noted: six percent increased the use of collateral in spite of the new restriction (but perhaps as a way to offset the weakening of other remedies), two percent lengthened maturities (some reported this move to increase revenues) and a few firms (1/2 of one percent) reported some lower rates.

The impact of laws and regulations [on these policies] were clear, at least in the minds of the respondents. More than 88 percent cited regulatory restrictions. More than 61 percent blamed higher costs, including the cost of compliance with regulations (5%), paper work (16%) and legal costs (2%). Six percent cited the low return on consumer lending, 38 percent blamed the quality of loans and 18 percent cited economic conditions as major causes. When asked specifically about changes in lending standards and rates charged (whether or not these were among the three most important policy changes), a similar pattern of results emerged, with regulation-related responses dominating (in frequency) references to economic conditions or the cost of funds. . . .

Overall, it appears that the effects were fairly pervasive. This is emphasized by the fact that the largest banks were, on balance, the most restrictive in their response. Although many factors could cause some of the reported changes in lending policy, the banks reported reasons related to regulations most frequently in open-ended questions about the reasons for policy changes.[53]

E. Summary of empirical evidence

All of the econometric studies conducted on the topic leave no doubt that the predictions of economic theory are supported in investigations of the potential impact of creditors' remedy restrictions. That is, these studies demonstrate repeatedly that curtailment of creditors' remedies either significantly increases loan rates or reduces credit availability. Further, the increases in loan rates or reductions in credit availability tend to fall heaviest on the highest-risk classes of borrowers.

IV. The presiding officer's treatment of the economic evidence

In August 1978, following completion of the hearings, the FTC official presiding over the rule-making proceedings issued his report,[54] recommending that the Commission adopt most of the rule as originally proposed. In so concluding, he discounted the evidence and analysis discussed in this chapter.

There are, however, two major deficiencies in the presiding officer's evaluation of the economic evidence presented. First, he frequently overlooked or downgraded most of the substantive evidence that economists presented, often because of technical quibbles raised about sampling procedures. Second, and contrastingly, he apparently gave considerable weight to ad hoc evidence presented by various consumer advocate attorneys, who used *no* systematic sampling procedure at all to validate the accuracy of their observations. Overall, then, he seemed to take the view that what certain attorneys said – mostly favorable to the rule – was worth taking into account, whereas what economists said – mostly critical of the rule – was not. The presiding officer's approach led to the overlooking or downgrading of evidence that economists presented, even though that evidence *uniformly* indicated that creditors' remedy restrictions, such as those proposed in the Trade Regulation Rule, would tend to increase the price or restrict the availability of consumer credit – particularly to high-risk customers.

The major technique that the presiding officer used to dismiss the economic evidence was to cite a technical criticism of an investigator's work by another party. Then, regardless of whether that criticism was justified or whether additional studies free of the initial technical problems had been conducted, he ignored or downgraded the results. He used this technique to the greatest extent in dismissing the findings of Barth and Yezer and of the National Commission on Consumer Finance (NCCF).

The Barth and Yezer study is of particular interest because the preliminary versions of their report did, indeed, contain some methodological defects. They corrected those mistakes, and the work that they submitted as their final testimony was, overall, objective and scholarly.[55] Although their initial methodology was suspect, they corrected it, and their final results should have been viewed as more reliable. Nonetheless, the presiding officer did not analyze the merits of their actual testimony. Instead, after noting that Barth and Yezer's earlier work contained some deficiencies and that their methodology had changed over time, he discounted their findings because in his view their methodology was suspect and arbitrary.

Given the reluctance of the presiding officer to accept the full implications (as discussed in the preceding section) of Barth and Yezer's actual testimony, it is surprising that he accepted the methodological criticisms that Barth and Yezer made of the NCCF's findings. Further, the presiding officer's evaluation of the NCCF data totally ignored my testimony and the related working paper with Frew. Those studies used different procedures to reinvestigate the NCCF's findings, showing that further analysis of the data supported the NCCF's findings that a number of the remedy restrictions proposed in the FTC Rule tended to reduce the availability or increase the price of credit in states where remedies had been proscribed.

Moreover, the presiding officer ignored or overlooked other economic evidence suggesting that remedy restrictions had a significant effect on the price or availability of loan rates. In addition to the studies based on NCCF data, he also ignored my testimony (and the related working paper submitted in evidence) that used Federal Reserve data on individual banks and found that banks located in states with substantial restrictions on creditors' remedies charged higher rates on their auto and personal loans. Further, in determining the likely amount of rate increase from the rule, the presiding officer considered the Barth and Yezer findings with respect to changes in the nominal finance charge (APR1), which is constrained by legal rate ceilings in many states, and ignored the total cost of obtaining credit once all fees and insurance charges are included (APR2). APR2 increased much more than APR1 in states where creditors' remedies were restricted. Since APR2 measures the full cost of borrowing, and it can vary even when APR1 cannot (owing to rate-ceiling restrictions), it was the more appropriate variable to consider. Even though he noted that restrictive rate ceilings complicated one of their related studies, the presiding officer did not give a reason for ignoring Barth and Yezer's APR2 results.[56]

Finally, the presiding officer accepted ill-founded criticisms as a rationale for ignoring the economic findings. In particular, he echoed the National Consumer Law Center in criticizing the Purdue studies of creditors' responses to the Wisconsin Consumer Act (which paralleled in many respects the proposed TRR) by noting that over the period studied, many other things changed, such as the state of the economy and certain rate-ceiling statutes. The Purdue studies, however, used "open-ended" questions that asked creditors to cite any policy changes that they had made, together with the reasons for those changes. In response, lending institutions frequently cited changes in the state of the economy and in rate ceilings as reasons for changing their loan policies, credit availability, or credit scoring standards. Nonetheless, the most frequent reasons that consumer finance companies gave for restricting credit availability following enactment of the Wisconsin Consumer Act related to changes in consumer laws and regulations and the following increases in creditors' losses and delinquencies. This was shown in my testimony as well as in the accompanying Credit Research Center Working Paper (No. 13), which was submitted as an exhibit.[57]

A second reason that the presiding officer gave for ignoring the Purdue studies was that they were all subject to the criticisms that the National Consumer Law Center made of Dunkelberg's study. Aside from claiming that other things had changed over the period of the study (as noted above), the NCLC's principal criticism was that only one-third of all Wisconsin banks responded to the Purdue questionnaire. My studies of finance companies, however, obtained responses from all auto finance companies and nearly all consumer finance companies operating in the state. Whatever the merits of the NCLC criticism as it applied to the Dunkelberg study, it was inapplicable to the other studies.

Thus, as to costs, the presiding officer overlooked substantive studies without having sound reasons for treating them so lightly. In concluding that restrictions on remedies would have only a "slight" effect on the credit markets, he incorrectly dismissed studies (all of the substantive economic studies conducted by Barth and Yezer, the National Commission on Consumer Finance, Dunkelberg, myself, and others) that provided empirical evidence contradicting his conclusion.

As to the presiding officer's conclusions on the benefits of the rule, our discussion can be brief. In contrast to his tendency to discount the substantive economic evidence presented, the presiding officer gave considerable weight to ad hoc observations of consumer-interest lawyers. Thus, when such lawyers reported that they thought that consumer credit-collection problems had declined in Wisconsin after the passage of the Wisconsin Consumer Act, he accepted those subjective judgments (which have to be viewed as casual empiricism at best) uncritically.[58] He neither questioned the randomness or completeness of the sampling procedures upon which those judgments were based, nor raised the question of whether that result occurred in part because the consumers who were most likely to experience credit-collection problems could not get credit as frequently after the WCA was enacted.

V. Conclusions: economic trade-offs associated with the proposed Trade Regulation Rule

Significant creditor remedy restrictions will cause some people to pay more for consumer credit or to be deprived of access to credit. Of course, some of those that are still able to obtain credit under a restrictive remedy environment will be willing to pay somewhat more to obtain credit with fewer remedies, and all will be insured against the operation of certain remedies if they should default on their consumer loans. For some individuals who continue to obtain credit, the expected benefit from the remedy restrictions *may* exceed the expected cost. Yet if the benefit to consumers *generally* exceeded the increased costs, creditors previously would have had an incentive to provide a contract with less restrictive remedies. Since the credit market has not produced the contract that the BCP desires, the evidence suggests that the additional benefit from mandated restrictions on creditors' remedies would not exceed the costs.

Because the empirical evidence indicates that costs of remedy restriction will exceed benefits, the BCP is left with two possible arguments. The first is that a better wealth distribution would result from the remedy restrictions. The second is that those who would be denied credit as a result of remedy restrictions would be better off anyway, because they are not capable of using credit wisely and should first try to save in advance of purchasing.[59]

The wealth-redistribution argument is invalid, as all available empirical evidence shows that the individuals hit hardest by remedy restriction (in the sense that they would no longer be able to obtain credit *even if* they could use it to their advantage) will be among the *poorest,* most marginal credit risks, in our society. This is not the type of wealth redistribution that most people would likely favor, unless they felt that such individuals were too ignorant to make wise credit decisions.

The consumer-ignorance argument, however, is particularly disturbing because it implies a degree of intellectual arrogance on the part of the regulators. It essentially assumes that the omniscient regulator knows better than the consumer whether credit use is or is not good for him or her. Further, the BCP case for consumer ignorance is not well developed. The data they cite from Caplovitz show, as Johnson pointed out,[60] that consumer debtors are somewhat better educated than average. Additional documentation is lacking about the extent of consumer ignorance. Thus, to support the BCP position, one must have *faith* that consumers cannot adequately take care of themselves. Only if one takes the paternalistic view that regulators know better than consumers what is good for them can one justify the BCP's position.

On the other hand, those that find that credit markets tend to be efficient and that consumers can make judgments that are in their best interest would not agree with the BCP position. Consumers should not be coerced into having their welfare decreased.

12 Regulating postpurchase relations: mobile homes

LOUIS DE ALESSI

In May 1975, the Federal Trade Commission (FTC) proposed the Mobile Home Sales and Service Trade Regulation Rule (TRR).[1] The TRR followed closely in form and substance the consent orders accepted on March 3 and 4, 1975, from four leading mobile home (MH) manufacturers.[2]

The stated purpose of the TRR is to remedy the alleged failure of MH manufacturers and dealers to perform warranty service adequately. The most important provisions of the TRR require MH warrantors to establish procedures for performing warranty repairs within specified time limits (e.g., begin major repairs within three business days from date of notification), maintain records on warranty repairs, perform two on-site inspections (one before or at the time of tender of possession and another within 90 days thereafter),[3] sign formal contracts with dealers and third parties delegated authority for warranty service, establish procedures for screening and monitoring dealers and third parties, and use disclaimers, limitations, labels, and certificates only as prescribed. If these provisions become law, failure to comply could entail fines of up to $10,000 per day per violation.

This chapter examines the rationale and the consequences of the proposed TRR. Section I contains a discussion of the evidence, the theoretical framework, and the value criteria used by the FTC in proposing the TRR. Section II contains an analysis of the nature and role of warranties, and Section III a description of the MH industry. To examine the economic consequences of the consent decrees and of the proposed TRR, Section IV focuses on MH prices and output, Section V on consumer welfare, and Section VI on the structure of the industry. Section VII contains a few concluding remarks.

I. Evidence and theory underlying the rule

The Bureau of Consumer Protection (BCP) initiated its investigation of the MH industry in August 1972. The BCP selected a sample of 16 firms and required them to provide detailed information on their organizational structure and operating procedures. It also held hearings in six locations across the United States and interviewed a number of state officials, manufacturers, dealers, and consumers. The BCP then issued a report summarizing its findings, stating the case for regulation, and detailing the provisions of the proposed TRR.[4]

Surprisingly, the BCP report does not contain an explicit statement regarding either the theory (or theories) used in collecting and analyzing data or the criteria used in assessing their significance. It also fails to contain or to suggest the existence of any systematic body of empirical evidence supporting the BCP's criticism of current market solutions and choice of remedies. Indeed, it fails to offer any data that would provide a basis for assessing the consequences of the proposed TRR. It offers absolutely no evidence on which to make a judgment.[5]

The BCP report suggests a fundamental lack of understanding of economic theory and its application as well as of the most rudimentary rules of statistical evidence. For example, much of the report (and apparently, much of the initial investigation) focused on the existence of individual consumer complaints, which was taken as *per se* evidence that manufacturers and dealers were taking advantage of consumers, and on the lack of more formal contractual and monitoring arrangements. These conditions were viewed as obvious and easily remedied weaknesses of the market. Moreover, the production of higher-quality MHs and warranties seems to have been viewed as costless, and the administration of the proposed TRR as effective, costless, and preferable to any other alternative.

Based on the BCP's suppositions, all consumers, especially lower-income consumers who are more likely to purchase lower-quality MHs, would benefit from the regulation. If higher quality is not costless, however, the belief that the TRR will redistribute income from unscrupulous or misguided manufacturers and dealers to uninformed or incompetent consumers is sharply inconsistent with the FTC staff's own view of the demand and supply conditions within the highly competitive MH industry. Thus, the Bureau of Economics has argued that the price elasticity of MH demand is relatively low (-0.38),[6] whereas the BCP has implied that the price elasticity of MH supply is relatively high.[7] Under these conditions, most of the increase in costs will be borne by consumers in the form of higher prices. Moreover, the increase in prices will be larger for lower-quality units, impinging most severely on lower-income consumers and pricing at least some of the latter out of the market.

The general tone of the BCP statement suggests that the decision to obtain the consent decrees and to propose the TRR rested on a lack of understanding and mistrust of the market and on the faith that regulation will help lower-income consumers. The BCP actions did not rest on a rigorous examination of existing market conditions and of the consequences of the proposed legislation.

II. The nature of warranties and their role in the marketplace

A consumer's demand for a MH is determined by the prices of MHs, by the prices of substitutes and complements, and by the consumer's wealth, stock of assets, opportunity cost of time, tastes, and household production function. The last defines the individual's comparative advantage in the performance of various household activities, including the repair and maintenance of assets.

As a first approximation, assume that information and transaction (including enforcement) costs are zero. All other things being the same, a consumer will choose the MH with the lowest expected present-value cost of repairs, thereby providing a manufacturer with the incentive to reduce such costs. Reducing the frequency and severity of defects, however, is costly and results in higher MH prices. Accordingly, in competitive equilibrium a manufacturer will reduce the frequency and severity of each defect until the marginal cost of doing so will just equal the marginal cost of repairs to consumers. Producers and consumers will specialize in those cost-reducing activities in which each has a comparative advantage, and this will minimize the full price (the sum of production costs and expected repair costs) of each MH type.

Differences in consumer demands imply that manufacturers will specialize in the production of MH lines with different profiles of defect characteristics. The prices of these homes, controlling for all other variables, will then differ by the market-determined present value to consumers of the differences in the repair costs and inconvenience associated with the expected defect profiles. Moreover, regardless of which party is initially liable for the consequences of defects, warranties will be provided by their least-cost producers, the market price of each warranty will be equal to its true actuarial value, and the defects will be repaired by their least-cost producer.

In the real world, of course, information and transaction costs are positive and, like all other economic costs, eventually rise at the margin. This, however, does not imply that consumers find themselves at a disadvantage in their dealings with manufacturers. Competition among producers and continuing relationships between producers and consumers effectively curb the concentration of economic power. Moreover, as information costs increase, expert buyers (e.g., retailers) enter the market on behalf of consumers. As a result, consumers incur lower search costs by learning about the quality of a few retailers rather than about the quality of the myriad of products the retailers handle. Of course, this does *not* imply that dealers will stock only higher-quality units. Consumers with a higher tolerance for inconvenience, a lower opportunity cost of time, a lower income, or a comparative advantage in making repairs will prefer lower-priced, lower-quality goods. Accordingly, manufacturers and dealers will provide a range of quality.

To lower search costs to consumers, manufacturers and dealers will also find it profitable to offer warranties for sale jointly with some products. Warranties will be used as a signaling device to inform consumers of the relative quality of the products offered, and liability will be partitioned among parties according to their comparative advantage in reducing the incidence and severity of various defects. Moreover, difference in the demands of individual consumers will induce manufacturers to provide warranties of varying quality, including different probability distributions regarding the extent to which various clauses will be honored.

The existence of positive information and transaction costs has other important implications. First, because costs must be incurred to establish the validity of consumer claims, it will not pay to reduce errors to zero. As a result, some wrongful claims will be honored and some rightful claims will not.[8] Second, because contractual and organizational arrangements are costly to make, they will not be fully specified. In competitive markets, prices reflect demand and supply conditions, transmitting information quickly and cheaply while simultaneously providing economic agents with the incentive to respond. A myriad of production, employment, and consumption decisions are made continuously and simultaneously, without central direction and, typically, without formal contracts or formal organizational structures for internal monitoring. In the vast number of instances, formal arrangements are sufficiently costly that their lack *per se* is neutral with respect to how well the market is functioning.

Under real-world conditions, in a well-functioning market, some goods are defective, some wrongful claims are honored, and some warranties are breached. Thus, instances of such events are irrelevant in assessing the market solution. For that purpose, it is necessary to establish whether the frequency and severity of defects and of breaches are "too" great according to appropriate criteria. Moreover, if the market solution is found wanting, it does not follow that government regulation is desirable. Government decision makers also operate under positive information and transaction costs; more important, their incentive structure typically is not designed to yield Pareto-optimal solutions. Accordingly, government intervention must be justified on the basis that it yields a preferred solution under the real-world conditions in which both government and private decision makers operate.

III. Characteristics of the mobile home industry

There is every indication that the MH industry is highly competitive. Indeed, the FTC staff[9] as well as the economists testifying for and against[10] the proposed TRR seem to agree that there are no legal barriers to entry, that economies of scale are exhausted at relatively low levels of output, that the costs of entry for manufacturers and dealers are relatively low, and that concentration is not a problem. The available evidence supports these views.

First, the MH industry contains a relatively large number of manufacturers with plants located throughout the United States. Thus, the 246,000 units shipped in 1976 were produced by 221 manufacturers using 499 plants located in 39 states.[11] More specifically, 127 firms produced fewer than 500 units per year, 43 produced between 500 and 1,000 units per year, 41 between 1,000 and 5,000 units per year, and 10 produced more than 5,000 units per year.[12] Altogether, national concentration ratios are sufficiently low (e.g., the four-firm concentration ratio is about 28 percent)[13] that even proponents of the TRR do not use them to support their case.[14] Although some regional markets exhibit relatively higher concentration ratios,[15] the threat of competition from neighboring regions as well as from new entrants severely limits the scope for noncompetitive activities.

Second, legal barriers to entry are negligible. Individuals prepared to meet safety, construction, and similar regulations are able to establish new firms, open new plants, or ship units into new areas.

Third, costs of setting up a plant are relatively small.[16] The typical plant consists of 65,000 square feet of rented space, about $100,000 in equipment, and a production line designed to allow semiskilled workers using power tools to assemble ready-made components into a finished unit in a few hours. Manufacturers typically purchase materials on credit and carry low inventories of parts and finished units. Under these conditions, the initial investment for establishing a viable plant can be relatively low—$200,000 in the mid-1970s.[17] Plants apparently are small because the major economies of scale are exhausted at relatively small volumes of output, thereafter being offset by the higher costs of shipping the finished product to more distant markets; the average MH is set up on a site within 300 miles of the plant that manufactured it.

Fourth, the MH industry is highly competitive at the retail level. There are no legal barriers to entry, and the costs of opening a dealership are relatively low.[18] In the mid-1970s, more than 10,000 dealers were in business. Most manufacturers (85 percent) sell their output through independent dealers,[19] and the few dealers who are part of vertically integrated organizations typically round out their offerings with MHs produced by other manufacturers.[20] Indeed, in 1974 about 75 percent of the dealers represented three or more manufacturers, and 41 percent represented five or more.[21] Thus, each dealer typically provides customers with some choices regarding size, floor plan, quality, and prices from competing manufacturers. Since consumers on average visit four dealerships before making a purchase, even first-time buyers presumably examine the products of a dozen manufacturers.[22] More important, first-time buyers receive the benefit of the experience acquired by repeat buyers. Manufacturers' and dealers' behavior is determined by consumers' choices at the margin, and those of repeat buyers may be expected to be systematic; among other things, purchasers typically site their MHs in MH parks and MH subdivisions, and thus are able to acquire product information at a very low cost and to act upon it on subsequent purchases. Finally, contractual arrangements between dealers and manufacturers frequently are informal, facilitating changes in representation and entry of new firms.[23]

Turning to other characteristics of the industry, MH buyers typically have lower income and are younger than all U.S. families. In 1969, the median income of families living in owner-occupied MHs was about 18 percent less than that for all U.S. families. The percentage of heads of household under 25 years of age was twice (15 versus 7.4 percent) the estimate for all U.S. households, and that for heads aged 65 or older was about the same (18 versus 19.4 percent).[24]

The diversity in the characteristics of MH buyers implies differences in their MH demand. Not surprisingly, MHs exhibit great price variations within and across size categories,[25] reflecting differences in the quality of design, materials, workmanship, furnishings, options, and warranty service.

MHs have become an increasingly important source of U.S. housing. Shipments increased from 63 thousand units, all 8 feet wide, in 1950 to a peak of 576 thousand units, mostly 12 feet wide and larger, in 1972. More important, during this period MH shipments represented an increasing proportion of the sum of new MHs shipped and single-family private (SF) housing starts,[26] increasing from 9 percent in 1960 to more than 30 percent from 1969 to 1973.

One reason for the growing popularity of MHs has been that, at least until the mid-1970s, their prices were lower than those of conventional housing[27] and were increasing more slowly. From 1964 through 1972, residential construction costs in 1967 constant dollars increased by about 23 percent, an average rate of about 2.6 percent per year (Table 12.1). During

Table 12.1. Mobile home average prices and residential housing construction cost index (1964–77)

	(A)	(B)	(C)	(D)	(E)	(F)	(G)	(H)
Year	MH retail sales (millions of dollars)	MH average real price (1967 dollars)	MH average size (ft²)ᵃ	MH average real price/ft² (1967 dollars)ᵃ	Residential construction cost index (1967 dollars)	MH change in average real price (%)	MH change in real price/ft² (%)	Change in residential construction cost index (%)
1964	1,071.4	6,028			94.3	-3.3		1.6
1965	1,212.2	5,926			95.7	-1.7		1.5
1966	1,238.6	5,864			97.0	-1.0		1.4
1967	1,370.1	5,700			106.0	-2.8		3.2
1968	1,907.7	5,758			103.0	1.0		3.0
1969	2,496.8	5,510	684	8.06	105.8	-4.3		2.7
1970	2,451.3	5,254	732	7.18	105.3	-4.6	-10.9	-0.5
1971	3,297.2	5,479	780	7.02	109.6	4.3	-1.2	4.1
1972	4,002.8	5,547	831ᵇ	6.67	116.4	1.2	-5.0	6.2
1973	4,406.4	5,839	882	6.62	119.6	5.3	-0.7	2.7
1974	3,217.7	6,607	910	7.26	116.5	13.2	9.7	-2.6
1975	2,469.6	7,203	955	7.54	113.8	9.0	3.9	-2.3
1976	3,136.6	7,474	966	7.74	116.4	3.8	2.7	2.3
1977	4,100.0	8,504	977	8.70	119.3	13.8	12.4	2.5

(A) MHI, *Quick Facts*, May 1977, p. 12. Estimates for 1977 provided to the author by MHI.

(B) $B_t = [(A_t/S_t)/I_t] \times 100$, where A_t is retail sales (column A), S_t is total mobile home shipments, and I_t is the consumer price index for all items (1967 = 100).

(C) MHI, *Quick Facts*, 1977.

(D) $D_t = C_t/B_t$.

(E) $E_t = [(R_t/68.6)/(I_t/100)] \times 100$, where R_t is the "Residences" Boeckh Index (U.S. Department of Commerce, *Construction Review*, various dates). E converts the residential construction index to a 1967 base and then adjusts it to reflect 1967 dollars.

(F) $F_t = [(B_t/B_{t-1}) - 1] \times 100$.

(G) $G_t = [(D_t/D_{t-1}) - 1] \times 100$.

(H) $H_t = [(E_t/E_{t-1}) - 1] \times 100$.

ᵃ Data prior to 1969 are not available.

the same period, the average MH retail price in 1967 constant dollars *decreased* by 8 percent, an average rate of decline of about 1 percent per year (Table 12.1). Adjusting for such things as the increase in MH sizes, the constant-quality, constant-dollars MH price undoubtedly decreased by an even greater percentage. Indeed, from 1969 (the earliest year for which reliable data are available) through 1972, MH prices per square foot in 1967 dollars *decreased* at an average annual rate of over 6 percent (Table 12.1).

The economic downturn of 1973–5 adversely affected both the MH and SF housing markets, but MHs recovered more slowly. Thus, by 1977 MH shipments were 54 percent *lower* than they had been in 1972, whereas SF housing starts were 11 percent *higher*. A preliminary explanation of the phenomenon is fairly straightforward: the relative prices of MHs increased. Thus, whereas the residential construction index in real terms increased by 2.5 percent between 1972 and 1977, the average real price of MHs increased by 53 percent, and the average real price of MHs per square foot increased by 30 percent (Table 12.1).[28] The rapid recovery of SF housing starts apparently was abetted not only by the income effect associated with the upswing, but by the substitution effect resulting from the more rapidly increasing MH prices.[29]

The preceding comments indicate that MH shipments are highly sensitive to MH prices and to general economic conditions. Accordingly, the proposed TRR could have a profound effect on the health and structure of the industry and on the welfare of its customers.

IV. Consequences of mobile home regulation

Compliance with the proposed TRR will increase MH production costs, yielding a decrease in supply, and will increase MH quality, yielding an increase in demand. This section explores the possible magnitudes of these shifts in demand and supply curves and their effect on MH prices and sales.

A. *Decrease in supply*

Compliance implies higher production costs. Although some manufacturers will be able to substitute higher-quality materials, workmanship, and production standards for some warranty service, thereby incurring lower cost increases, the scope for such substitution is limited. First, the higher construction standards imposed by HUD presumably have already reduced the range of options. Second, a significant portion of the anticipated cost increases associated with the proposed TRR will be due to additional activities, such as screening and monitoring dealers, more formal contracting procedures, collecting and reporting data, which have to be incurred regardless of the quality of the output.

A rough estimate of the increase in production costs can be obtained from testimony submitted to the FTC in 1977. Allen R. Ferguson, testifying in support of the TRR, estimated that MH prices on average would increase by no more than $272.[30] First, he estimated that the two on-site inspections would involve $192 for three person-days of labor (two on the job and one travel at $8 per hour), $50 for replacement parts at wholesale prices, and $10 for travel expenses, yielding a total of $252. Second, he estimated that the various administrative and record-keeping requirements would involve a full-time administrator at $20,000 per year, two clerks at $10,000 each per year, 50 percent overhead, and $40,000 for travel and other administrative expenses, yielding $100,000 per year, or $20 per unit at an average output of 5,000 units per year; as output per firm has been about 1,000 units per year, however, $20 per unit presumably would underestimate actual administrative and record-keeping expenses. Ferguson noted that the total of $272 per unit did not include startup costs; on the other hand, he believed that it overestimated repairs in the field. Accordingly, he concluded that $272 was an upper bound. Among other things, however, his estimate ignored legal fees as well as manufacturer's and dealer's markups.

Additional legal fees for complying with the contracting provisions of the TRR were estimated by James E. Lavasque at $55 per MH.[31] His firm, however, was one of the few that was vertically integrated and would thus have a smaller increase in legal fees. If the additional legal fees incurred by a nonintegrated company were no higher, surely a conservative assumption, Ferguson's estimate would be increased by $55 to $327. Lavasque's final estimates allowed for a manufacturer's markup of 10 percent and a dealer's markup of 30 percent.[32] Applying the overall markup of 42 percent increases Ferguson's estimate to $464.

The other estimates available are by manufacturers or on their behalf.[33] Lavasque testified that the costs of the units produced by his company would increase by $209 to $368 each.[34] The low estimate allowed $80 for two on-site inspections by dealers (each inspection was assumed to involve 4 hours of labor, including travel time, at $6 per hour plus $16 travel cost on an average round trip of 100 miles); it also allowed $12 for record-keeping and administrative costs and $55 for legal services. The higher estimate allowed for greater travel time if the inspections were to be performed by the manufacturer. Both estimates excluded additional parts. Recall, however, that this firm was vertically integrated and produced high-quality output. Assuming conservatively that legal and administrative costs would be no higher and adding an allowance of $71 for replacement parts (Ferguson's $50 plus markup) to Lavasque's average estimate of $289 would yield a minimum cost increase of $360 for nonintegrated companies producing units of average price and quality.

Michael Mann, testifying on behalf of the Manufactured Housing Institute, estimated the increase in costs at $500 to $550 per unit based on a survey of MH manufacturers.[35] Mann calculated that shifting liability for the setup from the dealer to the manufacturer would entail a loss in efficiency of $200 to $300 per unit, an average of $250. He then estimated clerical and administrative costs at $18 per unit for the larger and $46 per unit for the smaller manufacturers; incremental warranty service at $60 for the larger and $90 for the smaller manufacturers; and inspection costs at $150 to $200, independent of firm size, for an average of $175. These figures yield total per unit costs of $503 for the larger and $563 for the smaller manufacturers. Mann did not include legal costs because only one respondent identified them ($143 per unit). Taking Mann's low estimate of $503, deducting $250 for setup (not included in the other estimates), adding $55 for legal fees, and applying a markup of 42 percent yields $437.

Other manufacturers also estimated the increase in costs associated with the TRR but did not indicate how the numbers were computed. Thus, Don L. Greenwalt testified that just providing warranty service within the time limits required would increase his company's production costs by about $200 per unit,[36] Philip S. Davis claimed that his client would incur unit costs of $400 on the two inspections alone,[37] and John P. Williams asserted that the cost of a unit produced by his firm would increase by $700, of which $200 would be attributable to the setup responsibilities.[38]

The time and data necessary to produce an independent, more accurate estimate of the expected cost increase are beyond the scope of this study. The data examined, however, are sufficiently similar to offer a hint. The estimates vary between $360 and $700 per unit, with those worked out with some care clustered between $360 and $464, for an average of $420. Recall, however, that all the estimates (except for Williams') exclude any allowance for higher setup costs, which Mann assessed at $250 per unit. The estimates also do not allow for the probability that a firm will be fined for failing to comply; at a rate of $10,000 per day per violation, even a fairly low probability of detection and conviction could prove costly. More important, the estimates do not allow for the increased uncertainty occasioned by the prospects of government intervention. Based on these slender reeds, an increase in costs of $400 per unit, which would yield a $400 shift upward in MH supply, would surely underestimate the increase in costs that will in fact occur.

B. Increase in demand

Compliance with the TRR presumably will cause some increase in MH quality. This implies an increase in demand. Although rigorous estimates of the expected increase in demand are not available, information generated in the course of the FTC proceedings offers some clues.

As a first step, consider the frequency with which warranties are breached. Data from the Consumer Protection Agency of South Carolina from January 1, 1975, to October 15, 1977, reveal at most 24 warranty-related complaints for every 1,000 MHs shipped into the state.[39] If only 3 percent of all complaints are filed,[40] an extremely generous estimate, then the maximum possible breach rate is 80 percent. MH survey data suggest a much lower estimate. A consumer group, with FTC funding, surveyed a sample of 1,864 MH owners in Ohio and reported that 41 percent claimed to have been unsuccessful in having warranty repairs completed to their satisfaction.[41] Relying on a different survey, Ferguson noted that about 40 percent of defects remain unrepaired.[42] Not all complaints are legitimate, however, and at least some legitimate complaints are trivial. As a generous estimate, suppose that 40 percent of all MH warranties are breached.

Next, consider the effect of the TRR in reducing the frequency of breaches. According to another survey funded by the FTC, 29 to 38 percent of the respondents – all California MH owners – claimed that warranty problems had not been resolved to their full satisfaction.[43] For a number of years, however, California has enforced stricter regulations than those proposed in the TRR.[44] If the Ohio data are taken to reflect pre-TRR conditions and the California data post-TRR conditions, it appears that the TRR would reduce the frequency of breaches at most by one-fourth. To ensure that the breach rate is over- rather than underestimated, however, suppose that the TRR would reduce the breach rate from 40 percent to zero.

In estimating the possible decreases in repair costs and inconvenience to consumers occasioned by the TRR, the experience of the Commodore Corporation offers some clues. As part of its consent agreement, Commodore was required to write to all retail customers to whom it had sold MHs between July 10, 1972, and July 30, 1974, and to complete all legitimate claims for repairs. The resulting repair costs averaged $50 per unit.[45] Although the number of units repaired was unspecified, presumably it was small because it was equal to only 0.5 percent of all warranty repairs undertaken by Commodore after the consent decree. Because the FTC chose to prosecute, Commodore's record presumably was worse than average. Accordingly, its data would overestimate the reduction in repair bills to consumers. On the other hand, the $50 was a residual after repairs by owners. To err on the side of overestimating the benefits, quadruple the amount to $200 and suppose that it applies to all instances in which dealers and producers fail to satisfy customer complaints. Given a reduction in the breach rate from 40 to 0 percent, this would reduce a customer's expected repair costs by $0.4 \times \$200$, or by $80, assuming risk neutrality. To allow for faster repair service and reduced inconvenience, increase the possible benefits from $80 to $100, yielding an upward shift of $100 in the demand curve. Although this estimate is weak, its computation is intended to overestimate expected gains to consumers in order to give the TRR the benefit of the doubt.

C. Effect of the TRR on MH prices and sales

The demand and supply data developed so far provide a basis for estimating the effect of the TRR on MH prices and on MH quantities sold.[46] If the supply curve is relatively flat, an increase in production costs of $400 per unit implies an increase in retail prices of $360 to $400,[47] the price effect depending almost entirely on the size of the shift in the supply curve. It also implies a decrease in sales of 2,000 to 7,000 units, the size of this effect depending primarily upon the price elasticity of and the shift in MH demand.[48] On the general suppositions that the supply curve is highly elastic ($n_s = 10$) and that the demand curve is relatively elastic ($n_d = -1$), an increase in production costs of $400 per unit and an increase in demand of $100 per unit would yield a minimum increase in price of about $370 and a minimum decrease in industry sales of about 5,000 units.

In concluding this section, it is tempting to estimate the costs and benefits of the proposed TRR. Granting the poor quality of the data and recalling that the assumptions made strongly favor the TRR, some rough calculations suggest annual costs of $104 million,[49] annual benefits of $26 million,[50] and a net annual welfare loss of $78 million.[51] This yields a present-value deadweight loss of about $780 million[52] in 1977 dollars or well over $1 billion in current (1980) dollars. Even in the face of grossly overestimated benefits, costs would have to be less than one-fourth the amount estimated for the TRR to yield a net benefit.[53]

V. Impact on consumers and producers

The various gains and losses discussed in the preceding section do little more than hint at the actual magnitudes involved. More accurate estimates undoubtedly would be helpful. Overall estimates, however, fail to indicate the incidence of the costs and the distribution of the gains, information that is crucial in comparing alternatives. Accordingly, the next task will be to examine the consequences of the proposed legislation on different groups of consumers and on the structure and performance of the industry.

A. Consumers

Some producers will cease offering warranties, and their retail prices will decrease to reflect the lower cost of their product. To the extent that these warranties covered the provision of services in which manufacturers had a comparative advantage, consumers will confront higher costs to obtain comparable services from alternative sources. As a result, consumers will pay a higher full price and will be worse off. Note that producers of the lowest-quality MHs will face the highest compliance costs and will have the greatest incentive to cease offering warranties.

Most MH manufacturers may be expected to comply. Manufacturers typically are not yet well known to consumers. Up to some point, therefore, warranties are still worth offering as a signaling device to consumers. Compliance with the TRR, however, will result in a proportionately greater increase in prices for lower- than for higher-priced MHs. First, because the cost of implementing some of the major provisions of the TRR (e.g., administrative, record-keeping procedures, and on-site inspections) are largely independent of MH prices and quality, they will affect all MH prices by similar amounts. Second, to the extent that various provisions of the TRR result in lower frequency of repair and in better warranty service, producers of higher-priced units who already provide higher-quality warranty service will incur smaller cost increases. At worst, the TRR will force these firms to substitute higher-cost techniques required by the FTC for the lower-cost techniques previously used, and only the differential cost would be reflected in higher prices.

Some indication of the effect of the TRR on the MH price structure may be obtained from the frequency distribution of retail sales in various price categories.[54] If the estimated increase in average retail prices of $370 is applied to the data for the U.S. as a whole, the prices of units below the 10th percentile would increase by 5.7 percent or more, those below the 25th percentile by 3.7 percent or more, those at the 50th percentile by 2.9 percent, those above the 75th percentile by 2.2 percent or less, and those above the 90th percentile by 1.6 percent or less. Thus, the TRR will reduce relative price differentials. Indeed, because producers of lower-priced, lower-quality MHs will incur higher compliance costs than will producers of higher-priced, higher-quality MHs, price differentials will be narrowed even further. Lowering the relative prices of the highest-priced units will make them more attractive to consumers, who will buy relatively more of them. As a corollary, producers of these MHs will benefit relative to producers of smaller, lower-quality MHs.

Lower-income consumers typically will be worse off. These consumers by definition have a stricter budget constraint and are thus the most likely buyers of lower-priced, lower-quality MHs. These homes will exhibit the highest percentage increase in price and may be expected to exhibit the largest percentage decrease in sales. Some lower-income consumers will simply be priced out of the market, and they will be worse off. The lower-income consumers who, as a result of the TRR, will buy higher-quality, higher-priced MHs but who would have preferred to buy lower-quality, lower-priced MHs, no longer available, will also be worse off. This group includes individuals who had a comparative advantage in performing their own repairs, or had a greater tolerance for inconvenience, or, at existing prices, preferred better medical care, better food, or other things to better MH warranties.

Higher-income consumers typically will also lose, but to a much lesser extent. The increase in prices will be smaller, and fewer buyers of higher-quality MHs will be priced out of any given quality range. Nevertheless, some will be induced to buy lower-quality MHs than they otherwise would have purchased. To the extent that consumers pay a higher price for the same quality or get lower quality at the same price, clearly they are worse off.

Some consumers will gain from the proposed TRR. The TRR will result in greater standardization of certain product characteristics, and economies from larger planned volume of output imply that the prices of the latter will be lower than they would have been otherwise. Accordingly, individuals who would have bought them at a higher price will benefit. Although some consumers will gain on individual items, however, they will lose on others, and on balance the probability that they will gain is small.

The effect of the proposed TRR on search costs is less clear. The proposed TRR presumably will yield more uniformly reliable warranties, and this will lower search costs. On the other hand, the TRR will reduce the number of dealers and the number of manufacturers represented by each dealer; consumers will have to travel farther and visit more dealerships, increasing search costs. The net effect will depend upon the specific circumstances surrounding specific consumers. Because the quality of the warranty is only one characteristic of a MH, however, the presumption is that search costs will increase.

The discussion so far suggests that the TRR will harm consumers and that it will harm lower-income relatively more than higher-income consumers. More lower-income consumers will be priced out of the market, and some of those who are not will be induced to buy a less preferred, higher price–quality combination. As noted earlier, there is no evidence that the market conditions (high information and transaction costs, closed markets) that are necessary (but not sufficient) to suggest otherwise in fact exist.

Moreover, the impact on consumers will not be uniform across regions. Thus, although only 12 percent of all units sold nationally in July 1977 retailed for less than $8,000, the corresponding figure for the East South Central region was 38 percent. Indeed, in the latter region units selling for $10,000 or less accounted for 59 percent of all sales, whereas the corresponding figure for the Pacific and for the Mountain States was zero percent.[55] This evidence is supported by annual data showing that the average retail price of MHs sold in the West since 1974 has been 50 percent higher than the average retail price of those sold in the South.[56] Stricter regulation in California and other western states relative to southern states no doubt accounts for much of this price differential. Thus, consumers in southern states will be much more affected by the TRR than consumers in western states.

B. Manufacturers and dealers

The proposed TRR will change the relative cost of engaging in various business activities within the MH industry. As shown below, this will yield a reduction in the number of manufacturers, in the number of dealers, and in the number of firms represented by each dealer. It may also be expected to yield an increase in concentration and in vertical integration. Depending upon how strictly the TRR will be interpreted and enforced, the changes in the structure of the MH industry could be profound.

Under the conditions postulated earlier, MH sales will decrease by at least 2 percent, or about 5,000 units. Many firms will sell less, and some will exit. Those firms currently holding a comparative advantage in the production of lower-quality MHs will be most likely to exit, along with other firms that, for individual reasons, will also be unable or unwilling to adjust. If the cost effects of the TRR were neutral with respect to firm size, the historical relationship between shipments and number of firms in the industry suggests that at least six firms and 18 plants will exit.[57]

The cost effects of the TRR, however, do not seem neutral with respect to firm size. Some compliance costs, such as keeping up with the flow of TRR-related regulations, will be invariant with respect to output, yielding higher unit costs to smaller firms. Other compliance costs, such as screening and monitoring dealers, typically will increase less than proportionately with output, again imposing relatively higher costs on smaller firms. Moreover, the variance in quality among firms presumably will be greater in the case of smaller than of larger firms, because smaller firms may be expected to include a greater proportion both of fly-by-night operators and of high-quality custom shops. Smaller firms with a comparative advantage in the production of low-quality MHs will incur higher-than-average compliance costs and will be more likely to exit. Higher-quality firms typically ship their output further, and therefore will incur higher than average monitoring and setup costs. As a result, some low-volume producers of higher-quality units may also be squeezed out of the market. Although the TRR imposes somewhat weaker constraints on firms producing fewer than 5,000 units per year, the practical consequences of this differential treatment seem negligible. On balance, the TRR will encourage the exit and discourage the entry of smaller firms. Concentration will increase.

Next, consider the effect of the TRR on the number of plants operated by a manufacturer. Increased monitoring and administrative costs, holding other things constant, will increase the cost of operating separate plants. Up to some point, this cost increase will offset the lower transportation costs obtained by having more plants located closer to markets, and the manufacturer will have the incentive to concentrate production in fewer plants. The experience of the firms that signed consent decrees is consistent with this implication.[58] Following the consent decrees, the number of plants operated by Fleetwood decreased by 19 percent (from 36 to 29), whereas those operated by Skyline decreased by 16 percent (from 38 to 32), yielding an average decrease of 18 percent.[59] Over the same period, the average number of MH plants per manufacturer decreased by 13 percent (from 2.60 to 2.26), a decrease of just two-thirds the rate experienced by the signatories.

As noted earlier, however, the TRR will impose higher costs on smaller firms, often one-plant operations. Some of these firms will leave, yielding an increase in the average number of plants per firm. The exit of smaller firms also implies an increased demand for the output of the remaining (larger) firms, increasing the profitability of establishing plants in the vacated markets. On balance, therefore, the effect of the TRR on the number of plants per firm seems indeterminate.

The effect of the TRR on MH dealers is more straightforward. The requirement that manufacturers screen, contract with, monitor, and generally supervise dealers more closely will decrease the profitability to a manufacturer of using lower-quality, lower-volume dealers located farther from the manufacturer's home office. Accordingly, producers will use fewer dealers with these characteristics. The same provisions of the TRR also increase the cost to dealers of representing a manufacturer, and they will represent fewer of them. In the process, of course, some dealers will go out of business.

There is some evidence that the TRR will yield a decrease in the number of dealers. Thus, Fleetwood, Redman, and Commodore reported to the FTC that no more than 5 percent of the dealers they dropped during the mid-1970s was attributable to the FTC order.[60] During the period in question, however, the number of dealers within the industry decreased by 21 percent, from 12,480 in 1974 to 9,865 in 1976. It seems reasonable to suppose that at least some of the dealers who were squeezed out by the general downturn in economic conditions were precisely those who would have been squeezed out by the TRR. Some of the weaker dealers presumably exited before the signatories had a chance to sever relations with them, suggesting that an exit of 200 dealers (5 percent of 10,000) would underestimate the effect of the TRR on the dealer population.

The closer dealer–manufacturer relationship required by the FTC also implies a decrease in the relative cost of operating vertically integrated firms. Existing firms of this type will be more likely to survive and to prosper, and other firms will be encouraged to adopt this organizational structure. The competitive advantage, however, could be relatively small and partially offset by the threat of antitrust suits by independent dealers.

Finally, the TRR will adversely affect the ability of manufacturers, dealers, and consumers to specialize in those activities in which each has a comparative advantage and to adjust more quickly and cheaply to changes in economic conditions. More important, it will deflect the entrepreneurial process of discovery away from preferred solutions (e.g., the more efficient production of desired goods, including the introduction of innovative, lower-cost warranties) and toward unintended and undesired side effects.[61] The result will be higher production costs and higher full prices to consumers.

VI. Conclusions

The FTC's case for the proposed Mobile Home Trade Regulation Rule seems to be wholly impressionistic. The BCP Statement of Position contains no empirical evidence bearing on whether consumers are or are not getting the quality of mobile homes and MH warranties that they are paying for. Indeed, apart from a five-page introductory profile of the industry, which is described as competitive, the statement contains no systematic evidence of any kind. Moreover, it contains no statement either of the theory (or theories) used in collecting and analyzing data or of the criteria used in assessing the significance of the findings. Indeed, there is no indication that the BCP undertook an objective, systematic analysis of the industry and of the consequences of the TRR, either before or during the hearings.

The evidence suggests that the MH industry is competitive. At least until recently, there were no legal barriers to entry, and the amount of capital desirable to open either manufacturing or retailing facilities was relatively small. Other bits of evidence suggest that MHs were produced in a wide range of quality and sizes in response to consumer wants. Given this setting, the main consequences of implementing the TRR appear to be as follows. First, production costs will increase, yielding a decrease in supply. Second, the quality of MHs will increase, yielding an increase in demand. Under the conditions estimated in this chapter, retail prices will increase by at least $370, and sales will decrease by at least 5,000 units; the TRR will yield annual costs of $104 million, benefits of $26 million, and a deadweight loss of $78 million, yielding a present-value deadweight loss of $780 million in 1977 dollars, or well over $1 billion in current (1980) dollars. Other considerations, including some allowance for growth in sales over time, suggest that the present-value deadweight loss would be substantially larger.

Mobile homes are a major source of lower-income housing. As a result of the TRR, lower-income consumers in general will be worse off. The prices of lower-quality units will increase more (absolutely as well as relatively) than those of higher-priced units, and relatively more lower-income buyers will be either squeezed out of the market or induced to spend more on MHs and less on other goods (e.g., food, medical care) than they would have preferred. Moreover, the impact of the TRR will be strongest in southern states, where relatively more lower-priced units are currently sold.

Turning to the structure of the industry, the main effect of the TRR will be to reduce the number of competitors. There will be decreases in the number of firms, in the number of plants, in the number of dealers, and in the number of dealers represented by each firm, and there will be an increase in concentration and in vertical integration.

The analysis and the evidence presented in this chapter suggest that the TRR will reduce consumer welfare, especially that of lower-income consumers. It will also decrease the welfare of most producers, particularly small ones. On these grounds, it has little to recommend it.

Acknowledgments

The author thanks Dennis Murphy, Bureau of Economics, FTC, and Stephen Meyer, Bureau of Consumer Protection, FTC, for pointing out substantive statements in the public record; H. E. Blomgren, Vice President of the Indiana Manufactured Housing Association, J. Brown Hardison, publisher of *Mobile-Modular Housing Dealer,* and others within the industry for providing information about mobile homes; and Kenneth W. Clarkson, Timothy J. Muris, and Patrick O. Gudridge for their helpful comments.

13 Regulating information: advertising overview

MARK F. GRADY

This chapter examines the legal rules that the FTC has evolved to judge advertising. The FTC has set the wrong objective for these rules in that the agency has tried to increase the reliability of all advertising, both the kind that consumers use as a complement or guide to their own product search activities and the kind that consumers use as a substitute for their own search. Instead, the agency should police only the reliability of the "search substitute" kind of advertising. This is the approach of the common law of fraud. FTC advertising rules based on this approach would be more enforceable for the agency, more predictable to advertisers, and more beneficial to consumers.

Section I summarizes the relevant economic principles. Section II describes the common-law approach in terms of these principles. Section III describes current FTC advertising doctrines, analyzes their consumer welfare consequences relative to the common-law approach, and proposes two alternative kinds of regulatory reform.

I. The economics of deceptive advertising

A. The theory of advertising

The main economic justification for advertising is that it reduces consumer search costs and makes consumer search more effective. Consumers constantly expend resources to find the goods and services that best serve their wants. Any device that reduces these search costs produces benefits.[1] Aside from the direct benefit of the time and other resources that consumers save, consumers receive two other benefits from advertising. First, when search costs are reduced, consumers are more likely to find the good rather than the bad buys; second, when sellers know that consumers are more likely to find the good buys, they will be less disposed and less able to offer bad buys.

Phillip Nelson says that understanding how advertising reduces search costs begins with distinguishing two kinds of attributes that products have.[2] One is a "search quality," which is an attribute that consumers can evaluate prior to purchase (e.g., the "style" of a dress). The second kind is an "experience quality," which consumers can evaluate only after purchase (e.g., that taste of a brand of soup).

Nelson says that with experience goods (i.e., goods whose experience qualities dominate), consumers can use advertising as a "guide" to their search for the best buys in the market, largely without paying any attention to the contents of the advertising. Under Nelson's theory, consumers search competing experience goods by buying and trying them. Nelson argues that the profitability of experience goods advertising is higher for good buys than for bad buys, because advertising a good buy will win repeat sales as well as initial sales, whereas advertising a bad buy will at best earn initial sales only. If this is so, the best buys will tend to be those that are most heavily advertised, because it will be most profitable to advertise those goods that can be expected to win common consumer acceptance. It thus becomes a good strategy for consumers searching for an experience good to pay little attention to the contents of advertising and to rely merely on its existence and volume as a guide to which experience goods to try first in the search process. If advertising did not increase the productivity of consumer search, Nelson argues, consumers would learn not to use it as a guide to their search activities, because experience with advertised goods would eventually demonstrate its unreliability as a guide to search.

Under Nelson's theory, the search process for search goods (i.e., goods whose search qualities dominate) does not necessarily involve buying competing products and trying them, because consumers can evaluate search goods before purchase. Rather than guide search, search goods advertising provides what Nelson calls "hard information." For instance, showing a picture of a dress provides hard information about its style. Nelson concludes that the contents of search goods advertising are often significant, but that the contents of experience goods advertising are not as significant as the volume of it.

Nelson's theory has several implications regarding deception in advertising. For search goods, it will rarely pay to engage in false advertising, because consumers can discover the falsity *before* purchase. This factor, in combination with the cost of processing nonbuying customers and the cost of losing credibility for future ads, generally makes the deceptive advertising of search goods unprofitable even without legal sanctions.

For experience goods, however, Nelson finds that deceptive advertising can be profitable, because it will earn initial sales, even if it will not yield many repeat sales after consumers learn the truth from their trial of the product. Nelson says that consumers can be sure that the contents of experience goods advertising are reliable only when very narrow "authenticating" conditions are met. Nelson says that the only kind of claim that meets these conditions is one that identifies product function.

Despite this conclusion about the unreliability of the contents of experience goods advertising, Nelson argues that laws against deceptive advertising are usually unwise. He concedes that "they can – at a cost – make more information available to consumers from advertising"[3] but argues that these laws actually increase deceptive advertising for two reasons. First, they give consumers more confidence that the contents of advertising are true. This will increase sellers' incentives to deceive, unless the law is perfectly enforced, which would be nonoptimal. Second, he says that most consumers, not being legal experts, will misunderstand the domain of the law's protection and will sometimes think that a claim is reliable when really it is not.

Nelson's arguments against deceptive advertising laws are incorrect. We are certainly wise to have a law of contracts, even if the consequences are that more bargains are broken (because more are made) and that buyers sometimes think that they have a legally enforceable agreement when they do not. In addition, we observe consumers relying on advertising claims that are unreliable under Nelson's theory. Under Nelson's theory it would be unwise for consumers to believe a seller's claim about the BTU rating of an air conditioner or even about the net weight of a can of peas, yet few consumers are so skeptical.

Rather than distinguishing advertising that contains "hard information" from advertising that only "guides" consumer search, it is more useful to distinguish between advertising that consumers use as a "substitute" for their search and advertising that consumers use as a "complement" to their search. What Nelson calls "hard information" actually reduces the marginal productivity of consumer search and is a substitute for it. If a consumer relies on a seller's claim of the BTU rating of an air conditioner, it will not be as productive for that consumer to insist on conducting his or her own experiments of its cooling power in the showroom. On the other hand, for the reasons Nelson explains, other kinds of advertising claims increase the marginal productivity of search by guiding or "complementing" it instead of substituting for it. However, advertising is not the usual kind of complementary resource that increases the amount of other resources used with it. Consumers in the possession of "search complement" can actually search less for the same reason that Robinson Crusoe might spend less labor husking coconuts if someone gave him a high-speed coconut husker. Because his costs of transacting with other consumers are prohibitively high, he produces food only for his own consumption just as consumers often search only for their own consumption.

of information because of the high transaction costs of selling information to other consumers. Search complement can also make consumers search more. "Search substitute," on the other hand, will always make consumers search less. The distinguishing economic difference is that search complement increases the productivity of consumer search, whereas search substitute reduces its productivity.

The contents of advertising will often increase the productivity of search. For instance, an advertisement's emphasis on an attribute will attract consumers who especially value this attribute, or those normally associated with it, and will turn away consumers who especially value other attributes that are normally traded off against the attribute emphasized. One supermarket might offer low prices but relatively long checkout lines, little variety, high stockout rates, and whatever other attributes must be sacrificed to sustain the low prices. A competitive supermarket might provide higher prices but better service. A consumer seeing a supermarket ad that says "check out our unbelievably low prices" can come to three possible conclusions: that the claim is "false," that the advertising supermarket is more technically efficient than its competitors and is able to pass these efficiency savings on to its customers, or that the service offered by the advertising store is worse than at competing stores. Consumers would like to be able to distinguish among these three possibilities without having to visit the store, but even if they cannot, this kind of ad can help different segments of consumers guide their search. For a consumer looking for low prices (even if it means poor service), it makes sense to try the supermarket that advertises low prices first rather than one that advertises "gourmet foods."

For the same reason, it makes sense for a consumer looking for some exotic food not stocked at most supermarkets to avoid the store that advertises "check out our unbelievably low prices." A seller thus has little incentive to emphasize one attribute rather than another in search complement advertising, unless the seller thinks that the consumer segment attracted by the emphasized attribute will buy or continue to buy once these consumers have learned the truth from inspection or experience. This tends to make search complement advertising reliable in the absence of any law or regulation.

It is not necessary to assume that all consumers use advertising in the same way. Heavy advertising of a product may attract those segments of consumers that have found that products with similar advertising practices usually meet their wants better than others. But there seem to be other consumer segments, whose members have tastes different from common tastes, that would use advertising as a means of deciding which products to avoid. For instance, a consumer looking for extremely high quality pipe tobacco might consciously avoid searching advertised brands and might especially avoid the brands that are most heavily advertised. Such a consumer would have implicitly figured out that his own values for this product are not common enough to support advertising. Even in this situation, advertising increases the productivity of both the attracted and the turned-away consumer segments by complementing or guiding the search activities of both.

Further, the seller's media selection can also complement consumer search. As Nelson says, "What is a high-utility brand for some consumers will be a low-utility brand for others. . . . In consequence, the producer distributes his advertisements among media so that his message is seen by those who are most likely to repeat purchase of his brand. An esoteric, high-price soup gets advertised in the *New Yorker,* whereas Campbell's Soup displays its wares in *Good Housekeeping.*"[4] Even the knowledge that a product "advertises in *Life*" can be useful to consumers with experience with other products advertised in that same magazine.

Finally, the "style" of an advertisement can complement search by appealing to segments attracted or turned away by different artwork. For example, very expensive stores frequently use very simple artwork. This kind of appeal can be fully "rational" if consumers and sellers come to an implicit common understanding of the way style signals quality, as seems to be the case.

In summary, advertising can be a complement to consumer search and help guide it in several different ways. First, the fact that a brand advertises or advertises heavily can help guide consumers who have found that advertised brands tend to be better buys (or worse buys) for them than unadvertised or less heavily advertised brands. Second, knowing the media in which a brand advertises can help consumers who have discovered that brands advertised in particular media tend to be better buys (or worse buys) for them than other brands. Third, the style of an advertisement can help consumers identify whether the seller believes that the product will appeal to the consumer groups of which they are members. Finally, and most important to the following discussion, when advertising emphasizes a particular attribute, it can help consumers who have a preference for (or against) those attributes normally associated with the emphasized one. This emphasis signals to consumers an increase in probability that the advertised brand has the attribute emphasized and reduces the probability that the brand has attributes that are normally traded off against the emphasized one.

B. Search complement and search substitute

How do sellers decide whether to provide consumers with information that is a complement to consumer search or to provide information that is a substitute for consumer search? An example of a search substitute claim would be any that describes some sort of technical or otherwise objective specification of a product, such as a horsepower or BTU rating. An example of a search complement claim would be any that invites consumer search (e.g., "Taste for yourself why it costs so much"). The next section will elaborate upon this distinction.

Advertising is very much like exchange between producers, except that buyers usually do not transfer product information to sellers. Both buyers and sellers produce information about products. When a seller has a comparative advantage at producing information that a buyer wishes to use, it benefits both parties for the seller to produce it for the buyer's consumption rather than for the buyer to produce it for himself at greater cost. Neither buyers nor sellers invariably have a comparative advantage at search. (A seller's production of information, just like the buyer's production of information for himself, will sometimes also be called "search.") Sometimes sellers can more cheaply produce information about a particular product attribute than buyers can (e.g., the age of wine), and other times it is buyers who can more cheaply produce information about a product attribute (e.g., the taste of wine). Buyers will usually have a comparative advantage at searching such attributes as how products taste, how they smell, and how they look when worn. But if each buyer had to rely exclusively on his own production of product information, buyers would incur much higher costs to use it and would use much less of it.

A seller will wish to provide search substitute about those product attributes for which the seller has a comparative advantage at search and will wish to provide search complement about those attributes for which buyers have a comparative advantage at search. If buyers can search more cheaply themselves, they will not wish to pay for the search that the seller must do to provide search substitute. This does not mean, however, that sellers will always provide search substitute when they have a comparative advantage at search. They may, instead, not provide any information because the cost is too high relative to demand for this information or, as will be explained more fully below, sellers may provide search complement because of high "transaction costs" in providing search substitute.

Whether it is buyer or seller who can more cheaply produce product information will vary between different buyers and different sellers even for the same product. One would suppose that buyers would generally have a comparative advantage at evaluating experience qualities of inexpensive, nondurable goods and search qualities of all goods, because consumer search is cheap in these instances. Sellers would more likely have a comparative advantage at evaluating experience qualities of expensive durable goods, because neither prepurchase inspection nor experience is an entirely satisfactory way for consumers to evaluate these products. We would thus expect to find that the advertising of cheap nondurables would contain proportionately less search substitute and more search complement information than the advertising of expensive durables. Casual observation seems to bear this out. For example, it is extremely rare to find technical specifications in advertising of cheap nondurables.

Beyond these considerations, there will often be economies of scale in product evaluation that will also tend to give sellers a comparative advantage at search, for instance when evaluation can be best accomplished with some costly fixed asset, such as a testing machine, a survey of some sort, or specialized expertise. Sellers will not always provide search substitute in these situations, because it is often costly for sellers to provide enough facts to make consumers want to use the information provided as a substitute for search, and it is often costly for consumers to understand the significance of complicated facts in terms of their own values. These difficulties in communication will be called transaction costs, and they reduce the scale of advertising, particularly search substitute advertising.

Buyers will be most willing to substitute seller-provided information for their own search when the information (1) has a fixed meaning that (2) does not incorporate a value judgment by the seller and (3) can be cheaply interpreted by the buyer in a way that lets him or her form his or her own value judgment about the product. This kind of information reduces the risk that the buyer will incur the cost of getting something that he or she does not want. Claims about measurements of product volume, weight, and length meet these criteria, and we observe consumers substituting seller statements about these attributes for their own search, even though consumer search of these attributes is itself relatively cheap in most instances. (We do not observe consumers weighing prepackaged, weight-marked vegetables.) When the government standardizes weights and measures of this kind, it effectively reduces the transaction costs buyers and sellers incur to exchange information through advertising. Individual buyers can also invest in reducing transaction costs by learning how to interpret more specialized product measurements (e.g., the harmonic distortion rating of a stereo amplifier).

A major difference between search complement and search substitute goes beyond the examples given at the beginning of this discussion, however, because the higher consumer search costs are, the more likely a buyer will want to use even value-laden information provided by a seller as a substitute for search. For instance, a buyer is more likely to treat as search substitute a physician's statement that he or she "needs an operation" than a clothier's statement that he or she "needs this suit." These complications will be analyzed in the next section, as the difference between search complement and search substitute is more clearly defined.

II. The economic policy of the common law of fraud

The common law of fraud establishes rules to make information exchanges more efficient, just as the law of contracts establishes rules to make exchanges of other goods and services more efficient. Market forces, especially those involving the principle of comparative advantages and the existence of transaction costs, will cause sellers to provide consumers with both search substitute information and search complement information.

In a world where sellers were perfectly honest and in the absence of any law of fraud, buyers would still have the problem of distinguishing information intended as search complement from information intended as search substitute. Now, if we introduce the possibility that some sellers are dishonest, consumers have an additional, separate problem of distinguishing reliable search substitute from unreliable search substitute. Quite apart from the legal system, there are market signals available for this purpose, such as the seller's reputation in the community, length of time at a particular location, size, and dependence on repeat sales. Even with a law of fraud, we observe consumers relying on these market signals for the purpose of assessing the reliability of information, because the legal system is costly to invoke.

The law of fraud, does, however, allow consumers to rely less on these market signals of honesty. There are several benefits from this. Relying on the legal system is often cheaper for buyers than relying on market signals of honesty, because it is often costly for sellers to invest in giving the correct signals (e.g., by increasing their scale of business) and it is costly for buyers to assess these signals (e.g., by finding people who have dealt with the seller in the past). Because it is sometimes cheaper for consumers to rely on the law rather than on market signals, there are several derivative benefits. Consumers can rely more often on the kind of seller-provided information that the law protects. The proportion of reliable information of this kind should increase, because unreliable information will carry a legal as well as a market penalty. Because of this, consumers should make better purchase decisions.

There is a basic similarity between the way that the law of fraud works and the way that the law of contracts works. For both, the law's protection is invoked by the consent of the parties, inferred from their conduct. The law of fraud creates a framework by which buyers and sellers "agree" when the buyer may, with the law's protection, treat seller-provided information as a substitute for the buyer's search. (The law of contracts creates a framework by which buyer and seller "agree" when a transfer of goods is legally enforceable. This equally metaphorical "agreement" to invoke the protection of the law of contracts is different from the underlying agreement to transfer the goods, which may or may not be legally enforceable.)

Under the law of fraud, when a seller (or buyer) wishes to provide reliable information, he or she must phrase the statement such that it objectively appears worthy of being used as a substitute for search. Whether a statement is phrased as search substitute is a matter of relating the nature of the words used to the subject matter of the claim. At one extreme, claims that objectively appear most worthy of being treated as search substitute will be phrased (1) in a positive way, without any expression of doubt; (2) in a factual rather than in a value-laden way; (3) in a specific rather than in a general or indefinite way; and (4) in a temperate rather than in an exaggerated way. At the other extreme, claims that are phrased with doubt or in a value-laden, indefinite, or exaggerated way generally do not have the law's protection as a substitute for search.[5] By making this kind of distinction, the law follows common expectations and is easily understood by nonlawyers; but if the law were different, expectations would also be somewhat different. The law of fraud has two technical names for claims that are ordinarily not to be treated as search substitute. A "statement of opinion" is a value-laden or otherwise indefinite statement. For instance, a seller will not ordinarily be liable for saying how much land is worth or how much profit a business will make in the future.[6] "Puffery" is an exaggerated statement that is usually also value-laden. For this reason, it is often seen as a particular kind of opinion statement and the two names are often used interchangeably. To illustrate, a seller will not be liable for saying that "there is no better land in Vermont"[7] or that a used car was a "dandy" or a "bear-cat" or that a film should be a "block-buster."[8]

The kinds of statements that are search substitute, assuming that they concern matters susceptible of the seller's knowledge,[9] are called "statements of fact." For instance, a seller will ordinarily be liable for misrepresenting the price at which a stock was selling on the market[10] or that a car was the latest model.[11]

This system of invoking the law's protection through the phrasing of claims is flexible. In theory, practically any claim about any product attribute can be stated as opinion or as fact. A seller can say "this car goes to beat the band," which is search complement of the puffery variety or, alternatively, "this car has been tested at zero to sixty in five seconds," which is a statement of fact that the buyer should be able to treat as search substitute. Whether a seller provides fact or opinion will depend largely on the principle of comparative advantage and transaction costs, as described earlier.

The idea that opinion is indeed search complement is reflected in the law of fraud in several ways. For instance, we find courts saying, "An indefinite representation ought to put the person to whom it is made on inquiry."[12] In fact, the common law seems based on the idea that a buyer can use information either as search substitute or as search complement. If a buyer treats a claim as a mere invitation to conduct his or her own investigation, the buyer cannot recover even if the claim is a statement of fact.[13]

Although the main determinant of the difference between fact and opinion is phrasing, courts treat this as a matter of degree. In deciding whether a seller's statement is actionable, the courts also look to the circumstances surrounding the transaction, and buyer and seller accordingly must also bear these circumstances in mind when claims are phrased in general or value-laden terms. The law also follows common expectations in defining these relevant circumstances. As suggested in the preceding section, value-laden information presents a special problem, because there are some technical subjects upon which transaction costs are so high that hardly anything can be said by an expert seller to a lay buyer that is not laden with the expert's value judgment. This problem goes beyond technical subjects. For instance, it would be difficult for a seller to describe a vacation house, a piece of land, or a book in terms that are entirely factual or value-free. The higher the buyer's own search costs on the subject matter of the seller's claim and the higher the transaction costs of factual communication, the more economic it becomes for the buyer to rely on value-laden information as a substitute for search, even if it means increasing the risk that the buyer will get a product that he or she does not want. Accordingly, the first test of opinion is whether the transaction costs of providing more factual information would be excessive. The second test is whether the buyer's search costs are high relative to the seller's. The higher the transaction costs of providing more factual information and the higher the buyer's search costs relative to the seller's, the more reasonable it is to infer that the parties have transacted in search substitute. The third test is whether the seller has significantly more information about the product than the buyer.

Expert sellers speaking on technical subjects is one area where all three of these tests are met. Typically, the transaction costs of more factual communication are high, the buyer's search costs are also high, and the seller typically has much more information about the product than does the buyer. Accordingly, when a surgeon provides information to a lay buyer about the value of an operation[14] or when a jeweler provides information to a lay buyer about the value of a diamond,[15] the law will treat the information as search substitute, even though the phrasing is relatively general or value-laden.

When the buyer is also an expert, the transaction costs of providing more factual information are less, and general or value-laden information will ordinarily not be actionable.[16] With value-laden information provided by an expert, there is still the flexibility to phrase the information as search complement through including an expression of doubt (e.g., "this operation could well do you good, but it is difficult to predict"[17]).

The courts have held that high buyer search costs are an independent factor in construing information as search substitute, even in nontechnical areas. For instance, value-laden statements about land or property at a distance will often be considered actionable search substitute, whereas the same kinds of statements about nearby land will be nonactionable search complement.[18] But it is the buyer's search costs, not the distance, that are determinative. In one case, even though the property was located at some distance, the court denied liability for a value-laden sales description because there were "two or three trains per day affording easy access" and "over a week elapsed between the making of these representations and the closing of the deal, within which time there was ample opportunity for . . . [the buyer] to have inspected . . . [the goods]."[19] In other words, the court did not think that the buyer's search costs were sufficiently high and held that the seller's statement in these circumstances was more properly construed as search complement. Courts also consider factors that make search especially costly for a particular buyer, when these factors are known to the seller. For instance, it makes a difference that the buyer is an invalid and unable to search.[20]

A very similar consideration is whether the seller has more facts about the product than the buyer. Of course, this is typically the case, but especially when this superiority of knowledge on the part of the seller is combined with high search costs on the part of the buyer, the courts are likely to hold a relatively general or value-laden statement to be actionable search substitute. For instance, when a seller of real property told a buyer that the current tenant was "most desirable," the court held the seller liable when it turned out that the tenant had been in arrears on the rent:

Where the facts are equally well known to both parties, what one of them says to the other is frequently nothing but an expression of opinion. . . . But if the facts are not equally well known to both sides, then a statement of opinion by one who knows the facts best involves very often a statement of a material fact, for he impliedly states that he knows facts which justify his opinion.[21]

Whether the phrasing of a claim is actionable or not often depends, at least implicitly, on the transaction costs of making the claim more factual. In a relatively old case, a warehouseman stated that his building was "fireproof" to a purchaser of his services. Even though the word "fireproof" was somewhat general or value laden, the transaction costs of providing more factual information were high enough, relative to the benefit to the buyer in being able to make a more accurate purchase decision based on more specific facts, for the court to hold it actionable.[22] In more modern times, this probably would not be a close issue, and the tendency of the law is to make more general statements actionable, other circumstances being equal.[23] But the rule is still clear that a sufficiently general or value-laden statement will not be actionable,[24] although there are differences from state to state on how general the statement must be to avoid liability. High transaction costs of providing more factual information should be used only in connection with the other factors, such as high buyer search costs relative to the seller's search costs, and the courts follow this practice, as the cases discussed above indicate.

The risk that a buyer incurs in using value-laden information is that he or she will get something that he or she does not want, owing to the possibility that the buyer's values differ from the seller's. In ordinary sales transactions, it is predictable that the seller would naturally tend to look at the product more favorably than would most buyers.[25] When a seller purports to be disinterested or interested in favor of the buyer, the buyer's risk of relying on value-laden information is reduced, and it becomes more reasonable to construe this information as search substitute. For instance, a buyer was able to recover against a defendant who, posing as a disinterested party, made a statement about the value of land, when in fact the defendant was representing the seller.[26] The buyer's own high search costs will also be a factor that the courts consider in this situation.[27] Similarly, under some circumstances the buyer may wish to rely on the seller's values as much as or more than on his or her own, and create a fiduciary relationship for this purpose. Accordingly, the law often construes a value-laden statement by one fiduciary to another as search substitute.[28]

To summarize, in construing search substitute, the law looks first at the phrasing of the claim. If the claim is value-laden, general or indefinite, a claim will more likely be construed as search substitute (1) if the transaction costs of providing more factual information are high, (2) if the buyer's search costs are high relative to the seller's, (3) if the seller knows more facts about the product than the buyer, (4) if the seller is posing as a disinterested person or a person interested in the buyer's favor, or (5) if a fiduciary relationship exists between buyer and seller.

These rules can be used in a flexible and relatively accurate way by buyers and sellers bargaining for the law's protection in a face-to-face setting. Imagine a buyer on a used-car lot:

Seller: This car is just great. (search complement)
Buyer: How many miles does it have on it?
Seller: 78,000. (search substitute)
Buyer: What parts have you replaced?
Seller: The battery and the clutch are brand new. (search substitute) I don't think you'd be disappointed with it. (search complement)
Buyer: How does it handle on the road?

Seller: Why don't you take a test drive and see for yourself? (search complement)

Buyer: What are these rust spots? Is the damage extensive?

Seller: I doubt that it is, but it is hard to say for sure. (search complement) We haven't patched it with resin or anything. (search substitute) But if you're looking for something a little better, why don't you step over here? (search complement)

Ironically, a major reason for the reliability of seller-provided information is that much of it is so obviously unreliable and can be clearly indentified as such by those seeking to make decisions based on it. A seller bent on deception is not likely to use exaggerated lies or vague statements, and the existence of these statements, paradoxically, is evidence of honesty.

III. FTC regulation of advertising

There are two legal doctrines that the FTC uses to regulate advertising. The older doctrine prohibits "deceptive" advertising, and the newer doctrine prohibits "unsubstantiated" advertising. Currently, the FTC uses both, although during the past decade the agency has relied increasingly on the unsubstantiated advertising doctrine.

A. The deceptive advertising doctrine

Section 5 of the Federal Trade Commission Act does not define "deceptive advertising," only declares "unfair or deceptive acts or practices" unlawful.[29] As discussed in Chapter 4, the courts, and the agency itself, have had considerable flexibility in specifying the kind of advertising that is unlawfully deceptive. The FTC may prohibit any advertising that has a "capacity and tendency" to deceive,[30] by proving that at least a "significant minority" of consumers exposed to it were deceived.[31] There are two parts to this proof: first, showing that a significant minority of the consumers interpreted the claim in some way that could have influenced their decisions,[32] and, second, showing that the advertisement, so interpreted, was false.

In many FTC cases, the main controversy centers on whether a significant minority of consumers did indeed interpret the claim to mean something that was false. The courts have given the agency a great amount of discretion on this issue, and instances in which the courts have reversed the agency are rare.[33] Although the agency is "not required to sample public opinion,"[34] it will admit survey evidence offered by the respondent to prove that the meaning attached to the claim by the agency was held by an insignificant minority of consumers.[35] The Commission, however, often uses this evidence to prove its own case. In one case of this type, the agency held that 14 percent of consumers holding the false interpretation was enough;[36] in another, 15.3 percent was enough;[37] and in still another, 9 percent was enough to hold the ad deceptive.[38] There have been at least a few cases, however, in which the agency has found ads deceptive, even though the proportion of consumers holding the false interpretation was surely less than these figures, though no survey demonstrated it.[39] Thus, to the agency, a "significant minority" appears to be a "nontrivial" minority. The courts and the FTC justify holding claims deceptive when relatively few consumers are deceived as a means of protecting consumers of low intelligence,[40] as discussed in Chapter 4.

Although some courts once held that the FTC could not proceed against "statements of opinion" as "opinion" is defined under the common law of fraud,[41] current FTC law creates only an exception for "puffery" that is much narrower than the common-law exception.

Exactly what is permissible puffery under agency law practically defies description and is more a matter of unstated prosecutorial discretion than anything else. Nowhere have the courts or the Commission given a definition that they have consistently followed. It is clear, however, from past decisions that the phrasing of a claim in general, indefinite, value-laden, or exaggerated terms will not bar liability. For instance, the agency has successfully challenged ads that "Dannon is known as nature's perfect food that science made better,"[42] that a deodorant "kills strongest odors,"[43] as well as the claims "always milder" for a brand of cigarettes[44] and "improved health" for a shoe insert.[45] On the other hand, either the agency or the courts have found *nonactionable* the claims that a toothpaste will "beautify the smile,"[46] that a diet plan is "easy,"[47] and that a deodorant is "dry."[48] The difference between these two sets of claims is not clear. Both the actionable and nonactionable ones seem phrased in much the same value-laden, general, vague, or exaggerated way.

One possible difference between them may be that consumer search costs are generally higher (relative to seller's) for the actionable claims than for the nonactionable ones. For instance, it may be cheaper for consumers to discover whether a deodorant is "dry" than whether it "kills strongest odors." Consumers probably have more of a comparative advantage in discovering whether a toothpaste "beautifies the smile" than they have in discovering whether a shoe insert "improves health." If this is the rule, it is nowhere stated explicitly and its application is necessarily extremely uncertain.

Nonetheless, there must be some kind of rule that precludes liability for claims at which consumers have a significant comparative advantage at search, or else there would be more extreme prosecutions than there are currently. For instance, is it a violation for an advertiser to say that "spinach tastes good"? The agency would probably never prosecute this kind of claim even if it could be shown that a significant minority of consumers would hold it false. Yet if this claim is false to a significant minority of consumers, it would seem to be unlawful under the Commission's frequently stated advertising rules. This ambiguous interplay between the stated advertising rules and the largely unstated rules of prosecutorial discretion creates a real problem for advertisers, because they cannot tell what claims are permissible search complement and what claims are not. It is clear from the examples that the agency does regulate some search complement advertising (e.g., that a deodorant "kills strongest odors" or that a brand of cigarettes is "always milder"). Indeed, regulating the reliability of search complement seems to be conscious. Under current law, the agency does not have to find, or even assume as a conceptual matter, that any of the consumers that interpreted the claims as alleged substituted these interpretations for their own search. The agency only has to believe that the claim could have influenced consumer decisions, even if it only influenced their decisions to search, not to buy, and the consumers learned the true facts before purchase.[49]

It would thus appear that relatively few consumers benefit from a typical FTC deceptive advertising prosecution in the same way that consumers benefit from the common law of fraud. They would be the consumers who would interpret the claim in the same way that the agency does in finding deception and then use this interpretation as a substitute for their search. Because the proportion of consumers placing the false interpretation on the claim can be lower than 10 percent the proportion substituting the false interpretation for their own search is probably well below this figure in many cases.

Because it imposes a very similar cost, the nature of the cost to consumers from the agency's doctrine of deceptive advertising will be analyzed next in connection with the *Pfizer* doctrine of unsubstantiated advertising.

B. The Pfizer doctrine of unsubstantiated advertising

In the past decade the agency has relied less and less on its doctrine of deceptive advertising and increasingly on the newer *Pfizer* doctrine of unsubstantiated advertising, especially in agency prosecutions against national, as opposed to local, advertising. The *Pfizer* doctrine works in the same way as the doctrine of deceptive advertising, except that the agency does not have to prove that the alleged interpretation is false, only that the advertiser did not, before the ad was run, have evidence that proved the truth of each interpretation that would be placed on the claim by a nontrivial minority of consumers.

In *Pfizer,* the literal claims contained in the challenged advertisement were that Pfizer's sunburn painkiller, "Un-Burn," "stops sunburn pain in . . . less time than it takes . . . to slip out of [a] bikini,'' that it ''re-lieves pain fast,'' and that it ''actually anesthetizes nerves.''[50] The agency's complaint alleged that these product claims also implied a ''sub-stantiation claim'': that *Pfizer* had ''adequate and well-controlled scien-tific studies or tests'' that supported the product claims. The complaint also alleged, as a separate count, that it was ''unfair'' under the FTC Act to make such product claims without having prior studies and tests, re-gardless of whether it was deceptive to fail to have these studies or tests.

At trial, Pfizer defended itself against the deception count of the com-plaint by arguing that the phrasing of the advertisement and its general tone could not have implied, even to a minority of consumers, that the product claim was based on ''adequate and well-controlled scientific tests.'' As a defense to the unfairness count and as an alternative defense to the deception count, Pfizer also introduced evidence that, before run-ning the ad, it did perform a review of the medical and pharmacological literatures to establish that the active ingredient was an effective topical anesthetic. Additionally, Pfizer introduced results from a scientific test, performed *after* the agency issued the complaint, which showed that Un-Burn was effective in relieving sunburn pain. Based on this evidence, the agency's trial judge held for Pfizer. The FTC prosecutors then appealed to the full Commission.

The five comissioners dismissed the deception count because they agreed with Pfizer that the claims did not imply the existence of well-con-trolled scientific tests or studies. As to the unfairness count, the commis-sioners said that the complaint was wrong to say that product claims, like the ones Pfizer made, always required substantiation in the form of scien-tific tests. Instead, the commissioners announced the more flexible rule that it was unfair to make a product claim without having a prior ''reason-able basis.'' Sometimes a ''reasonable basis'' would be scientific tests and studies, but other times, the commissioners said, a different kind of sub-stantiation would do, perhaps a literature review. In any event, there should be a ''written report'' setting out the ''reasonable basis'' prepared prior to the time the ad is run. What will constitute a ''reasonable basis'' for any particular product claim, the commissioners said, will depend on ''the interplay of overlapping considerations such as'':

(1) The type and specificity of the claim made – *e.g.*, safety, efficacy, dietary, health, medical; (2) the type of product – *e.g.*, food, drug, potentially hazardous consumer product, other consumer product; (3) the possible consequences of a false claim – *e.g.*, personal injury, property damage; (4) the degree of reliance by consumers on the claims; (5) the type, and accessibility, of evidence adequate to form a reasonable basis for making particular claims.[51]

Returning to the facts of the case, the commissioners held that the sci-entific tests that Pfizer introduced could not be a ''reasonable basis'' because Pfizer did not have these tests before it ran the advertisement. The literature review, the commissioners said, could have been a reasonable basis, but it was difficult to tell, because the case was tried on the theory that a scientific test was needed. From the evidence received at trial, the commissioners said that they could not tell whether the people in the firm looked at enough literature before the ad was run. Rather than remanding the case to the trial judge for more evidence, however, the commissioners dismissed the complaint against Pfizer, but announced for the future that all "affirmative product claims" would have to be substantiated with a prior "reasonable basis."

The justification that the agency gave for the *Pfizer* doctrine was explicitly economic:

Given the imbalance of knowledge and resources between a business enterprise and each of its customers, economically it is more rational, and imposes far less cost on society, to require a manufacturer to confirm his affirmative product claims rather than impose a burden upon each individual consumer to test, investigate, or experiment for himself. The manufacturer has the ability, the know-how, the equipment, the time and the resources to undertake such information by testing or otherwise – the consumer usually does not.[52]

In essence, the agency seems to argue that sellers always have a comparative advantage at search. But as noted in the first section, this is not true for many product attributes, such as how food or drink products taste to consumers or how products look on consumers.

That consumers sometimes have a comparative advantage at search is not, however, a completely adequate criticism of the *Pfizer* doctrine. For as a matter of prosecutorial discretion, the agency generally does not prosecute claims about how products taste or look, although some advertisers prepare "reasonable basis" reports for such claims. Although it is unstated, there is the same rule under the *Pfizer* doctrine that the agency will generally not prosecute claims at which consumers have a significant comparative advantage at search. The agency may have been seeking to convey this idea by saying that only *"affirmative* product claims" have to be substantiated, although it has not explained what "affirmative" means in this context. *Pfizer* itself comes very close to being a case where consumers, and not the seller, had a comparative advantage at search, but it is plausible that it would be less costly to society for Pfizer to perform a test once, even if it is a more costly test than that of an individual consumer, than for individual consumers to run their own tests by trying the product. Nevertheless, this is not a sufficient defense of the *Pfizer* doctrine, for reasons that will become apparent.

Since 1972, when the *Pfizer* case was decided, the ad substantiation program has become the principal means by which the FTC regulates national advertising. The program works in enforcement "rounds." To encourage compliance with the obligation to prepare "reasonable basis" reports, the agency will select a particular type of claim (e.g., tire performance claims) and will then collect the leading advertisements making this type of claim and subpoena the substantiation that the advertiser is supposed to have had before making the claim. The subpoenas will not require substantiation for the literal text of the claim but for each interpretation that the agency lists. When the subpoena returns come back, the agency will issue a complaint if it believes that inadequate substantiation was submitted for at least one of these interpretations and that this interpretation was one that a "substantial minority of consumers" placed on the claim. The substantiating evidence submitted by the advertisers are often voluminous reports,[53] with much of the data submitted extremely technical and beyond the understanding of nonexperts.[54] The large volume and technical nature of the substantiation reports became an issue in congressional hearings, because it was originally hoped that consumers, or the news media, would seek to inspect the substantiation to gain information about products. When this did not happen, the principal objective of the program came to be seen as deterring unreliable claims.

Once an advertiser loses a substantiation prosecution, it is subjected to a particularized substantiation requirement for the future in making similar claims. In most cases these substantiation requirements are quite stringent. For instance, the agency successfully challenged a General Motors advertisement that said: "There's only one way, really, to find out what a Chevy Vega is all about, and that's to drive one. *Road and Track* Magazine drove one and wound up saying . . . 'Vega is beyond a doubt the best handling passenger car ever built in the U.S.'"[55]

The Commission believed that a significant minority of consumers would interpret this claim to mean that the Vega was the best handling car in America, not merely that *Road and Track* said it was. When GM was unable to prove that GM itself had substantiation, the FTC required GM, before making any comparative handling claim in the future, to perform a specified "scientific test." The order stipulated:

The word "handling" shall be defined in terms of the response of the vehicle: (a) under conditions where rapid steering inputs in evasive or emergency maneuvers are necessary; (b) under cornering conditions at speeds in excess of 30 miles per hour in which levels of lateral acceleration in excess of .2g are attained; and (c) in gusty crosswinds, on rough roads and under severe steering-braking conditions.[56]

This definition essentially determines the kind of scientific handling test that GM needs for future handling claims.

In a very recent case, the agency challenged an advertising program by Kroger in which the grocery chain sent out "price patrols" to conduct "shopping basket" price comparisons of its competition to signal consumers its corporate decision to become an "everyday low price merchant."[57] The FTC trial judge found some problems with the representativeness of the price patrol "shopping basket" samples, so he deemed the surveys to be inadequate substantiation for the comparative price claims. His order, which is now on appeal to the commissioners, specifies that any similar "comparative retail food price claim" that Kroger makes in the future must be substantiated by price surveys following procedures that the order specifies. The trial judge found that a "conservative estimate" of the annual cost of a similar survey was $644,020 for 100 markets.[58] Under the order, even an "indirect" comparative price claim would have to be substantiated by some kind of survey, and this would presumably include a claim of "bargain" or "discount" prices, or "check out our un-believably low prices."[59] A substantiation order becomes something very much to be avoided by an advertiser that wishes to continue to include search complement in advertising.

C. Consumer welfare consequences

For several reasons, it seems improbable that the costs of the FTC's advertising regulation can be justified by improvements in the reliability of search substitute in advertising. As noted in previous sections, the advertising claims challenged by the FTC are often false or unsubstantiated only in the sense that an interpretation held by a minority of consumers is false or unsubstantiated. In the majority of cases, the interpretation placed on the claim by most consumers is true. There is, in addition, little reason to believe that even those consumers who place a false interpretation on the challenged ads typically use their interpretations as a substitute for search. In the *Pfizer* case itself, the low cost of consumer search should have discouraged consumers from using the claim as anything but search complement, even if it had been phrased in entirely factual terms. As it was, at least the "slip-out-of-a-bikini" claim was phrased in such a way that the agency expressly held that not even a minority of consumers would assume that it was based on reliable evidence. Although some consumers may be led astray by many advertising claims, it is at least dubious that consumers who are habitually led astray also habitually substitute their false interpretations for search. Because this kind of behavior would lead to bad purchase decisions, there should at least be a kind of negative conditioning over time, even if the process is not fully conscious. It is far more likely that a consumer who would habitually place false interpretations on advertising would eventually learn to rely on sources of information that are easier to use, such as observing the purchase decisions of others or relying on well-known trademarks.

FTC law in its current form does not improve the efficiency of transactions in search substitute, because the FTC rules are so uncertain that they do not allow the development of any kind of understanding between sellers and consumers about which claims are search substitute and which claims are search complement. This is in sharp contrast to the common law system, under which consumers can generally determine fairly accurately which claims have the law's protection of reliability as search substitute and which do not. As a practical matter, the FTC must enforce its own rules selectively, because its laws make so much unlawful. But because consumers cannot readily determine the agency's rules of prosecutorial discretion – it is extremely difficult for a trained lawyer to do so – consumers cannot tell which claims have the FTC's protection of reliability if used as search substitute. Accordingly, the FTC rules do not significantly help consumers substitute advertising for their own search.

Even if the agency had the resources to enforce strictly its substantiation requirements for all "affirmative product claims," it is doubtful that many consumers would use advertising more often as a substitute for search. Claims on many technical subjects involve very high transaction costs if these claims are to be made factually. For instance, it would be costly both for GM to express and for consumers to understand the detailed factual results of the scientific test that the agency has mandated for comparative handling claims. Under these circumstances, it is likely that most claims about the "handling" of automobiles will continue to be made in value-laden terms (except, perhaps, to small segments of consumers who have invested in the ability to interpret technical, factual handling claims). If handling claims continue to be made in value-laden terms, there may be little incentive for consumers to substitute these claims for their own search, even if they know that the agency-ordained scientific test stands behind these claims. For consumers to want to substitute value-laden claims for their own search, they need some assurance that the agency's values in designing the test are the same as their own. In the context of the GM claim, many consumers might especially value handling in tight parking spots or in ordinary driving more than handling under the extreme conditions dictated by the agency. If this is so, and if there is no necessary association between the two types of handling, many consumers would be unwise to treat the value-laden claim as search substitute, even if it is fully substantiated to the agency's satisfaction. In short, the FTC cannot be a fiduciary to millions of different consumers as long as they have conflicting values. The degree to which consumers rely on claims as search substitute will be limited by the transaction costs of making these claims factual, whatever the agency does in its ad substantiation program.

There is good reason to believe that sellers would have the correct incentives to choose properly between search substitute and search complement in the absence of FTC regulation. If a seller has a comparative advantage at search and if the transaction costs of making a factual claim are less than the consumer search costs avoided by the seller's making a factual claim, the seller's incentive is to offer search substitute. The market should reward sellers that reduce search costs for their customers, because consumers should be willing to pay higher prices for lower search costs. The FTC's advertising regulation may distort these decisions and result in an inefficient selection of search substitute over search complement.

Search complement claims can be especially costly to substantiate, because if a seller wants to make this kind of claim at all, it frequently indicates that the transaction costs of a more factual claim are high (or that consumers have a comparative advantage at search). Substantiating a nonfactual or value-laden claim is likely to be more costly than substantiating a factual or non-value-laden claim. For this reason, the FTC's advertising regulation probably tends to cause advertisers to shift in favor of factual claims. Yet it may be more useful for consumers to know that Kroger has staked its valuable reputation against a search complement claim of "discount" or "bargain" prices than for consumers to have the information from Kroger that eggs this week are x cents, that Bartlett pears are y cents, and so forth.

Superimposed on the tendency of advertisers to shift inefficiently in favor of factual or search substitute claims is the overriding effect of the regulation to reduce all kinds of advertising, both search complement and search substitute. In addition, advertisers will more often make completely vacuous claims that are not subject to a coherent FTC challenge. That is, if the advertiser finds it uneconomic to make a substantiative factual claim, the alternatives are to make no claim at all or a claim that is entirely meaningless. (A meaningless claim can still convey information through the advertiser's media selection and through volume.) Yet under some circumstances, consumers would find unsubstantiative opinion claims more useful than meaningless claims.

The ad substantiation program, which imposes the cost of preparing a costly "reasonable basis" report, even for claims that are known to be true without prior substantiation, seems especially undesirable from a consumer welfare point of view. The only possible justification for this requirement is the administrative savings from eliminating the agency's obligation under the deceptive advertising doctrine to prove claims false. It is extremely doubtful that these savings are worth the cost of the many reports that must be prepared needlessly. These costs are passed on to consumers, and to some extent they must deter useful advertising, as firms seek to avoid these costs.

Balanced against the cost of FTC advertising regulation is mainly the possibility that it increases the reliability of search complement. But as discussed earlier, market regulation of search complement is especially effective, at least relative to market regulation of the reliability of search substitute. The market provides no substantial or lasting reward for a seller that provides unreliable search complement, because the consumer search induced by the information will usually uncover its unreliability before purchase or, in the case of cheap nondurables, before repeat purchase. The chief instance in which the agency itself has specifically found unreliable search complement to be a consumer problem is in the practice of "bait and switch." Under this kind of scheme, an unscrupulous seller lures a consumer into the store with a false claim about one product, invariably a consumer durable, and then switches the sales pitch to try to convince the consumer to buy something else. The consumers who are misled by this practice seem to disregard ordinary market signals of reliability, as the sellers that the agency has prosecuted for this deception generally appear to be obviously disreputable retailers.[60] The consumer injury in this kind of case is also problematical, because consumers typically learn the true facts before they purchase. Whatever special problems may be raised by bait and switch, and possible similar practices that are occasionally profitable, unreliable search complement does not seem to be a major problem in the economy. Usually, an advertiser has a large economic incentive to target search complement on those consumer segments that are most likely to be satisfied after they have searched through inspection or experience, because this kind of advertising is most profitable. It seems dubious that any further improvements in the quality of search complement accomplished by the FTC outweigh the costs imposed on consumers by the substantiation expenses that are passed back to them.

If, as seems probable, the FTC's regulation makes advertising more costly and less efficient, there are several more general effects. Consumer search costs will increase and individual sellers will confront more inelastic demand curves and will be given a kind of monopoly power that would not otherwise exist.[61] An extreme case of this phenomenon would be obvious if the whole supermarket industry were placed under the Kroger order. Prices should be higher in such a regulated market for the same reasons that prices are higher in markets where advertising is forbidden outright.

D. Possible reforms

The common law suggests two possibilities for the reform of FTC advertising regulation so as to make it more beneficial to consumers. The first possibility would be for the agency to establish some symbol for advertisers to use to code search substitute, perhaps similar to the symbol for registered trademarks. The agency would then confine its regulatory efforts to advertising claims that bear the symbol. Unlike current FTC law, this system would give consumers (and sellers) a clear understanding of which claims have the FTC's protection as search substitute, and this system would not have misallocative effects. The disadvantage of this idea is that it could be awkward, especially for broadcast advertising and oral sales presentations. Although printed advertising might be easily and conspicuously coded, broadcast advertising could be coded only with a visual overlay or with some sort of formula phrase or word, such as the use of a phrase containing a codeword (e.g., "You can 'rely on the fact' that Farmer Brown's bacon contains no nitrites."). An advantage of this system is that it would provide a marketplace test for the usefulness of the agency's advertising regulation. The more advertisers that use the symbol or the codeword, the more it would indicate that the agency is providing a useful service to consumers.

The second possibility for reform would be for the agency to make the phrasing of claims relevant to the issue of deception. Following the modern common law, claims phrased in value-laden, general, indefinite, or obviously exaggerated terms would not be actionable. In deciding close cases, it would seem appropriate for the agency to follow principles similar to fraud principles. A value-laden claim would be more likely actionable (1) the higher consumer search costs relative to the seller's, (2) the more information possessed by the seller relative to the buyer, and (3) the higher the transaction costs of providing more factual information.[62] These principles should only be used to decide close cases, however, because if there is not sufficient flexibility to phrase claims on any subject either as nonactionable search complement or as actionable search substitute, use of these principles could lead to the same problems created by current law.

In any event, the agency should overrule the *Pfizer* doctrine and rely exclusively on the doctrine of deceptive advertising. Even if there are administrative savings from the agency's not having to prove claims false, it would be cheaper for consumers for the agency directly to shift the burden of proof on the issue of falsity rather than doing this indirectly. This reform would save consumers the expense of paying for "reasonable basis" reports for claims that are obviously true.

IV. Conclusions

The courts' and the agency's failure to preserve in some way the common-law distinction between fact and opinion in FTC advertising law has led to a set of rules that imposes unnecessary costs on consumers and makes advertising less useful to them than it might be. The legislative history of the Federal Trade Commission Act indicates that the Congress intended this distinction to be preserved. Senator Wheeler, one of the sponsors of the legislation that gave the agency its comprehensive authority to regulate advertising, assured his fellow senators in the floor debate:

The object of the proposed legislation is not to stop the issuing of exaggerated opinions with reference to one's own articles. . . . [T]he courts have recognized the difference between simply puffing one's own product in a general statement by saying, for example, "It is the best car manufactured," and misrepresenting a definite fact with reference to the product. If an automobile manufacturer said, "This automobile has a self-starter on it," when as matter of fact the automobile did not have a self-starter on it, that statement would be a definite, positive misrepresentation of a provable fact. However, if the manufacturer said, "My car is the best car on the market for the money," there would be a vast difference of opinion in the general public's mind as to whether it was or not, and a great many persons might say it was the best, whereas a great many persons might say it was not. It would be a very difficult thing to prove that the car was not just what the manufacturer said it was. Those are things which are generally recognized by the courts as not capable of being reached by any law.[63]

The courts and the agency should return to these principles.

14   Special statutes: the structure and operation of the Magnuson-Moss Warranty Act

GEORGE L. PRIEST

In January 1975, the Magnuson-Moss Warranty Act became law,[1] imposing, for the first time, the forceful hand of federal regulation on the content of consumer product warranties. Prior to the passage of the Warranty Act, warranty content had remained within the jurisdiction of the individual state legislatures. Indeed, scarcely a decade earlier, 49 of the 50 state legislatures had completed the most comprehensive reform of sales law in the country's history: the enactment in each state of the identical statute, the Uniform Commercial Code. The Code, however, establishes only a structure for the effectuation of agreements between buyers and sellers and has little direct effect on warranty content. The Warranty Act, on the other hand, is designed as a powerful regulatory instrument for the influence of warranty terms for the benefit of consumer buyers. The Act prescribes specific provisions that must be included in consumer warranties, and it delegates authority to the Federal Trade Commission both to enforce these prescriptions and to promulgate rules and regulations for specific industries.

Despite the differences between the methods of the Warranty Act and the Commercial Code, however, the Congress chose to build upon the provisions of the Code rather than to scrap them. Thus, to predict the effects of the Warranty Act, one must compare carefully consumer rights and remedies under the Uniform Commercial Code with the rights and remedies created by the Warranty Act. Section I discusses the general objectives of the Magnuson-Moss Act. Section II considers the Act's provisions in detail and compares them to the analogous law of the Uniform Commercial Code to determine the net effect of the Act on consumer warranty law. Finally, Section III investigates the effect of the Act in a different way. It compares the content of a set of warranties issued prior to the enactment of the Magnuson-Moss Act with the warranties for the same products issued subsequent to the Act to determine the Act's influence on warranty practices.

246

I. The rationale of the Warranty Act

Prior to 1975, when the Magnuson-Moss Act was enacted, the Congress commissioned three studies of warranty practices, the first with respect to appliances, the second with respect to automobiles, and the third with respect to a more comprehensive set of consumer durables.[2] The general findings and conclusions of these studies were similar: Consumers possessed little information about warranty content or warranty practices. Furthermore, consumers, as a general proposition, were unable to bargain effectively with manufacturers who unilaterally dictated warranty terms. As a consequence, the coverage actually offered in consumer product warranties was extremely limited and was subject to little influence from the forces of competition. The Magnuson-Moss Warranty Act was designed to address these problems.[3]

The general approach of the Warranty Act may be summarized as follows:

1. The Act places extensive requirements on sellers to disclose the terms of product warranties *prior* to the consumer's purchase of the product.[4] These requirements are designed to enable consumers to make more informed product choices and, concomitantly, to stimulate competition over the extent of warranty protection between the manufacturers of *all* consumer products.

2. The Act requires manufacturers to make the terms of their warranties more intelligible to consumers by requiring expression in "simple and readily understood language" and by requiring manufacturers to designate the warranty, conspicuously, as either "Full" or "Limited." The language requirement is designed to reduce consumer confusion by eliminating the legal terminology characteristic of most warranties. Similarly, the designation requirement seeks to enable consumers to compare more readily the warranty protection offered for competing products by simplifying the categories of warranty coverage. To qualify as a Full Warranty, a warranty must offer certain minimum elements of protection. Warranties not meeting these requirements must be labeled as "Limited." The drafters hoped that these designations would lead to the widespread adoption of Full warranties because of competitive pressures and that further competition would ensue over the duration of Full warranty protection.[5] Of course, it was hoped that the competition over warranty protection generated by the disclosure and designation requirements would lead, ultimately, to the manufacture of products of higher quality.[6]

3. The Act seeks to enhance the substantive position of consumers relative to manufacturers. First, it amends the law of warranties in various ways. A manufacturer offering a written warranty, whether Full or Limited, is prohibited from disclaiming the implied warranties during the

written warranty's duration. In addition, warrantors are prohibited from requiring as a condition of warranty effectiveness that a buyer use any other particular product or service (the "tie-in" prohibition). And a manufacturer who offers a Full warranty (which, of course, the drafters hoped would occur) is prohibited from disclaiming the implied warranties at all. Such warranties will run, presumably, until the expiration of the statute of limitations.[7] Furthermore, the Full warrantor must either fix or replace a defective good, or refund the purchase price at no charge to the buyer.

Second, the Act attempts to improve the ability of consumers to pursue remedies for defective products. The Act empowers manufacturers to establish methods it calls "informal dispute settlement mechanisms," hopefully less cumbersome and costly than the judicial system, for more rapid and effective resolution of consumer complaints. The Act provides that once such a "mechanism" meets standards promulgated by the Federal Trade Commission, the manufacturer may preclude the consumer from bringing a civil action under the Act (but not under the Uniform Commercial Code or other state law) until resort to the "mechanism" has been exhausted.

In addition, when it becomes necessary for a consumer to seek relief in a court of law, the Act empowers courts to award attorneys' fees and court costs to successful consumer litigants. It was hoped that the award of fees and costs would stimulate warranty litigation and that greater levels of warranty litigation would cause manufacturers to improve product performance.[8]

4. Finally, the Warranty Act delegates to the Federal Trade Commission extraordinary authority to define the specific contours that the various policies and requirements of the Act will assume. The delegation to the Commission is so extensive, in fact, that it is not exaggeration to conclude that the Congress has given the Commission authority to determine whether the Act will have any effect at all. For example, many of the statute's central requirements become effective only after the Federal Trade Commission promulgates specific rules. The requirement that a warranty's terms be disclosed clearly and conspicuously is made expressly subject to rules to be determined by the Commission. The statute itself sets forth only a list of items of information and delegates to the Commission the choice of which, if any, of them are to be required disclosed.[9] Similarly, the statute charges the Commission to promulgate a rule defining the conditions under which suppliers are obliged to make the terms of warranties available to buyers prior to sale. The statute itself, however, gives no guidance as to what these conditions ought to be.[10] The minimum procedural and administrative requirements for an effective "informal dispute settlement mechanism" are left to the Commission to determine.[11]

This list does not exhaust the areas in which the Commission may determine the effectiveness of the Act. The Commission is specifically granted authority to waive in individual cases various of the statute's specific requirements. The Commission may waive the designation requirement,[12] the tie-in prohibition,[13] and the provisions acknowledging the Warranty Act's supercession of state law.[14] More important, the Act grants the Commission residual authority to impose much more significant and intrusive control over the content of product warranties. The Commission is expressly authorized to promulgate detailed substantive warranty provisions for individual products or industries.[15] Furthermore, the Commission is given express authority to redefine the minimum requirements for qualification as a Full warranty under the Act.[16] The Commission, of course, possesses primary authority to enforce the various requirements under the Federal Trade Commission Act.[17]

The wide discretion afforded the Commission is a significant aspect of the legislation. Although some delegation of definitional powers must be expected, perhaps, in any regulatory measure meant to control the behavior of manufacturers of thousands of different products, the broad delegation of the Warranty Act has never been explained or justified.

II. How the Magnuson-Moss Act has changed warranty law: the choice between a Full and a Limited warranty

This section discusses the requirements of the Warranty Act and the Commission's regulations implementing the Act, and compares them to the case law of the Uniform Commercial Code and other current law. First, Section II.A discusses the requirements of the Act that apply to all written consumer product warranties:[18] the intelligibility and disclosure requirements, the prohibition of tying arrangements, and the provision for informal dispute settlement mechanisms. Next, Sections II.B and II.C discuss the differences under the Act between Full and Limited warranties, particularly the warrantor's freedom to disclaim implied warranties, the parties entitled to sue for breach of warranty, and the remedies available upon breach.

A. Requirements for all written warranties

1. The disclosure and availability of warranty terms

The Commission has promulgated two rules regarding the provision of warranty information. The Commission's disclosure rule[19] lists six separate categories of information regarding protection that a warrantor must present in "a single document," designated "clearly and conspicuously," and drafted in "simple and readily understood language."[20] In general, the Commission has required the disclosure of the central provisions of the warranty in terms of characteristics covered, duration, allocation of costs, and limitations of liability, as well as a detailed explanation of the remedies available to disappointed consumers and the procedures that a consumer must follow to obtain them. The Commission has also required that all written warranties incorporate three paragraphs, each stating that the specific terms of the warranty may not be enforceable, depending upon state law.[21] The requirement of these paragraphs by the Commission is a peculiar method of implementing a policy of clarification and simplification of warranty terms. The paragraphs are designed, with good intentions, to suggest to consumers that their rights may not be foreclosed by specific warranty terms. But they are certain to cause substantial consumer confusion over what remedies in fact *are* available, confusion that can be reduced only by resort to legal counsel.

As mentioned, the rule requires each of the six categories of information and the three paragraphs to be disclosed "clearly and conspicuously." In addition, in separate provisions, the Act requires the limitation of consequential damages in a Full warranty, the disclaimer of implied warranties in a Limited warranty, and the very designation of each warranty as either Full or Limited for a specified duration to appear "conspicuously."[22] As of November 1979, there is no reported case law on the definition of "conspicuousness" under the Act.[23] Under the Uniform Commercial Code, however, a term is defined as "conspicuous" as a function of its apparent importance relative to other terms of the warranty. Thus, a provision is "conspicuous" if it appears as a "printed heading in capitals" or "in larger or other contrasting type or color" or written so "that a reasonable person . . . ought to have noticed it."[24] The Code's requirement of conspicuousness for the disclaimer of implied warranties, as we shall see, has played an important substantive role in consumer warranty disputes. Courts have routinely refused to give effect to central terms limiting a warrantor's liability that were not immediately apparent to consumers on the face of the document itself.[25]

The Commission's promiscuous use of the conspicuousness requirement, however, can lead only to its trivialization. The Commission and the Act require virtually *every* term of a product warranty to appear "conspicuously." A warranty, of course, would be rendered incomprehensible if the 13 or 14 provisions were required to appear "conspicuously" by way of contrasting colors or types. The requirement of uniformly conspicuous display, however, also means that a court can no longer compare the relative prominence of the more and less central terms to determine what is likely to be conspicuous to a consumer. As a consequence, the now elaborate Code case law, which has had the effect of drastically limiting a warrantor's ability to disclaim liability, is made obsolete.

The Commission has also promulgated a rule requiring warrantors and retailers of warranted products to make the texts of warranties available to consumers prior to the time of purchase.[26] The rule suggests, as one means of compliance, the posting of a warranty alongside each particular product,[27] a requirement that could impose marketing costs of extraordinary dimension. The rule, however, authorizes less drastic means of compliance, one of which is the collection of copies of the various warranties in binders. Furthermore, through publication of an advisory opinion, the Commission has indicated that the collection of warranties can be maintained on ultrafiche cards, one of which can comprise as many as 2,800 pages of information.[28]

Except for the Uniform Commercial Code's requirements of the conspicuous disclosure of warranty disclaimers[29] and occasional state consumer legislation,[30] the disclosure and presale availability requirements of the Warranty Act are novel. The requirements, at the least, will cause warrantors to redraft and repackage warranties and will cause retailers to post signs and maintain current copies. These efforts, of course, cannot be made costlessly, but the sensitivity that the Commission has shown to the exigencies of effective marketing has probably allowed these costs in the aggregate to be kept small. Currently, there are no persuasive theories available regarding the level of information about product quality and warranty protection that consumers possess prior to their purchase of the good. Thus, it is currently impossible to predict the effect of the Act's requirements on consumer product choice.

2. Warranty tying arrangements

The Magnuson-Moss Act prohibits warrantors from establishing, as a condition for the effectiveness of a warranty, that a consumer use any article or service identified by brand, trade name, or corporate name, unless the article or service is provided to the consumer without charge. The Act authorizes the Commission, however, to waive the prohibition if the warrantor can "satisfy" the Commission that the warranted product will function properly only if the tied article is used and if the Commission feels that a waiver is in the public interest.[31]

The Warranty Act's prohibition of tying arrangements is substantially more restrictive than current interpretations of the Clayton and Sherman Act[32] prohibitions of tying arrangements. The prohibition in the antitrust laws is based upon the theory that a tying arrangement is a means by which a manufacturer with market power with respect to one product can lever supracompetitive returns from sales of another product. The legal standards for proof of a violation derive from the empirical prerequisites of the theory. In general, it must be shown that a firm (1) possesses market power with respect to the tying product, (2) has exercised the power (through some form of coercion of the victim), (3) has affected some greater than *de minimus*) commerce involving the tied product.[33] In the past decade, courts have imposed very rigorous standards for the establishment of these necessary elements of an offense.[34]

The prohibition of tying arrangements in the Warranty Act requires proof of none of the three elements of the antitrust offense. It is unlikely that a tying arrangement in the context of a warranty would satisfy current requirements for proof of either market power, coercion, or effect on commerce.[35] Indeed, the prohibition of the Warranty Act is so comprehensive that it is unnecessary to even suggest that the warrantor stood to gain from the imposition of the tie. It is a violation if a warrantor specifies the product of another manufacturer with whom the warrantor has no commercial relationship. This point is not academic. In 1976, the Coleman Company, a manufacturer of mobile home furnaces, sought a waiver under the Magnuson-Moss Act for a condition of its warranty that any associated equipment that a consumer might buy (such as "conversion blowers, gas valves, limit switches," etc.) be approved by Underwriters' Laboratories, an independent testing agency, or the American Gas Association.[36] The Commission, under the Warranty Act, denied the application.[37]

If the Commission acts to enforce such a policy, its effect will be to completely extirpate tying arrangements in the context of product warranties. The Act empowers a consumer to sue only if he can prove damage,[38] but it empowers suit by the Federal Trade Commission for any violation.[39] It is less clear how the elimination of tying arrangements in warranties will affect warrantor behavior. It is difficult to argue a priori that the prohibition will significantly harm warrantors. But it is even more difficult to explain how consumers might be benefited. The theory underlying the prohibition of tying arrangements in the antitrust laws is sufficiently fragile that it is unlikely that such arrangements threaten consumer welfare even when market power appears to be significant, coercion appears obvious, and the effect on commerce great.[40] Firms that have developed complementary products or extensive specialized service facilities, however, will face greater obstacles in informing consumers of their availability and convincing consumers of their attributes.

3. Informal dispute settlement mechanisms

As explained above, disillusionment with common-law litigation as an effective means of consumer redress led the Congress to provide a structure in the Warranty Act for the institution by warrantors of informal procedures for the resolution of consumer complaints: what the Act calls "informal dispute settlement mechanisms."[41] The Act delegates to the Commission authority to define the minimum requirements for such mechanisms, and provides that if an established mechanism meets the Commission's standards, a consumer can be constrained from seeking relief under the Warranty Act in a court of law until mechanism remedies have been exhausted. The Warranty Act, however, does not give decisions by a mechanism the force of law. A mechanism's decision is only "admissible in evidence" in a subsequent legal suit.[42] The establishment of a mechanism cannot constrain a consumer from seeking relief under another state law, such as the Uniform Commercial Code, before or after resort to the mechanism.

The Commission has promulgated minimum standards for qualifying mechanisms that require a warrantor to establish a set of written procedures for the resolution of consumer disputes and a staff to administer them.[43] The staff must be insulated from interest in the dispute. No member may have "a direct involvement in the manufacture, distribution, sale or service of any product." In addition, the warrantor must commit funds in advance to finance mechanism operations. The mechanism may not levy charges on consumers. It must make decisions within 40 days of the consumer's complaint. It must maintain records on each dispute for a period of 4 years, including all the evidence introduced or compiled, and an index of disputes involving each warrantor, organized by brand name and product model. Furthermore, the warrantor must submit annually to an audit of the mechanism, reviewing the various indexes and determining whether the mechanism has complied with the Commission's standards. A report of the audit must be submitted to the Federal Trade Commission. Finally, a warrantor is required to disclose to consumers, "clearly and conspicuously," the availability of the mechanism, its procedures, and the precise actions that must be taken to prosecute a claim.

Weighed against the limited benefits to warrantors of establishing a qualifying mechanism, these various requirements seem sufficiently burdensome to deter serious consideration of the institution as a consumer dispute resolution device. Decision by the mechanism does not bind the consumer. The exhaustion requirement may postpone legal action, but by Commission rules only for 40 days, a period of trivial significance given current backlogs for civil suits. Furthermore, the effect on a jury of evidence of a mechanism decision favorable to a warrantor is problematic. Finally, since the Act does not legally bind a warrantor to a mechanism's decision, it is not obvious that consumers will regard mechanism procedures as worthwhile. Indeed, the informal dispute settlement mechanism, as an institution, possesses less actual force than the typical complaint desk. The corporate value of establishing a mechanism is comparable only to alternative forms of public relations. Yet the burdens imposed on warrantors who choose to comply with the Act's requirements are substantial. The independent funding, the assignment of a staff insulated from any involvement with the manufacture or sale of the product, the elaborate record keeping, and the submission to an annual audit represent, in sum, a significant investment of resources.[44]

It is thus not surprising to discover that, as of November 1979, Commission qualification for an informal dispute settlement mechanism has been sought by, of all the potential warrantors in the country, only one firm. And the single firm establishing a mechanism, the National Association of Home Builders,[45] had initiated a dispute settlement procedure as early as 1973, which it amended – with some difficulty[46] – to comply with the Commission's rules.

Other organizations and firms, however, have established procedures for the settlement of consumer disputes without attempting to obtain certification under the Warranty Act. Typically, these procedures differ from mechanism procedures under the Warranty Act in significant respects and resemble more the procedures of commercial arbitration.[47] The General Motors Corporation, for example, recently has tested a consumer settlement project that requires both the consumer and the dealer to submit to binding arbitration. The Ford Motor Company has established a Consumer Appeals Board, whose decisions are binding on the dealer but not on the customer. The Better Business Bureau has maintained a consumer complaint forum for many years. The adoption of such procedures by private firms suggests the existence of consumer demand for simplified methods for the resolution of disputes involving warranties. Although the Commission possesses the authority to soften the requirements it imposes on warrantors seeking certification of settlement mechanisms, it cannot – without legislative amendment – make the settlement mechanism of the Warranty Act binding on the parties and thus a more attractive substitute for civil litigation.

4. Attorneys' fees

The Warranty Act allows successful consumer plaintiffs to recover attorneys' fees and court costs for any violation of the Act.[48] The effect of an award of attorneys' fees is to stimulate litigation by plaintiffs with claims involving small dollar amounts for which, without the prospect of recovering fees, the expected judgment is less than the expected costs of obtaining it. Because consumer product warranty suits, in the absence of personal injury, involve relatively small amounts, the award of attorneys' fees may prove to be an important stimulus to litigation.

The award of fees also may influence the nature of the claims litigated. As mentioned earlier, a consumer may file suit for any violation of the

Act, but may recover only actual damages.[49] In general, the only actual damages worth recovering under the Act will be the consumer's loss from a defective product violating the Federal Minimum Standards.[50] It is likely to be very difficult for a consumer to demonstrate anything more than nominal damages for a violation of any other of the Act's provisions, such as the disclosure, designation, and presale availability requirements or the tying arrangement prohibition.

The award of attorneys' fees and court costs, of course, will not influence the level of actual damages in such cases. But enterprising attorneys, able to find plaintiffs willing to lend their names and causes of action, may find it worthwhile to prosecute such claims. It is too early to determine the influence of the Act on warranty litigation. An official of the Commission has informed me, however, that between 1976 and September 1979, attorneys' fees were awarded in every Magnuson-Moss decision.[51]

B. Differences between Full and Limited warranties in the context of the Uniform Commercial Code: disclaimers and privity

This section and the one that follows consider what is substantively the most significant aspect of the Warranty Act: the distinction between Full and Limited warranties. The Act requires Full warranties to meet the statute's Federal Minimum Standards of warranty protection (and the various regulations interpreting those standards), whereas Limited warranties, except with respect to disclaimers, must meet only the requirements of the Uniform Commercial Code. The drafters of the Warranty Act thought that the Federal Minimum Standards provided greater consumer protection than the Code did, and they hoped that competition would induce warrantors to offer Full warranties. To evaluate these efforts, it is first necessary to see how extensive the legal difference between Full and Limited warranties really is.

1. Disclaimers of implied warranties

The official text of the Uniform Commercial Code provides for the implication in every sales contract of a warranty that goods are merchantable, if the seller is a merchant with respect to goods of that kind,[52] and that the goods are fit for a particular purpose, if the seller has reason to know of the buyer's purpose and that the buyer is relying on the seller's judgment in the selection of the goods.[53] The Code also provides, however, that a written term in a contract (or in the warranty itself) excluding or modifying the duration of these warranties, will be given effect as long as it appears conspicuously, mentions "merchantability," and does not lead to an unconscionable result.[54]

The Warranty Act changed these rules. A supplier who offers a Full warranty may impose no limitation whatsoever on the duration of the implied warranties.[55] Thus, the supplier will be liable for a breach of warranty unless the product remains "merchantable" or fit for its "purpose" under the definitions of the Code until a given state's statute of limitation expires.[56] Any term in the same contract disclaiming this liability is ineffective.[57] Furthermore, the Warranty Act prohibits all other (Limited) warrantors from disclaiming the implied warranties during the duration of the written warranty.[58] Thus, under the Act, if a manufacturer offers a Limited warranty for any performance characteristic of the good for any period, and the good fails to remain merchantable and fit for its purpose as defined under the Code during that period, the manufacturer will be liable for breach of warranty. According to the text of the Uniform Commercial Code, of course, the manufacturer could have warranted a single characteristic of the good while disclaiming liability for all other characteristics including its merchantability and fitness for the buyer's purpose, as long as the disclaimer was conspicuous, mentioned "merchantability," and was not unconscionable.

As mentioned earlier, the limitation of a supplier's ability under the Code to disclaim or exclude implied warranties has been viewed as one of the principal achievements of the Warranty Act. And the prohibition on disclaimers of the implied warranties has been celebrated as significantly improving the rights of consumer–buyers relative to suppliers.[59] The effect of the Warranty Act's prohibition of disclaimers, however, has been overstated. Prior to the Act, several states, either through the enactment of separate consumer protection bills or by amendment of their versions of the Uniform Commercial Code, prohibited disclaimers of the implied warranties.[60] Because such prohibitions apply to all consumer sale contracts, their effect is equivalent to the Warranty Act's requirement for Full warranties and is broader than the Act's requirement for all other (Limited) warranties. Thus, the Warranty Act's prohibition of disclaimers will have no independent effect on the sale of consumer products within these states.[61]

Furthermore, although the Uniform Commercial Code empowers a seller to disclaim the implied warranties, courts frequently have refused to give such disclaimers effect. Indeed, in reported cases between 1965 and 1977, disclaimers of implied warranties have been held ineffective in 67 percent of cases.[62] This statistic is surprising since the Code's requirements for an effective disclaimer seem purely formal. A disclaimer must only mention "merchantability" and be "conspicuous," a requirement satisfied by appearance as "a printed heading in capitals" or "in larger or other contrasting type or color."[63] Judicial standards for compliance with these requirements, however, have been exceptionally strict. In separate cases, for example, a disclaimer has been held ineffective because inconspicuous where the disclaimer appeared only in a separate "Warranty Facts" book,[64] appeared only on the final page of such a book,[65] and notwithstanding the underscoring of the disclaimer in the contract.[66] This case law, together with the special legislation of the various states, of course, suggests that the effect of the Magnuson-Moss Act's provisions prohibiting disclaimers of the implied warranties is not likely to constitute either the significant addition to consumer rights or the burden to suppliers that might otherwise have been expected.

2. Privity of contract

The Uniform Commercial Code offers three alternative provisions dealing with rights of action for breach of warranty of individuals not party to the sale contract.[67] Each alternative provision has some support, but many states have adopted individual variations. The provision most commonly adopted is the most restrictive, alternative A, in force in 25 jurisdictions. It empowers suits by persons in the buyer's family or household and guests "who may reasonably be expected to use, consume or be affected by the goods" if the person has suffered injury to his person. In 21 other jurisdictions, however, at the minimum, a suit may be brought by *any* person "who may reasonably be expected to use, consume or be affected by the goods" where either personal or property injury is suffered.

The Magnuson-Moss Act does nothing to reconcile these individual state differences, but it extends a right of action to a set of consumers who, prior to the Act's passage, faced great difficulties bringing suit: transferees of the buyer, including bailees, lessees, and vendees.[68] Most readings of the various Code privity provisions preclude these persons from bringing suit.[69] Indeed, even in jurisdictions that have attempted to eliminate privity requirements altogether, it is difficult for vendees and lessees to recover, because the subsequent sale or lease generally establishes a separate and independent allocation of risks.[70] In empirical terms, the most significant of those granted rights of action by the Magnuson-Moss Act would be vendees and purchasers of used consumer goods.[71] Thus, the Act's extension of rights of actions is most likely to influence the warranty policies respecting goods for which secondhand markets exist.

C. Differences between Full and Limited warranties in the context of the Uniform Commercial Code: breach and remedy under Full and Limited warranties

The most significant distinction between Full and Limited warranties under the Magnuson-Moss Act concerns the standards for determining breach of warranty and the remedies available to a consumer once the warranty has been breached. Consumers buying products with Limited warranties must rely solely on the standards and remedies of the Uniform Commercial Code. Consumers buying products with Full warranties, on the other hand, may invoke the standards and remedies of the Act's Federal Minimum Standards.[72] These standards include a prohibition of the placement of any duty on a consumer as a condition of recovery beyond notification of the defect, unless the duty is shown to the Commission to be "reasonable." The Commission, in 1977, proposed a rule defining eight "duties" that it would consider unreasonable and violative of the Act.[73] As of November 1979, the Commission's promulgation of a final Reasonable Duties rule is imminent. The rule, I am informed, will closely resemble the 1977 Proposed Rule.[74]

1. Standards for recovery: the issue of breach

a. The notification requirement. The Warranty Act's Federal Minimum Standards acknowledge that notification may be required of a consumer as a condition for securing a remedy,[75] but the Federal Trade Commission has specified in its proposed Reasonable Duties rules that a warrantor may not require that the consumer's notice be in writing.[76] If a warrantor offers a Full warranty, "any communication reasonably calculated to inform the warrantor of the defect" will constitute sufficient notice. The Uniform Commercial Code, on the other hand, sets forth very clearly that notification of the seller is a condition for both rejection and revocation of acceptance, although the Code does not make clear whether the notification must be in writing.[77]

Formal manifestation of a notice of rejection or revocation of acceptance, however, has never been an important issue in the courts. Some decisions interpreting the Code have allowed a buyer to return defective goods to the seller even though there was no communication between them that could reasonably be construed as a notification of the defect. In *Testo v. Russ Dunmire Oldsmobile, Inc.*[78] and *Fenton v. Contemporary Dev. Co.,*[79] the notification requirement was found to be satisfied by the buyer's filing suit and refusing to allow the seller to cure (repair). In another case, the notice requirement was satisfied by vague complaints and a refusal to continue payments.[80]

Although there have been Code decisions denying rejection where the buyer failed to notify the seller,[81] a broader view suggests that the Code's notification requirement has been invoked chiefly where the buyer's response to the discovery of a defect or the nature of his complaints to the seller provides evidence of the conformity of the goods with the warranties of the contract.[82] If this is the function that courts have given the notification requirement of the Code, the concerns of the Commission's Reasonable Duties rule are misplaced, because it is irrelevant whether or not the buyer's communication is in writing.

b. The reasonable time requirement. The Uniform Commercial Code requires generally that a buyer notify the warrantor of the defect within a reasonable period.[83] Consistent with its general policy of freedom of contract, however, the Code gives effect to any particular period of time for the buyer's notification established in the sale contract. The Warranty Act may be read, similarly, as establishing a requirement that a consumer notify the warrantor within a reasonable time of discovering the defect.[84] The Commission, however, has explained that it feels consumers buying products with Full warranties must be protected from the imposition by warrantors of restrictive time limitations for notice.[85] Thus, in its Reasonable Duties rule, the Commission has prohibited parties from agreeing on any specific time for the buyer's notification unless the period is found to be "reasonable."[86]

As a general matter, however, courts applying the Code's provisions have not enforced such time restrictions without regard to the reasonableness of the restriction, given the necessities of the seller and the burdens on the buyer.[87] Rather, the Code's reasonable time requirement has served two functions. First, the requirement has allowed courts to place incentives on the parties to discover defects and notify the warrantor within an efficient period of time, weighing the costs to the buyer of discovery against the costs to the seller of delay. Second, the requirement, like the notification requirement, has been invoked where the time or manner of the buyer's rejection or revocation has indicated that the tender, although alleged to be defective, actually complies with the contract.[88] Indeed, between 1954 and 1976, the Code's reasonable time requirement has *never* been invoked to deny rejection or revocation of acceptance by a consumer buyer.[89] Thus, the restrictive interpretation of the Commission's Reasonable Duties rule will only duplicate standards developed in Code litigation.

c. Damage by the buyer or his unreasonable use. The Federal Minimum Standards for Full warranties provide that a warrantor may defend an action for breach "if he can show that the defect, malfunction, or failure of [the] product to conform with a written warranty was caused by damage (not resulting from defect or malfunction) while in the possession of the consumer, or [from the consumer's] unreasonable use. . . ."[90] There are two analogous provisions of the Uniform Commercial Code that control products covered by Limited warranties. The Code provides that a buyer may not reject goods "if he does any act inconsistent with the seller's ownership" of them.[91] Furthermore, a buyer may not revoke acceptance of goods if there has occurred "any substantial change in condition of the goods which is not caused by their own defects."[92]

The Code's "act-inconsistent" provision has been invoked in two sets of cases: when the buyer's actions with respect to the goods – for example, his continued use of or payment for the goods after rejection – has indicated either that the goods conform to his purposes,[93] or that the goods, although defective, are more valuable to the buyer than to the seller for resale.[94] In the first set of cases, denying rejection simply enforces the terms of the contract; and in the second set, it reduces the joint costs to the parties, because it is cheaper, for the buyer and seller jointly, for the buyer to keep the goods and recover damages than to reject and force their resale by the seller.

The act-inconsistent provision, however, can be invoked only when the buyer attempts to reject the goods and is inapplicable when the buyer admits his acceptance but claims to revoke it.[95] No analogous Code provision empowers a court to deny revocation of acceptance based upon subsequent *actions* of the buyer with respect to the goods. The provision prohibiting revocation after a "substantial change in condition of the goods" is available, but because the provision focuses on changes in the goods themselves rather than on the behavior of the buyer, it is not always apposite and has been employed only infrequently.[96]

In many respects, it is more critical in revocation of acceptance than in rejection cases for a court to superintend the buyer's actions. In general, the stakes are higher in revocation cases than in rejection cases because the buyer, at the time of revocation, has used the goods for his own purposes for some period of time. Not only will the goods have depreciated, but they often will have been altered by the buyer to better fit his needs prior to the discovery of the defect. As a result, the seller, required by the Code to return the purchase price and reclaim the defective goods, will suffer typically a greater loss where the buyer revokes acceptance than where he rejects. Since ultimately the parties will be affected by the costs of breach of warranty, it may be appropriate for courts to minimize costs by examining the implications on the issues of breach and remedy of the buyer's actions with respect to goods claimed to be defective. Indeed, courts have responded to the statutory omission of a revocation provision focusing attention on the buyer's use of defective goods by creating a novel doctrine of the buyer's "waiver" of the right to revoke, by actions similar to those found "inconsistent with the seller's ownership" in rejection cases.[97]

The "unreasonable use" defense of the Federal Minimum Standards for Full warranties differs from the Code's provisions in substantial respects. First, the Standards shift the burden to the seller to prove the effect of the buyer's unreasonable use. More important, the Standards provide a defense only when the unreasonable use of the buyer has *caused* the defect. Under the Code, uses of the buyer that have been found sufficient to preclude rejection and revocation of acceptance are not only uses that cause disrepair, but also uses that indicate that the goods conform to the buyer's original purposes and that rescission by the buyer is not the appropriate remedy. As a consequence, when products are covered by Full rather than by Limited warranties, it is less likely that a buyer will be held to have waived his right of rescission because of subsequent use of the goods.

    d. Additional requirements for rescission affecting Limited warranties. There are two further limitations on a buyer's rescission under the Uniform Commercial Code that are absent from the Federal Minimum Standards. To revoke acceptance under the Code, a buyer must show that he accepted the goods without knowledge of the defect and that the defect substantially impairs the value of the goods to him.[98] It is not likely, however, that either of these restrictions will differentially affect consumer recoveries under Full or Limited warranties.

    Technically, a warrantor offering a Full warranty is required by the Act to remedy a defective product although the buyer purchased the goods knowing of the defect. Had the warrantor offered a Limited warranty, of course, the Code would provide a complete defense. Even under the Federal Minimum Standards, however, the warrantor, if conscious of the defect, may retract the Full warranty and either sell the product "as is," that is, without a warranty, or subject to a Limited warranty. Thus, the Code provision will only be of advantage to a warrantor where the consumer possesses knowledge about the product that the warrantor does not. And it is not implausible in such contexts that the common-law concepts of assumption of risk and commercial fair dealing might lead a court to deny recovery, notwithstanding the letter of the Federal Minimum Standards.

    The Code provision requiring the showing of a substantial impairment of value to the buyer is likely to be subjected to similar treatment. Although the requirement has been litigated frequently, it has been invoked in Code decisions chiefly to deny revocation when the defect in the goods has appeared trivial.[99] Furthermore, the Code case law shows that however convenient the substantiality requirement may be as a legal ground for such a decision, there are other means by which courts can deny recovery for trivial defects. The Code's rejection provision, for example, does not incorporate a substantiality requirement, but courts, similarly, have refused rejection for trivial defects,[100] principally by construction of the contract.[101] In every rescission case, a court must determine whether or not the tendered goods conform to the description in the contract or, more broadly, to the parties' agreement. To conclude that a defect is trivial is to decide only that the goods conform in all essential respects. Although the Federal Minimum Standards fail to incorporate a substantiality of defect requirement, courts applying them must still decide whether or not the goods are in fact defective or fail to conform to the warranty.[102] Thus, products covered by Full warranties under the Minimum Standards are likely to be subjected to the same scrutiny as are products covered by Limited warranties under the Code.

2. Remedies for breach

a. Cure of defective tender. Both the Uniform Commercial Code and the Federal Minimum Standards provide the opportunity for the seller to cure (repair) a defective tender prior to the institution of litigation by the buyer. The potential advantages of the seller's cure to both parties is apparent. The buyer is saved the costs of shopping for a replacement. The seller saves the difference between the costs of cure and either the diminution in the value of the goods because of the defect and because of depreciation while in the buyer's possession if the buyer has sought damages, or the diminution in value plus the costs of resale if the buyer has sought rescission. These savings, however, only indicate why the parties might agree for the seller to cure the defect. Where the seller's right to cure is institutionalized for all cases, other problems develop.

In general, it is advantageous for a buyer who has discovered a defect in the goods to rescind the contract and recover the purchase price rather than to seek damages where between the time of agreement and the discovery of the defect, the price of the goods has declined, or the buyer has obtained new information about the goods showing them to be unsuitable for his purposes. The Code, however, does not empower the seller to recover damages (for the difference in value) in such cases. Thus, to the extent that buyers are successful in rescinding in these circumstances, the risk of a decline in the market price and the risk of the inappropriateness of the goods – risks normally borne in a sales contract by the buyer – are shifted to the seller. In fact, a buyer in such a case has an incentive to conjure up defects or to exaggerate the materiality of real defects in order to justify rescission.

The gain to a buyer from rescission, of course, represents a loss to the seller, and sellers can be expected under such conditions to attempt to prevent the buyer's rescission. One method of preventing rescission under the Uniform Commercial Code, for example, is by curing the defect. But the seller's cure in such a case may no longer reduce the joint costs of breach. When the price of the goods or the buyer's information about the goods has remained constant, the diminution in the value of the goods because of the defect establishes an upward constraint on the seller's investment in cure that is consistent with joint maximization of value. When the market price has declined, or when the goods have depreciated while in the hands of the buyer, the seller faces an incentive to invest additional amounts in cure, which may, in sum, be greater than the joint value to the parties of the investment.

The Uniform Commercial Code gives the seller an absolute right to cure a defect either before the time for performance or for "a further reasonable time" if the seller had reasonable grounds to believe that the initial tender would be acceptable.[103] Courts have enforced this right when buyers have attempted to refuse the seller's cure.[104] Courts possess scant authority under the Code, however, to control a seller's excessive investment in cure. Prior to the time for performance, there are no limits to a seller's cure. There are decisions, however, holding that a seller did not complete cure within the "further reasonable time" that the Code allows when the seller believed that the initial tender would be acceptable.[105] To date, however, courts have announced such holdings only in cases in which sellers have made what appear to be exceptionally extravagant investments in cure. Thus, the Code's cure provision has not yet provided a carefully designed constraint on the level of the seller's investment in cure.[106]

The provisions of the Federal Minimum Standards that address the seller's cure reverse the positions of the sellers and buyers under the Code. Like the Code, the Act gives a warrantor a right to cure defects.[107] But the Federal Minimum Standards provide that a consumer may insist upon refund or replacement of defective goods "after a reasonable number of attempts by the warrantor to remedy" the defect.[108] The focus of the Federal Minimum Standards on the number of attempts by the seller may enable closer judicial supervision of the seller's investment in cure than the Code's focus on the passage of time after the buyer's complaint.

The Federal Minimum Standards, however, create a novel difficulty in the definition of "remedy." A consumer's remedy for breach of a Full warranty is repair, replacement of the defective product, or, finally, refund of the purchase price. A warrantor may refund the price to the consumer, however, only if he "is unable to provide replacement" *and* if "repair is not commercially practicable" or will be untimely.[109] The Federal Minimum Standards do not provide for recovery of damages by consumers and, in fact, specifically preempt the Code's damage remedies that otherwise might be available.[110]

The remedies of the Federal Minimum Standards will be indistinguishable from those of the Code when the price of the goods has declined subsequent to the agreement. But when the price of the goods has increased, the consumer will be in the position under the Federal Minimum

Standards of the seller under the Code. Where price has increased, the *seller* will prefer to refund the original price and to sell the goods after repair at the higher market price. Under the Code, the buyer upon breach could recover damages equal to the difference between the contract price and market price in addition to refund.[111] The buyer cannot recover such damages, however, under the Federal Minimum Standards, just as the seller, in the reciprocal situation, could not recover damages under the Code where the price of the goods declined subsequent to the agreement. Thus, under the Federal Minimum Standards, the consumer will face the incentive to insist on excessive and extravagant investments in cure that the seller faced under the Code. As a consequence, in an economy more characterized by increasing than declining prices, the consumer is in a less advantageous position under a Full warranty than under a Limited warranty.

b. Incidental charges to the consumer. The Warranty Act requires, where a Full warranty is offered, that a warrantor remedy a defect "without charge" to the consumer[112] and prescribes that if repair requires the replacement of a component part of a consumer product, the remedy under the Federal Minimum Standards "shall include installing the part in the product without charge."[113] These provisions seem to require a warrantor to bear the costs of the parts and labor necessary to effect the repair. Liability for incidental costs, however, is ambiguous under the Warranty Act. One central provision of the Standards specifies that a warrantor "shall not impose any duty other than notification upon any consumer as a condition for securing [a] remedy,"[114] suggesting that the warrantor may not require the consumer to incur expenses such as shipping the defective product to the warrantor for repair. But a subsequent section qualifies this reading by interpreting the Standards as "not necessarily requir[ing] the warrantor to compensate the consumer for incidental expenses."[115]

The Commission has attempted to resolve this ambiguity by proposing a rule defining the "duties" of consumers that it considers reasonable under the Federal Minimum Standards.[116] The rule places liability for incidental expenses on the warrantor, who must either incur (or reimburse the consumer for incurring) the costs of mailing or shipping the defective product for repair.[117] In addition, if the product weighs more than 35 pounds, possesses "hazardous handling characteristics" (such as sharp edges), or is not designed "for convenient handling," the warrantor must arrange for shipment of the product.[118] Similarly, if the product is built-in, the warrantor must arrange for its removal and its reinstallation, unless these tasks can be performed "by the average consumer without special tools, skills or [and?] without the expenditure of a substantial amount of time."[119]

It is interesting to note that the same responsibilities are placed, in the first instance, on warrantors by the Uniform Commercial Code, applicable to sales of products with Limited warranties. The Code clearly provides that the only "duty" of a buyer after rejection or revocation of acceptance is to hold the defective goods, "with reasonable care, at the seller's disposition for a time sufficient to permit the *seller* to remove them" (emphasis added).[120] Furthermore, the expenses that a buyer may recover from a seller are perhaps more extensive under the Code than under the Commission's proposed Reasonable Duties rule. A buyer may recover "expenses reasonably incurred in inspection, receipt, transportation and care and custody of goods," as well as "any other reasonable expense incident to the . . . breach."[121]

The chief difference between the Code and the Federal Minimum Standards, however, is that the Code allows the buyer and seller to amend their contract to place the burden of incidental expenses on the buyer. The Federal Minimum Standards, on the other hand, require that a firm offering a Full warranty bear all these expenses.[122] As a result, any agreement between the parties with respect to the costs of shipment or repair will be ineffective.

As we shall see in Section III, prior to the Warranty Act, a substantial number of manufacturers incorporated provisions in warranties placing the burden of the costs of transporting defective goods and other incidental expenses on buyers. Although the drafters of the Warranty Act were suspicious of unilateral "agreements" of that nature, it is not implausible, in many cases, that the total costs to the parties will be lower if the buyer bears them than if the seller does. Certainly, buyers, in general, possess better information than manufacturers (although perhaps not than retailers) of the most convenient means of shipping products from their homes or particular communities. Furthermore, where a product must be built-in to an existing structure, it is plausible that the buyer will be in a better position than the seller to choose a location and a method of installation for the product that minimizes costs. Where the seller must reimburse all costs of removal and installation should the product prove defective, the buyer has no incentive to choose a location for the product that optimizes the seller's costs of removal and the buyer's costs of convenience. Of course, if the joint costs to the parties are lower when liability is placed on the buyer, both parties will be better off by arranging for such an assignment of liability. Consumers on average will be fully compensated for their expenditures because the *full cost* of the product will be lower. Thus, to the extent that there are efficiencies in placing liability for incidental expenses on buyers of particular products, manufacturers of these products are less likely to benefit from offering Full warranties rather than Limited warranties.

c. Measuring the refund. At common law, the rescission of a sales contract required the restoration of the status quo prior to the contract: the buyer was required to return the goods and the seller to return the purchase price. In some cases, however, courts modified this general remedy by allowing the seller to deduct from the purchase price the value of the buyer's use of the property between performance and rescission. Such deductions were made routinely in judgments rescinding land sale contracts, where the buyer had occupied the land subsequent to performance,[123] and not infrequently in judgments rescinding service contracts, such as insurance contracts, where the buyer had received services subsequent to performance.[124] Deduction of the value of the buyer's use was unusual, however, in the rescission of sales contracts, largely, in my view, because of the common law requirement in sales cases that a rescinding buyer tender the goods in the same condition in which received.[125] Although a rental value could probably have been computed for most goods, if the buyer had not made use of them, consideration of a deduction seemed academic.

The Uniform Commercial Code relaxed the requirement that a rescinding buyer tender goods exactly in the condition in which received, perhaps because of the perception that as the complexity of products increases, the difficulty increases of discovering defects in them prior to acceptance and use. By the Code remedy of revocation of acceptance, a buyer may rescind a contract for the sale of goods after substantial use, if he can show that the defect was difficult to discover.[126] And there have been Code decisions granting rescission after periods of use as long as two years.[127]

The Uniform Commercial Code, however, did not amend the common law rule in sale of goods cases denying deduction of the buyer's use. There is no Code provision to authorize the deduction of the value received by the buyer during possession prior to rescission. Thus, a rescinding buyer gains a private benefit equal to the value of the use of the goods. This private benefit to the buyer is unrelated to the seller's breach. A breaching seller suffers the full loss from the breach by being forced to repay the full purchase price in exchange for the defective goods.

Courts applying the Uniform Commercial Code have not been insensitive to the additional loss suffered by a seller where the buyer has used the goods prior to rescission. But the comprehensive provision of damage remedies in the Code and the notable absence of a provision authorizing deduction have proven to be significant constraints. In many cases involving substantial use by the buyer, courts have denied rescission despite the presence of defects, relegating the buyer to the recovery of damages.[128] In these cases, the buyers are made to suffer for the absence of a deduction provision in the Code. In a few jurisdictions, however – at current count, eight – courts have deducted amounts equal to the value of the buyer's use, notwithstanding the Code's failure to empower such a remedy.[129]

It appeared that the Warranty Act would correct the Code's statutory omission, at least with respect to products sold with Full warranties. The drafters of the Warranty Act defined the remedy of "refund" in the context of the Federal Minimum Standards as equal to the original purchase price "less reasonable depreciation based on actual use where permitted by rules of the Commission."[130] In 1976, the Commission proposed a depreciation rule[131] that, although peculiar in some respects,[132] would have largely removed the incentives that buyers otherwise face of rescinding after using the product. The Federal Trade Commission, however, has decided not to promulgate a final Depreciation rule.[133] Thus, far from reforming the Code's provisions, at least for Full warranties, the Federal Minimum Standards exacerbate the problem, because the Warranty Act clearly precludes a court from allowing a deduction and precludes the parties from agreeing to a deduction under a Full warranty until the Commission has promulgated a rule. If a warrantor offers a Limited warranty, of course, he retains the possibility of obtaining a deduction under the Uniform Commercial Code or of incorporating a provision in the warranty agreeing to a deduction. The Commission's reluctance to promulgate a rule thus makes a Full warranty less attractive than a Limited warranty not only to manufacturers but also to consumers.

D. Summary

This section has shown that the net effect of the Magnuson-Moss Act on the law of warranties has been modest. Although there are some changes with respect to tying arrangements and disclaimers of the implied warranties, the most significant effects of the Act are the requirements that warrantors redraft warranties to make them understandable, to disclose terms more fully, and to make warranties available to consumers prior to sale. If warranty practices are sensitive to the information that consumers possess about warranty terms and to consumer preferences (as the drafters of the Act believed), these provisions may have a substantial effect.[134] Currently, however, we have no theory with which to estimate what the effect will be.

III. The Magnuson-Moss Act and specific warranty terms: warranties for consumer durables, 1974 and 1978

This section examines the effects of the Magnuson-Moss Act in a manner different from that of the preceding section. It presents the preliminary results of a comparison of the provisions of warranties of 43 consumer products offered in 1974, prior to the enactment of the Magnuson-Moss Act, with warranties of the same products offered in 1978, a year and a half after the Act's implementation.[135] The study compares warranties, principally, of the major consumer durables: refrigerators, freezers, ranges, washers and dryers, air conditioners, television and stereo sets, automobiles, mobile homes, travel trailers, recreational vehicles, and coaches. Because the sample is limited to warranties of durables, it is probably not representative of the written warranties of all products. But it is likely that the sample describes the warranties attending a large proportion of consumer purchases weighted by dollar volume.

It is important to appreciate the difficulty of attributing any observed changes in warranty provisions to the Magnuson-Moss Act itself and thus the necessarily limited and preliminary nature of the findings. The Act, as we have seen, places certain direct limitations on warranty provisions, such as limitations on the availability of disclaimers of the implied warranties, of restrictions of coverage to the original purchaser, and so forth. With a single exception, however, these limitations are only effective if the warrantor offers a Full rather than a Limited warranty. Since the Act leaves the warrantor free to choose between Full and Limited coverage, it is possible that the warranties in the sample will not change at all subsequent to the Act, except for the single exception of the limitation on Limited warranties with respect to disclaimers of the implied warranties. More generally, we might predict that those warrantors who find valuable specific provisions prohibited by the Federal Minimum Standards are less likely to adopt Full warranties. There are no current theories, however, suggesting why one provision or another might be more or less valuable to a warrantor of a particular product. In the absence of such a theory, of course, we cannot confidently attribute any change observed in warranty provisions before and after the Act to the Act itself, as opposed to other changes in the costs of or demand for coverage of which we have no evidence.

As indicated in Section II, the most significant change of law of the Magnuson-Moss Act that affects warranties for all products is the extensive requirement of disclosure, designation, and simplification of warranty terms and the requirement that warranties be made available to consumers prior to the time of purchase. The justification for such requirements, of course, is the belief that more warranty information will lead to different product choices by consumers in response to the greater information available, and to enhanced competition between warrantors over warranty terms. Unfortunately again, however, we lack a theory explaining consumer choice of warranty coverage. Thus, again, it is difficult to determine which changes observed in warranty provisions, if any, may be attributed to the Magnuson-Moss Act itself.

Table 14.1. *Content of product warranties, 1974 and 1978*

1. Duration
   Product groups with firms increasing: electric ranges, stereo sets, automobiles, mobile homes, recreational vehicles, coaches

   Product groups with firms decreasing: freezers, washers, air conditioners, television sets, travel trailers

   Mixed changes: refrigerators

   Product groups with no change: cookware, gas ranges, dryers

	Number of firms incorporating	
	1974	*1978*
2. Disclaimers or limitations (1978) of implied warranties	17	15
3. Exclusion of consequential damages	14	31
4. Exclusion of incidental damages	7	20
5. Limitation to original purchaser	19	15
6. Transport charges to buyer	28	20
7. Registration card required	12	4
8. Authorized service center only	34	28
9. Coverage limited to home use	16	15
10. Appeal process (Major Appliance Center Action Panel)	4	0
Total firms = 43		

Source: Warranties provided by the Federal Trade Commission, June 1978.

Table 14.1 indicates how, in general, the provisions of consumer product warranties changed after the enactment of the Warranty Act. It presents the total number of warranties within the 1974 and 1978 samples in which, for example, implied warranties were disclaimed (in 1974) or limited (in 1978) (row 2) or consequential damages were excluded (row 3).

Row 1 shows changes in the duration of warranty coverage and indicates the product groups in which at least one firm changed the duration of its coverage. The duration of coverage cannot be standardized because of differences in coverage of individual product characteristics and in coverage for subsequent parts and labor expenses. We may observe, however, that within six product groups, the only changes were increases in duration; within five product groups, decreases; within one product group, the changes were mixed; and there were no changes in duration within three product groups. If one believed that warrantors sought to achieve some constant level of payouts over the two periods, one might attribute the decreases in warranty duration to the other of the Act's restrictions on warrantors. The (slightly) more extensive increases in duration, however, are inconsistent with this explanation. On the other hand, one might attribute the changes to more informed consumer choice in response to increased disclosure and simplification of warranty terms. This hypothesis, however, does not explain changes across product groups, such as why a television warrantor decreased duration and a stereo warrantor increased duration. In sum, we have no basis for attributing the changes in warranty duration to the Act itself.

Table 14.1 shows that for the principal provisions defining liability and remedies – the provisions disclaiming the implied warranties and excluding consequential and incidental damages (rows 2 to 4) – there have occurred very curious changes. Although the number of firms disclaiming the implied warranties or, in 1978, limiting them to the duration of the warranty, has declined, the number excluding consequential and incidental damages has increased dramatically. Firms offering Full warranties, of course, are prohibited from any form of disclaimer of the implied warranties, which may account for the decline in frequency of that provision. The sharp increase in the exclusion of damages, however, may represent a response.[136]

Rows 5 to 7 address provisions directly affected by the choice between a Full and a Limited warranty. Manufacturers offering Full warranties may not limit coverage to the original purchaser (row 5), assess transportation charges to the buyer (row 6), or require submission of a registration card as a condition of coverage (row 7). Table 14.1 indicates that the frequency of each of the provisions has declined in 1978, which may represent a direct effect of the Act. The analysis of the decline in the assessment of transport charges to the buyer (row 6), however, must be qualified. The specific assessment of transportation charges achieves an effect similar to the exclusion of incidental damages. Although the number of warranties including the former provision (row 6) has declined, the number of warranties including the latter provision (row 4) has increased, and increased by a greater amount. The net effect is in doubt.

The Act provides that a Full warrantor may not condition coverage on the use of any particular service unless the service is provided without charge. Row 8 indicates some decline in the frequency of such a restriction. Row 9 shows an incidental decline in the limitation of coverage to domestic use of the product. Finally, the Act seems to have caused manufacturers to withdraw provisions in warranties for the reference of consumer disputes to the Major Appliance Center Action Panel (MACAP), sponsored by a group of manufacturing trade associates (row 10). It is likely, however, that reference to the panel has been deleted, because MACAP has not sought qualification as an "informal dispute settlement mechanism" under the Act. Thus, the deletion of these provisions does not necessarily indicate that fewer manufacturers are making use of

MACAP, or other informal processes not qualifying under the Act, for the resolution of consumer disputes.

In sum, if the composite figures in Table 14.1 are representative of the level of consumer warranty protection, the Magnuson-Moss Act can be concluded to have had some positive effect on the position of consumers, but an effect that is probably modest.[137] The Act seems to have made warranty provisions regarding transportation charges, the submission of registration cards, and the required use of authorized service centers more favorable to consumers. In addition, the disclaimer of implied warranties, already constrained by judicial interpretation of the Uniform Commercial Code, has diminished in frequency and, of course, in effectiveness even under a Limited warranty.

It is not evident, however, that these particular changes constitute a significant advance for consumer interests. The authorized service center requirement and the assessment of the costs of transporting the defective product to the repair shop cannot be regarded as major burdens on consumers. And the registration card requirement appeared relatively infrequently in warranties prior to the Act (in 28 percent of them). It seems, as a first approximation, an equally significant consequence of the Act that the number of firms excluding liability for consequential and incidental damages has greatly increased.

To this point, we have not considered a warrantor's choice between a Full and Limited warranty under the Magnuson-Moss Act. Of the 43 warrantors represented in the sample, 20 adopted Full warranties and 23 adopted Limited warranties. For five product groups – cookware, refrigerators, freezers, washers, and dryers – each of the firms in the sample adopted a Full warranty.[138] For five other product groups – television sets, stereo sets, travel trailers, recreational vehicles, and coaches – each of the firms adopted a Limited warranty. In the remaining five product groups, the adoptions of the firms were mixed.

Table 14.2 provides a better indication of some of the characteristics of firms that adopted Full and Limited warranties. It segregates firms imposing particular restrictions in 1974 warranties by whether they offered Full or Limited warranties in 1978. Table 14.2 indicates, for example, that of the 17 firms disclaiming the implied warranties in 1974 (row 1), 6 offered Full and 11 offered Limited warranties in 1978.

Table 14.2, first, confirms the suppositions drawn from Table 14.1. We know, of course, that the Federal Minimum Standards for Full warranties prohibits the inclusion in 1978 Full warranties of disclaimers of implied warranties (row 1), limitations on coverage to the original purchaser (row 4), the imposition of transport charges to the buyer (row 5), and the requirement of submission of a registration card (row 6). Thus, the decline

Table 14.2. *Firms imposing restrictions in 1974 by offer of Full or Limited warranty in 1978 (number and proportion)*

	(1) Total number imposing (1974)	(2) 1978 Full warrantors (total = 20) Number imposing	(3) Percent of 20	(4) 1978 Limited warrantors (total = 23) Number imposing	(5) Percent of 23
1. Disclaimer of implied warranties	17	6	30	11	48
2. Exclusion of consequential damages	14	4	20	10	43
3. Exclusion of incidental damages	7	4	20	3	13
4. Limitation to original purchaser	19	5	25	14	61
5. Transport charges to buyer	28	8	40	20	87
6. Registration card required	12	4	20	8	35
7. Authorized service center only	34	11	55	23	100
8. Coverage limited to home use	16	11	55	5	22
Composite proportion, all restrictions			32		53

Source: Warranties provided by the Federal Trade Commission, June 1978.

in the frequency of these various provisions between 1974 and 1978 can now be directly attributed to the Act. Because they chose to offer Full warranties in 1978, the six, five, eight, and four firms, respectively, that imposed the various provisions in 1974 (column 2) could not impose them in 1978. It should be noted, however, that the frequency of each of these provisions declined between 1974 and 1978 by *less* than the number of firms offering Full warranties in 1978. Thus, some firms must have added new and additional restrictions to their Limited warranties in 1978, subsequent to the Act.

Table 14.2 indicates, second, the extent to which, in general, the imposition of a particular restriction by a firm in 1974 made the choice more likely in 1978 of a Limited than of a Full warranty. For example, of the 19 firms that limited coverage to the original purchaser in 1974 (row 4), 5 chose Full warranties in 1978 and 14 chose Limited warranties. Similarly, of firms imposing transport charges on the buyer, 8 chose Full and 20 Limited warranties in 1978. Table 14.2 also suggests the relative significance of individual provisions to Full and Limited warrantors. Thus, com-

Table 14.3. *Disclaimers of the implied warranties and exclusions of damages, 1974 and 1978, by firms offering Full warranties in 1978 (of 20 firms)*

	Number of firms (1974)	Number of firms (1978)
1. Disclaimers of the implied war-ranties	6	0
2. Transport charges to the buyer	8	0
3. Exclusion of consequential dam-ages	4	14
4. Exclusion of incidential damages	4	9

Source: Warranties provided by the Federal Trade Commission, June 1978.

paring columns 3 and 5, we may observe that 55 percent of firms offering Full warranties required service at an authorized center, whereas 100 percent of firms offering Limited warranties imposed such a requirement. Similarly, 87 percent of firms offering Limited warranties imposed transport charges on buyers in 1974, whereas only 40 percent of firms offering Full warranties imposed such charges in 1974. These results again suggest, as a general proposition, as we might expect, that firms offering relatively more liberal coverage in 1974 were more likely to offer Full than Limited warranties in 1978. Surprisingly, row 8 indicates that of the 16 firms limiting coverage to home use, 11 chose Full and 5 Limited warranties in 1978. This finding suggests that the home-use restriction is product-specific rather than a general characteristic of liberal or restrictive warranty policy.

Finally, Table 14.3 directly investigates whether the changes in warranty terms subsequent to the Act that are adverse to consumers, including the increases in exclusions of consequential and incidental damages, are related to restrictions placed on warrantors by the Federal Minimum Standards.[139] Table 14.3 shows, for those firms offering Full warranties in 1978, the frequency of disclaimers of the implied warranties, impositions of transport charges on buyers, and exclusions of consequential and incidental damages in 1974 and 1978. The Federal Minimum Standards, of course, prohibit Full warrantors from disclaiming the implied warranties and from allocating transport charges to buyers, and Table 14.3 indicates the direct effect of the prohibition (rows 1 and 2).

We have observed earlier, however, that the exclusion of incidental damages is closely related to the allocation of transport costs to the buyer, because transport costs are one of the elements of incidental damages in the law. Table 14.3 indicates that there has occurred a dramatic increase in the exclusion of such damages by Full warrantors subsequent to the

Act (from 20 to 45 percent of those firms), an increase that appears more plausibly now to be a response to the restrictions of the Federal Minimum Standards.

There is a similar relationship between consequential damages and the implied warranties. The implied warranties constitute a general obligation (to be defined by the courts) with respect to product defects.[140] These general obligations are likely to be more significant to firms that face large damage judgments when products are defective. Consequential damages, of course, are all losses beyond the value of the defective product itself. Thus, firms prohibited by the Federal Minimum Standards from limiting their general liability by a disclaimer of implied warranties would seem to be the firms that would find the exclusion of consequential damages more advantageous. A comparison of rows 1 and 3 of Table 14.3 indicates what appears to be a response to the Federal Minimum Standards. Six firms removed disclaimers of the implied warranties in 1978, but an additional ten firms added exclusions of consequential damages.

IV. Conclusions

Although the Magnuson-Moss Act has been trumpeted as a major reform of the law of consumer warranties,[141] the legal analysis of Section II and the empirical analysis of Section III suggest that the Act has had only a limited influence on the level of warranty protection. The empirical findings of Section III are preliminary and alone are insufficient to support such a claim. But the legal analysis of Section II suggests a similar conclusion. The Magnuson-Moss Act has changed the details of warranty law but not the substance. It has, of course, required the redrafting and repackaging of consumer warranties, has changed some aspects of the law of tying arrangements, and allows for the recovery of fees and costs. Although the Act appears to grant new remedial opportunities to consumers, however, its provisions, once litigated, are likely to dictate legal resolutions for the most part similar to those of the Uniform Commercial Code.

The empirical study of product warranties shows that, although there has occurred a substantial reduction in the frequency of some restrictions in warranties, the frequency of others, in particular the exclusions of liability for consequential and incidental damages, has greatly increased, apparently in response to the Act. Other data show that the influence of the Magnuson-Moss Act has been marginal. Firms offering more protective warranties in 1978 are generally the same firms that offered the more protective warranties prior to the enactment of the Magnuson-Moss Act.

It is very difficult to evaluate the effects of the Act, because we lack both a theory of the role of the warranty in the selection of a product for purchase and a theory of the determinants of warranty content. Certainly various of the Act's requirements, in particular the presale availability requirement, will increase costs to manufacturers; it is likely that there will be some benefit to consumers. In the absence of either theory or more detailed data, however, it is impossible to estimate the net effects of the Act.

Acknowledgments

The author wishes to thank Lawrence Kanter and Jacqueline Schmitt of the Federal Trade Commission for the provision of the warranties examined in Part III of the Article and for valuable counsel. The author also is grateful to William Lundquist, Robert E. Priest, Carol S. Maue, Timothy Johnson, Daniel Meyer, and Kenneth Landau for valuable research assistance.

Part III

Conclusions and reforms

Introduction

It is time to link our knowledge of the environment in which the Commission operates with our knowledge of the impacts of FTC activities. By drawing on the first two parts of this book and on an analysis of the FTC's internal structure and employee incentives that is developed within the chapter, Chapter 15 attempts to explain why the agency takes some of its actions. This explanation leads to our final chapter, proposals for reform. Understanding the underlying causes of FTC actions suggests several changes in the FTC's constraints to improve performance. We also discuss the most prominent of the many reforms suggested during recent attacks on the FTC by business managers, politicians, and others.

15 Commission performance, incentives, and behavior

KENNETH W. CLARKSON AND TIMOTHY J. MURIS

This chapter discusses the common threads uniting Commission actions and begins to develop an explanation of how those threads relate to the agency's constraints and to the incentives of its employees. Relying extensively on Chapters 6 through 14, Section I summarizes the major characteristics of FTC activities. Section II briefly discusses the importance of the external constraints revealed in Part I of the book. Section III analyzes the FTC's internal organization and its relationship with the external constraints. Internally, the Commission is replete with important conflicts among its levels of authority, among its different types of professionals, and among its bureaus. Although the external constraints arising from Congress and other sources leave the Commission largely unconstrained, its internal organization creates constraints that guide much of the Commission's behavior. Section IV analyzes the incentives of FTC personnel, emphasizing the contribution of the lack of external constraints to the formation of human capital among FTC employees. Finally, Section V illustrates how the external constraints, the internal constraints, and the personnel incentives interact to produce FTC behavior.

I. Characteristics of FTC actions

Although Chapters 6 through 14 do not evaluate a completely random sample of the hundreds of Commission programs, they not only discuss programs representative of those undertaken since 1970,[1] but also emphasize the cases with which the agency claims to have had its greatest impact. The following two sections examine these cases both to reveal that, despite its good intentions, the Commission's performance remains poor, and to show that FTC actions contain important, recurring themes.

A. *Good intentions, poor performance*

Despite good-faith attempts to improve performance during the past decade, the FTC still does not adequately meet its goal of benefiting consumers. On several dimensions, the agency performs poorly. Most important, many (although by no means all) Commission actions harm consumers. The antitrust attacks against efficient practices described in Chapters 6 and 9, the substantial failure of FTC rule making described in Chapters 10 through 12, and the misguided advertising regulation dissected in Chapter 13 all reveal an agency intending to benefit consumers, but harming them instead. Moreover, even if they do not harm consumers, some of the Commission's programs are not worth doing. For example, the Magnuson-Moss Warranty Act (see Chapter 14) at best duplicates the protection provided by decisions interpreting the Uniform Commercial Code. Further, even if the line-of-business (LB) program (see Chapter 7) produced accurate information, firms are unlikely to find that information useful.

Another Commission failing is its mishandling of cases that might otherwise be beneficial. For example, in the Xerox litigation discussed in Chapter 8, the Commission's failure to pursue a sound theory – indeed it seemed to lack any theory at all – reduced the possibility that the proceeding would benefit consumers. Further, although its performance was improving in late 1979, Chapter 10 reveals that the FTC's mishandling of the funeral program prevented emphasis on the anticonsumer, cartel-like activities that appear to permeate the industry. A related point concerns the FTC's attempt to pursue programs beyond its institutional competence. For example, even if meaningful LB data were useful, FTC provision of such data is virtually impossible. Although such production would be a problem even for an agency versed in complex economic issues, it is a special problem for the FTC. In case after case, Chapters 6 through 14 reveal an agency refusing to face tough economic issues, or mishandling the ones it does face.

B. *Recurring themes*

FTC programs since 1970 contain several recurring themes. To begin with, the Commission's approach is more aggregated and quasilegislative than previously. Both its increased rule making and its focus on entire industries with multiple problems show this preference. Consequently, Commission proceedings have become more complex in both the facts at issue and the relevant legal theory.[2]

Moreover, fundamental inconsistencies regarding economic analysis emerge among FTC programs. For example, particularly within the BCP, as Chapter 10 details, some FTC actions deregulate an industry on the theory that market forces best protect consumers, while others regulate an industry on the basis of hostility to market forces.[3] In general, the agency takes three approaches to economic analysis. Sometimes, as in its deregulatory rules and its deemphasis of Robinson-Patman cases, the FTC concurs with the nearly unanimous view of economists. In other cases, the Commission enthusiastically chooses one side in a raging debate among economists, as in its adoption of LB and the market concentration doctrine. In still other cases, the FTC runs against mainstream economic analysis, as in its downgrading of the cost considerations in rule making (see Chapters 10 through 12), its bringing of "practice" cases (see Chapters 6 and 9), and its frequent refusal to allow economic concerns to complicate its simple, per se approach (see Chapters 6, 9, and 13). In this last group of cases, the agency often not only deemphasizes economists' data, but also relies on ad hoc impressions of industry participants or observers (see especially Chapters 10 through 12).

What are we to make of the FTC's poor performance, its shift toward larger cases, and the inconsistencies underlying its actions? The remainder of this chapter attempts to formulate a theory explaining the FTC's behavior in enforcing its statutes. That theory relies on properly identifying the constraints and incentives that guide FTC decision makers. As Chapters 2 through 5 demonstrate, the external constraints often permit wide discretion in choosing among possible courses of action. We next turn to those external constraints.

II. External constraints: the role of the political environment

This section examines the influence that the combined effect of the external constraints has on Commission behavior. In general, unless all constraints push the Commission in the same direction, a historically unusual occurrence, the Commission remains largely unconstrained from without. Furthermore, except in determining the parameters of permissible behavior, the external constraints have little influence upon the specific allocation of resources within the Commission.

To understand the effects of external constraints and the Commission's reactions to them, we focus on the congressional and executive branches of government.[4] Figure 1 depicts polar opinions of Congress on the horizontal plane and the executive branch on the vertical plane, illustrating ambivalent reactions to the agency in general or on a specific issue.

An activist opinion is at one end of the spectrum, and a nonactivist opinion at the other. Activist is defined as favoring FTC intervention and nonactivist as opposing intervention. The pure activist and nonactivist positions are extremes. To be at either extreme, Congress must be able to support its position with both budget changes and legislation. Thus, the

CONGRESS

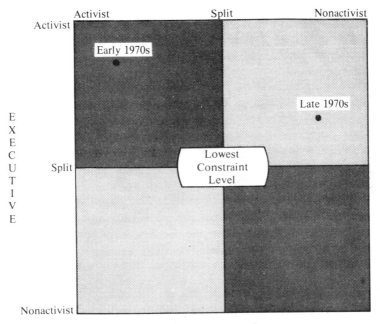

Figure 1. External attitudes and agency constraints.

extreme positions are rare. Congress may have a strong position toward the FTC, but the political environment may still be split if proponents of the dominant position cannot change the budget and pass legislation.

The vertical plane shows the objectives of the executive branch, again ranging from the pure activist to the pure nonactivist. As with Congress, a situation between the two extremes is normal, reflecting either a dispute within the executive branch or, perhaps more likely, no strong feelings toward the FTC. If both Congress and the executive branch are split (see the center of Figure 1 labeled "lowest constraint level"), no agreement exists on the direction the Commission should take. In such situations, the agency will have its greatest discretion.

Any movement from the center decreases the Commission's freedom, at least marginally. Probably the most effective constraint occurs when both Congress and the executive are nonactivist, meaning that they will block the agency with budget cuts and restrictive legislation if necessary. Even here, however, as explained in Chapter 3, an activist FTC could successfully continue most of its activities in all but the most hostile political environment. On the other hand, Congress and the executive branch can both be activist, as in the early 1970s, a position depicted on the upper left-hand corner of Figure 1 by the point "early 1970s." (Section V of this chapter discusses this point and the late 1970s in greater detail.) With this constraint, the agency will receive budget increases, new legislation, and other "encouragement" to be activist. The FTC has more freedom with this constraint than it would when facing the opposite extreme of a nonactivist environment. For example, legislation forbidding the FTC to pursue a certain course constrains the agency more than legislation expanding the FTC's power because of Congress's inability to specify precisely the contours of FTC activism.

Thus, in most cases, the projects that the FTC in fact pursues cannot be understood as a function only, or normally even primarily, of the external constraints. To understand the agency, one needs also to understand the FTC's internal structure and the incentives of those who control that structure. We turn to the internal structure next. Section IV then discusses employee incentives.

III. FTC organization and resulting conflicts

Given that the courts' broad interpretation of Section 5 of the FTC Act leaves the Commission great discretion in defining what is "unfair and deceptive" and that the other external constraints are usually as ineffective as that of the judiciary, FTC officials have very broad parameters within which to work. Not surprisingly, this lack of external guidance leads to conflicts between bureaus and individuals within the Commission. After an overview of the FTC's structure, we then discuss these intraagency conflicts.

A. Organization

Since the Weinberger reorganization of 1970, the basic structure of the FTC has remained unchanged. These units are of various sizes, as their fiscal year 1978 expenditures reveal (see Figure 2). We discuss next the individual units.

1. Commissioners

Five commissioners are appointed for staggered seven-year terms by the president of the United States with the advice and consent of the Senate. The president designates one of the five as chairman, and only three may belong to the same political party.

Since 1950, the chairman has had executive and administrative responsibilities for the Commission, including management and personnel. As to

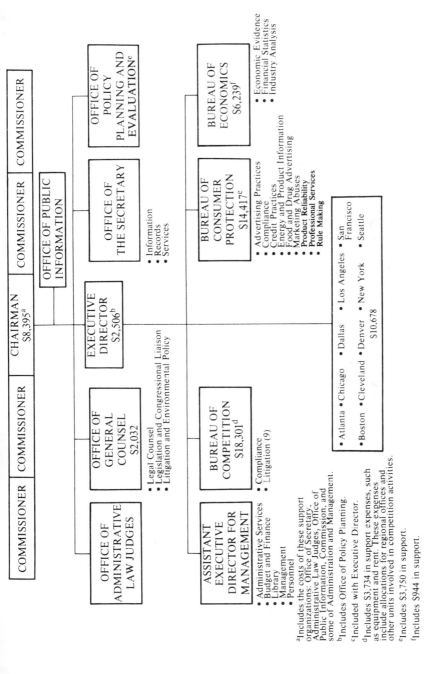

| COMMISSIONER | COMMISSIONER | COMMISSIONER | CHAIRMAN $8,395[a] | COMMISSIONER | COMMISSIONER | COMMISSIONER |

OFFICE OF PUBLIC INFORMATION

OFFICE OF ADMINISTRATIVE LAW JUDGES

OFFICE OF GENERAL COUNSEL $2,032
• Legal Counsel
• Legislation and Congressional Liaison
• Litigation and Environmental Policy

EXECUTIVE DIRECTOR $2,506[b]

OFFICE OF THE SECRETARY
• Information
• Records
• Services

OFFICE OF POLICY PLANNING AND EVALUATION[c]

ASSISTANT EXECUTIVE DIRECTOR FOR MANAGEMENT
• Administrative Services
• Budget and Finance
• Library
• Management
• Personnel

BUREAU OF COMPETITION $18,301[d]
• Compliance
• Litigation (9)

BUREAU OF CONSUMER PROTECTION $14,417[e]
• Advertising Practices
• Compliance
• Credit Practices
• Energy and Product Information
• Food and Drug Advertising
• Marketing Abuses
• Product Reliability
• Professional Services
• Rule Making

BUREAU OF ECONOMICS $6,239[f]
• Economic Evidence
• Financial Statistics
• Industry Analysis

• Atlanta • Chicago • Dallas • Los Angeles • San Francisco
• Boston • Cleveland • Denver • New York • Seattle
$10,678

[a]Includes the costs of these support organizations: Office of Secretary, Administrative Law Judges, Office of Public Information, Commission, and some of Administration and Management.

[b]Includes Office of Policy Planning.

[c]Included with Executive Director.

[d]Includes $3,734 in support expenses, such as equipment and rent. These expenses include allocations for regional offices and other units involved in competition activities.

[e]Includes $3,750 in support.

[f]Includes $944 in support.

Figure 2. Federal Trade Commission organization with fiscal year 1978 budget allocations (dollars in thousands). (From FTC fiscal year 1979 budget submission to Congress.)

personnel, however, the full Commission must approve appointments of the director of public information, general counsel, chief administrative law judge, the secretary, executive director, director of policy planning, and the directors of the Bureau of Competition, the Bureau of Consumer Protection, and the Bureau of Economics.[5]

2. The operating bureaus

Each bureau is comprised of several individual units, each headed by assistant directors. After a Pertschuk Administration reorganization, the Bureau of Competition (BC), which directs FTC antitrust activities, has 13 assistant directors who supervise activity in various programs, such as mergers, transportation, and food. Most of the attorneys are involved in investigation, litigation, and compliance, although some are assigned to divisions for planning and evaluation. At any one time, most of these employees are involved in litigating cases in which the Commission has issued a complaint. For example, during calendar year 1973, 65 to 70 percent of the bureau's working resources went to litigation.[6]

The Bureau of Consumer Protection (BCP) considers practices allegedly deceptive or unfair to consumers. As with the Bureau of Competition, the Pertschuk Administration reorganized the BCP.[7] Ten assistant directors currently supervise such program areas as marketing abuses, credit practices, and planning. Unlike competition, where there are no trade regulation rules (although some are under consideration), at least half of BCP's staff is engaged in rule making or rule enforcement.[8]

Throughout most of the 1970s, the Bureau of Economics (BE) has operated three units. A division of economic evidence works with the Bureau of Competition to investigate and evaluate possible law violations. As of fiscal 1979, another division has been systematically involved with consumer protection. Before this time, BE worked only occasionally with BCP, usually concerning trade regulation rules. The Division of Industry Analysis conducts studies of various industries and practices. Finally, the Division of Financial Statistics collects and analyzes financial data from a large number of corporations, in some instances publishing aggregated statistics. In the future, the major work of this division will be the annual line-of-business report, discussed in Chapter 7.

3. Regional offices

The remaining operating units of the Commission are the regional offices, using roughly 15 to 20 percent of the Commission's resources.[9] These 10 offices, which since 1970 have had the power to initiate investigations, have triggered controversy both within and without the FTC.

Critics question the need for their existence and assert that these offices have a disproportionate share of the problems that allegedly plague the FTC, such as delay and lack of priority setting. It is further charged that their role is not adequately defined and that they are ineffectively used, overly reviewed from above, and inadequately managed from within.[10]

Whatever the merits of these charges, the Pertschuk Administration has attempted something of a "housecleaning." Between June 1977 and March 1978, during four regional office evaluations, Los Angeles and New York did not receive completely favorable reports and now have new directors.[11] Additionally, the Washington regional office was even closed.

4. Supporting units

Of the three major supporting units, the executive director is the Commission's chief operating officer. The director has executive and administrative supervision over all FTC offices and supposedly implements Commission policy, coordinating related activities when necessary. The executive director's impact upon the Commission's activities is difficult to specify. Procedurally, that is, in "making the trains run on time," the executive director plays a dominant role. Substantively, the question of "where the trains are headed," the executive director's role depends to a significant extent on the power that the chairman delegates. The executive director can influence policy, such as when the director occasionally referees staff disputes. For example, when the Office of Policy Planning and Evaluation (OPPE) had difficulty obtaining documents from the BC, the chairman designated the executive director to resolve the dispute. Further, in a step that may someday enormously influence the manner in which the Commission makes decisions, R. T. McNamar, executive director from the fall of 1973 until the summer of 1977, played the central role in devising the planning and budgeting procedures discussed later in this chapter. Third, the executive director has had a continuing and prominent role in the relationship between the regional offices and the agency's officials in Washington, including determination of the nature of activities the regional offices shall pursue.

The second support unit is the general counsel's office. As the Commission's lawyer, the general counsel appears in federal court, advises on legal matters, and serves as liaison with many other federal agencies. In addition, the general counsel's office has normally been responsible for the liaison between Congress and the Commission, although the chairman's office occasionally performs much of this function. Although lacking a major substantive role, the general counsel can be important in phrasing advisory legal opinions. As we saw in Chapter 4, the Commission historically has had broad discretion in determining what practices are illegal, and thus this function has not been crucial. There is some indication that the office may be more involved in substantive matters under the Pertschuk Administration. For example, the general counsel was in charge of a task force on Commission remedies.

Finally, the Office of Policy Planning, before mid-1977 the Office of Policy Planning and Evaluation, concentrates on "think pieces" by working on task forces and planning sessions that are innovations of Chairman Pertschuk. These sessions review all the activities of the agency in a particular area, such as energy,[12] and may evaluate or propose new initiatives. The history and operation of the Office of Policy Planning will be discussed in more detail below.

B. Intraagency conflicts

At any given time the chairman may be vying against the rest of the Commission, the staff may be attempting to sidestep the wishes of the Commission, the lawyers may be working against the economists, or the planners may be competing with the staff. Two central actors exist, the chairman and the staff, and we discuss the role of each in detail.

1. The role of the chairman

The chairman holds the most powerful position within the agency, strongly influencing "budget, appointments, and administration—and consequently the initiative."[13] Although technically the full Commission must approve the selection of upper-level officials, during the 1970s the chairman made his selections with little or no consultation with other commissioners.[14] As to management, without even perfunctory consultation required, the full Commission is not involved.[15]

Much of the chairman's power stems from his relationship with the staff. We shall see when discussing case selection that the Commission's role is minor relative to that of the staff. Nevertheless, the chairman's role in selecting and, to some extent, managing the staff gives him important leverage. The chairman can have the staff work on projects of his choosing, at least to the extent that the agency's resources are not already committed to other projects. Further, the chairman can affect the timing of matters as the staff presents them to the full Commission, a power that, as economists have shown, influences decisions.[16]

The chairman wields considerable influence through appointment and management functions, as seen in recent case selection "tools." During the Kirkpatrick years, the planning staff and the operating bureaus developed a much-ballyhooed prototype resource allocation model (PRAM) for predicting which antitrust cases to pursue. Upon Lewis Engman's arrival, the project was abandoned. During the Engman–Collier chairmanships, the staff designed "policy protocols," listing questions to be addressed each time the staff brought a case involving an activity for which a protocol existed. Although the Commission adopted two protocols and staff work was proceeding upon many others, Chairman Pertschuk abandoned this project, at least in the form that the previous chairman envisioned.

Besides direct influence over staff appointments and activities, the chairman's leadership role increases the office's power. A perhaps extreme example is children's advertising. In 1977, the Commission stated that it intended "to judge each advertisement on the basis of the particular circumstances. . . . There are distinct advantages in proceeding on a case-by-case basis where, as in this instance, the evidence is less than clear cut." One year later the Commission, unchanged except for a new chairman who made children's advertising his top priority, unanimously held a different view. Having previously rejected a proposed *guide* on TV advertising of premiums to children, this time the Commission unanimously agreed that the solution to the problem was a *rule-making* proceeding that is considering regulations far stronger than the guide that the Commission rejected.[17]

The chairman also significantly influences budget priorities. Under Kirkpatrick, consumer protection received more money than antitrust. Engman changed this, and Collier concurred. Of course, other changes occurred in the Commission during the 1970s, but the chairman, not the other commissioners, set the tone in budget priorities.

a. The chairman versus the commissioners. The other commissioners have relatively little power. They do vote on complaints, investigations, and so on; but, as we shall see later, this power is ill suited to influence the agency's conduct. Indeed, in terms of affecting the FTC's activities, an individual commissioner is less important than such top staff members as the directors of the Bureaus of Competition and Consumer Protection. Only in adjudication and in votes on whether to promulgate rules are the other commissioners equal to the chairman.[18] This, however, is a difficult tool with which to control the agency's activities. Cases and promulgated rules are infrequent and may turn on points unrelated to broad policy considerations. Moreover, a commissioner who wants the agency to investigate specific industries or practices cannot use administrative or rule-making decisions to force the staff to fulfill these desires.

b. The chairman versus the staff. Some constraints on the chairman are more effective than those provided by the other commissioners. One of the most important is the inventory of matters existing upon the chairman's arrival. A chairman has considerable power over resources not already committed to specific tasks, but cannot unilaterally end projects that have already begun if they had previous Commission support. Working with the appointed bureau directors, the chairman may decide that some matters should end, but implementing such a decision can be costly. Termination must usually proceed through the Commission, where the chairman's vote is only one of five. Staff members who have worked on the threatened project may become disgruntled and uncooperative. Because the project may have been announced (often with considerable fanfare) to the public and Congress, its supporters outside the Commission may also resist its abandonment and hence cost time and effort. Although the chairman can successfully end an investigation, he is much more constrained in closing matters than in beginning a project. Thus, the fewer noncommitted resources, the more constrained is the chairman. (The effects that the staff's attitude has on the chairman and the Commission is also important and will be discussed below.)

Another constraint is lack of information about intra-FTC activities. Before 1974, the chairman (or anyone else for that matter) could rarely gain precise knowledge of the staff's activities, available resources, and so on. In 1974, the Commission began steps toward a budgeting and planning system to eliminate this problem. As we shall see, the system has been, at best, only a partial success.

2. The role of the staff

The staff's central role is best seen through its impact on case selection.

a. Case selection: the Commission versus the staff.

a. Case selection: the Commission versus the staff. Before 1970, the staff selected cases for the agency to pursue, with the commissioners possessing a "veto power."[19] The Commission participated by exercising that power. If they opposed a certain type of case, they gave the staff the message by vetoing the complaint or investigation. Further, a staff loss in adjudication before the Commission was another signal to end a particular type of case. The method of case selection used by the staff before 1970 relied more on complaints than on internal planning procedures.

Although the planning and budgeting tools described below have made some changes, the staff still largely chooses projects, with the commissioners possessing only a veto power. Most cases and rules proceed similarly. The staff presents a proposed investigation to the Commission, usually at the stage when it desires subpoena power. The Commission has before it only this one investigation; no discussion of similar investigations takes place, nor is a menu of possible projects provided. (The new planning procedures described below are attempting to change this approach.) In other words, the Commission still views the proposed case isolated from other possible projects. If a commissioner or other member of the staff questions the desirability or necessity of the investigation, the staff often argues that it merely wants to discover the facts. Accompanied by the staff's description of possible monopoly or deception, this is usually enough to rebut the criticism successfully. Further, rejection of a staff proposal could harm morale, particularly if the Commission did not state what it would prefer that the staff do instead, a task that is extremely difficult for the commissioners, who have only small staffs. Rejection also opens the Commission to possible adverse publicity and criticism from Congress for refusing even to investigate the facts of a possibly illegal activity. Thus, the recommended investigations are usually approved, often with extensive publicity.

Months or, if it is a major matter, years later the staff returns to seek a complaint, proposal of a rule, or closing. At this complaint stage, the matter is again presented to the Commission in isolated fashion. No attempt is made to compare this case with other cases or to consider it as part of overall Commission priorities. Until about 1975, there was not even an estimate of the direct cost to the Commission of further action.

When a complaint is issued or a rule proposed, the amount of resources already spent plays a key, albeit perverse, role. Rather than realizing that past costs are sunk and therefore irrelevant to current decisions, the opposite notion prevails, reflecting distaste for "wasting" already spent resources. Indeed, the staff evokes this attitude, asking how the Commission could discard years of work. Further, the staff now has a vital stake in a "yes" vote. With a "no" vote, staff members, who must have litigation experience to maximize their value in this job market, see their investment in a good prospect lost. Thus, faced with a yes or no decision, the commissioners are under great pressure to say yes. They can usually give the staff nothing in return for rejection; nor can they argue that they are allocating their scarce resources among a range of possible activities. With rule making, the commissioners have somewhat more flexibility because the Commission can propose only parts of a rule or list other parts as staff proposals upon which the Commission desires comment.

The commission will sometimes vote "no" or, more likely, send the case back to the staff for further investigation. Nevertheless, compared to a system that allowed the Commission broader choices than yes or no, the Commission's role is limited relative to that of the staff. Commission review at this level does create delay, triggering criticism of the Commission by the staff and outsiders.[20] When the role of the Commission in case selection is understood, however, delay becomes understandable: Commission efforts at planning cause delay. By frequent review of the staff, the Commission exercises what limited control it can; the more review, the more chance commissioners have of control.

Currently in the competition area, agency lawyers must work with economists in choosing cases. The conflict between these groups will be discussed in more detail in the next section. In consumer protection, a shift away from acting primarily on complaint letters has occurred, although complaints still produce an occasional case (as they do for competition as well). Staff initiatives and even some program creation from outside BCP now determine case selection. Occasionally, individual staff members initiate major projects, as when a staff attorney's reading of Jessica Mitford's *The American Way of Death* led to the creation of the funeral industry program.[21] More frequently, however, project creation has been a group effort. For example, the 1970s saw an effort within the BCP's Division of National Advertising to produce new remedies. Also, a conscious decision to shift to rule making was made, with some of the major rules produced by a special unit that Lewis Engman initiated to force the staff to provide more detailed and uniform information in various cases. Further, the occupational licensure program was proposed by the Office of Policy Planning, approved by the Commission, and thus placed into the bureau from without.

The interjection of the occupational licensure program can be partly explained by the Office of Policy Planning's greater emphasis on economic input. Except for occupational licensure, at least until 1976, there was almost no economic input in the activities of the Bureau of Consumer Protection. An evaluation committee, created in 1976 to produce economic input, has not been as influential as the BC evaluation committee. Economists have generally been less interested in BCP than in BC, a phenomenon that is discussed in Section V. With the 1978 creation of a special unit within the Bureau of Economics to work with the Bureau of Consumer Protection and with the Commission now requiring Bureau of Economics's involvement in rules, this has begun to change.

Outside the context of the planning and budgeting process described below, the Commission has occasionally tried to force the staff to provide more detailed and uniform information in various cases. Rather than attempting to establish priorities among different types of cases, the goal was primarily better information on individual cases. Two such attempts are illustrative.

In the fall of 1973, newly appointed Commissioner Mayo Thompson asked that estimates of costs and benefits be required when the staff requested a complaint.[22] Among other things, Thompson asserted that mergers should be permitted unless the price would rise or quality would fall because of the merger. Hence, he wanted data on these issues. Thompson's efforts culminated in a Commission meeting at the end of

1973 that, in terms of the information that the staff produced in future cases, had no lasting effect.

Second, Chairmen Engman and Collier advocated that policy protocols be adopted for the major classes of matters before the Commission. These protocols would "provide criteria which can be used to evaluate each Commission enforcement proceeding. All costs and benefits cannot be measured in absolute terms, but it is possible to formulate a series of questions which will elicit the type of information relevant in making a policy [as contrasted with a legal] decision."[23] Although these protocols were staff creations, they were in part negotiated by the Office of Policy Planning from a different legal and economic perspective than the staff's. Further, there was some indication from the Commission that the questions should produce detailed information, not just vague generalities, to assist the Commission in gaining more control over case selection. The two protocols that were adopted – involving bait and switch and unsubstantiated advertising claims – did present numerous questions that could lead to more detailed and uniform information being presented to the Commission. As previously mentioned, this project was terminated when Pertschuk became chairman.

b. *Conflicts among the staff.* Because the various staff units within the Commission have a great deal of autonomy, their decision makers lack a Commission-wide perspective, but look instead at matters only as they influence their particular unit. This territorial attitude helps explain the considerable hostility between units and makes projects that require cooperation more difficult to complete. Consider the 1977 comments of the director of the Bureau of Consumer Protection:

As a newcomer, and even from my position of relative isolation over the past few weeks, I've been struck by the pervasive hostility and adversarial attitude that exists between various units of BCP as well as between BCP and the Regional Offices. Instead of directing our energies toward targeted respondents, we seem to be about taking shots at each other and at the Commission. I am not sure whether the alarming level of paranoia is cause or effect.[24]

The hostility between economists and lawyers is a prime example of staff conflict. Case selection in the Bureau of Competition is performed by an evaluation committee comprised of lawyers and economists. Although the director of the Bureau of Competition is not bound by the advice he receives from other members of the committee, in practice that advice is very influential. The committee was begun in the early 1970s, and the presence of the economists gives them the important voice that they previously lacked. The economists cannot be ignored because they have the right to go to the Commission and disagree when the Bureau of Competition requests compulsory process or a complaint. This right is exercised, and although they lose many (probably a majority) of their disputes with the lawyers, the economists win enough to hold the attention of the attorneys.[25]

The economists' role is controversial. Many attorneys, sometimes even those at the top of the bureau, are dissatisfied with the economists' substantive positions, with their right to comment, and with what they perceive as the undue delay that the economists cause.[26] The economists have been very influential, although it is impossible to measure the exact extent of that influence. Some examples, however, are revealing. The economists' opposition to Robinson-Patman is now shared by most BC attorneys.[27] The Commission brings few Robinson-Patman Act cases today, and those that it does usually cause controversy between the lawyers and economists.[28]

Further, particularly in the early and mid-1970s, the economists' selection criteria became prominent. The leaders of the Bureau of Economics were advocates of the market-concentration doctrine, which focuses on concentration and profits as signals for antitrust enforcement. The Commission embarked on several cases and investigations that attack industrial structure, including most of its industry-wide programs discussed in Chapter 6.

3. Planning versus the case-by-case approach

Another major conflict in Commission decision making – involving both conflicts among the staff and between the Commission and the staff – arises between the planned (at the Commission level) and the case-by-case approaches for selecting actions. In the case-by-case approach discussed above, the staff has a great deal of discretion in its choices of cases. This makes it very difficult for the Commission to supervise staff activities and expenditures. The staff desires to be monitored as little as possible, whereas the Commission would prefer having the control over case selection that planning and monitoring would bring. In this section we discuss the role that planning has played in the Commission during the past 10 years.

Before 1970 practically no planning apparatus existed at the FTC. Case selection was largely in response to complaints,[29] with no specific budgeting procedure to present proposals to the Commission and to set specific priorities among varying alternatives. Thus, to the extent that it existed, "planning" was reactive, resulting in the charges of ineffectiveness discussed in Chapter 1. In response to the criticism, one of the major changes was the June 1970 creation of the Office of Policy Planning and Evaluation, which was given the responsibility to help the Commission better utilize resources.

Three distinct periods may be distinguished in this office's history. First, the office emphasized cooperation with the operating bureaus on case-selection criteria. The prototype resource allocation model (PRAM), mentioned earlier in the chapter, was a major product of this cooperation. The office also undertook other efforts aimed at planning and budgeting, including a Policy Profile Task Force Report to provide "a conceptual framework within which activities of the . . . [operating bureaus] could be organized, classified and compared,"[30] an annual planning report, and a report on the fiscal 1975 budget in which the office listed possible goals that the Commission might wish to pursue. This work had minimal effect upon Commission case selection. Because PRAM never became operational, it cannot be said to have had a major impact.[31] Further, the other projects were not influential. As outgoing FTC Commissioner Mary Gardner Jones stated in October 1973, "Planning has not yet become operational at the Commission."[32]

Second, from 1974 through 1976, the office, with almost a complete change in personnel, concentrated on three projects, emphasizing its role of giving the Commission an independent evaluation of the staff's activities. The office presented written evaluations of the Commission's programs, including advice on the amount of consumer benefit from each, and suggestions for new programs. In cooperation with the operating bureaus, it also worked on policy protocols to develop questions that would elicit better information which the Commission could use to assess the public interest of particular cases. Finally, using quantitative techniques, the office began to evaluate the impact of past Commission actions.

These activities, particularly the independent review of Commission programs, were extremely controversial.[33] The office was largely unsuccessful in stopping the actions that it opposed, although it had considerable success in helping create new programs, such as the Commission's occupational licensure effort and other programs scrutinizing state and federal regulation. Further, the office's insistence that economic analysis underlie all FTC cases did force heightened awareness of economics among the staff and Commission. The protocols, largely abandoned by Pertschuk, have not had lasting effect. The impact evaluation program, which began in earnest under Chairman Collier, is a potentially important device and is discussed below.

Most of the office's evaluative work occurred in the context of the budget procedure that began in 1974, when the Commission basically started over in its efforts to establish a system for controlling resource allocation. Because these efforts are still influential today, we will discuss them in some detail. If the Commission was to control resource allocations, then data on how the staff was spending its time were vital. A management information review committee produced a report in mid-1974 that led to a computerized reporting system to "record the resources spent on and time consumed by every active matter in the Commission."[34] Staff members complete weekly activity reports to record the time worked on various matters, with the time then allocated to the appropriate programs for use by program managers and other interested individuals.

Simultaneously, a program budget system devised for the formation of the fiscal year 1976 budget divided the work of Consumer Protection and Competition into programs. Competition programs are broad, covering matters such as food, energy, mergers, and distributional restraints. Consumer protection programs are usually more specific, focusing on individual activities such as a particular rule making. (Consumer protection programs have tended to become somewhat larger in recent years.)

The procedure established then is still used. In May or June, the operating units formulate their requests, which the executive director uses in preparing a draft budget for the Commission. Although there is undoubtedly guidance from the chairman (which may be increasing with the Pertschuk administration's emphasis on avoiding staff conflict) and perhaps from other commissioners, the staff recommendations are generally independent products. Until 1977, OPPE presented an independent evaluation of the recommendations. At the end of July the Commission reviews the various recommendations. In a one- or two-day meeting, the Commission has the opportunity to consider the budget without having to vote on a final package. During this session, formal votes are seldom taken, the commissioners merely expressing their opinions. During August, when the Commission is not in session, the executive director works with the chairman to assemble the budget, using the Commission's guidance from the meeting to arrive at final totals.[35] At least during the Engman and Collier years, during August there were extensive negotiations among the chairman, executive director, and bureau directors. Finally, in September the budget is presented to the Commission for its vote and is then transmitted to OMB.

Since 1975, there has also been a midyear review to reallocate resources based upon staff proposals (including until 1977 those of OPPE). Chairman Collier instituted quarterly budget sessions, which continue today.

The planning and budgeting process has changed somewhat since Chairman Pertschuk's arrival in 1977. Moving to avoid confrontation within the staff, Chairman Pertschuk reconstituted the Office of Policy Planning. Again with almost entirely new personnel, the office began its third and current era. The evaluation function has been entirely eliminated, leaving the Commission without any independent evaluation of the staff's budget proposals. The OPP is now heavily involved with the task forces and planning sessions implemented by Pertschuk. Although not new devices at the Commission,[36] they have never been used on as broad a scale. Because they are just beginning to produce, their impact is indeterminate.

Another recent development in the budget process is zero base budgeting, required by the Carter Administration, forcing the commissioners to rank programs in their order of preference. This process may allow OMB, the staff, or the Commission to decide which programs are marginal.

The link between the planning and budget procedures and the manner in which individual projects are selected is not at all clear. Further, although these procedures were designed to give the Commission control over resource allocation, the staff still determines most case selection, with the Commission possessing a veto power.

For at least four reasons, control over case selection through the planning and budget process has been largely unsuccessful. First, the link between budgeting and individual case selection is tenuous at best. From the standpoint of both the Commission and the staff, case selection proceeds basically as it did before the new budget process began in 1974. Because the budget process was simply imposed upon the existing procedures for case selection, this is not surprising.

Second, the staff is ineffectively monitored to see that its programs use resources appropriately under the budget. The manner in which the budget is compiled and cases are handled discourages a close link between budget and case selection. Once a project is funded past the stage of proposing a rule or issuing a complaint, the Commission does not closely scrutinize resources devoted to the relevant program. Mergers provide an illustration of Commission failure to monitor ongoing agency enforcement. The program manager determines long in advance how much merger activity the staff will want to attack. If the staff presents more or fewer merger cases, the Commission will examine these cases individually, not as part of a limited number of merger resources that it decided to spend. In other words, if the Commission decides that it wants 30 person-years spent on mergers, it will normally do virtually nothing to require 30 person-years on mergers. It imposes no penalties for staff failure to comply with the budget.

A third reason that the program budget does not greatly constrain the staff in its case selection is that the staff retains considerable flexibility. When planning the fiscal year 1977 budget, for example, the Commission allotted an increase of nearly $1 million in its horizontal restraints program. At least some of the commissioners wanted the staff to pursue more horizontal cases, particularly involving price fixing. Although the Commission continues to express this desire,[37] the resources allocated were never fully spent, nor did the staff significantly increase its attack on horizontal price fixing.[38] A similar scenario occurred with information disclosure.[39] With the removal of evaluation from the Office of Policy Planning, one potential check on staff manipulation of the budget has ended.

Finally, poor information exacerbates Commission difficulty in controlling resource allocation. Because staff members lack the incentive to complete time sheets and monitor cases that private law firms have from the need to bill clients, the data in the information system is often inadequate.[40]

The new procedures do cause some effective reallocation of resources, and the quarterly budget and other planning sessions do increase at least the opportunity for control over the staff. Relative to the staff's processes, however, these activities have had little impact. Until there is a closer link between case selection and budgeting and planning, the Commission will have little more than a case-by-case veto over resource allocation.[41]

The Pertschuk changes may integrate case selection more fully into the planning system, although it is too early to determine their impact. The planning sessions and task forces give the commissioners an opportunity to examine a menu of activities, not just cases on an isolated basis. They also allow the Commission a voice at a very early stage of project development. Further, to the extent that they are devoted to new program development, they give (at least) the chairman more control over resource allocation by allowing him increased opportunity to structure projects through the top staff. Regardless of their impact on the Commissioners, these new activities may assist the staff in improving its own case-selection techniques. Finally, the FTC funds impact evaluations, basically devices by which the effect of various Commission projects and rules are analyzed, at about $1 million annually.[42] Because Commission projects are limited in variety and because the agency tends to repeat "successes," impact evaluations could have a major influence upon case selection. Projects that produce benefits would presumably be repeated; projects that do not fulfill predictions of the staff could be de-emphasized. At least, these evaluations should have the salutary effect of forcing the staff to make predictions.

IV. FTC personnel incentives

The relative weakness of the external constraints increases the influence of the agency's internal structure on FTC behavior. Before fully comprehending that influence, however, we must analyze the participants' incentives. We first consider the differences between constraints and incentives arising in government agencies and those in profit-seeking firms. Then, we discuss the importance of FTC experience to agency attorneys.

A. *Governmental constraints and incentives*[43]

Contrasting the constraints on government employees with those on employees in a proprietary, profit-seeking enterprise is revealing.[44] Managers of a profit enterprise strive to maximize the wealth of the firm's owners. Government managers lack this (or any other) single purpose. Ownership rights in government enterprises differ from those in profit-seeking institutions in two important ways. First, governments do not sell the rights to the capitalized value of their future benefits and liabilities. If an FTC official saves consumers millions of dollars, neither that person nor the Commission has rights to the savings. Second, government decision makers lack the exclusive right to the flow of money attributable to their actions, a right that exists in profit-seeking firms.

These differences yield differences between the performances of government and profit-maximizing institutions. Both institutions introduce controls to reduce undesired behavior by decision makers. Owners of profit organizations often assign some of the residual claim to decision makers through, for example, stock ownership, thereby indirectly monitoring their activities. Taxpayers do not do this, leaving government decision makers with less concern for their behavior's impact on the organization's costs and revenues. The result is that the wealth of managers in firms is tied much more closely to the wealth of the owners of the firm than the wealth of managers in government is tied to the wealth of taxpayers.

The lack of the overriding constraint that wealth maximizing imposes (unprofitable firms are less likely to survive than profitable ones), coupled with the weakness of existing external constraints, enhances the importance of individual preferences in analyzing government performance. In this sense, people do matter. Of many possible preferences (i.e., sources of utility), we discuss two that are often complementary, one for power, the other for wealth. Both are available within existing FTC constraints. A person's preference for power manifests itself in a desire to reshape society in his or her own image. An individual with this preference will be attracted to organizations that lack the discipline of profit or other stringent constraints.[45] Although this preference undoubtedly has had some impact on the agency, given that most FTC employees choose to stay with the agency for only a few years, the preference for wealth appears more important and will be discussed in detail.

B. *Human capital development of attorneys*

Except for the few key positions within the Bureau of Economics, all important FTC substantive decision makers are attorneys. Moreover, attorneys comprise approximately 75 percent of the professional staff.[46] The available evidence suggests that attorneys have used the FTC to enhance their marketability for future employment, thus investing in their human capital.[47] The turnover rate among attorneys has approached 20 percent annually,[48] and a 1976 study revealed that 89 percent of all attorneys who joined the FTC in 1972–75 expected to leave in two years or less.[49] Perhaps more important proof of the investment nature of FTC employment is that in the 1970s attorneys who left the FTC increasingly also left government, indicating that they were taking more lucrative jobs in private firms.[50] Top officials also turn over frequently, leaving for private law practice in even higher percentages than lower staff.[51]

In at least four ways, agency attorneys use FTC experience to increase their value to private law firms. First, particularly for young attorneys, FTC employment provides valuable training, including the study of applicable statutory laws, court decisions, regulations, and the Commission's rules of procedure. Because litigation and its rule-making counterpart are the most important experience young attorneys receive, they desire to work on projects complex enough to guarantee litigation of legally sophisticated issues, yet not requiring a long tenure to receive the necessary experience. Second, particularly for higher staff, who less frequently need this on-the-job training, mere appointment to their position represents a certification of prominence that has significant value in the job market.[52]

Third, increases in private legal fees spent to litigate FTC issues enhance the marketability of FTC employees, at least to the extent that current increases raise the probability of future higher fees. Budget increases further this goal. Moreover, private fees probably rise, all else equal, when the FTC pursues more projects with multiple respondents, as with the 1970s emphasis on rule making and the market concentration doctrine. Law firms that represent multiple respondents often duplicate work, partly for ethical reasons (one law firm will often have difficulty representing more than one respondent) and partly because the respondents' legal positions may vary. Further, coordination costs among the private firms may exceed those within the agency, thereby raising private legal fees.

A fourth method to increase value, closely related to the third method, is to obtain expertise in crucial areas. Thus, those FTC employees (usually higher-level staff) who invented and perfected the agency's new "lore,"[53] such as structure cases and rule making, enhanced their value. Because the benefits of such expertise fall unevenly among FTC attorneys, because in the 1970s the new projects were often extremely complex, and because young (and usually low-level) attorneys desire at least some cases of lesser complexity, another source of conflict exists within the agency.[54]

C. Economists[55]

Economists turn over at roughly half the rate of attorneys,[56] with those who leave going to other agencies, not private firms. If the FTC is not a way-station to private firms, then what are the economists' incentives? Because their outside employment opportunities are relatively poor compared to their attorney counterparts, economists have a greater stake in enhancing their individual influence within the agency, which in turn increases future income opportunities in the Commission. Economists' influence rises with the number of cases requiring evidence and theories that economists have a comparative advantage in developing.[57] Because attorneys need theories that support FTC action, economists face an important constraint: Theories that reduce the FTC's role will meet intense hostility.[58] How the economists have increased their influence despite this constraint is one of the major developments in the agency since 1970. We discuss this occurrence next, as we summarize our theory of FTC action.

V. Toward an explanation of FTC behavior

We are now ready to explain the FTC's behavior summarized in Section I. Section II discussed the unusual conditions necessary for external constraints to exert major control on agency action. Section III detailed the conflicts within the agency over case selection. Section IV explained the importance for agency attorneys of FTC experience as an investment in their human capital. We hypothesize that an interaction of the phenomena discussed in these three sections provides the foundation for understanding FTC behavior.[59] This section illustrates that interaction by discussing both the key changes made in the agency's overall approach to regulation since 1970 and the nature of agency case selection.

A. The FTC's overall approach to regulation

1. The early 1970s

As Chapter 1 detailed, the FTC was transformed during this period. Changes in the external constraints were crucial. As Figure 1 (p. 283) shows, the external forces coalesced to help create an activist agency. Five important groups outside the Commission might have influenced the agency –the White House, Congress, courts, consumers, and producers. None opposed reform; some enthusiastically supported it. Consumerists, who in the late 1960s became politically powerful, strongly supported change.[60] Indeed, some of its proponents attained prominent positions within the Commission. Producers, to the extent they had influence (at least from 1969 through 1970) spoke mainly through the ABA Report (many of whose authors were attorneys for prominent corporations), and thus were extremely critical of the FTC.[61] The White House enthusiastically supported change, at least initially, as did the courts through the *S&H* decision. Most important, until about 1978, Congress enthusiastically supported expanded powers. As Chapter 2 detailed, Congress moved quickly to remedy alleged defects in the agency's statutes. Moreover, between 1970 and 1976 the FTC's budget doubled, representing an increase of 40 percent in real dollars.

Within the agency, no important resistance to change existed. Because case closings and budget increases freed considerable resources and because the political environment supported change, the power of an activist chairman was at its height, particularly during the crucial chairmanships of Weinberger and Kirkpatrick. To the extent that other commissioners had a voice, they either did not oppose reform or could not muster enough support from within or without the FTC to stop the changes. Intransigent personnel were not a large problem, as a dramatic turnover in the entire professional staff was accomplished.[62]

2. The late 1970s

By 1978, much of Congress opposed an activist FTC. (Figure 1 depicts this change in the political environment.) For example, what had begun in 1977 as yet another bill to increase FTC power was killed by the House in 1978 because it lacked a one-house legislative veto for FTC rules.[63] From fiscal year 1978 to fiscal year 1980, congressional appropriations for the FTC fell approximately 3 percent per year, after adjustment for inflation.[64] Opposition grew during the late 1970s, but because the FTC already had sufficient authority and resources to pursue major regulation of much of the business community and because congressional oversight could not deter the FTC, the opponents turned to new legislation to "tame" the FTC. As Chapter 16 discusses, the two main planks of the legislation, the legislative veto and specific industry exemptions, do not affect the source of the FTC's problems: the agency's lack of effective constraints. Consequently, even if passed, such legislation is unlikely to end the problems detailed in this book.

In any event, the imminent threat of new legislation changed the external constraint on the FTC. To maintain its authority – and particularly the top staff have a strong incentive to see their investment protected (see Section IV.B) – in late 1979 the agency launched an effective lobbying and publicity counterattack.[65] Second, the FTC created an impression of softening its activism. For example, discussions of greatly increasing the scope of activities subject to regulation ended and some rule-making proceedings were curtailed.[66]

Despite the undoubted importance of the external constraints in fueling the changes of the early 1970s and in forcing the FTC to invest large resources to defend itself in 1979, these constraints provide only very general guidance for understanding the details of FTC behavior summarized in Section I of this chapter. At most, the political environment has expanded or contracted the parameters within which the agency acts, parameters that during the 1970s became wide indeed. For a better understanding of FTC performance, we must return to the agency procedures.

B. Case and project selection

To illustrate the importance of the interaction of the internal constraints and employee incentives, we discuss six attributes of agency case and project selection.

1. Market concentration doctrine

As Chapter 6 details, the Commission has substituted cases employing the market concentration doctrine for those under the Robinson-Patman Act. Independent of the relative merits of these two types of cases, this substitution served at least two important purposes. First, it was a mutually satisfactory resolution to the dispute between lawyers and economists over the Robinson-Patman (RP) Act. Second, it increased the complexity of FTC cases. When the economists received a voice in selecting cases, a clash over RP became inevitable. Robinson-Patman cases had little need for any expertise of economists and thus could not increase their influence. Moreover, Bureau of Economics support of RP would have spawned derision from the academy. To the economists, the market concentration doctrine provided the ideal vehicle for increasing their influence. As Chapter 6 explains, the doctrine gave them a central role in case selection and an important, but less crucial role, in case preparation. Further, although academic support for the doctrine decreased dramatically during the 1970s, considerable respectable support remained.

To FTC attorneys, recommending RP complaints risked the Commission following the economists' advice to vote against the complaint. Although the economists probably lost more battles with the lawyers than they won, the damage to a staff attorney's career is significant when he loses a case on which he has invested a year or so of work. Moreover, the Weinberger-Kirkpatrick personnel changes provided a unique opportunity to deemphasize RP. Attorneys knowledgeable in the arcane law of the Robinson-Patman Act lost positions of power; indeed, most left the agency entirely. The market concentration doctrine had attractive features for the attorneys who replaced them. Although some cases using the doctrine were extremely complex, and thus of dubious value to young lawyers, they involved multiple respondents and important expansions of authority, attractive features to higher staff. Further, for young lawyers, the market concentration doctrine supported many manageable cases, particularly through its justification of a strong merger program.

2. The inconsistent use of economic analysis

Section I.B of this chapter summarized the agency's inconsistent attitudes toward economic analysis. In fact, the attitudes contain a common link: The agency's position toward economics usually justifies expansion of FTC power. Thus, the Commission agrees with economists concerning deregulation to support a new FTC power, preemption of anticompetitive state laws; the agency favors some economists over others to embrace the market concentration doctrine, thereby supporting activist antitrust policy;[67] and the agency ignores economic analysis when acceptance would prohibit some of its rule-making proceedings. Further, ignoring economic analysis permits the agency to mix practice cases with structure cases, thereby resolving a conflict among the staff over complexity.[68] In short, inconsistent use of economic analysis is used to enhance the human capital of FTC attorneys.

3. Lack of price fixing

Although horizontal price fixing is one of the few business practices that almost all economists condemn, the FTC fails to attack this practice. Because neither FTC attorneys nor economists benefit from ordinary price-fixing cases, this failure is hardly surprising. For attorneys, two disadvantages exist. If criminal violations are discovered, the case may be shifted to the Department of Justice, thus decreasing its investment potential. Second, litigating these cases often requires functions identical to those of the Department of Justice, decreasing their investment value because of the competition in the private market with Justice attorneys. FTC attorneys are of more value if their Justice Department counterparts are complements, not substitutes.[69] For economists, ordinary price-fixing cases provide no special role, given the law's focus on the act of fixing prices, not on its economic consequences.[70]

4. Consumer protection rule making

At least two points deserve attention. First, emphasis on rule making contributed to human capital. Rule making provided on-the-job training in a vital new area of agency activity. Compared to less emphasis on rules, it probably increased private attorneys' fees through duplication of effort and the open-ended nature of the proceedings, and it increased the value of specific individuals who became experts in the new activity.[71] Although most rule proceedings are longer than originally planned, their length is not as serious an obstacle to young consumer protection attorneys as the length of structural cases is to young antitrust attorneys. This conclusion follows because some of the attributes of rule making most important for private practice – preparation for and participation in public hearings – occur at an earlier stage than analogous important parts of a structure case. Moreover, the agency continues many manageable consumer protection cases, thereby partly minimizing any problem of young attorney frustration.

Second, the conflicting nature of FTC project selection and the incentives of agency employees illuminate the past and the expected future roles of economists in consumer protection rule making. During the 1970s, neither economists nor lawyers enthusiastically supported the several attempts to increase economist involvement in rule making. Economics lacked a theory of consumer protection that would serve the same purposes that the market concentration doctrine serves for antitrust. Without such a theory and with standard economic analysis often extremely critical of BCP rules (see Chapters 10 through 12), economists could offer only opposition to, not a justification for increased FTC authority. Attorneys, of course, would hardly welcome such conflict.

By 1979, however, at least in part because of legal requirements within the rule-making process, economists had become involved in consumer protection rules. We predict that these economists will make two contributions. First, they will judge rules by their costs and benefits, a subject on which economists have a comparative advantage over attorneys. Given the nature of BCP rules, conflict resembling that over RP will occur, particularly in the short term. Second, some economists will attempt to develop a justification for activist rule making. The amorphous market failure concept may provide such a justification.[72] Independent of the merits of this concept as applied to particular settings, it offers economists a device to increase their influence and lawyers a device to avoid conflicts, yet still pursue activist rules.

5. Delay

Delays inevitably result as a function of conflict resolution within the Commission involving the commissioners, top staff, lower staff, and the economists. Moreover, in a hostile political environment, delay will increase because commissioners may hesitate to make tough decisions during the hostility and because action that even most of the Commission supports may exacerbate the hostility.

6. *Reorganization*

When a chairman – the most powerful person in the agency – has strong preferences inconsistent with the likely results under the existing internal organization, he will reorganize if his expected tenure allows recovery of any costs of the reorganization.[73] Reorganizations destroy existing power blocs, penalize disfavored employees, and reward favored ones. The Weinberger reorganization discussed in Chapter 1 is a classic example of the chairman's use of this power.

VI. Conclusion

This chapter has provided the foundation for a theory of FTC performance. The interaction of the agency with the political environment, the resolution of conflicts, the desire of FTC attorneys to improve their wealth, and the desire of economists to increase their individual influence all appear to shape the agency. For these variables to explain behavior, decision makers need not understand their nature any more than billiard players need to understand the laws of physics. Nor is there a need for FTC decision makers consciously to weigh alternatives in such terms as impact on their wealth or on the political environment. It is only necessary that we have appropriately specified both the constraints facing the agency and those sources of utility that most influence the relevant individuals' behavior. Of course, the ultimate value of our approach of focusing on constraints and the resulting options must await additional evidence from other agencies and from other periods of FTC history. This book, after all, is but a case study of one agency during one period of time. Nevertheless, we have attempted to show that careful use of this analytical approach can enhance understanding of agency behavior.

This chapter has taken agency constraints as given. Next, we consider how specific changes in constraints will alter performance.

16   What can be done?

TIMOTHY J. MURIS

Despite its increased powers and more competent personnel – two re-forms that the FTC's 1969 critics maintained were necessary – the agency's overall performance remains poor. Indeed, measured by the agency's impact on the economy, matters have deteriorated. Although performance has not changed, the scope of activities has: In the 1960s, the FTC attempted little; in the 1970s, it attempted much. This chapter considers what changes, if any, can improve performance. Section I considers the question of abolishing the agency, and Sections II and III consider those changes that would likely be unsuccessful and successful, respectively, in improving performance. Because higher-quality personnel have not improved matters, we concentrate on changes in the Commission's environment.[1]

I. Abolition

In determining whether the FTC is worth sustaining, we must articulate the appropriate decision criterion. To justify an FTC, it is not enough that markets may fail, that consumers are sometimes subject to fraud, or that business managers occasionally fix prices or engage in other practices that harm consumers. Rather, we must consider whether the benefits of the agency exceed the costs, given the best institutional setting that we are likely to achieve in an imperfect world. Given its current set of weak con-straints, the costs of the agency appear to exceed the benefits, with this book yet another in a long line of studies to find the FTC wanting. Before concluding that the agency should be eliminated, however, we must consider two elements.

The first is the value of the agency as a "safety valve." By referring a matter to the FTC, Congress can sometimes vent much of the steam from an issue that has attracted public attention.[2] As poorly as the FTC might handle the issue, the Commission is somewhat shielded from political pressure and can more easily delay action to allow time for more careful reflection. Thus, the FTC may perform certain functions better than Congress. Proponents of this theory offer the FTC's largest action, its suit to break up the oil industry, as an example. This case began during the height of public animosity toward the oil industry, and its existence has perhaps deflated the attacks on the industry enough to prevent ill-considered legislation.

The theory is difficult to evaluate, either in general or as applied to the oil industry. Congress members do frequently refer matters to the agency and do use agency action to answer constituent demands for correction of their problems. What would happen without the FTC, however, is unknown. Perhaps the best that can be said is that the "safety-valve" theory is plausible and serves to remind us that, even without the FTC, an absence of harmful regulation would not necessarily result. If our choice was only between the FTC of the 1970s and abolition with no replacement, we would favor abolition. Such congressional restraint, however, appears unlikely.

The second consideration in determining whether to abolish the FTC is whether specific changes can reduce the costs of agency actions while raising the benefits. We believe that such changes are possible. The next two sections of this chapter focus on changes both likely to fail and to succeed.

II. Modifications unlikely to improve FTC performance

A. Legislative veto

Although the legislative veto is the most widely discussed legislative reform of the FTC, it is not desirable for three reasons. First, as explained in Chapter 3, the veto would only occasionally be effective. The number of rules that the Commission passes will likely be so numerous, the information necessary to evaluate them critically so great, and the political pressures surrounding rules so varying that the veto is unlikely to result in continuous, close scrutiny of the agency.

Second, even when the legislative veto influences the FTC, consumers will not always benefit. This problem stems from the divergence between the influence and nature of producer and consumer interests. Producer interests will tend to be more influential in Congress because they are more concentrated,[3] with the effect of this phenomenon on FTC rules varying. With FTC rules harmful to both businesses and to consumers as a class (e.g., the mobile homes rule discussed in Chapter 13), successful producer lobbying would benefit consumers. In other rules, producer and consumer interests differ, as in the rules attacking the professions described in Chapter 10. Because some of the most beneficial FTC rules involve industries with influential members in every congressional district in the United States – professions, for example – this problem will be serious. Another reason that the veto will not always benefit consumers is that consumer interests differ from those of consumerists to the extent that the latter are not representative of consumers as a class, as the evidence in Chapter 3 suggests.[4] For example, consumerists with a higher-than-average preference for quality may effectively lobby the Congress to not veto rules (e.g., mobile homes) that reflect this preference. The third reason why the veto is not desirable is that business leaders and legislators tend to look upon the legislative veto as "the solution" to the problem of the FTC. This quick-fix attitude decreases the possibility of potentially more effective reforms becoming law.

Rather than the kind of hit-or-miss supervision that would occur under a legislative veto, detailed and continuous supervision of FTC actions is needed. Judicial focus on the substantive criteria of FTC decisions would provide such supervision. Because such a procedure would probably require a legislative change,[5] we will discuss it when we focus on the institution that would be the primary constraining force, the judiciary.

B. *Industry exemptions*

Throughout 1979, as the unpopularity of the FTC grew, several firms and even entire industries attempted to have Congress end funding for FTC investigations regarding them or to have their industries exempted from the FTC Act.[6] This is a poor strategy for dealing with the FTC. Because only a handful of industries are likely to win congressional approval, the exemption strategy leaves the problems of the FTC uncorrected for consumers in industries still subject to FTC scrutiny. Moreover, exemptions provide no guidance to the FTC other than to avoid regulating industries with political clout. This message embodies an additional problem inherent within the exemption strategy. By seeking exemptions, critics of the FTC appeared motivated by a desire to protect "special interests," rather than to remedy the agency's poor performance. The exemption strategy thus allowed the FTC to portray itself as a victim of special interests, rather than as the seriously defective organization that this book reveals it to be.

C. *"Revolving door"*

Agency personnel are often criticized for moving between the agency and the industries it regulates. FTC attorneys move from representing the Commission to representing private clients before the Commission (except in cases on which they were involved during their agency tenure). Because the wealth of these attorneys is positively linked to an activist agency regardless of the agency's impact on consumers, this book offers a new argument to curtail the "revolving door" between FTC employment and private clients before the agency, particularly for the higher-level staff who are most influential in decision making. By itself, however, this reform is unlikely to improve performance. If constraints on the FTC remain weak, then individual preferences remain important. When the importance of wealth is reduced, another preference will be pursued, and there is no reason to believe that benefiting consumers as a class will receive high priority.

III. Modifications likely to improve FTC performance

A. Congress: budget moratorium

A five-year moratorium on budget increases should be instituted – a freeze that, given inflation, would effectively halve the agency. Nevertheless, this would leave adequate resources for current beneficial projects and would create an incentive for reform. At the end of five years, if the reforms suggested here have been implemented and performance has improved, Congress could reconsider the budget.

B. Judiciary

As indicated in Chapter 4, the Commission is free within very wide parameters to decide what is legal and illegal under Section 5 of the FTC Act. If the judiciary is to provide an effective constraint, this discretion must be narrowed.

What form of judicial constraint will improve FTC performance? This depends upon what one believes the FTC's mission ought to be. Fortunately, a consensus exists on this point. Both the critics of 1969 and those who have since praised or damned the FTC have concluded that the agency must be evaluated according to how well it protects the economic well-being of consumers. To determine whether a particular action benefits consumers, economic analysis is appropriate and accordingly should be the touchstone for legality under the FTC Act.[7] Both deception and unfairness should be defined economically.[8] As Chapter 13 implies, deception should be defined to eliminate the fools test and to include a materiality element. Thus, an act or practice would not be deceptive unless it misled a reasonable person and unless the misleading aspect caused consumers to change position to their detriment. Unfairness, whether in terms of acts, practices, or methods of competition, should be defined in terms of actual injury to consumers where market forces and private law are inadequate to prevent the injury. For actions in which the Commission's remedy would cause a major change in industry practices, such as rule making, deconcentration, mandatory warranties, or information disclosure, we would further require cost/benefit analysis, reviewable in the courts.[9]

This approach will focus decisions on consumer welfare, giving the courts a tool to narrow FTC discretion. The Commission acts in the name of protecting the consumer, and economic analysis is the ideal tool to determine whether a proceeding in fact serves that end. Of course, objections to our approach will arise, particularly to the cost/benefit analysis. Most prominent among them is that benefits and costs cannot be appropriately measured. For four reasons, this objection should not bar the proposed reform. First, skepticism about such statements is needed to avoid chicanery:

If there is a demand for information, the cry goes out that what the organization does cannot be measured. . . . Oftentimes this is another way of saying, "Mind your own business." Sometimes the line taken is that the work is so subtle that it resists any tests. On other occasions the point is made that only those schooled in esoteric arts can properly understand what the organization does and they can barely communicate to the uninitiated. There are men so convinced of the ultimate righteousness of their cause that they cannot imagine why anyone would wish to know how well they are doing in handling our common difficulties. Their activities are literally priceless; vulgar notions of cost and benefit do not apply to them.[10]

Second, the FTC will not base its judgments on noneconomic criteria (such as distributional effects) that would complicate cost/benefit analysis. The focus will be only on the economic welfare of consumers as a group. Third, the FTC will rarely be involved in resolving great scientific controversies that complicate cost/benefit analysis in areas such as nuclear power. Fourth, the FTC would not always need to show with certainty that benefits exceed cost. Where the agency's evidence does not prove that the benefits exceed the cost, but does show that sufficient benefits are likely but cannot be demonstrated at the time of the proceeding, the FTC rule or orders should be approved with an automatic five-year sunset provision. At the end of the five years, if the agency cannot then show that benefits exceed costs, the rule or order will lapse. This procedure would allow the agency to collect before and after data to demonstrate the net benefits of its action.[11]

The cost/benefit standard alone will not guarantee an end to anticonsumer regulation. The Commission would still have broad discretion in some cases, particularly where evidence is in serious conflict. Requiring the FTC to show that its cases produce benefits exceeding costs would at the very least, however, limit FTC discretion to impose costly regulation upon consumers without compensating benefits. It would be an important step toward transforming the agency from a lawless one (i.e., not subject to meaningful court review) to one based upon the appropriate rule of law: the welfare of consumers.

If the FTC Act is not changed to narrow the agency's discretion, other appropriate alternative steps would be to eliminate its unfairness jurisdiction or at least to prevent the FTC from proceeding on an industry-wide basis via rule making or the notice provisions of Section 5(m) of the FTC Act.[12] Because these reforms would still leave the agency broad discretion in areas where it could act and would eliminate some of the most beneficial FTC activities (e.g., the attack on anticompetitive state laws), the cost/benefit approach is superior.

To strengthen cost/benefit review, groups appearing before the Commission must also improve their performance. Businesses subject to Commission regulation tend to avoid making their case against the FTC on the substantive ground of consumer welfare.[13] Even within FTC rule making, where the stakes are high and the statute requires findings concerning the impact of the rule on consumers, many industries have instead opposed the Commission procedurally, politically, and even on grounds that the agency will destroy the industry.[14] Careful economic analysis supported by hard data has been the exception, not the rule. This absence of economic analysis has made it easier for the FTC staff and the Commission to conclude that the practices they subject to scrutiny do not benefit consumers.

More careful rebuttal of the substantive merits of FTC proposals will help constrain the agency in at least three ways. Most important, such business action will increase the effectiveness of court review, even under a cost/benefit standard. Second, these arguments are more likely to be persuasive to the FTC than those based on procedure, politics, or scare tactics. Third, business focus on the welfare of consumers will provide for more informed discussion of FTC actions in the press, the Congress, and the academy.

C. Executive

The executive branch should encourage cost/benefit analysis. Current executive regulations to provide such analysis, however, do not impose sufficient penalties for noncompliance or poor analysis.[15] Thus, the executive branch should support judicial review of the cost/benefit test or penalize noncompliance through the budget process.

D. Within the Commission

1. Use of economics

As we have indicated, a major failure of the Commission is mishandling economic analysis. To correct this failure, it is not enough for the Commission or the chairman to order the staff to be more attuned to economics and to cost/benefit analysis; instead, the approach must be institutionalized. We recommend four changes. First, we would establish an office whose sole function is to serve as a "devil's advocate." This office would report to the Commission, reviewing major staff proposals to highlight factual, theoretical, and legal defects. With access to different and opposing sources of information, the Commission should be capable of reaching better decisions. Although this approach may appear too adversarial to some, it simply recognizes the reality at the FTC. As Chapter 15 indicates, the staff in effect already acts as an advocate when making proposals to the Commission. Without the active support of at least the chairman, however, the advocate will have little effect. Unless the operating staff knows that the advocate has support at the Commission level, they can ignore the advocate and even curtail its information sources. Because the advocate's effectiveness will thus turn to some extent on who the chairman is, this reform is more fragile than the external ones.[16]

Second, the impacts of major theories under which the Commission brings projects, such as its various theories of advertising deception and anticompetitive practices, should be tested via evaluations of test cases and rules. These evaluations would study the results of past actions to see if they had attained the intended effects. Although the Commission has recently begun this procedure, we would expand it and would remove testing from control of the staff who were originally responsible for the project. That staff should have input to the evaluation, but not control.

A third internal change concerns the Bureau of Economics. We would institute a system of peer review to allow professional feedback from outside the FTC. A board of prominent industrial organization economists, representing a cross section of views, should periodically analyze and critically comment upon major bureau memoranda concerning cases and rules. As Chapter 15 detailed, the bureau has an incentive to support some theories independent of their merits. For this reason, economists who favor those theories are likely to seek FTC employment in disproportionate numbers. Improving contacts with and feedback from the leaders of the economics profession would not correct this problem, but at least would militate against any tendency of the bureau to become isolated from expert comment on the quality of its work.[17]

Finally, we would require the staff, when making proposals, to weigh explicitly various alternatives. Thus, whenever the FTC is considering an action, the staff would have to determine the precise objectives of the action, alternative solutions to the problem, including market-enhancing options, and the expected costs and benefits. Like other internal constraints, these suggested changes will succeed only if accompanied by strong leadership or if incorporated into the formal decision-making process.

2. Abolishing adjudication

Critics have frequently suggested that the Commission be stripped of its adjudicative authority.[18] Although this reform would remove any appearance of impropriety from the prosecutor acting as judge and jury,[19] it would not necessarily have a significant beneficial impact on the outcome of FTC cases. Because Bureau of Consumer Protection projects increasingly have relied upon rules and because our cost/benefit approach discussed below would appropriately reform that activity, we here focus on the effect of removing adjudication of FTC cases brought under antitrust theories.

Determining the precise effect of this change would require a comparison of the constraints and incentives of federal court judges with those of Federal Trade Commissioners, a comparison that we cannot completely perform here because a study of judges is beyond the scope of this book. We do note, however, that at least two variables appear to be vital to determining the effect. One involves the Supreme Court, which ultimately decides the meaning of antitrust law, regardless of whether cases are originally heard in the FTC or in the federal courts. The Court consequently will have a key influence in determining the outcome of FTC antitrust cases. The second concerns judicial treatment of factual issues. Removal of adjudication would be important if we could assume that federal judges are less likely to find for the agency on close questions of fact – a perhaps plausible assumption because judges are less closely tied to the agency than commissioners are. Removal would be beneficial, however, only if we could further assume that federal judges would do a better overall job of evaluating factual questions. The lifetime tenure and the higher prestige of federal judgeships provide some reasons to believe that this would be so. That commissioners have more experience with antitrust than most judges have does not mean that judges will do a poorer job, given that the FTC possesses no expertise that judges could not easily acquire.

Of course, these two variables are interrelated. The Court could leave considerable discretion in trial court judges by making the law turn on many factual questions. Alternatively, the Court could narrow the range of discretion of the trial court judge. For example, in merger cases in the

1960s, district court judges repeatedly found for defendants, only to be reversed by the Supreme Court, with the Court severely limiting the district courts' power to question the government's judgment as to the legality of a merger.[20] If the Court takes this attitude in antitrust cases, putting FTC cases in federal courts would have a marginal impact. On the other hand, the current Court has reinterpreted the law both to make government success less automatic and to make factual matters more important. In this new judicial environment, removing FTC antitrust adjudication to the federal courts could influence the agency. There appears no harm from the change and some chance for benefit.

IV. Conclusions

In front of the main FTC building in Washington, a statue depicts a man – the FTC – attempting to rein in an unruly horse – American industry. The reality has changed: The FTC has become the horse and consumers the man. Although it is uncertain whether the agency can be reined in to serve its beneficial purposes, the reforms outlined in this chapter attempt to attack the heart of the problem: the weakness of the FTC's constraints. Since 1970, the FTC's budget and power have grown dramatically, without a corresponding increase in the ability of other institutions to check them. So powerful and harmful an agency must be constrained. Consumers simply cannot afford otherwise.

Notes

1. Introduction

1 *Washington Post,* February 6, 1977, p. C-1.
2 For several examples of such trivia, see Chapter 4. Of course, the Commission engaged in many diverse activities over the years. Although some of these were major and innovative, such as the 1964 cigarette rule, which asserted that the FTC possessed substantive rule-making power, most of the innovations dealt with trivia.
3 See Gerard C. Henderson, *The Federal Trade Commission* (New Haven, Conn.: Yale University Press, 1924); George J. Alexander, *Honesty and Competition: False-Advertising Law and Policy under FTC Administration* (Syracuse, N.Y.: Syracuse University Press, 1967); Commission on Organization of the Executive Branch of the Government (Hoover Commission), *Task Force Report on Regulatory Commissions* (1949), app. N; James M. Landis, *Report on Regulatory Agencies to the President-elect* (1960), 230–41; Carl A. Auerbach, "The Federal Trade Commission: Internal Organization and Procedure," 48 *Minnesota Law Review* 383 (1964). See also Robert Heller & Associates, Inc., *Federal Trade Commission Management Survey Report* (1954); U.S. Civil Service Commission, *Evaluation of Personnel Management, Federal Trade Commission* (1965); see, generally, "Federal Trade Commission Silver Anniversary Issue," 8 *George Washington Law Review* 249 (1940); "Symposium on the Federal Trade Commission: A Program of Enforcement," 38 *Indiana Law Journal* 319 (1963); "The Fiftieth Anniversary of the Federal Trade Commission," 64 *Columbia Law Review* 385 (1964). For a personal, and very stinging, criticism of the FTC, see Lowell B. Mason, *The Language of Dissent* (Cleveland, Ohio: World Publishing Co., 1959).
4 See Commission on Organization of the Executive Branch of the Government (Hoover Commission), *Task Force Report, supra* note 3, at 41.
5 Edward F. Cox, Robert C. Fellmeth, and John E. Schultz, *The Nader Report on the Federal Trade Commission* (New York: Barron Press, 1969); reprinted as *The Consumer and the Federal Trade Commission,* 115 *Congressional Record* (Part 2) 1539 (1969).
6 *Id.,* at 150. Like some other charges, this one may have been overstated. "Bright men did not apply" may have been just as appropriate. The reasons why many top law students may have shunned the FTC –

for example, the agency was absorbed in trivia and poorly run – demonstrate, however, that the central theme of the report was correct. For a detailed critique of some of the report's excesses, see Ernest T. Gellhorn, "Book Review: *The Consumer and the Federal Trade Commission,*" 68 *Michigan Law Review* 151 (1969).

7 See Burton A. Weisbrod, ed., *Public Interest Law: An Economic and Institutional Analysis* (Berkeley, Calif.: University of California Press, 1978); Senate Committee on Government Operations, *Study on Federal Regulations: The Regulatory Appointments Process* (1977), ch. 13.

8 *Hearings on FTC before the Subcommittee on Independent Offices and Department of Housing and Urban Development of the House Committee on Appropriations,* 91st Cong., 1st Sess. (February 5, 1969). This Nader report dealt only with Commission consumer protection activities. Another Nader report – Mark J. Green, Beverly C. Moore, and Bruce Wasserstein, *The Closed Enterprise System: Ralph Nader's Study Group on Antitrust Enforcement* (New York: Grossman, 1972) – discussed FTC antitrust activities, again very critically.

9 *Hearings on FTC, supra* note 8, at 23.

10 See American Bar Association, *Report of the ABA Commission to Study the Federal Trade Commission* (1969), p. 86.

11 *Id.,* at 3.

12 *The Ash Report,* an internal government report released in January 1971, recommended that the FTC be abolished, with its consumer protection responsibilities vested in a new Federal Trade Practices Agency headed by a single administrator and the antitrust responsibility transferred to a new Federal Antitrust Board. Although this report generated considerable controversy, it seems to have had little or no direct impact upon the Commission. This report was reprinted in Roy L. Ash *et al.,* "Ash Report on the FTC: Antitrust Moving to the White House?," 4 *Antitrust Law and Economics Review* 21 (Fall 1970).

13 *Hearings on FTC Appropriations before the Subcommittee on Agriculture and Environmental and Consumer Protection Appropriations of the House Committee on Appropriations,* 92nd Cong., 1st Sess., 3 (1971), pp. 213–14. See also 457 *Antitrust and Trade Regulation Report* (BNA) (April 14, 1970), p. X-1. There is some disagreement about the number of cases closed, with estimates ranging from 450 to 700.

14 434 *Antitrust and Trade Regulation Report* (BNA) (November 4, 1969), p. X-2. Chapter 15 will briefly discuss the relation of the criticism of the FTC discussed here to the changes in the FTC that are also described in Chapter 1.

15 Senate Committee on Government Operations report, *supra* note 7, at 210.

16 *Id.,* at 212. Further, Weinberger had earlier seemed to encourage the regional offices by allowing them greater freedom to conduct their own investigations.

17 465 *Antitrust and Trade Regulation Report* (BNA) (June 9, 1970), at A-1.

18 Senate Committee on Government Operations report, *supra* note 7, at 209.

19 *Id.,* at 209.

20 *Id.,* at 213.

21 *Id.*, at 214.
22 *Id.*, at 215–28.
23 See, e.g., Judy Gardner, "FTC Seeks Wider Impact in Antitrust Work: Puts New Emphasis on Planning," 4 *National Journal* 1151 (1972); 554 *Antitrust and Trade Regulation Report* (BNA) (August 22, 1972), at A-6 (discussing ABA antitrust law panel that found new vitality in FTC). But see Subcommittee on Commerce and Finance (Senate Committee on Interstate and Foreign Commerce), 93rd Cong., 1st Sess., *Staff Report: The Federal Trade Commission – 1974* (1975), arguing that the criticism of the Nader and ABA reports as to lack of output, poor planning, and inadequate management still applied. Although the report is correct in stating that the FTC oversold its planning accomplishments, and many cases in litigation in 1974 were as dubious as those that the ABA had criticized, its major conclusion – that the FTC's output was declining – is misinformed. The number of complaints and investigations did drop, but focus on such data ignores the shift to very large cases and rules that was under way. For the FTC's response, see 688 *Antitrust and Trade Regulation Report* (BNA) (May 8, 1976), at A-1.
24 During Paul Rand Dixon's short tenure as acting chairman of the FTC in early 1976, he attempted to reinvigorate Robinson-Patman Act enforcement. Although he apparently was successful in getting some investigations started, he did not have a major impact in terms of resources spent or complaints brought. For recent evidence that the FTC still engages in some Robinson-Patman Act enforcement, see *FTC: Watch* (July 12, 1978), p. 1.
25 For discussion of FTC goals and policies under Pertschuk, see *Law and Business, A Dialogue with the Federal Trade Commission* (New York: Harcourt Brace Jovanovich, 1979).
26 See the introduction to Part II.
27 For an explanation of the standard utility maximization approach, see Roger L. Miller, *Intermediate Microeconomics: Theory, Issues, and Applications* (New York: McGraw-Hill Book Company, 1978), ch. 2.
28 See, e.g., the sources cited in notes 3, 5, and 10 *supra.*
29 Part I also employs some economic and political analyses.
30 Applying the utility maximization theorem to governmental employees has recently significantly enhanced the understanding of bureaucratic decision making. In particular,. see Kenneth W. Clarkson and Donald L. Martin, eds., *The Economics of Nonproprietary Organizations* (Greenwich, Conn.: JAI Press, 1980). This approach permits specific implications (or predictions as we often call them in this book) to be derived from the conjunction of the proper identification of both external and internal constraints facing FTC decision makers with the basic utility maximization theorems of economics. Of course, if one could *also* identify preferences of individual Commission decision makers *ex ante,* the predictions would be more accurate. At present, however, there is no accurate method for identifying preferences of each FTC decision maker.

2. Statutory powers

1 See FTC Budget Justification to Congress for Fiscal Year 1980. We do not discuss all 27 statutes in this chapter.

2 15 U.S.C. § 45 (1976).
3 38 Stat. 717 (1938).
4 15 U.S.C. §§ 12–27 (1976).
5 87 Stat. 591 (1973).
6 See the article cited in Chapter 1 *supra*, at note 1. Although National Petroleum Refiners Association v. FTC, 482 F.2d 672 (D.C. Cir. 1973) *cert. denied* 415 U.S. 951 (1974), had given the agency substantive rule-making power, the Improvements Act removed any lingering doubt about the Commission's rule-making ability.
7 See, e.g., FTC Budget Justification to Congress for Fiscal Year 1977 (1976), p. 51.
8 Wool Products Labeling Act of 1940, 54 Stat. 1128 (1940) [current version at 15 U.S.C. §§ 68–68j (1976)]; Fur Products Labeling Act of 1951, 65 Stat. 175 (1951) [current version at 15 U.S.C. §§ 1051–1127 (1976)]; Textile Fiber Products Identification Act of 1958, 72 Stat. 1717 (1958) [current version at 15 U.S.C. §§ 70–70k (1976)].
9 For description of the problems that these statutes cause for consumers, see Alan Stone, *Economic Regulation in the Public Interest* (Ithaca, N.Y.: Cornell University Press, 1977), ch. 9.
10 See FTC Annual Report for 1970; FTC Budget Justification to Congress for Fiscal Year 1979.
11 15 U.S.C. §§ 1451–61 (1976); Federal Cigarette Labeling and Advertising Act of 1966, 79 Stat. 282 (1966) [current version at 15 U.S.C. §§ 1331–39 (1976)]; Truth in Lending Act, 82 Stat. 146 (1968) [current version at 15 U.S.C. § 1601 *et seq.* (1976)]. Further, three additional special statutes are Export Trade Act, 40 Stat. 516 (1918) [current version at 15 U.S.C. §§ 61–65 (1976)]; Lanham Trademark Act of 1946, 60 Stat. 427 (1946) [current version at 15 U.S.C. § 1051 *et seq.* (1976)]; Packers & Stockyards Act, 42 Stat. 159 (1921) [current version at 7 U.S.C. § 181 *et seq.* (1976)].
12 Fair Credit Billing Act, 84 Stat. 1128 (1970) [codified at 15 U.S.C. § 1681 *et seq.* (1976)]; Consumer Leasing Act, 90 Stat. 257 (1976) [codified at 15 U.S.C. § 1667 (1976)]; Fair Debt Collection Practices Act, 91 Stat. 874 (1977) [codified at 15 U.S.C. § 1692 (Supp. I 1977)].
13 In 1978, the Commission received four other special statutes regarding energy resources. Petroleum Marketing Practices Act, 92 Stat. 322 (1978); Outer Continental Shelf Lands Act Amendment of 1978, 92 Stat. 629 (1978); National Energy Conservation Policy Act, 92 Stat. 3200 (1978); Power Plant and Industrial Fuel Ore Act of 1978, 92 Stat. 3289 (1978).
14 See Budget Justification to Congress for Fiscal Year 1979.

3. Legislative constraints

1 We speak of Congress taking an action for convenience. Of course, it is more appropriate to discuss Congress in terms of its myriad subparts.
2 The Congress also participates in the appointments process for top FTC officials, a constraint discussed in Chapter 5.
3 Richard F. Fenno, Jr., *The Power of the Purse; Appropriations Politics in Congress* (Boston: Little, Brown and Company, 1966). See also Aaron B. Wildavsky, *The Politics of the Budgetary Process* (Boston: Little, Brown and Company, 1964).

4 Fenno, *supra* note 3.
5 A measure that focuses on the difference between the OMB approved request and congressional appropriation may be crude, since either the FTC could modify its request to OMB or OMB could modify its allowance (the offered request to Congress) to meet expected congressional action. Despite these problems the measure is useful when the congressional appropriation is above or below the official request to Congress. More important, the change in congressional appropriations over time has been positive.
6 *Condominium Consumer Protection Act of 1975: Hearings before the Senate Committee on Banking, Housing and Urban Affairs,* 94th Cong., 1st Sess. (1975). See also *Federal Trade Commission Condominium Decision and Operations: Hearing before the Subcommittee on Commerce, Consumer and Monetary Affairs of the House Committee on Government Operations,* 94th Cong., 1st Sess. (April 30, 1975); *Condominium Development and Sales Practices: Hearing before the Subcommittee on General Oversight and Renegotiation of the House Committee on Banking, Currency and Housing,* 94th Cong., 2nd Sess. (May 19, 1976).
7 Calculated from the data given in note 3 *supra.*
8 *Budget of the U.S. Government Appendix, Department of State, Justice, and Commerce, the Judiciary, and Related Agencies and Appropriations: Hearings before the Subcommittee on State, Justice, Commerce, and the Judiciary Appropriations for Fiscal Years 1976–1979.* (Washington, D.C.: U.S. Government Printing Office, 1970–80). 92 Stat. 1040 (1978).
9 92 Stat. 1040 (1978).
10 Letter from the Comptroller General of the United States to John E. Moss, Chairman, Subcommittee on Commerce and Finance (July 24, 1974).
11 House Committee on Appropriations, *Report on the Agriculture-Environmental and Consumer Protection Appropriation Bill,* H.R. Rep. No. 1120, 93rd Cong., 2d Sess. 12 (1977), p. 12.
12 A letter supplied by GAO identified 15 documents issued between 1970 and 1977 that dealt with the FTC. Nine of the 15 documents were letters sent by GAO to the FTC or Congress members, dealing with topics such as the Flammable Fabric Act, government procurement, the line-of-business program, information search and copy fees, and the monitoring of the oil industry. The other six documents dealt with fees and charges of regulatory agencies, the advertisement substantiation program, the Webb-Pomerene Act, the energy industry, and GAO's responsibilities under the Federal Reports Act. Based on a survey of official documents and interviews with previous and present FTC commissioners and officials, the effects of GAO inquiries were minimal.
13 Letter from the Comptroller General of the United States to the Chairman of the Committee of Appropriations, House of Representatives (March 5, 1975).
14 Subcommittee on Oversight and Investigation of the Senate Committee on Interstate and Foreign Commerce, *Federal Regulation and Regulatory Reform* (1975 and 1978) (hereinafter 1975 and 1978 Moss Questionnaires).
15 *Oversight Hearings into the Federal Trade Commission Bureau of Consumer Protection (Delays in Rulemaking – Regulation of Advertising):*

Hearings before the Subcommittee on Commerce, Consumer and Monetary Affairs of the House Committee on Governmental Operations, 94th Cong., 2d Sess. (1976).

16 Nominations: Hearings before the Senate Commerce Committee, 94th Cong., 2d Sess. (1976).

17 See, e.g., *Regulations of Various Federal Regulatory Agencies and Their Effect on Small Business: Hearings before the Subcommittee on Activities of Regulatory Agencies of the House Committee on Small Business,* Part IV, 94th Cong., 2d Sess. (1976).

18 *Regulation of Various Federal Regulatory Agencies and Their Effect on Small Business: Hearings before the Subcommittee on Activities of Regulatory Agencies of the House Committee on Small Business,* Part V, 94th Cong., 2d Sess. (1976), at 61.

19 The agency must respond in good faith to congressional inquiries to avoid congressional attacks on its authority and budget unrelated to the substance of FTC programs.

20 This may be changing with funerals.

21 For one scenario, see *FTC: Watch* (November 30, 1979), pp. 8–11.

22 See, e.g., the House version of the FTC appropriations Bill (H.R. 2313) passed with amendments on November 27, 1979, reported in 125 *Congressional Record* H1189. The amendments included a one-house legislative veto and restrictions on FTC action concerning trademarks, agricultural cooperatives, and the funeral industry. See also the discussion of the political environment in Chapter 15, Sections II and V, *infra.*

23 See *Wall Street Journal,* September 4, 1979, pp. 1, 31. See also Chapter 10. As Chapters 10 and 15 describe, however, the FTC still continues many controversial initiatives virtually unchanged.

24 See, generally, Chapters 6 to 14 *infra.*

25 See 835 *Antitrust and Trade Regulation Report* (BNA) (October 20, 1977), p. A-2.

26 See 883 *Antitrust Trade and Regulation Report* (BNA) (October 5, 1978), p. A-5.

27 See, generally, Charles C. Clapp, *The Congressman: His Work As He Sees It* (Garden City, N.Y.: Doubleday & Co., 1964).

28 This may be confirmed by examining the choice of committee by senior congressional members.

29 In our discussion we assume that the groups are formulated with well-defined purposes. It is beyond the scope of this study to investigate the free-rider and other problems associated with group activity. See, for example, Mancur Olson, Jr., *The Logic of Collective Action: Public Goods and the Theory of Groups,* 2d ed. (New York: Schocken Books, 1971); George J. Stigler, "Free-Riders and Collective Action: An Appendix to Theories of Economic Regulation," 5 *Bell Journal of Economics* 359 (Autumn 1974), pp. 359–65.

30 Morris P. Fiorina, *Congress: Keystone of the Washington Establishment* (New Haven, Conn.: Yale University Press, 1977).

31 James M. Buchanan and Marilyn R. Flowers, *The Public Finances* (Homewood, Ill.: Richard D. Irwin, 1975) pp. 113–14; Kenneth Arrow, *Social Choice and Individual Values* (New York: John Wiley & Sons, 1963).

32 Priscilla A. LaBarbera, "An Empirical Investigation of Consumer Participants in Federal Trade Commission Consumer Protection Rule-making Procedures" (unpublished Ph.D dissertation, Michigan State University,

1975). See also 663 *Antitrust and Trade Regulation Report* (BNA) (October 9, 1973).

33 Notable exceptions include a statistical analysis of FTC Robinson-Patman Act enforcement for 1954 through 1970. In the fiscal year 1971 appropriation hearings, one letter charging lack of oversight was included with the budget. The fiscal year 1972 Senate authorization hearings included a Federal Trade Commission response to the appropriation committee report on the FTC.

34 Table 3.3 gives a sample of questions.

35 *Shortage of Home Canning Equipment: Hearing before The Subcommittee on Commodities and Services of the Subcommittee on Activities of Regulatory Agencies of the House Committee on Small Business*, Part V, 94th Cong., 2d Sess. (1976), at 61.

36 Ernest T. Gellhorn and Harold H. Bruff, "Congressional Control of Administrative Regulation: A Study of Legislative Vetoes," 90 *Harvard Law Review* 1369 (1977).

37 See H.R. 3822 (1978). This legislative veto provision did not become law.

38 H.R. 2313 is a 1980 authorization bill. See 914 *Antitrust and Trade Regulation Report* (BNA) (May 17, 1979).

39 Gellhorn and Bruff, *supra* note 36, at 1422–23 (footnote omitted).

40 See Kenneth W. Clarkson, *Food Stamps and Nutrition* (Washington, D.C.: American Enterprise Institute, 1975), pp. 73–74.

4. Judicial constraints

1 In keeping with the theme of this study, procedural matters (e.g., enforcement of subpoenas) will not be discussed. We treat as substantive the question of what evidence the FTC needs to prove before a court will sustain its findings.

2 In determining whether a practice is legal, a reviewing court may disagree with the agency position because of "insufficient facts." See, e.g., note 63 and accompanying text below. Although our focus will be on FTC freedom to define what practices are illegal, we are not asserting that there is an easily discernible line between questions of law and those of fact.

3 253 U.S. 421 (1920). Because the FTC is a party to all cases, we will not list it in citing the case. The nongovernment party will be listed only when not mentioned in the text.

4 258 F. 314, 317 (2d Cir. 1919).

5 253 U.S. 421, 427 (1920).

6 *Id.*, at 436.

7 280 U.S. 19 (1929).

8 *Id.*, at 28.

9 283 U.S. 643 (1931).

10 *Id.*, at 649.

11 291 U.S. 67 (1934).

12 64 F.2d 618 (9th Cir. 1933).

13 291 U.S. 67, 76 (1934).

14 See S. Forrester Davidson, "The Place of the Federal Trade Commission in Administrative Law," 8 *George Washington Law Review* 280 (1939), pp. 303–4.

15 291 U.S. 304 (1934).
16 *Id.*, at 314.
17 302 U.S. 112 (1937).
18 86 F.2d 692, 695–96 (1936).
19 302 U.S. 112, 116 (1937).
20 *Ibid.*
21 The distinction made here between consumer protection and antitrust follows that of current FTC enforcement as discussed in the introduction to Part II.
22 George J. Alexander, *Honesty and Competition: False-Advertising Law and Policy under FTC Administration* (Syracuse, N.Y.: Syracuse University Press, 1967), p. 8 (footnote omitted).
23 Mary Carter Paint, 382 U.S. 46 (1965). See Robert Pitofsky, "Beyond Nader: Consumer Protection and the Regulation of Advertising," 90 *Harvard Law Review* 661 (1977), pp. 688–89.
24 Gelb, 144 F.2d 580 (2d Cir. 1944).
25 See Alexander, *supra* note 22, at 69, for a detailed discussion; Chapter 13 *infra*.
26 See Ernest T. Gellhorn, "Proof of Consumer Deception before the Federal Trade Commission," 17 *Kansas Law Review* 559 (1969), for a leading article on this point.
27 See Pitofsky, *supra* note 23, at 677–78.
28 See, e.g., Zenith Radio Corp., 143 F.2d 29 (7th Cir. 1944).
29 See, generally, Frederick M. Rowe, *Price Discrimination under the Robinson-Patman Act* (Boston: Little, Brown and Company, 1964).
30 See note 43 *infra* and accompanying text.
31 U.S. v. Von's Grocery, 384 U.S. 270, 301 (1966) (Stewart, J., dissenting).
32 See Chapter 2 *supra*. James C. Lang, "The Legislative History of the Federal Trade Commission Act," 13 *Washburn Law Journal* 6 (1974).
33 384 U.S. 316, 320 (1966).
34 339 F.2d 45 (8th Cir. 1965).
35 384 U.S. 316, 321–22 (footnote omitted).
36 Continental TV v. GTE Sylvania, 433 U.S. 36 (1977).
37 405 U.S. 233 (1972).
38 *Id.*, at 244.
39 327 U.S. 608, 612–13 (1946).
40 See, e.g., ITT Continental Baking Co., 532 F.2d 207 (2d Cir. 1976) for a listing of many of the cases.
41 There may be some limits to the FTC's discretion. For example, the Pertschuk Administration has discussed moving against practices of a different nature than those traditionally attacked, including sex discrimination and hiring of illegal aliens. See, e.g., 892 *Antitrust and Trade Regulation Report* (BNA) (December 14, 1978), p. A-23. A court would probably not consider the cases discussed in this chapter as dispositive of an FTC attack on such practices.
42 545 *Antitrust and Trade Regulation Report* (BNA) (January 11, 1972), p. A-6. In another interview, the current director of the Bureau of Consumer Protection expressed a more cautious view of his bureau's power under Section 5, perhaps reflecting awareness of the possible limitations upon FTC freedom discussed in Section IV *infra*. See 848 *Antitrust and Trade Regulation Report* (BNA) (January 26, 1978), p. A-15.
43 See A. Everette MacIntyre and Joachin J. Volhard, "The FTC and Incipient Unfairness," 41 *George Washington Law Review* 407 (1973), pp. 433–35.

44 Bunte Brothers, Inc., 312 U.S. 349 (1940) (not in commerce); National Casualty Co., 357 U.S. 560 (1958) (McCarron-Ferguson Act prevented FTC authority over advertising of insurance company).
45 Warner-Lambert Co., 562 F.2d 749 (D.C. Cir. 1977), *cert. denied*, 435 U.S. 950 (1978) (corrective advertising); Firestone Tire and Rubber Co., 481 F.2d 246 (6th Cir. 1973), *cert. denied*, 414 U.S. 1112 (1973) (substantiation). These doctrines are discussed in Chapter 13 *infra*.
46 L. G. Balfour Co., 442 F.2d 1 (7th Cir. 1971).
47 Spiegel, Inc., 494 F.2d 59 (7th Cir. 1971), *cert. denied*, 419 U.S. 896 (1974). Spiegel, in its advertising circulars, offered products on a 30-day "free trial" or at a "percentage off." These offers were subject to the customer meeting Spiegel's credit qualifications, a requirement mentioned in small print on some of the offers and stated in the Spiegel catalog. Further, the customer submitted credit-related data with the order. The Commission claimed that the circulars had a capacity to mislead the public because they allegedly created the impression that the offer was unconditional when actually it depended on the customer's credit rating. The court agreed with the Commission that the offer was misleading. Judge Pell, in a convincing dissent, stated that the Commission had found "a detriment to the public interest in the situation of deadbeats being deceived into thinking that they are going to receive a free trial of, or discount on, merchandise which they could not realistically purchase on either a cash or a deferred basis." *Id.*, at 65. Moreover, that the order form requested credit information would certainly inform anyone of reasonable intelligence that the merchandise would only be sent to good credit risks.
48 Cinderella Career and Finishing Schools, Inc., 425 F.2d 583 (D.C. Cir. 1970).
49 Marco Sales Co., 452 F.2d 1 (2d Cir. 1971).
50 Bendix Corp., 450 F.2d 534 (6th Cir. 1971).
51 Heater, 503 F.2d 321 (9th Cir. 1974).
52 BOC Int'l., 557 F.2d 24 (2d Cir. 1977).
53 Spiegel, Inc., 540 F.2d 287 (7th Cir. 1976); Golden Grain Macaroni Co., 472 F.2d 882 (9th Cir. 1972), *cert. denied*, 491 U.S. 918 (1973); Beatrice Foods Co., 540 F.2d 303 (7th Cir. 1976); Abex Corp., 420 F.2d 928 (6th Cir. 1970), *cert. denied*, 400 U.S. 865 (1970).
54 Harbor Banana Distributors, 499 F.2d 395 (5th Cir. 1974); SCM Corp., 565 F.2d 807 (2d Cir. 1977); U.S. Steel Corp., 426 F.2d 592 (6th Cir. 1970).
55 Respectively, Papercraft Corp., 472 F.2d 927 (7th Cir. 1973); National Dynamics Corp., 492 F.2d 1333 (2d Cir. 1974), *cert. denied*, 419 U.S. 993 (1975) (other parts of order also overturned); ITT Continental Baking Co., 532 F.2d 207 (2d Cir. 1976). The last case, however, could arguably be said to represent close judicial scrutiny, as discussed in Section IV of this chapter.
56 See Virginia State Board of Pharmacy v. State Citizens Consumer Council, 425 U.S. 748 (1976); Bates v. State Bar of Arizona, 433 U.S. 350 (1977). More recently, however, the Court has retreated from protection of commercial speech. See Friedman v. Rogers, 440 U.S. 1 (1978).
57 Beneficial Corp., 542 F.2d 611 (3d Cir. 1976), *cert. denied*, 430 U.S. 983 (1977). The other three cases are L. G. Balfour Co., 422 F.2d 1 (7th Cir. 1971); National Egg Commission, 517 F.2d 485 (7th Cir. 1975), *cert. denied*, 426 U.S. 919 (1976); Standard Oil of Calif., 577 F.2d 653 (9th Cir. 1978).
58 542 F.2d 611, 618–19 (3d Cir. 1976). The court's principle of close scrutiny was clear, but its application to the facts of the case was not, given the FTC's

explicit finding that a narrower remedy would be unsatisfactory. *Id.*, at 621–22 (Van Dusen, J., dissenting and concurring in part).

59 One court, however, relying in part on *Friedman,* note 56 *supra,* affirmed the FTC's power to impose prior substantiation, at least where the remedy was a reasonable one for past violations of the FTC Act. See Jay Norris, 598 F.2d 1244, 1251–52 (2d Cir. 1979).

60 See Warner-Lambert Co., 562 F.2d 749 (D.C. Cir. 1977), *cert. denied,* 435 U.S. 950 (1978); Nat'l Egg Comm'n, 517 F.2d 485 (7th Cir. 1975), *cert. denied,* 426 U.S. 919 (1976).

61 See Richard B. Stewart, "The Reformation of American Administrative Law," 88 *Harvard Law Review* 1667 (1975), upon which this paragraph draws heavily.

62 See James V. DeLong, "Informal Rulemaking and the Integration of Law and Policy," 65 *Virginia Law Review* 257 (1979). Whether the recent Supreme Court decision in Vermont Yankee Nuclear Power Corp. v. Natural Resources Defense Counsel, Inc., 435 U.S. 519 (1978) will significantly curtail the recent closer scrutiny remains to be seen. See DeLong, at 309–19.

63 518 F.2d 33 (7th Cir. 1975).

64 561 F.2d 357, 364 (D.C. Cir. 1977).

65 See Warner-Lambert Co., 562 F.2d 749 (D.C. Cir. 1977); Standard Oil of Calif., 577 F.2d 653 (9th Cir. 1978).

66 577 F.2d 653, 657 (9th Cir. 1978).

67 See U.S. v. General Dynamics, 415 U.S. 486 (1974) (horizontal merger); U.S. v. Marine Bancorporation, 418 U.S. 602 (1974) (conglomerate merger); Continental TV v. GTE Sylvania, 433 U.S. 36 (1977) (overruling *Schwinn*).

68 557 F.2d 24 (2d Cir. 1977). A further indication of this possibility is the FTC's mixed record in obtaining injunctions to stop mergers. See, e.g., Tenneco, Inc., 433 F. Supp. 105 (D.D.C. 1977).

69 See, e.g., U.S. v. Falstaff, 410 U.S. 526 (1973).

70 See, e.g., Alterman Foods, Inc., 497 F.2d 933 (5th Cir. 1974); see also Perpetual Federal Savings, 90 FTC 608 (1977) (Section 5 used to close jurisdictional gap in Clayton Act, Section 8).

71 But see Atlantic Richfield Co., 549 F.2d 289, 291–92, n.1 (4th Cir. 1977), indicating some judicial unwillingness to use Section 5 as a separate basis for reviewing mergers.

72 See, e.g., answer to 1975 Moss Questionnaire, question 3. This questionnaire is discussed in Chapter 3 *supra,* at note 14 and accompanying text.

5. Executive constraints

1 The Civil Service Commission, since January 1, 1979, the Office of Personnel Management, pursuant to Executive Order 12107 of December 28, 1978, is listed as part of the Executive Branch even though it is independent of presidential authority in the same manner that the FTC is. According to the *United States Government Manual,* the Commission is listed as one of the independent establishments underneath the Executive Branch.

2 Senate Committee on Government Operations, *Study on Federal Regulation: The Regulatory Appointments Process,* vol. 1, S. Doc. No. 25, 95th Cong., 1st Sess. (1977), p. 205.

3 *Ibid.*; see also Edward F. Cox, Robert C. Fellmeth, and John E. Schultz, *The Nader Report on the Federal Trade Commission* (New York: Barron Press,

1969); reprinted as *The Consumer and the Federal Trade Commission*, 115 *Congressional Record* (Part 2) 1539–68 (1969).

4 Senate Committee on Government Operations report, *supra* note 2, at 154.

5 *Id.*, at 217.

6 *Id.*, at 191–92. Some reorganizations require the president's approval.

7 Although several executive orders apply directly to the FTC, most do not impose any constraint on Commission activities. According to the Commission, the major executive orders are as follows: E.O. 9809 gives the FTC the responsibility to compile financial statistics on American industry. E.O. 9833, 10090, and 10980 permit the Commission to inspect corporate income tax returns. E.O. 10033 requires the FTC to furnish statistics to international bodies of which the United States is a member. Reorganization Plan No. 8 of May 15, 1950, transferred to the chairman certain executive and administrative functions of the Commission. This power that the chairman derives is important and will be discussed in Chapter 15. Reorganization Plan No. 4 of 1961 authorizes the Commission to delegate its functions to subordinates. E.O. 12022 established the National Commission for the Review of Antitrust Laws and Procedures of which the FTC chairman was made a member. Although the Commission is not subject to E.O. 12044, it attempts to develop its regulations according to that Order's goals of providing simple, clear, effective and not unnecessarily burdensome regulations. Source: 1978 Moss Questionnaire, *supra* Chapter 3, at note 14, question 21.

8 Apparently because of its size, the *Exxon* case has even been brought to the attention of the president, or at least to that of his staff.

9 Based on an interview with previous OMB examiners.

10 OMB is authorized by statute, 31 U.S.C. § 16 (1976), to prepare the budget under such rules and regulations as the president shall prescribe. This includes the authority to assemble, correlate, revise, reduce, or increase requests for appropriations from the various departments and agencies.

11 Based on interviews with FTC and OMB officials.

12 See, e.g., letter from Executive Director of the FTC to Associate Director of Economics and Government, Office of Management and Budget (November 17, 1975).

13 1978 Moss Questionnaire, *supra* note 7, question 23.

14 1975 Moss Questionnaire, *supra* note 7, question 81.

15 OMB examiners have told us that the FTC is generally very cooperative and that the informal interaction produces more valuable information than does the formal budget process.

16 1978 Moss Questionnaire, *supra* note 7, question 21. Each of these circulars provides specific procedures for carrying out governmental activities.

17 Our evidence is based primarily on interviews with previous high-level officials within the Commission as well as OMB examiners.

18 Based on interviews with FTC and congressional officials.

19 1975 Moss Questionnaire, *supra* note 7, question 82.

20 1975 Moss Questionnaire, *supra* note 7, question 71.

21 Most FTC employees fall within the "GS" or general schedule, the basic pay schedule for most civilian government employees in lower- and middle-level positions. The GS is divided into 18 grades, ranging from GS-1 to GS-18. Jobs are classified according to the difficulty and responsibility of the work as defined by statute, 5 U.S.C. § 5104 (1976). Upper-level positions, such as cabinet officers, their deputies, and the heads of various agencies and their

assistants, are paid according to the Executive Schedule, which has five levels as defined by 5 U.S.C. § 5311 (1976).

22 Based on interviews with civil service officials.

23 Very few FTC employees, especially attorneys, are military veterans. Veteran attorneys receive the same protection as veterans in competitive positions, and thus may be fired only for abuse.

24 If an employee can make out a *prima facie* case of being fired for an unconstitutional reason, he is entitled to a hearing to present his case even though the terms of his employment are that he may be fired without cause. Board of Regents v. Roth, 408 U.S. 564, 575 n. 14 (1972).

25 See *Report to the Chairman of the Federal Trade Commission: Attorney and Attorney Manager Recruitment, Selection and Retention* (Meredith Associates, Inc., July 15, 1976).

26 For example, in the five years prior to the 1975 Moss Questionnaire, the Civil Service Commission denied 7 of the 10 supergrade positions requested by the FTC. 1975 Moss Questionnaire, *supra* note 7, question 83. The 1978 Questionnaire, however, listed 10 requests for additional positions after June 1, 1975. Of the 9 requests which the Civil Service Commission had acted upon at the time of the answer, 7 were approved. 1978 Moss Questionnaire, *supra* note 7, question 25.

27 Prior to the Magnuson-Moss Act, the Justice Department generally followed Commission recommendations on filing suits and making appeals. The 1978 Moss Questionnaire identified two instances in the previous five years in which the Justice Department had failed to seek *certiorari* following an FTC request to do so. The questionnaire also identified only two cases in which the Attorney General refused to follow the Commission's recommendations that civil penalties be sought. All actions for civil penalties related to consumer protection matters within the five years prior to the questionnaire were filed by the Justice Department. Of the three criminal actions the Attorney General refused to prosecute, one was recertified as a civil action and litigated and another was later certified and prosecuted. 1978 Moss Questionnaire, *supra* note 7, question 26.

28 Moss Questionnaire 1978, *supra* note 7, question 24.

29 Senate Committee on Governmental Affairs, *Study on Federal Regulation: Regulatory Organization*, vol. 5, S. Doc. 91, 95th Cong., 2d Sess. (1977), pp. 251–54.

30 *Id.*; Edwin S. Rockefeller, *Desk Book of FTC Practice and Procedure* (New York: Practicing Law Institute, 1976), pp. 35–38.

Part II. Nature and consequence of FTC actions

1 See Chapter 1 *supra*.

2 *Id.* See also the FTC's March 5, 1976, letter to Senator Moss, in which it called its new antitrust enforcement one of the 25 most important steps in improving consumer welfare. See also 1978 Moss Questionnaire, *supra* Chapter 3, at note 14, question 3. Indeed, all the activities discussed in Part II are mentioned in some form in either or both Commission documents.

3 For a detailed account of the development of the Pertschuk administration, see the issues of *FTC: Watch*.

4 See Chapter 5 *infra*, note 8 and accompanying text.

5 See Chapter 1 *supra*, note 1.

6 Ellis discusses several others. Important examples not discussed in our book include the proposed health spa and hearing-aid rules.

6. Bureau of Competition

1 See Robert H. Bork, *The Antitrust Paradox: A Policy at War with Itself,* (New York: Basic Books, 1978); Wesley J. Liebeler, "Market Power and Competitive Superiority in Concentrated Industries," 25 *U.C.L.A. Law Review* 1231 (1978).

2 The FTC budget was prepared on a program basis beginning with fiscal year 1975. Through that year, the justification for FTC budget requests may be found in the reports of hearings before the Agriculture, Environment and Consumer Protection Subcommittee of the House Committee on Appropriations. Subsequent justifications may be found in reports of hearings before the Department of State, Justice, and Commerce, the Judiciary and Related Agencies Subcommittee.

3 The ranking itself was done in a memorandum dated March 30, 1972, from the Bureau of Economics and the Office of Policy Planning and Evaluation to the Commission (PRAM memo). It is discussed in Paul D. Scanlon, "FTC and Phase II: The McGovern Papers," 5 *Antitrust Law and Economics Review* 19 (No. 3, 1972); Donald Bumpass, "The Social Costs of Monopoly: They May Be Greater Than We Thought," 9 *Antitrust Law and Economics Review* 91 (No. 2, 1977). The relevant memoranda were also forwarded to Congressman Moss and are available in his subcommittee's files. For a discussion of the economic model on which this ranking was based, see Liebeler, *supra* note 1.

4 See Federal Trade Commission, *FTC Annual Report* for 1972, pp. 43–44.

5 See Liebeler, *supra* note 1, at 1267.

6 See Harold Demsetz, "Industry Structure, Market Rivalry, and Public Policy," 16 *Journal of Law and Economics* 1 (1973); Harold Demsetz, "Two Systems of Belief about Monopoly," in Harvey J. Goldschmid, H. Michael Mann, and J. Fred Weston, eds., *Industrial Concentration: The New Learning* (Boston: Little, Brown and Company, 1974), pp. 164–84.

7 Oliver E. Williamson, "Economics as an Antitrust Defense: The Welfare Tradeoffs," 58 *American Economic Review* 18 (1968); Oliver E. Williamson, "Economics as an Antitrust Defense Revisited," 125 *University of Pennsylvania Law Review* 699 (1977); Liebeler, *supra* note 1, at 1262.

8 See Charles E. Mueller, "Sources of Monopoly Power: A Phenomenon Called 'Product Differentiation,'" 2 *Antitrust Law and Economics Review* 59 (No. 4, 1969).

9 See also H. Michael Mann and J. W. Meehan, Jr., "Structural Antitrust Cases: The Benefit–Cost Underpinnings," 42 *George Washington Law Review* 921 (1974); Elizabeth Dole, "Cost–Benefit Analysis versus Protecting the Vulnerable: The FTC's Special Interest Groups," 9 *Antitrust Law and Economics Review* 15 (No. 2, 1977).

10 See *FTC: Watch* (April 21, 1978), p. 10.

11 See Wesley J. Liebeler, "Integration and Competition," in Edward J. Mitchell, ed., *Vertical Integration in the Oil Industry* (Washington, D.C.: American Enterprise Institute, 1976), p. 10.

12 See Richard A. Posner, "Antitrust Policy and the Supreme Court: An Analysis of the Restricted Distribution, Horizontal Merger and Potential Competition Decisions," 75 *Columbia Law Review* 282 (1975).

13 General Mills, 83 FTC 696 (1973).

14 United Brands, 83 FTC 1614 (1973).
15 Ash Grove Cement, 85 FTC 1123 (1975); OKC Cement, 77 FTC 1342.
16 Great Lakes Carbon, 82 FTC 1123 (1975); Coors, 83 FTC 32 (1973); Chock Full O' Nuts, 83 FTC 575 (1973).
17 Although the Commission states that the 16 firms that entered did so after 1935, it appears that they actually entered after 1945. Great Lakes Carbon, Administrative Law Judge findings 181–207, 82 FTC 1529, at 1581–92. See also *id.*, at 1664.
18 The Commission's division of the market into an integrated and an unintegrated segment is a dubious proposition from an economic standpoint. Any market power in the unintegrated segment would be limited by the potential entry of other coke (i.e., by the elasticity of supply). If the market is viewed from the supply side, it is hard to see how the existence of a significant number of capable firms already in the business of processing coke can justifiably be ignored. Although it is true that the aluminum companies are not in the day-to-day business of selling coke to the unintegrated market, the relevant question is how much of a price increase it would take to get them there.
19 The extent of entry is not fully shown in the raw market share figures because the size of the market was rapidly expanding. In 1935 the coke that was being produced was piling up with no takers. In 1965 cokers in 45 refineries produced 6,640,907 tons of coke; in 1969 those figures were 52 and 10,056,920, respectively. Administrative Law Judge findings, *supra* note 17, at 1581. There had also been a sharp increase in the production of coke in other countries, which increased competition with the substantial U.S. exports, and it appeared that both the domestic and foreign production of coke were likely to continue to expand. *Id.*, at 1582–83. Under those circumstances, the possibility that GLC had the power to restrict output in the coke-processing industry cannot be seriously entertained.
20 *Id.*, at 1657–58.
21 Ronald H. Coase has equated this supersession of the market mechanism with the creation of a "firm." He states that "the distinguishing mark of the firm is the supersession of the price mechanism." Ronald H. Coase, "The Nature of the Firm," in George J. Stigler and Kenneth E. Boulding, eds., *Readings in Price Theory* (Chicago: Richard D. Irwin, 1952), p. 334. See also Oliver E. Williamson, *Markets and Hierarchies: Analysis and Antitrust Implications* (New York: The Free Press, 1975), ch. 5.
22 Transportation costs were an important factor in this specialization; it was customary for a processor to obtain a source of coke supply from a refinery within 200 miles of the refining plant. Administrative Law Judge findings, *supra* note 17, at 1573. In fact, many calciners were located adjacent to the supplying refinery.
23 *Id.*, at 1578.
24 See note 1 *supra* and Chapter 9 *infra*, at notes 1 and 2 with accompanying text.
25 83 FTC 32 (1973).
26 See Wesley G. Liebeler, "Toward a Consumers' Antitrust Law: The Federal Trade Commission and Vertical Mergers in the Cement Industry," 15 *U.C.L.A. Law Review* 1153 (1968), pp. 1178 ff.
27 If Coors has limited the returns of the dealers to a competitive rate, the dealers may be able to obtain a higher rate through cheating, hence may have an incentive to cheat.
28 83 FTC 32, 139 (1973).

29 See Coors v. FTC, 497 F.2d 1178 (10th Cir. 1974); U.S. v. Arnold, Schwinn, & Co., 388 U.S. 365 (1967).
30 See, e.g., FTC v. Gratz, 253 U.S. 421 (1920), which limited the FTC by finding that the words "unfair competition" were merely a codification of the preexisting common law. The FTC obtained a change in this ruling in FTC v. Winsted Hosiery Co., 258 U.S. 483 (1922). Compare also the FTC's reaction to FTC v. Raladam Co., 283 U.S. 643 (1931).
31 See, e.g., Judge Ely's opinion in GTE Sylvania, Inc. v. Continental TV, 537 F.2d 980 (9th Cir. 1976). Maxwell Blecher has described the Supreme Court decision in that case to overrule *Schwinn* as an example of the Supreme Court's finally deciding to go along with the rest of the federal judiciary.
32 Snap-On Tools Corp. v. FTC, 321 F.2d 825 (7th Cir. 1963).
33 Sandura Co. v. FTC, 339 F.2d 847 (6th Cir. 1964).
34 GTE Sylvania, *supra* note 31.
35 FTC opinion in Coca-Cola Co., decided on April 7, 1978, and reported in 861 *Antitrust and Trade Regulation Report* (BNA) (April 27, 1978), § F.
36 85 FTC 1123 (1975).
37 *Id.*, at 1165.
38 *Id.*, citing Marquette Cement Mfg. Co., 75 FTC 32, 96–97 (1969).
39 85 FTC 1123, 1148 (1975).
40 *Id.*, at 1149.
41 *Ibid.*
42 *Id.*, at 1150.
43 *FTC: Watch, supra* note 10.
44 See Lester G. Telser, "Why Should Manufacturers Want Fair Trade?" 3 *Journal of Law and Economics* 86 (1960); Liebeler, *supra* note 11, at 20.
45 See Fred C. Allvine and James M. Patterson, *Competition Ltd: The Marketing of Gasoline* (Bloomington, Ind.: Indiana University Press, 1972); review of the above by C. David Anderson, 82 *Yale Law Journal* 1355 (1973); Stark Richie, "Petroleum Dismemberment," 29 *Vanderbilt Law Review* 1131 (1976); Walter Adams, "Vertical Divestiture of the Petroleum Majors: An Affirmative Case," 30 *Vanderbilt Law Review* 1115 (1977).
46 See Liebeler, *supra* note 11, at 5–34.
47 The FTC staff has stated its rationale for bringing *Exxon* as follows: "The history of the Federal Trade Commission's activity in the petroleum industry has been characterized by a case-by-case attack on specific anticompetitive marketing practices. This approach has, in general, been of limited success in controlling wasteful marketing practices, dealer coercion, and the lack of competition in the petroleum industry. . . .

   "But the practice-by-practice approach to antitrust attack, which sought to correct specific anticompetitive conduct at the marketing level, did not adequately address the industry's vertically integrated structure or its multi-level behavior. The major oil companies operate on four levels – crude production, refining, transportation, and marketing. To fashion a remedy for one level without considering the performance of a company, or the industry, at the other levels, ignores the market power associated with vertical integration and limited competition."

   Adams, *supra* note 45, at 1117. This seems to say that *Exxon,* the aim of which in terms of remedy is obviously quite different from any of the previous individual cases, is designed to accomplish the purposes, primarily in terms of stopping alleged "anticompetitive conduct at the marketing level," which were not successfully accomplished by the case-by-case approach.
48 Excluding Cromwell Oil, 81 FTC 819 (1972), which involved a company sell-

ing distributorships and oil additives, and Occidental, 77 FTC 710 (1970), which did not involve petroleum products.

49 Occidental, 83 FTC 1374 (1974); Diamond Shamrock, 83 FTC 1389 (1974).

50 Standard of California, 83 FTC 852 (1973); Union Oil, 83 FTC 858 (1973).

51 Standard Oil (Indiana), 86 FTC 1570 (1975); Amerada Hess, 83 FTC 487 (1973).

52 Phillips Petroleum, 84 FTC 1666 (1974); Standard Oil (Ohio), FTC Docket No. 9810, *CCH Trade Regulation Reporter: FTC Complaints and Cases* 20,134 and 20,208 (1973).

53 Quoted in Bork, *supra* note 1, at 55.

54 *Ibid.*

55 Continental Oil, 72 FTC 850 (1967); Occidental Petroleum, 74 FTC 1191 (1968); Standard Oil (Indiana), 74 FTC 141 (1968).

56 Shell, 66 FTC 1336 (1964) (R-P case dismissed by FTC); Crown Central, 71 FTC 1470 (1967) (below-cost selling dismissed by FTC); Humble, 67 FTC 941 (1965) (R-P case dismissed by FTC); Amoco, 60 FTC 1786 (1962) (R-P case order vacated and FTC ordered to dismiss complaint in American Oil Co. v. FTC, 325 F.2d 101 [7th Cir., 1963]).

57 Pure, 66 FTC 1336 (1964); Sun, 67 FTC 341 (1965); Texaco, 66 FTC 1336 (1964); Shell, 54 FTC 1274 (1958).

58 Shell, 56 FTC 456 (1959); Shell, 49 FTC 1182 (1953); Mobil, 56 FTC 1209 (1960).

59 Sun, 63 FTC 1371 (1963); Standard (Indiana), 66 FTC 1336 (1964); Atlantic, 63 FTC 1407 (1963).

60 Gulf, 56 FTC 688 (1960).

61 Atlas, 48 FTC 53 (1951).

62 Goodrich, 69 FTC 22 (1966); Goodyear, 58 FTC 309 (1961); Firestone, 58 FTC 371 (1961).

63 Maryland Ann. Code Art. 56, §§ 157E(b)–(h) (1972) prohibits refiners from operating retail stations in the state.

64 See Frederick M. Scherer, *Industrial Market Structure and Economic Performance* (Chicago: Rand McNally & Company, 1970), p. 87; Oliver E. Williamson, "The Economics of Antitrust: Transaction Cost Considerations," 122 *University of Pennsylvania Law Review* 1439 (1974); Coase, *supra* note 21.

65 Continental TV, Inc. v. GTE Sylvania, 433 U.S. 36 (1977).

66 See the FTC opinion in Coca-Cola, *supra* note 35; FTC opinion on Fruehauf Corp., decided on February 22, 1978, and reported in 855 *Antitrust and Trade Regulation Report* (BNA) (March 16, 1978), § E.

67 Although some or all of the potential competition cases could have been classified as conglomerate, for convenience I have included them all in the category of horizontal mergers.

68 Sterling Drug, 80 FTC 477 (1972); Beatrice Foods, 81 FTC 481 (1972); Beatrice Foods, 86 FTC 1 (1975); Budd Co., 86 FTC 518 (1975).

69 Litton Industries, 86 FTC 589 (1933).

70 Resources budgeted for horizontal restraints and for vertical restraints, respectively, for the following four fiscal years are: FY 75: 10.1% and 12%; FY 76: 12.5% and 9.8%; FY 77: 20.3% and 5.1%; FY 77 (revised): 15.8% and 9.1%; FY 78: 15.5% and 9.7%. Engman's initiative is reflected in the initial FY 77 figures; after he left, those figures were adjusted downward and dropped slightly again in the FY 78 budget projections. See budget materials cited in note 12 *supra*.

71 Central California Lettuce Producers Cooperative, FTC Docket No. 8970,

CCH Trade Regulation Reporter: FTC Complaints and Cases 21,337 (July 25, 1977).

72 Although it is impossible to know precisely from the available budget documents, it appears that the Antitrust Division spends at least 33 percent of its resources on price fixing and on government restraints. On the other hand, the FTC's Bureau of Competition appears to spend less than 10 percent of its budget on these matters. See Justice Department 1978 Senate Appropriations Hearings and FTC Budget Materials discussed in note 2 *supra.*

Some of this large difference may be explained by the ability of the Justice Department to prosecute criminally. This fact, however, cannot justify the paucity of resources that the Bureau of Competition spends on price fixing and government regulation. Many important price-fixing cases are civil, including the two very successful cases that the FTC pursued in the 1960s. See note 79 *infra.* If the Commission could bring these cases, there seems no reason why it could not bring others. Further, although Justice's criminal power is not relevant in attacking government restraints, the Bureau of Competition has badly lagged behind the Antitrust Division in pursuing anticompetitive government regulation.

Finally, it is worth noting that the Bureau of Consumer Protection expends some of its resources attacking anticompetitive state laws. Combining this figure with the funds of the Competition Bureau would still leave the FTC commitment falling short of that of the Antitrust Division (in percentage terms).

73 Bakers of Washington, 64 FTC 1079 (1964); American Cyanimid, 63 FTC 1747 (1963); see Charles E. Mueller, "The New Antitrust: A 'Structural' Approach," 1 *Antitrust Law and Economics Review* 87 (No. 2, 1968); Peter M. Costello, "The Tetracycline Conspiracy: Structure, Conduct, and Performance in the Drug Industry," 1 *Antitrust Law and Economics Review* 2 (No. 4, 1968).

74 United Fruit, 82 FTC 53 (1973); Golden Grain Macaroni, 78 FTC 63 (1971).

75 Sterling Drug, 80 FTC 477 (1972); Beatrice Foods, 81 FTC 481 (1972).

76 Budd Co. 86 FTC 518 (1975), at 519.

77 *Id.*, at 552–55.

78 *Id.*, at 578.

79 United Fruit, 82 FTC 53 (1973); Sterling Drug, 80 FTC 477 (1972); Budd Co., 86 FTC 518 (1975); Kennecott Copper, 78 FTC 744 (1971); The Stanley Works, 78 FTC 1023 (1971); Papercraft, 78 FTC 1352 (1971); Bendix, 77 FTC 731 (1970); Beatrice Foods, 86 FTC 1 (1975). This antipathy toward efficiency took a reverse twist in Sterling Drug and Bendix, where either the Commission or the ALJ upheld the mergers' legality on the grounds, in part, that they did not contribute to efficiency.

80 Beatrice Foods, 86 FTC 1 (1975), at 65–66.

81 Avnet Inc., 82 FTC 391 (1973).

82 Jim Walter Corp., FTC Docket No. 8986, *CCH Trade Regulation Report: FTC Complaints and Cases* 21,379 (December 20, 1977).

83 Litton, 82 FTC 793 (1973), in which the FTC ended up with a finding that the acquisition was illegal but refused to order divestiture; Warner-Lambert, 87 FTC 812 (1976), in which partial divestiture was ordered; British Oxygen, 86 FTC 1241 (1975), in which the FTC held BOC to be a potential entrant into the U.S. industrial gas market and was reversed by the Court of Appeals in FTC v. British Oxygen Co., 529 F.2d 196 (3rd Cir. 1976); Liggett & Meyers, 87 FTC 1074 (1976), in which the merger was held illegal in part because the FTC believed advertising was a barrier to entry; RSR Corp., 88 FTC 800 (1976); American General Insurance, 89 FTC 557 (1977).

84 374 U.S. 321 (1963).
85 *Supra* note 82. The statement here was: "More importantly, relative ease of entry and the concomitant prospects for potential competition are not a substitute for the loss of substantial actual competition. As we have said before, 'even proof of low entry barriers . . . can be at most of slight exculpatory value in the face of probable anti-competitive effects, since all it suggests is that such effects may be smaller or shorter lived, not that they are unlikely to occur.'" *Id.*, at 21, 321.
86 See Chapter 1 *supra,* at note 11.

7. Information for antitrust and business activity

1 This statement was made in President Wilson's "Address to the Congress" on January 20, 1914. *Messages and Papers of the Presidents,* vol. 16, p. 7916.
2 "The Commission's objectives, as stated by it, are (a) to effectuate and foster resource allocation by competitors and potential competitors, investors, labor groups and others; and (b) to enable the Commission to pinpoint non-competitive markets for law enforcement purposes." Aluminum Co. of America, 390 F. Supp. 301, 307 (1975).
3 The difference amounts to more than the inclusion of Hartford Fire and other insurance and finance lines left blank in the 1971 report.
4 In the case of rivals (and even potential ones), information of this sort would be available both more promptly and in more detail in the industry's trade press.
5 F. M. Scherer, "Segmented Financial Reporting: Needs and Tradeoffs" (unpublished material, n.d.), p. 24.
6 "FASB Adopts Line of Business Reporting," *Financial Executive* (February 1977), pp. 8–9.
7 42 *Federal Register* 26009 (May 20, 1977).
8 Kenneth E. Boulding, "Economics and Accounting: The Uncongenial Twins," in William T. Baxter and Sidney Davidson, eds., *Studies in Accounting Theory* (Homewood, Ill.: Richard D. Irwin, 1962), p. 44.
9 See "Foreword" by Yale Brozen to Kenneth W. Clarkson, *Intangible Capital and Rates of Return* (Washington, D.C.: American Enterprise Institute, 1977), pp. 1–17, for a more detailed treatment.
10 The most explicit treatment of this problem can be found in Kenneth W. Clarkson, *Intangible Capital and Rates of Return* (Washington, D.C.: American Enterprise Institute, 1977).
11 John Maurice Clark, *Studies in the Economics of Overhead Costs* (Chicago: University of Chicago Press, 1923), p. 1.
12 Alfred E. Kahn, *The Economics of Regulation* (New York: John Wiley & Sons, 1970), vol. 1, p. 78.
13 Clark, *supra* note 11, at 1.
14 Robert K. Mautz and K. Fred Skousen, "Common Cost Allocation in Diversified Companies," *Financial Executive* (June 1968), pp. 15–25; reprinted in R. K. Mautz, *Financial Reporting by Diversified Companies* (New York: Financial Executives Research Foundation, 1968), app. E.
15 *Id.*, at 19.
16 *Id.*, at 21–23, tables 5 and 6.
17 *Id.*, at 15.
18 Scherer, *supra* note 5, at 40–43.
19 Robert K. Mautz, *Financial Reporting, supra* note 14, at 36, table 4.
20 *Id.*, at 37, table 5.

21 National Association of Cost Accountants, *Accounting for Intra-company Transfers* (June 1950), p. 37.
22 Federal Trade Commission, "Statement of Purpose," in *Line of Business Report of Program* (August 1973), p. 11.
23 R. H. Coase, "The Nature of the Firm," 4 *Economica* 386 (1937), p. 391.
24 The Bureau of Census of the Department of Commerce has developed a system of product classification for purposes of the census and other government statistical programs. Manufacturing activity is divided according to a Standard Industrial Classification (SIC) system. As this classification becomes more refined, more digits are used. For example, the two-digit classification "20" refers to all food and kindred products; the four-digit classification "2042," prepared animal feeds, would be a subset of the broader two-digit category. Seven digits is the narrowest classification.
25 Betty Bock, *Line of Business Reporting: Problems in the Formulation of a Data Program* (A Research Report from the Conference Board, November 1974), p. 20.
26 See Paul W. Cook, Jr., "Merger Law and Big Business: A Look Ahead," 40 *New York University Law Review* 710 (1965).
27 Bock, *supra* note 25, at 45–72.
28 *Id.*, at 64, table 12.
29 Bureau of Economics Staff Report, "1974 Form LB Revision," p. 13. We do not know the reason for the different estimates.
30 *Id.*, at 1.
31 In addition, the revenues of the secondary items of any selected "basic component" cannot exceed what they would be under the establishment-base rule.
32 Bock provides an example of how misleading the published data could be for an FTC category that comprises four products in *Line of Business Reporting, supra* note 25, at 39–43. Not only potential entrants would be sidetracked by the data, but respondent firms as well.
33 Richard G. Lipsey and Peter O. Steiner, *Economics,* 4th ed. (New York: Harper & Row, Publishers, 1975), p. 200.
34 Staff Report to the Federal Trade Commission, *Conglomerate Merger Performance: An Empirical Analysis of Nine Corporations* (November 1972), p. 135.
35 *Id.*, at 135–36. The only reason rates of return would not be equalized, according to this report, is because of risk differences in various industries. Under competition, no other reasons for profit rate differentials are recognized. But see Clarkson, *supra* note 10, at 59, for a list of reasons why rates of return would not be equalized under competitive conditions.
36 *Id.*, at 137.
37 Milton Friedman, *Price Theory* (Chicago: Aldine Publishing Company, 1976), p. 105.
38 In the long run, returns to entrepreneurial capacity can be above zero as long as the minimum average variable costs for the various firms in the industry are not identical. In the short run, there may be returns to fixed factors which are not permanent, tending to disappear as entry reduces demand. But they are *temporarily* price-determined and are therefore not truly "rents" but "quasi-rents." Returns to entrepreneurial capacity, on the other hand, are "rents."
39 See Harold Demsetz, *The Market Concentration Doctrine* (AEI-Hoover Policy Study, 1973); Yale Brozen, "Significance of Profit Data for Antitrust Policy," in J. Fred Weston and Sam Peltzman, eds., *Public Policy toward Merg-*

ers (Pacific Palisades, Calif.: Goodyear Publishing Co., 1969), pp. 110–127, esp. p. 119.

40 H. Michael Mann, "The Concentrated Industries Project," speech before the National Association of Manufacturers (November 11, 1971). Mann was, at the time, director of the FTC's Bureau of Economics.

41 For a survey see Leonard Weiss, "The Concentration–Profits Relationship and Antitrust," in Harvey J. Goldschmid *et al.*, eds. *Industrial Concentration: The New Learning* (Boston: Little, Brown and Company, 1974), pp. 184–232. On the relationship between a firm's market share and its profitability, see William G. Shepard, *The Treatment of Market Power* (New York: Columbia University Press, 1975), ch. 4; and more recently, Dennis C. Mueller, "The Persistence of Profits above the Norm," 44 *Economica* 369 (1977).

42 C. Reed Parker, "A View from Management – Comments," in Alfred Rappaport, Peter A. Firmin, and Stephen A. Zeff, eds., *Public Reporting by Conglomerates: The Issues, Problems, and Some Possible Solutions* (Englewood Cliffs, N.J.: Prentice-Hall, 1968), p. 72.

43 See George J. Benston, "The Federal Trade Commission's Line of Business Program: A Benefit–Cost Analysis," in Harvey J. Goldschmid, ed., *Business Disclosure: Government's Need to Know* (New York: McGraw Hill Book Company, 1979).

44 Bertrand Horwitz and Richard Kolodny, "Line of Business Reporting and Security Prices: An Analysis of an SEC Disclosure Rule," 8 *Bell Journal of Economics* 234 (1977).

45 D. W. Collins, "SEC Product-Line Reporting and Market Efficiency," 2 *Journal of Financial Economics* 125 (1975); "Predicting Earnings with Subentry Data: Some Further Evidence," 14 *Journal of Accounting Research* 163 (1976).

46 On the question of what information would be beneficial to investors in diversified companies, see Mautz, *Financial Reporting, supra* note 14, at 12, 95, 98, 115, 127. Mautz points out that in response to a carefully constructed questionnaire on financial analysis, growth potential and managerial ability were considered more important than other information, including profitability, in judging a corporation's potential. See Mautz, at 104–5.

47 "Supporting Statement, FTC Form LB 1974 Survey Version," *Hearings on FTC Appropriations before the Subcommittee on State, Justice, Commerce, Judiciary, and Related Agencies Appropriations of the Senate Committee on Appropriations*, 94th Cong., 1st Sess. 33 (June 1975), pp. 648–49.

8. Industry structure investigations

1 Xerox Corporation, 86 FTC 364 (1975).

2 *Id.*, at 367.

3 *Id.*, at 373–74.

4 *Id.*, at 367–68.

5 For an evaluation of the technological contribution of Xerox, see E. Blackstone, *The Copying Machine Industry* (unpublished doctoral dissertation, 1968), particularly p. 240.

6 The facts upon which the Commission would have relied if the proceeding had reached the hearing stage are summarized in a document designated "Complaint Counsel's Tentative Outline of the Types of Facts to be Proven in Support of the Complaint" [hereinafter "Tentative Outline"]. Paragraph 14a summarizes the facts relating to the aggregation of patents by Xerox.

7 For a general discussion of these strategic opportunities, see Fritz Machlup, "An Economic Review of the Patent System: Study of the Subcommittee on Patents, Trademarks and Copyrights of the United States Senate Committee on the Judiciary," 85th Cong., 2d Sess. (1958), p. 10; Phillip Areeda and Donald F. Turner, *Antitrust Law: An Analysis of Antitrust Principles and Their Application,* vol. 3 (Boston: Little, Brown and Company, 1978), p. 115.
8 See Blackstone, *supra* note 5, at 238.
9 This issue must be resolved doctrinally in the unfortunate context of the cases under Section 2 of the Sherman Act, 15 U.S.C. § 2 (1977), defining what conduct will be characterized as "exclusionary" and the even less satisfactory case law defining the term "unfair methods of competition" in the Federal Trade Commission Act, 15 U.S.C. § 45 (1977).
10 Xerox Corporation, 86 FTC 364, 367 (1975).
11 *Id.*, at 367–68.
12 *Ibid.*
13 *Ibid.*
14 *Ibid.*
15 *Ibid.*
16 *Ibid.*
17 *Ibid.*
18 *Ibid.*
19 The facts in this regard are set out in the various subparagraphs of ¶ 8 of the "Tentative Outline," *supra* note 6.
20 This policy was apparently undeviating until 1970, when some licenses were offered. "Tentative Outline," ¶¶ 8-50, 8-51.
21 Xerox Corporation, 86 FTC 364, 367–68 (1975).
22 See Areeda and Turner, *supra* note 7, vol. 3, pp. 13–35.
23 See Lawrence A. Sullivan, *Handbook of the Law of Antitrust* (St. Paul, Minn.: West Publishing Co., 1977), p. 508.
24 Automatic Radio Manufacturing Co., Inc. v. Hazelfine Research, Inc., 339 U.S. 827, 834 (1950).
25 Our analysis in this regard has been greatly aided by Areeda and Turner, *supra* note 7, vol. 3, pp. 114–33. Although their concern is in certain respects the same as ours (see vol. 3, p. 131), that (as is more fully developed later) joint profit maximization of patents covering substitutes may produce undesirable effects, their objections go further and seem to us to extend to conduct that is a legitimate exploitation of the patent monopoly. See Areeda and Turner, vol. 3, p. 115. Moreover, they conclude that monopoly power attributable to internally developed patents, even when offering opportunities to engage in undesirable conduct, should not be reached by the antitrust law (*id.*, vol. 3, p. 127).
26 Regarding the profit-maximizing behavior of a monopolist in products having interrelated demands, see J. R. Hicks, "Annual Survey of Economic Theory: Theory of Monopoly," 3 *Econometrica* 1 (1935), pp. 6–7, for a mathematical formulation. See also Martin J. Bailey, "Price and Output Determination by a Firm Selling Related Products," 44 *American Economic Review* 82 (1954), pp. 83–90.
27 If the monopolist can practice price discrimination by charging multiple prices for one or more of the substitutes, the analysis is complicated but essentially holds. Price discrimination is a device for varying price in order to exploit the differing intensities of demand manifested by consumers of the goods. As long, however, as the discrimination is not perfect, as was the case with

Xerox, consumers are only segregated into large subcategories of purchaser groups, and the advantages of practicing joint profit maximization remain. Under these circumstances, the relevant demand curves of each of the subgroups will exhibit the essential responsiveness to the price of substitutes which is required for joint profit maximization to be an effective strategy. It should be noted in passing that where perfect price discrimination is practical – through both intercustomer discrimination and multipart pricing – the allocative losses from monopolistic behavior disappear, although distributional objections may then be exacerbated. This theoretical possibility has little relevance to the present analysis.

28 In a private action, SCM Corp. v. Xerox Corp. (C.A. No. 15, 807 D. Conn.) there was testimony that Xerox did engage in pricing of this kind, Tr. 18, 699.
29 See United States v. Line Material Co. *et al.*, 333 U.S. 287 (1948), and cases in Ward S. Bowman, Jr., *Patent and Antitrust Law* (Chicago: University of Chicago Press, 1973), pp. 185–98.
30 In re Yarn Process Validity and Antitrust Litigation, 398 F. Supp. 31, 36 (S.D. Fla. 1975).
31 *Ibid.*
32 Bowman, *supra* note 29, at 206–7, argues that an acquisition of a patent which is "blocked" by a patent held by the acquiring company but which can be worked to produce a substitute for the product of the acquiring company should be judged under a "rule of reason."
33 Xerox Corporation, 86 FTC 364, 367 (1975).
34 E.g., "Tentative Outline," *supra* note 6, ¶¶ 14(a)-7, 14(c)-2, 14(c)-3.
35 *Id.*, ¶ 14(d)3–7.
36 The section below contains a number of factual descriptions of the industry during the 1970s. Our basic source for this information is a reporting service provided by Dataquest, Inc., a California research organization which is the acknowledged "scorekeeper" of the copier industry. Although this proprietary information is normally restricted to Dataquest clients, we make general reference to it by permission, which is gratefully acknowledged. In addition, specific reference is made to Dataquest, *New Plain Paper Copiers: Their Impact on Xerox Corporation* (February 1973), a report that substantially predicted the emergent competitive market conditions of the late 1970s at a time when the FTC order was quite speculative.
37 See FTC's "Complaint," In the Matter of Xerox Corporation, Docket No. 8909, at 9, where divestiture of Rank Xerox Ltd. is proposed.
38 The alleged insufficiency of three patents is a common refrain in the comments by Xerox's competitors on the proposed orders. For instance, see Van Dyk Research Corp., "Comments on Federal Trade Commission Docket No. 8909, Xerox Corp." (May 6, 1975), pp. 8–14.

9. Exclusionary practices

1 Ronald H. Coase, "Industrial Organization: A Proposal for Research," in V. Fuchs, ed., *Industrial Organization* (Washington, D.C.: National Bureau of Economic Research, 1972), p. 72.
2 Oliver E. Williamson, "Review of Bowman's *Patent and Antitrust Law*," 83 *Yale Law Journal* 647 (1974), p. 661.
3 Urban Land Institute Community Builders Council, *The Community Builders Handbook*, J. Ross McKeever, ed. (Washington, D.C.: Urban Land Institute, 1968), p. 264.

4 Remarks of Ernest G. Barnes, Assistant Director, Bureau of Competition, before the Annual Convention of the International Council of Shopping Centers, May 9, 1972; quoted in Steven G. Eagle, "Shopping Center Control: The Developer Besieged," 51 *Journal of Urban Law* 585 (1974); see also 577 *Antitrust and Trade Regulation Report* (BNA) (August 22, 1972), p. A-6.

5 Occasionally, this power is limited to tenants not on a preapproved list.

6 A tenant may sometimes receive the right to be one of a small number of stores in its specialty.

7 The analysis of Tysons Corner record and 85 FTC 970 (1975) and the collection of survey data cited in this chapter were performed as part of an impact evaluation of FTC shopping center actions conducted by the authors for the Commission.

8 See, e.g., Peoples Drug Stores, 87 FTC 1 (1976); Strawbridge and Clothier, 87 FTC 593 (1976); The Rouse Co., 85 FTC 848 (1975); Food Fair Stores, Inc., 86 FTC 706 (1975).

9 Continental TV v. GTE Sylvania, 433 U.S. 36 (1977). If circumstances justifying the practice would only occur very rarely and if those circumstances would be difficult to identify in practice, the restraint would probably be considered *per se* illegal. Further, although the courts may initially scrutinize a restraint under the rule of reason, experience may reveal that a *per se* approach is appropriate. Once a restraint is found to be *per se* illegal, justification evidence will not be allowed in subsequent cases.

10 *Id.*, at 49. Our discussion of the rule of reason is necessarily very brief. For more detailed treatment, see the *GTE* opinion and the sources cited therein.

11 Transcript of FTC Hearing Record in Tysons Corner, *Docket No. 8896* (May 7, 1974), at 375.

12 *Id.* (July 1, 1974), at 457.

13 City Stores had become a tenant by means of a suit for specific performance of an option to lease space for a department store in the center. The court ordered City Stores to be admitted to the center on terms essentially equal to those in the May Co. lease. See City Stores Co. v. Ammerman, 286 F. Supp. 766 (D.D.C. 1967), *aff'd per curiam*, 394 F.2d 950 (D.C. Cir. 1968). Neither court considered antitrust issues.

14 Transcript of FTC Proceedings in Tysons Corner, *supra* note 11, Oral Argument of March 13, 1975, at 34–36.

15 See, e.g., Gimbels Brothers, Inc., 83 FTC 1320 (1974).

16 Tysons Corner, 85 FTC 970 (1975), at 1011.

17 Even with Judge Needelman, this is sometimes not clear. See 85 FTC 970 (1975), at 998.

18 Direct costs include fuel, transportation, maintenance, and capital investment. Indirect costs include the value of time consumed in transportation to and from the point of purchase.

19 Indirect search costs are the value of time consumers spend finding purchase opportunities. Environmental amenities are characteristics of the physical shopping environment that customers consume but do not directly purchase.

20 Retailers may have a comparative advantage in selling rather than in monitoring and policing.

21 Five cities (Charlottesville, Va., Kalamazoo, Mich., Long Beach, Calif., Louisville, Ky., and Miami, Fla.) were chosen for conducting consumer and price–quality surveys. To choose the cities, we looked for comparability between shopping centers and conventional shopping areas based on size, environmental characteristics, and major department stores. The consumer

questionnaires (205 at shopping centers and 197 at conventional shopping areas) contained 14 questions and the price–quality survey contained 22 items. Detailed information on both the consumer and price–quality surveys are available from the authors. The limits of the data require calling it "preliminary." Because the sample is small in many cases and we are unable to isolate the test variable in others, we do not test for significance. Despite this shortcoming, the data in the aggregate support our hypotheses.

22 In four of the five areas surveyed, the average amount purchased per hour of time spent shopping was $4.74 higher in shopping centers than in their conventional counterparts. Only in Kalamazoo, Mich., was the average amount purchased per hour of time spent shopping higher (by $3.37) for the conventional shopping area than for the shopping center. Overall, the average for shopping centers (including Kalamazoo) was $15.98 or $4.00 more than the average in conventional shopping areas. This may be explained by the unusually high incidence of high income shoppers who frequent Kalamazoo's conventional shopping area. See note 26 *infra*.

23 The stores in conventional shopping areas studied averaged 30.9 percent clothing and shoes and 2.1 percent furniture. In contrast, stores in shopping centers averaged 31.7 percent clothing and shoes and no furniture. The nearness in the average of clothing and shoe stores is, however, misleading. The average appears artificially close because the Omni shopping center in Miami contains dozens of very small specialty shops that sell neither clothing nor shoes. The presence of these shops lowers the percentage of Omni clothing and shoe stores to a level well below that of the comparable downtown Miami area. Thus, if data were available by square foot, presumably the implication would be verified more strongly than by percentage of stores.

24 The coefficient of variation is the ratio of the standard deviation of a variable to its mean. In Kalamazoo, Mich., Long Beach, Calif., Louisville, Ky., and Miami, Fla., the coefficients of variation were lower for shopping centers by the following amounts respectively: 0.15, 0.08, 0.27, and 0.06.

25 In Charlottesville, Va., the coefficient of variation in the shopping center was 0.08 higher than that in the conventional shopping area. This may be attributed to the design at Barracks Road Shopping Center in Charlottesville. The center was established in 1959 and is laid out in roughly a straight line with parking immediately adjoining. Compared to most centers, there is a relatively wider range of quality among subsections, making the center effectively a combination of two different shopping centers. Despite this layout, however, the search costs of goods at Barracks Road are less than those of downtown Charlottesville. See Implication 6 and Table 9.9.

26 The one exception, Kalamazoo, Mich., may be a reflection of some unusual characteristics of the Kalamazoo downtown. These include a large, privately owned hotel complex that adjoins the conventional shopping area, a large work force of professional and other high-income individuals immediately adjoining the area, presence of a high-quality department store, and its close proximity to high-income suburbs.

27 Transportation time to and from shopping centers averaged 17.1 minutes, only 0.4 minute below the average for conventional shopping areas.

28 Of course, lower costs may also provide an explanation.

29 See 895 *Antitrust and Trade Regulation Report* (BNA) (January 1979), at A-13, summarizing statements of FTC staff.

30 Both quotes are from a speech made in Florida on October 18, 1972. See Emanuel B. Halpet, "The Antitrust Laws Visit Shopping Center Use Restrictions," 4 *Real Estate Law Journal* 3 (1975), pp. 25–26, nn. 65 & 66.

31 See notes 13 and 14 *supra*.
32 Urban Land Institute, *The Dollars and Cents of Shopping Centers* (Washington, D.C.: Urban Land Institutes, 1972), pp. 26, 110, and 1978, pp. 65, 161; Economic Report of the President, 1972 and 1978. *Dollars and Cents* is published in the spring of every third year and apparently contains data current as of the end of the preceding year. Since data on department stores are not available for neighborhood shopping centers, the closest substitute are data on variety stores (which are the largest stores in a shopping center this size). The data include all stores, not just those opened since 1972, and hence must be considered very carefully. About 20 percent of the 1978 data for regional centers, however, are from stores opened in the last six years, whereas about 36 percent of the information on neighborhood centers are from such stores.
33 See note 30 *supra*.
34 Urban Land Institute, *supra* note 32, 1972, p. 206, and 1978, p. 279.
35 *Ibid.*
36 *Id.*, 1972, pp. 24–25, and 1978, pp. 61, 63.

10. Legislative powers

1 15 U.S.C. § 57a (1976).
2 15 U.S.C. § 57a(a)(1)(B) (1976).
3 See the authorities collected in National Petroleum Refiners Association v. FTC, 482 F.2d 672 (D.C. Cir. 973), at 693–94, n. 27.
4 29 *Federal Register* 8325 (1964). The FTC had issued seven rules prior to the Cigarette Rule, but they were limited to requirements that products such as sleeping bags, simulated leather belts, and re-refined oil be accurately labeled. See 16 C.F.R. §§ 400–6 (1978).
5 15 U.S.C. §§ 1331–40 (1976).
6 36 *Federal Register* 23,883 (1971); 36 *Federal Register* 23,871 (1971). A number of rules addressing particular practices in specific industries had been issued in the period after the promulgation of the Cigarette Rule – see 16 C.F.R. §§ 409, 410, 413, 414, 417, 418 (1978) – as was a comprehensive disclosure rule regarding games of chance, 16 C.F.R. § 419 (1978).
7 National Petroleum Refiners Association v. FTC, 340 F. Supp. 1343 (D.D.C. 1972); *reversed,* 482 F.2d 672 (D.C. Cir. 1973); *cert. denied* 415 U.S. 951 (1974).
8 5 U.S.C. § 553 (1976).
9 15 U.S.C. § 57a(b) (1976).
10 15 U.S.C. § 57a(d)(1) (1976).
11 5 U.S.C. § 553 (1976).
12 15 U.S.C. § 57a(e) (1976).
13 43 *Federal Register* 23,992 (1978).
14 "Disclosure Requirements and Prohibitions Concerning Franchising and Business Opportunity Ventures," 43 *Federal Register* 59,614 (1978).
15 "Proprietary Vocational and Home Study Schools," 43 *Federal Register* 60,796 (1978).
16 925 *Antitrust and Trade Regulation Report* (BNA) (August 2, 1979), pp. G-3, G-5. The same agenda lists eight investigations now in progress that may result in a recommendation that the Commission promulgate a TRR, *id.*, at G-3.
17 29 *Federal Register* 8325, 8355 (1964).

18 FTC v. Sperry & Hutchinson Co., 405 U.S. 233, 244–45, n. 5. (1972).

19 43 *Federal Register* 59,614, 59,643 (1978) (Franchise Rule).

20 43 *Federal Register* 23,992 (1978) (Eyeglasses Rule).

21 See, e.g., Sissela Bok, *Lying: Moral Choice in Public and Private Life* (New York: Pantheon Books, 1978), especially the appendix, pp. 250–88.

22 43 *Federal Register* 23,997, 24,000 (1978).

23 *Id.*, at 24,000–1.

24 *Id.*, at 24,001. Someone at the Commission apparently recognized the embarrassment this statement could cause for some of its other TRRs that more overtly restrict market forces. Three subsequent paragraphs that seem to be late additions to the opinion seek to blunt the effect of this forthright acknowledgment of the primacy of the market and to justify in particular the TRR on "Preservation of Consumers' Claims and Remedies" [40 *Federal Register* 53,506 (1975); 16 C.F.R. § 433 (1978)] on the grounds that there the Commission found that only by intrusion into the market would "an efficient level of risk be achieved."

25 This assumes that the Commission is correct in its assertion of authority to preempt state law, a matter that is not free from doubt, as the FTC's analysis of its legal position indicates. 43 *Federal Register* 24,004–6 (1978).

26 Charles L. Schultze, *The Public Use of Private Interest* (Washington, D.C.: Brookings Institution, 1977), pp. 6, 13.

27 Jack F. Kahn, *Report of the Presiding Officer on Proposed Trade Regulation Rule concerning Funeral Industry Practices* (Washington, D.C.: FTC, July, 1977). The rule-making proceeding has yet to result in the issuance of a TRR by the Commission. On November 14, 1979, the House of Representatives voted 233 to 147 to prohibit issuance by the FTC of any rule regulating practices of the funeral industry. 940 *Antitrust and Trade Regulation Report* (BNA) (November 22, 1979), p. A-2.

28 *Id.*, at 34.

29 *Id.*, at 40–41 (immediate disposition services); 42–43 (memorial societies).

30 *Id.*, at 44–45, 47–49, 53.

31 *Id.*, at 135.

32 Bureau of Consumer Protection, *Funeral Industry Practices: Final Staff Report to the FTC and Proposed Trade Regulation Rule* (Washington, D.C.: FTC, June 1978), pp. 426–43, 125–38, 275–81, 408–43.

33 William C. Whitford, "The Functions of Disclosure Regulation in Consumer Transactions," 1973 *Wisconsin Law Review* 400 (1973), pp. 423–27.

34 *Id.*, at 423.

35 *Id.*, at 436.

36 George A. Akerloff, "The Market for 'Lemons': Quality Uncertainty and the Market Mechanism," 84 *Quarterly Journal of Economics* 488 (1970), pp. 499–510.

37 The rule includes specific requirements regarding the collection, verification, and maintenance of records of the information required to be disclosed. 43 *Federal Register* 60,796, 60,819 (1978).

38 Bureau of Consumer Protection, *Proprietary Vocational and Home Study Schools: Final Report to the FTC and Proposed Trade Regulation Rule* (Washington, D.C.: FTC, December 1976), p. 37.

39 *Id.*, at 38–39.

40 BCP Report (funeral industry) *supra* note 32, at 158–75; Report of Presiding Officer, *supra* note 27, at 23–25.

41 Report of Presiding Officer (funeral industry), *supra* note 27, at 28.

42 BCP Report (funeral industry), *supra* note 32, at 369.
43 See, e.g., *id.*, at 163–64; also Report of Presiding Officer (funeral industry), *supra* note 27, at 25, 61.
44 Memorandum: "Recommendation for Modification to the Funeral Rule as Proposed in the Staff Report" (January 29, 1979).
45 Memorandum: "Final Recommendations on the Proposed Funeral Industry TRR" (February 2, 1979).
46 Memorandum: "Response to Staff Memo Recommending Modifications in the Proposed Funeral Rule" (February 15, 1979).
47 44 *Federal Register* 10,993 (1979). Although no votes were taken, the Commission directed the staff to delete some and redraft other provisions of the proposed rule. Memorandum, "Summary of Actions taken at March 23, 1979, Mark-up Meeting" (April 16, 1979).
48 Memo, *supra* note 44, at 10.
49 Memo, *supra* note 46, at 22.
50 *Id.*, at 20.
51 Bureau of Consumer Protection, *Sale of Used Motor Vehicles: Final Staff Report to the FTC and Proposed Trade Regulation Rule* (Washington, D.C.: FTC, September 1978), p. 196, n.'271. In August 1979, the Director of the BCP indicated sharp disagreement with the Used Car Rule staff proposals, suggesting dealers should be allowed to avoid inspecting all used cars and to sell them with "No Promises." 927 *Antitrust and Trade Regulation Report* (BNA) (August 16, 1979), p. A-11. At oral argument, the Commission itself has expressed doubts about the practicability of the staff proposals. 932 *Antitrust and Trade Regulation Report* (BNA) (September 27, 1979), p. A-23.
52 This may not hold true for safety information, since some persons not parties to the transaction (e.g., future passengers, pedestrians, and other drivers) would bid for more safety defect disclosure. Since transaction costs prevent them from bidding, the market may undervalue safety information.
53 Akerloff, *supra* note 36.
54 BCP report (autos), *supra* note 51, at 460.
55 *Ibid.*
56 *Id.*, at 462–63.
57 It is not surprising that, as the BCP discovered, few used-car buyers arrange individual inspections. *Id.*, at 93–94. It is more efficient to buy from dealers who provide the service.
58 43 *Federal Register* 24,007–8 (1978).
59 *Id.*, at 24,001.
60 *Id.*, at 24,003.
61 The discussion here deals only with the costs reflected in the nominal price of the examinations and eyeglasses and does not take into account the additional savings in costs from "one-stop shopping" that consumers realize directly (from minimizing their own search, travel, contracting, etc., costs). The rule would not directly affect such economies, but the Commission ignores the effect they have upon consumers' incentive to shop separately for examinations and glasses.
62 BCP Report (autos), *supra* note 51, app. F.
63 *Id.*, at 452.
64 Of course, teachers could be hired on a percentage of fees received, in which case the payments to teachers would drop as students dropped out. But that merely changes the form of the transfer to teacher and does not reduce the resource inputs (teacher time); and, unless it is assumed that the school has an

employment monopoly, teachers would receive higher total salaries under a system in which their fees fluctuate with the number of students, since they would contract for compensation for the risk of their income's declining over the term.

65 For example, the rule as proposed by the original staff would require funeral homes to disclose to customers that cemeteries sell burial vaults in competition with funeral homes. It is not apparent why funeral homes rather than cemeteries are thought to be the most efficient providers of this information (nor why funeral homes should subsidize the cost of cemeteries' selling burial vaults).

66 The Presiding Officer cited evidence that supports this proposition. Report of Presiding Officer (funeral industry), *supra* note 27, at 63.

67 The Presiding Officer found that some funeral homes had substantial amounts tied up in cash advances. *Id.*, at 68.

68 *Id.*, at 68, n. 45; BCP report (funeral industry), *supra* note 32, at 250–51.

69 Memo, *supra* note 44, at 12.

70 15 U.S.C. § 57a(e)(3) (1976).

71 43 *Federal Register* 23,994–95 (1978).

72 BCP Report (autos), *supra* note 51, at 19–24. The BCP also relied upon the following studies to support its position: a telephone survey of used-car purchases, *id.*, at 24–28; a survey of consumer complaints about used cars, *id.*, at 28–30; a study of the files of two auto clubs' prepurchase inspections of used cars, *id.*, at 30–33; a shopping survey and a telephone survey both conducted by CALPIRG, *id.*, at 33–37. The BCP conceded that there were problems with CALPIRG's studies, *id.*, at 35 nn. 72, 76, 36; it relied upon them, nonetheless, *id.*, at 57.

73 *Id.*, at 242–44.

74 *Id.*, at 463, n. 24.

75 *Id.*, at 245.

76 *Id.*, at 246.

77 *Id.*, at 23.

78 Henry B. Cabell, *Report of the Presiding Officer on Proposed Trade Regulation Rule Concerning Credit Practices* (Washington, D.C.: FTC, August 1978), p. 335.

79 *Id.*, at 340.

80 Report of Presiding Officer (funeral industry), *supra* note 27, at 131.

11. Rewriting consumer contracts

1 The rule-making proceedings have yet to produce a final report. Details of the BCP's position come largely from a 610-page Memorandum submitted in 1974 by the BCP to the FTC in support of its proposals (hereinafter Memorandum).

2 Memorandum, p. 92.

3 *Id.*, at 31.

4 *Id.*, at 51, 54.

5 *Id.*, at 424.

6 *Id.*, at 441.

7 *Id.*, at 84–85.

8 *Id.*, at 91.

9 *Id.*, at 377–78.

10 David Caplowitz, *Debtors in Default* (New York: Bureau of Applied Social

Research, Columbia University, 1970); David Caplowitz, *Consumers in Trouble: A Study of Debtors in Default* (New York: The Free Press, 1974).

11 Robert W. Johnson, *Monograph No. 12, Cost/Benefit Analysis of Creditors' Remedies* (West Lafayette, Ind.: Credit Research Center, Purdue University, 1978).

12 *Id.*, at 6.

13 Douglas F. Greer and Alan R. Feldman, "Creditors' Remedies and Contract Provisions: An Economic and Legal Analysis of Consumer Credit Collection," in *National Commission on Consumer Finance – Technical Studies,* vol. 5 (Washington, D.C.: U.S. Government Printing Office, 1973).

14 *Ibid.*

15 Johnson, *supra* note 11, at 24–28.

16 Johnson, *supra* note 11, at 20–24.

17 Memorandum, *supra* note 1, at 16.

18 Johnson, *supra* note 11, at 20–24; Gregory Boczar, "Competition Between Banks and Finance Companies: A Cross-Section Study of Personal Loan Debtors," 33 *Journal of Finance* 245 (1978).

19 Johnson, *supra* note 11, at 33.

20 *Id.*, at 36.

21 *Ibid.*

22 William C. Dunkelberg and James Stephenson, "Durable Goods Ownership and Rate of Return," in *National Commission on Consumer Finance – Technical Studies,* vol. 6 (Washington, D.C.: U.S. Government Printing Office, 1973).

23 Johnson, *supra* note 11, at 6.

24 *Ibid.*

25 Robert P. Shay, "The Impact of State Legal Rate Ceilings Upon the Availability and Price of Consumer Installment Credit," in *National Commission on Consumer Finance – Technical Studies,* vol. 4 (Washington, D.C.: U.S. Government Printing Office, 1973).

26 See note 10, *supra*.

27 Johnson, *supra* note 11, at 14.

28 Philip Schuchman, "Profit on Default: An Archival Study of Automobile Repossession and Resale," 22 *Stanford Law Review* 20 (1969). The BCP cited a study by Firmin and Simpson extensively in the Memorandum, *supra* note 1, but it provided no further reference. Apparently, that study was commissioned by the BCP for internal use and was not published.

29 Memorandum, p. 312.

30 Johnson, *supra* note 11, at 48–62.

31 Schuchman, *supra* note 28, at 42.

32 Stephen M. Crane, *The Aftermath of Repossession: Deficiency Suits for Automobile Credit Transactions in the District of Columbia* (Washington, D.C.: National Commission on Consumer Finance, unpublished report, n.d.), p. 23.

33 James Barth and Anthony Yezer, "Testimony at FTC Hearings on the Proposed Credit Practices Rule," *Hearing Exhibit 505,* (Washington, D.C., 1978).

34 *Id.*, at 6. APR2 was an APR figure adjusted for the cost of credit insurance fees and other noninterest charges included in the fees assessed on the loan. This adjustment allows for the fact that some creditors, in states where rate ceilings were restrictive, would adjust APR2 if their costs increased in lieu of adjusting APR1.

35 The total effect is subject to two caveats. First, the three- to five-percentage-point estimates of overall rate increases obtained by Barth and Yezer are, if anything, underestimates of the total impact of remedy restrictions, as they measure the incremental effect of FTC restrictions *relative to existing restrictions* in states from which *sample* loans were drawn. Second, these results may have been over inflated to some degree, *especially with respect to the impact that creditor* remedy restrictions have on the demand for credit by the fact that they were *estimated only for sample loans that experienced collection difficulties.* The demand for creditor remedy protection by people who expected that they might face repayment difficulties would be *particularly* elevated. Creditors who supplied debt to risky customers might also raise loan charges to compensate for that fact *but,* because they had less a priori knowledge than the consumer regarding the probability he would default (elsewise they probably would not have made loans to customers who later defaulted), the supply bias would be smaller than the bias in demand estimates.

36 Although the Barth and Yezer study indicates that, for the consumers they studied, the credit price increase resulting from the increase in demand when remedies were restricted would exceed the credit price increase that resulted from the reduction in credit supplies when remedies were restricted, they did not claim that this finding justified the FTCs proposed rule. In fact, no such claim can validly be made. What can be said is that the reduction in credit supply will *unambiguously reduce* the consumers' surplus *(welfare)* of consumers who would be in the consumer credit market had the rule not been passed. This welfare loss might be partially offset by gains to certain people.

In particular, because aggregate credit demand increases, some people will be willing to pay more to get credit in a restricted remedy environment – those people which we will call group A, likely have high expected probabilities of default; with reduced remedies, they will fear default less and bid up the price of credit. However, consumers with low expected probabilities of default (group B) will not increase their demand for credit, but must pay more to obtain it if they are to compete for credit with members of group A. Members of group B will lose consumers' surplus (welfare) while members of group A likely will gain. As a result of this redistribution, no net evaluation can be made of welfare changes caused by remedy restriction effects on demand without making interpersonal utility comparisons. However, the upshift in the supply curve *still* will *unambiguously* reduce the (consumers' surplus) welfare of all market participants.

It should also be pointed out that Barth and Yezer recognized that their atypical sample of consumers (i.e., people who eventually defaulted after borrowing from creditors who serviced the riskiest end of the market) might well have overstated the demand effect of remedy restrictions – as such consumers are exactly those whose demand for credit would be expected to increase most (because of their high potential for default) if the costs of default were to be reduced.

37 Barth and Yezer, *supra* note 33, at 10.

38 See note 36 *supra* for a discussion of welfare effects.

39 Richard L. Peterson and Michael D. Ginsberg, "Determinants of Commercial Banks' Auto Loan Rates," *Working Paper No. 6* (West Lafayette, Ind.: Credit Research Center, Purdue University, 1976).

40 Richard L. Peterson and Michael D. Ginsberg, "Regulatory Influences on Commercial Bank Consumer Loan Rates," in *Proceedings of a Conference*

on Bank Structure and Competition (Chicago: Federal Reserve Bank of Chicago, 1977), pp. 138–55.

41 This result (for attorneys' fees) was statistically significant. A test for confession of judgments, another remedy that the TRR would effect, was run with the result having the expected sign, although it was not statistically significant.

42 See also Greer and Feldman, *supra* note 13, at 43, where table 12A shows that 74 percent of respondent banks found attorneys' fees clauses moderately or substantially useful in collection.

43 Richard L. Peterson, "The Impact of Creditors' Remedies on Consumer Loan Charges," *Working Paper No. 15* (West Lafayette, Ind.: Credit Research Center, Purdue University, 1977).

44 Because the six states cited generally restrict either a creditor's ability to repossess an auto or his ability to obtain a full deficiency judgment (sometimes by making the creditor elect either repossession or a suit for the full unpaid debt), in some respects they parallel the proposed FTC Rule that would severely curtail or eliminate deficiency judgments.

45 Peterson, *supra* note 43, at 9–10.

46 Richard L. Peterson and James R. Frew, "Creditor Remedy Restrictions and Interstate Differences in Personal Loan Rates and Availability: A Supplementary Analysis," *Working Paper No. 14* (West Lafayette, Ind.: Credit Research Center, Purdue University, 1978), p. 14.

47 Richard L. Peterson, "The Impact of Restricted Creditors' Remedies on Automobile Finance Companies in Wisconsin," *Working Paper No. 12* (West Lafayette, Ind.: Credit Research Center, Purdue University, 1977).

48 Richard L. Peterson, "Changes in Finance Company Personal Loan Policies Following Enactment of the Wisconsin Consumer Act," *Working Paper No. 13* (West Lafayette, Ind.: Credit Research Center, Purdue University, 1977).

49 William C. Dunkelberg, "Banks' Lending Response to Restricted Creditors' Remedies," *Working Paper No. 20* (West Lafayette, Ind.: Credit Research Center, Purdue University, 1978).

50 A detailed comparison of the WCA and the TRR is provided by James L. Brown in app. C of the Dunkelberg study, *supra* note 49.

51 *Working Paper No. 12, supra* note 47, at 26.

52 *Working Paper No. 13, supra* note 48, at 1–30.

53 *Working Paper No. 20, supra* note 49, at 53–54.

54 Henry Cabell, *Report of the Presiding Officer on Proposed Trade Regulation Rule: Credit Practices* (Washington, D.C.: FTC, August 1978). The Presiding Officer's discussion of the economic evidence is at 287–350.

55 Although their sample was biased, as discussed in note 36 *supra,* this could not have justified the Presiding Officer completely dismissing the finding that remedy restrictions significantly affected credit costs – particularly since the bias was likely to affect estimates of remedy restrictions on credit demand substantially while affecting estimates of credit restrictions on credit supply little, if at all.

56 Cabell, *supra* note 54, at 298.

57 *Working Paper No. 13, supra* note 48.

58 Testimony of this sort was presented by James L. Brown, Esquire, Acting Director of the Center for Consumer Affairs, University of Wisconsin and Ronald Gall, Wisconsin Consumers League. References to both sets of testimony are made by Cabell, *supra* note 54, at 335 both in the text and in n. 42.

59 BCP statements that betray this attitude are collected in an FTC Office of Policy Planning and Evaluation memorandum from Timothy J. Muris to Wesley J. Liebeler (November 20, 1974) (memorandum placed on public rule-making record, September 1975).

60 Johnson, *supra* note 11, at 13–15.

12. Regulating postpurchase relations

1 Proposed Trade Regulation Rule, Mobile Homes Sales and Service (40 *Federal Register* 23334–23340) [hereinafter referred to as TRR]. Hearings on the TRR began in October 1977, and it is doubtful that a final rule will be promulgated before the end of 1981.

2 Redman Industries, Inc., 85 FTC 309 (1975); Fleetwood Enterprises, Inc., 85 FTC 414 (1975); Skyline Corp., 85 FTC 444 (1975); Commodore Corp., 85 FTC 472 (1975).

3 The two on-site inspections are intended to hold manufacturers liable for the setup.

4 *Staff Statement of Position, Proposed Trade Regulation Rule Regarding Mobile Home Sales and Service,* Federal Trade Commission (November 11, 1975).

5 A study exploring the possible economic consequences of the TRR is being prepared by the FTC and will be submitted to the hearing officer prior to the promulgation of a final rule. It seems peculiar that such a study was not prepared as a basis for deciding whether to propose the TRR and as a focus for the hearings.

6 R. Dennis Murphy, Rebuttal Submission regarding Testimony of Anthony M. Robinson (April 17, 1978), pp. 14–15.

7 Staff Statement, *supra* note 4, at 14–15.

8 Interestingly, one of the BCP's grounds for viewing MH warranties as unfair or deceptive is that they frequently exclude certain repairs and services which, in fact, are provided. See Staff Statement, *supra* note 4, at 48–50.

9 *Id.,* at 1–5.

10 E.g., Allen R. Ferguson, President, Public Interest Economics Foundation, Statement (September 19, 1977), p. 10, supporting rule; and Charles River Associates, Statement, The Economic Effects of the Federal Trade Commission's Proposed Rule Relating to Mobile Home Sales and Service (November, 1977), opposing rule. In this and subsequent footnotes, "Statement" refers to statements submitted for MH Rule Making Record.

11 *Data Sources.* MH shipments and sizes: MHI, *Data Books,* various annual issues. Number of MH firms and plants: MHI, *Flash Facts* (1969–73) and MHI, *Quick Facts* (1974–present), various annual issues. Number of MH dealers: provided to the author by *Mobile-Modular Housing Dealer.*

12 Letter from Elrick and Lavidge, Inc., to Manufactured Housing Institute (September 15, 1977).

13 *Id.* The usefulness of concentration ratios in assessing the existence of noncompetitive behavior is not clear. See Harold Demsetz, *The Market Concentration Doctrine* (Washington, D.C.: American Enterprise Institute, 1973).

14 E.g., Phillip Weitzman, Research Associate, National Social Science and Law Project, Inc., Statement (January 26, 1978), p. 12.

15 In 1977, four-firm concentration ratios for 25 states varied from 27 percent in

Kentucky, Missouri, and South Carolina to 71 percent in Wisconsin, with a median of 42 percent in Ohio and South Dakota. (Data provided to the author by the FTC.)

16 Unless otherwise noted, the source for all statements in this paragraph is Staff Statement, *supra* note 4, at 4.

17 Ferguson (Statement), *supra* note 10, at 9.

18 Staff Statement, *supra* note 4, at 4.

19 Arthur D. Bernhardt *et al., Structure, Operation, Performance and·Development Trends of the Mobile Home Industry* (unpublished manuscript, 1976), pp. 40–43. The study was prepared for HUD's Office of Policy Development and Research; references are to excerpts provided to the author by the FTC. According to Bernhardt, in 1975 the average manufacturer utilized about 405 dealers; approximately 9 percent used over 1,000 dealers each.

20 James E. Lavasque, President, Oakwood Homes Corp., Statement (October 1977), p. 4.

21 Owens/Corning Fiberglas Corporation, *Facts about the Mobile Home Buyer and the Mobile Home Dealer* (1975), p. 29.

22 Bernhardt, *supra* note 19.

23 Staff Statement, *supra* note 4, at 10–13. Moreover, national advertising (except for trade publications) is sponsored by trade associations, whereas local advertising is sponsored by dealers who typically represent several manufacturers. Bernhardt, *supra* note 19.

24 Staff Statement, *supra* note 4, at 5–7.

25 MH retail prices in July 1977 varied from less than $6,000 to more than $38,000. See *Mobile-Modular Housing Dealer* (September 1977), p. 36. There are substantial price variations within each size category; see MHI, 1976 *Data Book,* exhibit 14.

26 See *U.S. Survey of Current Business,* various issues.

27 In 1972, when MH shipments hit their peak, the average MH retail price was about $8.73 per square foot, including furnishings and appliances but excluding setup costs (about 15 percent of the retail price) and land; the average price of site-built homes reportedly was about $15.35 per square foot, excluding furnishings, appliances, and land; see *Quick Facts* (1977), pp. 3–4.

28 At least some of the increase in the relative prices of MHs was due to the actual and anticipated passage and implementation of various federal regulations. First, the Magnuson-Moss Warranty–Federal Trade Commission Act, enacted in January 1975 and implemented in December 1975, tightened the terms and conditions applicable to written warranties for consumer products. Second, the FTC consent decrees of 1975 foreshadowed the TRR. Third, the National Mobile Home Construction and Safety Standards Act of 1974, as implemented by subsequent regulations issued by the Department of Housing and Urban Development, imposed construction standards which, according to HUD's own conservative estimates, would have increased construction costs by about $400 per unit; HUD, *Inflation Impact Determination for Final Federal Mobile Home Construction and Safety Standards* (April 26, 1976).

29 The recovery of the MH industry was, no doubt, also inhibited by the large number of used MHs, frequently repossessed, which came on the market as MH owners (younger and less skilled than conventional house owners and therefore more adversely affected by the downturn) found it more difficult to maintain ownership. Moreover, finance companies apparently responded to

the higher perceived risk of MH loans by becoming more cautious in making such loans and by charging higher interest rates. See Richard X. Bove, Vice President–Research, Wertheim & Co., Inc., Member New York Stock Exchange, Inc., Statement (August 9, 1977). Although these factors help to explain why the *quantity* of MHs produced did not recover more quickly (the demand curve did not increase as much as otherwise), they fail to account for the observed increase in MH *prices*.

30 Ferguson (Statement), *supra* note 10, at 4–8.
31 Lavasque (Statement), *supra* note 20, exhibit 4.
32 *Ibid.* There is corroboration for a 30 percent dealer's markup. In 1976, the average MH retail price was $12,740 (table 1), while the wholesale value of the 247,734 units produced was $2,359 million or $9,552 per unit (*Annual Production Survey*, Tractor-Dealer Publishing Company, 1977). Thus, freight, insurance, and dealers' costs yield a markup of 33 percent.
33 An exception is Anthony M. Robinson, who testified on behalf of the Small Business Administration. He estimated that the proposed TRR would increase costs by a minimum of $300 per unit for larger and by $600 per unit for smaller firms (i.e., those with an output of less than 100 units per year). Anthony M. Robinson, U.S. Small Business Administration, Statement (undated), pp. 9–10. Robinson's calculations, however, are murky and rest on some apparent definitional errors sufficiently serious to destroy the usefulness of his estimates; see Murphy (Rebuttal: Robinson), *supra* note 6.
34 Lavasque (Statement), *supra* note 20, exhibit 4.
35 Charles River Associates (Statement), *supra* note 10. See also H. Michael Mann, Testimony, MH Hearings (January 13, 1978), pp. 6003–6134, esp. pp. 6068–69. Mann noted that the survey data were given with so much uncertainty and varied so much in magnitude to preclude determinative analysis; see Charles River Assoc. (Statement), p. 28. The quality of the survey methodology also left a great deal to be desired; see Mann (Hearings).
36 Don L. Greenwalt, President, C. and G. Corp., Statement (September 19, 1977), p. 6.
37 Philip S. Davis, Esq., Counsel, Lebanon Homes of New England, Inc., Statement (August 1977), p. 5.
38 John P. Williams, Vice President, Zimmer Homes Corp., Statement (August 1977), p. 7.
39 Harry B. Burchstead, Jr., Assistant Attorney-General of the State of South Carolina, Consumer Protection Division, Statement (1977) and Testimony, MH Hearings (November 2, 1977), pp. 2847–2958. Burchstead testified that 658 MH complaints had been filed between January 1, 1975, and October 15, 1977, either with his office or with the Manufactured Housing Inspector of the Inspection Services of the State Division of General Services. His office had files on 147 of the 169 complaints it had received between January 1, 1976, and October 15, 1977; of these, at most 90 (6 in the written testimony) involved a possible breach of warranty. Taking the ratio of 90 to 147 and multiplying it by 658 yields an estimate of 403 breach-related complaints. During the same period, 16,835 units were shipped to South Carolina; see MHI, *1976 Data Book* and MHI, *Mobile Home Shipments and Production* (December 1977), yielding a breach rate of 2.4 percent.

The frequency distribution of sales in various price ranges for the South Atlantic Region, which includes South Carolina, is quite similar to that for the United States as a whole [see "Retail Sales, Inventory and Prices," *Mobile-*

Modular Housing Dealer (1977, various monthly issues)]. If price is taken as an index of quality, including the quality of warranties, then the data from South Carolina can be taken as indicative of the United States as a whole.

40 Sentry Insurance, *Consumerism at the Crossroads* (1978), pp. 16–17. The report, based on a public opinion poll conducted by Louis Harris Associates for Sentry Insurance, was part of the submission of the Center for Auto Safety. The 3 percent estimate lacks any scientific basis and seems outlandish.

41 The Housing Advocate, Inc., *New Data on Non-respondents to the Housing Advocates, Inc., Ohio Mobile Homeowners Survey* (May 25, 1978), p. 21.

42 Ferguson (Statement), *supra* note 10, at 10.

43 Peter W. Sperlich, *Residing in a Mobile Home: A Survey of Consumer Experiences Regarding Product Satisfaction, Product Defects, and Warranty Service* (November 1977). Sperlich conducted the survey on behalf of Golden State Mobile Home Owners' League, Inc.

44 Herschel Elkins, Deputy Attorney General of the State of California, Head of Consumer Protection Unit of the Attorney General's Office, Testimony, MH Hearings (undated), pp. 4778–4853. See also Dennis B. Kavanagh, attorney representing Golden State Mobile Home Owners' League, Inc., Testimony, MH Hearings (December 12, 1977), excerpts, pp. 4177–4223. Apparently the seriousness of the complaints filed in California has decreased, shifting from matters affecting health and safety to those involving cosmetics. Elkins Testimony, pp. 4787–4788.

45 Letter written on behalf of the Commodore Corporation by Howard J. Kaslow, attorney, to Charles A. Taylor III, FTC (July 21, 1977).

46 For the sake of simplicity, demand and supply curves are taken to be linear over the relevant range at the 1977 equilibrium point of 265,640 units sold at an average price of $15,430. This equilibrium point reflects the responses of the four firms under order as well as the anticipations of other firms regarding implementation of the TRR; thus, output is smaller and (average) price is higher than otherwise would have been the case. Because the data are so weak and the effects at issue are so small, however, it seems best to recognize the matter simply as a limitation of the reported results.

47 In estimating the demand function, two alternative price elasticities of demand (n_d) are used. One is -0.38; as noted earlier, this seems favored by the FTC. The other is -1.0; this seems more likely to reflect the true long-run elasticity and is also useful in examining the sensitivity of the results to the coefficient used. Letting D = quantity demanded and P = price, the alternative demand functions then are: (a) $D = 366,583 - 6.54P$ for $n_d = -0.38$, and (b) $D = 531,280 - 17.22P$ for $n_d = -1.0$.

If the supply curve is perfectly flat, a $400 increase in production costs implies a $400 increase in retail prices. This is independent of the elasticity of or shift in demand; the quantity sold bears the full brunt of the adjustment.

If the supply curve is positively sloped but highly elastic, say with a price elasticity (n_s) of 10, however, then the supply function is $S = 172.16P - 2,390,760$ for $n_s = 10$. An increase of $400 in production costs, demand unchanged, then yields an increase in price of $385 if $n_d = -0.38$ and of $363 if $n_d = -1$. If demand increases by $100, the price increases are $389 and $372, respectively.

48 If the supply curve is infinitely elastic and demand is unchanged, a $400 increase in production costs yields a decrease in sales of 2,614 units if $n_d = -0.38$ and of 6,897 units if $n_d = -1$. If demand increases by $100, the net decreases in sales are 1,963 and 5,162 units, respectively.

If the supply curve has a price elasticity of 10 and demand is unchanged, a

$400 increase in production costs yields a decrease in sales of 2,487 units if $n_d = -0.38$ and of 6,315 units if $n_d = -1$. If demand increases by $100, the net decreases in sales are 1,859 and 4,748 units, respectively.

49 A decrease in supply of $400 per unit, an increase in demand of $100 per unit, a perfectly elastic supply, and a price elasticity of demand of -0.38 yield equilibrium sales of 263,680 units. This implies that the opportunity cost of the additional resources used to produce this output is (263,680) (400) = $105,472,000. For $n_d = -1$, costs are roughly the same: (260,467) (400) = $104,186,600.

50 Benefits were estimated at $100 per unit. For $n_d = -0.38$, sales of 263,680 units yield benefits of $26,368,000. For $n_d = -1$, sales of 260,467 units yield benefits of $26,046,700.

51 The difference between costs and benefits yields a net welfare loss of $79,104,000 for $n_d = -0.38$ and of $78,139,300$ for $n_d = -1$.

Under the conditions postulated here, the net change in welfare could be measured more precisely as the difference between the area bounded by the vertical axis, the old supply curve, and the old demand curve on the one hand, and the area bounded by the vertical axis, the new demand curve, and the new supply curve on the other hand. Then the deadweight loss is $79,344,900 for $n_d = -0.38$ and $78,979,745$ for $n_d = -1$. Thus, both estimates yield a deadweight loss of $79 million per year.

All the usual caveats apply regarding the usefulness of aggregate estimates of costs, benefits, and deadweight losses.

52 U.S. government decision makers are required to use a discount rate of 10 percent in computing the present value of future costs and benefits. See *Discount Rates To Be Used in Evaluating Time – Distributed Costs and Benefits,* Office of Management and Budget, Circular A-94 (March 27, 1972). A 10 percent discount rate is also indicated by recent estimates of the opportunity cost of capital. See Kenneth W. Clarkson, *Intangible Capital and Rates of Return* (Washington, D.C.: American Enterprise Institute, 1977), pp. 30–31.

53 Not only was the increase in production costs underestimated and the increase in benefits overestimated, but no allowance was made for government monitoring and enforcement costs. Even more important, the estimated deadweight loss is based on 1977 output, which was about half what it had been in the early 1970s and should be again by the mid-1980s.

54 *Mobile-Modular Housing Dealer* (September 1977), p. 36.

55 *Ibid.*

56 *Average sales price of new mobile homes placed for residential use[a]*

Year	North East	North Central	South	West	All Areas
1974	9,500	9,300	8,300	11,600	9,200
1975	10,600	10,700	9,000	13,600	10,900
1976	11,600	11,700	10,600	15,900	12,300
1977[b]	12,400	12,300	11,500	17,200	13,300

[a] Includes estimate of sales price for units leased.
[b] 1977 data are for the first quarter only.
Source: *Mobile-Modular Housing Dealer* (October 1977), p. 40.

57 During the period of industry contraction from 1974 to 1976, shipments fell by

83.2 thousand units, firms by 102 and plants by 301, yielding an exit of one firm per 816 and of one plant per 276 fewer units of output. Applying these estimates to a projected decrease in output of 5,000 units suggests an exit of about six firms and about 18 plants.

58 See Bove, *supra* note 29, at 5.
59 Moody's Investors' Services, Inc., *Moody's Handbook of Common Stocks* (Spring 1974, Spring 1976).
60 R. Dennis Murphy, Rebuttal Submission Regarding Testimony of Richard X. Bove (April 17, 1978), p. 3.
61 For an insightful discussion of this issue, see Israel M. Kirzner, *The Perils of Regulation: A Market Process Approach* (Coral Gables, Fla: University of Miami Law and Economics Center, 1978).

13. Regulating information

1 George J. Stigler, "The Economics of Information," 69 *Journal of Political Economy* 213 (1961).
2 Phillip Nelson, "Advertising as Information," 82 *Journal of Political Economy* 729 (1974).
3 *Id.*, at 750.
4 *Id.*, at 734.
5 See William L. Prosser, *Handbook of the Law of Torts,* 4th ed. (St. Paul, Minn.: West Publishing Co., 1971), pp. 720–24; Fowler V. Harper and Mary Coate McNeely, "A Synthesis of the Law of Misrepresentation," 22 *Minnesota Law Review* 939 (1938); W. Page Keeton, "Fraud: Misrepresentation of Opinion," 21 *Minnesota Law Review* 643 (1937).
6 E.g., Shine v. Dodge, 130 Me. 440, 157 A. 318 (1931).
7 Nichols v. Lane, 93 Vt. 87, 106 A. 592 (1919).
8 Bertram v. Reed Automobile Co., Inc., 49 S.W.2d 517 (Tex. Civ. App., 1932); Twentieth Century–Fox Distributing Corp. v. Lakeside Theaters, Inc., 267 So.2d 225 (La. App. 1972).
9 If a seller's statement concerns matters that he evidently could not know, it is generally not actionable – e.g., Harry V. Harris v. Delco Products, Inc., 305 Mass. 362, 25 N.E.2d 740 (1940).
10 Trust Co. of Norfolk v. Fletcher, 152 Va. 868, 148 S.E. 785 (1929). But a statement that a stock is a "good common stock" is not actionable. Mekrut v. Gould, 16 Misc.2d 326, 188 N.Y.S.2d 6, (Sup. 1959).
11 Pellette v. Mann Auto Co., 161 Kan. 16, 225 P. 1067 (1924).
12 Saxby v. Southern Land Co., 109 Va. 196, 63 S.W. 423 (1909). added).
13 McNabb v. Thomas, 190 F.2d 608, 611 (D.C. Cir. 1951); Sacramento Suburban Fruit Lands Co. v. Klaffenbach, 40 F.2d 899, 903 (9th Cir. 1930); Carpenter v. Hamilton, 18 Cal. App.2d 69, 62 P.2d 1397 (1936); Davis v. Bayne, 171 Wash. 1, 17 P.2d 618 (1932); Meland v. Youngberg, 124 Minn. 446, 145 N.W 167 (1914). See also Prosser, *supra* note 5, at 714–15.
14 E.g., Hedin v. Minneapolis Medical & Surgical Institute, 62 Minn. 146, 64 N.W. 158 (1895).
15 E.g., Pickard v. McCormick, 11 Mich. 68 (1862).
16 Vulcan Metals Co. v. Simmons Mfg. Co., 248 F. 853 (2d Cir. 1918). See also Bathchelder v. Birchard Motors, Inc., 120 Vt. 429, 144 A.2d 298 (1958).
17 E.g., Hedin v. Minneapolis Medical and Surgical Institute, 62 Minn. 146, 64 N.W. 158 (1895).
18 See, e.g., Morgan v. Dinges, 23 Neb. 271 (1888).

19 Wightman v. Tucker, 50 Ill. App. 75 (1893).
20 Bolds v. Woods, 9 Ind. App. 657 (1894) (seller held liable).
21 Smith v. Land and House Property Co., L.R. 28 Ch. Div. 7, 15 (1884). Accord Ryan v. Glenn, 344 F. Supp. 198 (N.D. Miss. 1972), aff'd, 489 F.2d 110 (5th Cir. 1974).
22 Hickey v. Morrell, 102 N.Y. 454 (1886).
23 Compare Lackey v. Ellingsen, 278 Ore. 11, 432 P.2d 307 (1967) with Henning v. Kyle, 190 Va. 247, 56 S.E.2d 67 (1949). Cf. Hauter v. Zogarts, 14 Cal.3d 104, 120 *California Reporter* 681, 534 P.2d 377 (1976).
24 Parker v. Arthur Murray, Inc., 10 Ill. App. 3d 1000, 295 N.E.2d 487 (1973) (statement that buyer had "exceptional potential to be a fine and accomplished dancer" not actionable).
25 See, e.g., Kimble v. Bangs, 144 Mass. 321, 11 N.E. 113 (1887).
26 Sorenson v. Greysolon Co., 170 Minn. 259, 212 N.W. 457 (1927).
27 Hassman v. First State Bank of Swatara, 183 Minn. 453, 236 N.W. 921 (1931).
28 See, e.g., Rogers v. Brummet, 92 Okla. 216, 220 P. 362 (1932) (principal and agent).
29 15 U.S.C. § 45(a)(1) (1976).
30 U.S. Retail Credit Association, Inc. v. FTC, 300 F.2d 212, 221 (4th Cir. 1962). Hereinafter, where the FTC is a party to the case, the agency's name will be omitted unless clarity requires it.
31 Heinz W. Kirchner, 63 FTC 1282, 1290 (1963), aff'd in Kirchner v. FTC, 337 F.2d 751 (9th Cir. 1964). See Rhodes Pharmacal Co., 49 FTC 263 (1951), *order modified and aff'd* in Rhodes Pharmacal Co. v. FTC, 208 F.2d 382 (7th Cir. 1953), *order restored in toto,* 348 U.S. 940 (1955) *(per curiam);* Giant Food, Inc. v. FTC, 322 F.2d 977, 981 (D.C. Cir. 1963), *cert. dismissed,* 376 U.S. 967 (1964).
32 Charles of the Ritz Distributors Corp., 143 F.2d 676, 680 (2d Cir. 1944). See also Colgate Palmolive, 380 U.S. 374, 391–92 (1965).
33 See Chapter 4, Section IIB *supra.*
34 Zenith Radio Corp., 143 F.2d 29 (7th Cir. 1944); J. B. Williams Co., 381 F.2d 884, 890 (6th Cir. 1967).
35 E.g., Korber Hats, Inc., 311 F.2d 358 (1st Cir. 1962); Exposition Press, Inc., 295 F.2d 869 (2d Cir. 1961), *cert. denied,* 370 U.S. 917 (1962).
36 Benrus Watch Co., Inc., 64 FTC 1018, 1032 (1964), aff'd, 352 F.2d 313 (8th Cir. 1965), *cert. denied,* 384 U.S. 939 (1966).
37 Firestone Tire and Rubber Co., 81 FTC 398 (1972), aff'd, 481 F.2d 246 (6th Cir.), *cert. denied,* 414 U.S. 1112 (1973).
38 Rhodes Pharmacal, 208 F.2d 382 (7th Cir. 1954), *reversed on other grounds,* 348 U.S. 940 (1955) *(per curiam).*
39 E.g., Gelb, 144 F.2d 580 (2d Cir. 1944).
40 E.g., Aronberg, 132 F.2d 165, 167 (7th Cir. 1942).
41 E.g., L. B. Silver Co., 289 F. 985 (6th Cir. 1923) (no deception in a hog breeder's advertisement that Ohio Improved Chesters were superior to Chester Whites because growers knew the underlying facts).
42 Dannon Milk Products, Inc., 61 FTC 840, 842 (1962).
43 Sebrone Co., 135 F.2d 676, 678 (7th Cir. 1943).
44 Liggett and Myers Tobacco Co., 55 FTC 354, 361 (1958).
45 Sewell, 353 U.S. 969 (1957) *(per curiam), reversing,* 240 F.2d 228, 231 (9th Cir. 1956).
46 Bristol-Myers Co., 46 FTC 162, 175 (1949), aff'd, 185 F.2d 58 (4th Cir. 1950).
47 Carlay Co., 153 F.2d 493, 496 (7th Cir. 1946).
48 Bristol-Myers Co. (Dry Ban), 85 FTC 688, 744 (1975).

49 Carter Products, 186 F.2d 821, 824 (7th Cir. 1951); Exposition Press, Inc., 295 F.2d 869, 873 (2d Cir. 1961). See Note, "Developments in the Law – Deceptive Advertising," 80 *Harvard Law Review* 1005 (1967), pp. 1059–60.
50 Pfizer, Inc., 81 FTC 23, 24 (1972).
51 *Id.*, at 64.
52 *Id.*, at 62.
53 Frank E. Moss and Consumer Subcommittee Staff, 92d Cong., 2d Sess., *Report to the Federal Trade Commission on Ad Substantiation Program Together with Supplementary Analysis of Submissions and Advertisers' Comments* (Committee Print, July 31, 1972).
54 *Advertising 1972: Hearings on S. 1461 before the Senate Committee on Commerce,* 92d Cong., 2d Sess. (1972) (statement of FTC Chairman Miles Kirkpatrick), p. 27.
55 General Motors Corp., 85 FTC 27, 29 (1975) (consent order).
56 *Id.*, at 33.
57 Kroger Co., FTC Docket 9102, slip opinion at p. 14 (FTC administrative law judge opinion filed June 11, 1979).
58 *Id.*, at 63.
59 See Tashof, 437 F.2d 707 (D.C. Cir. 1970) ("bargain" eyeglass prices must be substantiated by a survey of local competition).
60 See cases cited in George Eric Rosden and Peter Rosden, *The Law of Advertising,* vol. 2 (New York: Matthew Bender and Co., Inc., 1980) § 25.02, pp. 25.22 to 25.28.
61 See Stigler, *supra* note 1.
62 There should also be special rules for advertisers posing as disinterested parties, but these rules already exist.
63 80 *Congressional Record* 6592 (1936) (Wheeler-Lea Amendment).

14. Special statutes

1 Magnuson-Moss Warranty – Federal Trade Commission Improvement Act, Pub. L. No. 93–637, Tit. I, 88 Stat. 2183, 15 U.S.C. §§ 2301–12 (1976) [hereinafter cited solely by section number].
2 *Presidential Task Force on Appliance Warranties* (1969) as cited in H.R. Rep. No. 93-1107, 93rd Cong., 2nd Sess. 26–28 (1974) [hereinafter cited as 93-1107]; Federal Trade Commission, *Staff Report on Automobile Warranties* (1970) [hereinafter cited as FTC Automobile]; *Staff Report on Consumer Product Warranties,* House Interstate and Foreign Commerce Commission (September 17, 1974; mimeo) [hereinafter cited as 1974 Staff Report].
3 See also S. Rep. No. 93-151, 93rd Cong., 1st Sess. 4–7 (1973) [hereinafter cited as 93-151]; *Hearings on H.R. 20 and H.R. 5021 before the Subcommittee on Commerce and Finance of the House Committee on Interstate and Foreign Commerce,* 93rd Cong., 1st Sess., Serial No. 93-17 (1973); *Hearings on H.R. 6313 et al. before the Subcommittee on Commerce and Finance of the House Committee on Interstate and Foreign Commerce,* 92nd Cong., 1st Sess. (1971).
4 § 102. Details of the Warranty Act's provisions are discussed in Section II *infra.*
5 93-151, *supra* note 3, at 8. Also see Senator Magnuson's comments at 120 *Congressional Record* 40712 (1974).
6 93-151, *supra* note 3, at 7.

7 Under the Uniform Commercial Code, the statute of limitations is four years. U.C.C. § 2-725(1).

8 93-151, *supra* note 3, at 7.

9 § 102(b)(1)(B). The Commission may also determine the terms of service contracts that must be disclosed. *Id.*, at § 106(a).

10 § 102(b)(1)(A).

11 *Id.*, at § 110(a)(2). An additional illustration of the Commission's discretion: The statute defines the term "refund," a remedy available to consumers protected by Full warranties, as "actual purchase price (less reasonable depreciation based on actual use . . .)," but subject to Commission rule defining the measurement of "actual use" more precisely. Although the Commission once proposed a rule and offered it for public comment, it has decided not to promulgate a rule after all. Thus, the Commission, in effect, has repealed the statutory allowance of a deduction for depreciation. See § 102(12); 849 *Antitrust and Trade Regulation Report* (BNA) (February 2, 1978), at A-32.

12 § 103(c).

13 § 102(c).

14 § 111(c). The FTC also may prescribe rules for the extension of the duration of warranty coverage for any period during which the product is inoperable because of a defect, *id.*, at § 102(b)(3); and may determine whether or not a warrantor may require a product to be free of liens and encumbrances prior to remedying the defect, *id.*, at § 104(b)(2).

15 § 102(d). Warrantors are not required to incorporate these provisions into their warranties, although the FTC is delegated broad powers of persuasion through Section 5 enforcement powers. 14 U.S.C. § 45(a)(1) (1976). The Warranty Act specifically requires the Commission to promulgate a rule with respect to warranty practices in the sale of used motor vehicles, § 109(b). The Commission's proposed rule appears at 1977 *Trade Regulation Report* (CCH) ¶ 38,042, at 41,172 (FTC 1976). The FTC has also proposed a rule regarding Mobile Home Sales and Service that implicates warranty practices. See 42 *Federal Register* 26398 (1977). The content of these rules is beyond the scope of this chapter.

There remains a serious risk that promulgation by the Commission of industry-wide standards for warranties will facilitate collusion between competing firms over levels of warranty protection. See United States v. Greater Buffalo Roofing & Sheet Metal Contr's. Assn., 1977-1 *Trade Cases* (CCH) ¶ 61,491.

16 § 104(b)(3).

17 A violation of the Warranty Act constitutes a violation of the FTC Act. *Id.*, at § 110(b).

18 "Consumer product" is defined under the Act as "any tangible personal property . . . normally used for personal, family, or household purposes." § 101(1). Rights of action under the Act are afforded to all "consumers," which are defined as buyers of "consumer products." § 101(3). Thus, a merchant who purchases a product "normally used in the home" qualifies as a consumer and gains the benefit of the Act. The U.C.C., on the other hand, frequently distinguishes the responsibilities of merchants and consumers regardless of the nature of the product purchased. E.g., § 2-603.

19 16 C.F.R. § 701 (1977). The regulations are only applicable to products costing more than $15. *Id.*, at § 701.2.

20 16 C.F.R. § 701.3 (1977). Some individual states had enacted similar consumer disclosure acts prior to Magnuson-Moss. See, e.g., California's Song-Beverly Consumer Warranty Act, Cal. Civ. Code § 1790 *et seq.* (1973).

21 16 C.F.R. § 701.3(7)–(9) (1977). The Commission has also required that a warrantor supply a copy of the warranty with each item sold. 16 C.F.R. § 702.3(b) (1977).

22 §§ 104(a)(3), 108(b), 103(a). See also the requirement of conspicuous disclosure of Informal Dispute Settlement Mechanism procedures, 16 C.F.R. § 703 (1977) discussed *infra* in text following note 43.

23 Recently, however, an Administrative Law Judge has found a firm in violation of the designation requirement, § 103. In re George's Radio & TV, Docket No. 9115 (August 1, 1979). The opinion is not available. The decision currently is on appeal. See 925 *Antitrust and Trade Regulation Report* (BNA) (August 2, 1979), at A-22. The FTC has also claimed a violation of the designation requirement by the Virginia Home Manufacturing Corporation. 914 *Antitrust and Trade Regulation Report* (BNA) (May 17, 1979), at A-7.

24 U.C.C. § 1-201(10).

25 See Section IIB.1 *infra*.

26 16 C.F.R. § 702 (1977). The regulations are only applicable to products costing more than $15. *Id.*, at § 702.3. The Commission has brought several actions seeking to enforce the rule. 917 *Antitrust and Trade Regulation Report* (BNA) (June 7, 1979), at A-50 (Korvette's); 925 *Antitrust Trade and Regulation Report* (BNA) (August 2, 1979), at A-22 (George's Radio & TV); 884 *Antitrust and Trade Regulation Report* (BNA) (October 12, 1978), at A-17 (Montgomery Ward).

27 *Id.*, at § 702.3(a)(1)(i).

28 Sears, Roebuck and Co., 1977 *Trade Regulation Report* (CCH) ¶ 21,282 at 21,181–82 (FTC 1977). Also in Liberty Distributors, 42 *Federal Register* 39,381 (FTC 1977), the Commission relaxed its requirement that warranties be organized by product group.

29 U.C.C. § 2-316(2).

30 See note 20 *supra*.

31 § 102(c).

32 Clayton Act § 3, 15 U.S.C. § 15; Sherman Act, 15 U.S.C.A. § 1; Motion Picture Patents Co. v. Universal Film Mfg. Co., 243 U.S. 502 (1917).

33 Northern Pacific Railway Co. v. United States, 356 U.S. 1 (1958). See Lawrence A. Sullivan, *Handbook on the Law of Antitrust* (St. Paul, Minn.: West Publishing Co., 1977), pp. 434–44.

34 E.g., see SmithKline Corp. v. Eli Lilly & Co., 1976:2 Trade Cases (CCH), ¶ 61,199 (E.D. Pa. 1976) (market power); Response of Carolina, Inc., *et al.* v. Leasco Response, Inc., *et al.*, 1976-2 Trade Cases (CCH) ¶ 61,045 (5th Circ. 1976) (coercion); Watkins v. Kwik Photo, Inc., *et al.*, 1976-1 Trade Cases (CCH) ¶ 60,817 (S.D. Miss. 1975) (effect on tied product).

35 *Id.*

36 Coleman Company, Inc., 40 *Federal Register* 53,708 (FTC 1976).

37 847 *Antitrust and Trade Regulation Report* (BNA) (January 19, 1978), at A-12.

38 § 110(d)(1).

39 § 110(b).

40 See Richard A. Posner, *Antitrust Law: An Economic Perspective* (Chicago, Ill.: University of Chicago Press, 1976), p. 178.

41 § 110(a).

42 §§ 110(a)(2), (3).

43 All provisions referred to in this paragraph are from 16 C.F.R. § 703 (1977).

44 The record-keeping and recording requirements for audits of Informal Dispute Settlement Mechanisms may also expose warrantors to future liability under the FTC Act. The Commission recently has brought suit against the Ford

Motor Company claiming that Ford's inadequate response to discovery of a defect in 1974–77 models violated the FTC Act. 847 *Antitrust Trade and Regulation Report* (BNA) (January 19, 1978), at A-10. See also the FTC investigation of the warranty practices of the automobile rust-proofing industry. 1978 *Trade Regulation Report* (CCH) ¶ 10,201, at 18,104 (FTC, 1978).

45 The single qualifying mechanism is administered by the Home Owners Warranty Corporation.

46 See 1977 *Trade Regulation Report* (CCH) ¶ 50,314, 55,661 (FTC 1977).

47 The description of other settlement processes derives from a personal communication from Lawrence Kanter, Federal Trade Commission, June 1978, and from *The New York Times,* July 24, 1978, § A, p. 10, col. 1.

48 § 110(d)(2).

49 § 110(d)(1).

50 See Section II. B *infra*.

51 Personal communication to author from Rachel Miller, FTC, September 27, 1979.

52 U.C.C. § 2-314. Goods are "merchantable," in general, if they are "fit for ordinary purposes." U.C.C. § 2-314(2)(c). A "merchant" is defined as a person dealing in the goods or holding himself out as having knowledge or skill peculiar to the goods. U.C.C. § 2-104(1).

53 U.C.C. § 2-315. Other implied warranties may arise from a course of dealing or usage of trade. U.C.C. § 2-314(3).

54 U.C.C. §§ 2-316, 2-302.

55 § 104(a)(2).

56 The Code provides a four-year period of limitation, § 2-725(1), although there is some variation between states. See, e.g., California's Song-Beverly Act, *supra* note 20.

57 § 108(c). Such a disclaimer may also be deceptive under the Act. §§ 110(b), (c).

58 § 108(a).

59 Barclay Clark and Michael J. Davis, "Beefing Up Product Warranties: A New Dimension in Consumer Protection," 23 *Kansas Law Review* 567 (1975), pp. 610, 611, 616.

60 See *id*.

61 Much of this legislation applies only to consumers. Since the Warranty Act creates rights of action for merchants in some cases (see note 18 *supra*), the Magnuson-Moss Act may still affect some purchases within these states.

62 Derived from U.C.C. Reporting Service.

63 U.C.C. §§ 2-316(1), 1-201(10).

64 See Karczewski v. Ford Motor Co., 15 U.C.C. Rep. 605 (N.D. Ind. 1974) (dictum).

65 Pearson v. Franklin Laboratories, Inc., 254 N.W.2d 133 (S.D. 1977) (also in similar type).

66 Jones v. Abriani, 350 N.E.2d 635 (Ind. App. 1976).

67 U.C.C. § 2-318.

68 The Act defines as a "consumer" entitled to bring suit, § 110(d)(1), "any person to whom [a consumer] product is transferred during the duration of an implied or written warranty . . . and any other person who is entitled . . . under applicable state law to enforce the obligation of the warranty." § 101(3).

I have discovered only three Code cases in which transferees have been held entitled to recover: Lessees: Hiles Co. v. Johnson Pump Co., 560 P.2d 154, 21 U.C.C. Rep. 568 (Nev. 1977); Mack Trucks of Ark., Inc. v. Jet Asphalt & Rock Co., 246 Ark. 99, 437 S.W.2d 459, 6 U.C.C. Rep. 93 (1969) (under special statute relaxing privity requirements); bailee: Filler v. Rayex Corp., 8 U.C.C. Rep. 323 (7th Cir. 1970) (Indiana law). The first two of these cases did not involve consumer products; the last was a personal injury suit.

69 Some bailees, of course, may recover as members of the family or guests of the buyer. The Code allows the parties to agree as to who will be covered by the warranty. Otherwise, see, e.g., lessees: Barry v. Ivarson, Inc., 249 S.2d 44, 9 U.C.C. Rep. 404 (Fla. App. 1971); bailees: Harvey v. Sears, Roebuck & Co., 315 A.2d 599, 14 U.C.C. Rep. 327 (Del. Sup. 1973); donees: Ellis v. Rich's, Inc., 233 Ga. 573, 16 U.C.C. Rep. 683 (1975); vendees: Stewart v. Gainesville Glass Co., Inc., 233 Ga. 578, 16 U.C.C. Rep. 687 (1975). Each of these cases involved the sale of consumer goods.

70 But see Mack Trucks of Ark., Inc. v. Jet Asphalt & Rock Co., 246 Ark. 99, 437 S.W.2d 459, 6 U.C.C. Rep. 93 (1969) (but not consumer goods).

71 According to § 101(1), however, a "consumer product" is one purchased for personal use, not for resale. See § 101(3).

72 § 104.

73 1977 *Trade Regulation Report* (CCH) ¶ 40,017, 41,947 (FTC 1977) (Proposed rule).

74 Personal communication to author from Rachel Miller, Federal Trade Commission, September 27, 1979.

75 § 104(b)(1)(a).

76 16 C.F.R. § 705.3 (Proposed rule).

77 U.C.C. §§ 2-602(1), 2-608(2). See U.C.C. §§ 1-201(26), (27).

78 16 Wash. App. 39, 554 P.2d 349 (1976).

79 12 Wash. App. 315, 529 P.2d 883 (1974).

80 Performance Motors, Inc. v. Allen, 280 N.C. 385, 186 S.E.2d 161 (1972).

81 Bunch v. Signal Oil & Gas Co., 505 P.2d 41, 12 U.C.C. Rep. 112 (Colo. App. 1972); Southern Union Gas Co. v. Taylor, 486 P.2d 606, 9 U.C.C. Rep. 668 (N.M. 1971).

82 George L. Priest, "Breach and Remedy for the Tender of Nonconforming Goods under the Uniform Commercial Code: An Economic Approach," 91 *Harvard Law Review* 960 (1978), pp. 988–89.

83 Rejection: U.C.C. § 2-602; Revocation of acceptance: U.C.C. §§ 2-608, 2-607(3)(a).

84 The Act makes no specific reference to this requirement, but it allows warrantors to defend as "reasonable" any duty placed on consumers. § 104(b)(1).

85 1977 *Trade Regulation Report* (CCH) ¶ 40,107, 41,951, Comment 9 (FTC 1977).

86 16 C.F.R. § 705.3(h) (Proposed rule) (1977).

87 Courts have disregarded contractual specifications of notification periods in Q. Vandenberg & Sons, N.V. v. Siter, 204 Pa. Sup. Ct. 392, 204 A.2d 494 (1964), and Th. Van Huijstee, N.V. v. Faehndrich, 10 U.C.C. Rep. 598 (Civ. Ct. N.Y. 1972).

88 "Nonconforming Tenders," *supra* note 82, at 984–88, and cases cited therein.

89 A complete list of all cases in which the reasonable time requirement was litigated appears in the appendix, "Nonconforming Tenders," *supra* note 82, at 5–9.

90 § 104(c).

91 U.C.C. § 2-606(1)(c).

92 U.C.C. § 2-608(2).
93 See, e.g., Ingle v. Marked Tree Equipment Co., 244 Ark. 1166, 428 S.W.2d 286 (1968), and appendix, *supra* note 89, at 14–15.
94 See, e.g., Bowen v. Young, 507 S.W.2d 600 (Tex. Ct. App. 1974), and appendix, *supra* note 89, at 15.
95 U.C.C. § 2-608(3), however, provides that a buyer who revokes has the same duties as if he had rejected. To date, this provision has been invoked infrequently with respect to buyers' actions.
96 For a further discussion, see "Nonconforming Tenders," *supra* note 82, at 992.
97 "Nonconforming Tenders," *supra* note 82, at 991–94; and appendix, *supra* note 89, at 18–20.
98 U.C.C. § 2-608.
99 "Nonconforming Tenders," *supra* note 82, at 994; appendix, *supra* note 89, at 21–22.
100 U.C.C. § 2-601. For a summary of the outcomes of all rejection cases under the Code, 1954-77, see "Nonconforming Tenders," *supra* note 82, at 995–97.
101 E.g., Carnes Construction Co. v. Richards & Conover Steel Co., 10 U.C.C. Rep. 797 (Okla. Ct. App. 1972), discussed in appendix, *supra* note 89, at 3–4.
102 See § 104(c).
103 U.C.C. § 2-508.
104 E.g., Wilson v. Scampoli, 228 A.2d 848 (D.C. 1967); Bartus v. Riccardi, 284 N.Y.Supp.2d 222 (1967); Meads v. Davis, 206 S.E.2d 868, 15 U.C.C. Rep. 40 (N.C. Ct. App. 1974). But see Zabriskie Chevrolet, Inc. v. Smith, 99 N.J. Sup. 441, 240 A.2d 195 (Law Div. 1968); Bayne v. Nail Motors, 12 U.C.C. Rep. 1137 (Iowa Dist. Ct. 1973), in which the court concluded that cure would be ineffective.
105 Melby v. Hawkins Pontiac, Inc., 13 Wash. App. 745, 537 P.2d 807 (1975). See also Orange Motors v. Dade County Dairies, Inc., 258 So.2d 319 (Fla. Dist. Ct. App.), *cert. denied,* 263 So.2d 831 (1972). But see, Stofman v. Keenan Motors, 63 Pa.D. and C.2d 56, 14 U.C.C. Rep. 1252 (1973).
106 See "Nonconforming Tenders," *supra* note 82, at 980–81.
107 § 110(e). See also § 101(10).
108 § 104(a)(4).
109 § 101(10).
110 § 111(c)(1)(*B*).
111 U.C.C. §§ 2-712, 2-713.
112 § 104(a)(1). See note 115 *infra* for a definition.
113 § 104(a)(4).
114 § 104(b)(1).
115 § 104(d). "Without charge" is defined as not assessing the consumer for any costs incurred by the warrantor or his representatives.
116 16 C.F.R. § 705 (Proposed rule, 1977), promulgated pursuant to § 104(b)(3). For a discussion of the status of the rule, see note 74 *supra* and preceding text.
117 *Id.,* at § 705.3(a).
118 *Id.,* at § 705.3(b). This requirement, however, does not apply to defective automobiles.
119 *Id.,* at 705.3(d).
120 U.C.C. § 2-602(2)(b); see U.C.C. § 2-608(3).
121 U.C.C. § 2-715. Incidental damages, of course, are available when the buyer seeks damages as the principal remedy. U.C.C. §§ 2-712(2), 2-713(1).

122 § 104(a)(1) ("must . . . remedy . . . without charge . . ."); § 104(a)(4) (". . . replacement shall include installing . . . without charge. . . ."); § 104(d) ("may not assess the consumer for any costs . . ."). If the duties listed in the Commission rule are placed on a consumer, they will be considered by the Commission as unreasonable. Of course, the Commission's definitions may be subjected to judicial review.

123 E.g., Powers v. Wayside, Inc., 180 N.E.2d 677 (1962).

124 E.g., Bollenbach v. Continental Casualty Co., 414 P.2d 802 (Ore. 1966).

125 *Restatement of Contracts* § 349 (1932).

126 U.C.C. § 2-608.

127 Regents of the University of Colorado v. Pacific Pump & Supply, Inc., 528 P.2d 941 (Colo. Ct. App. 1974).

128 See "Nonconforming Tenders," *supra* note 82, at 992–94.

129 *Id.*, at note 95.

130 § 101(12).

131 1977 *Trade Regulation Report* (CCH), ¶ 40,015, 41,932 (FTC Proposed Rule 1976).

132 Under the proposed rule, the deduction would be calculated by determining the proportion of the period of the buyer's actual use to the life of the product and multiplying it by the sum of the purchase price, taxes, and delivery and installation charges. One difficulty with such a measure is the need to derive an estimate of a product's useful life, which the manufacturer of the product, of course, may want, for this purpose, to understate. In addition, the calculus does not estimate precisely the decline in value because of the buyer's use, but rather the decline in value over the period of possession assuming depreciation at a stable rate over the product's lifetime. This measure, however realistic for land sale contracts from which it was derived, will be inaccurate to the extent that different buyers use the product with differing intensities. Furthermore, it is unusual that the Commission would add delivery and installation charges to the purchase price for purposes of the deduction. The Federal Minimum Standards place liability for installation and removal charges on the seller, not the buyer. In many cases, the seller will neither have incurred nor have received payment for incurring the costs of delivery or installation. Yet, under the proposed rule, if, say, a buyer had possessed a product worth $100 for 20 percent of its useful life before discovering the defect, the seller could deduct from the $100 not only $20, but also 20 percent of the delivery and installation charges.

133 See note 11, *supra.*

134 A recently published study claims to show that a Wisconsin disclosure law for used car sales reduced prices by 12.2 percent. Kenneth McNeil, *et al.*, "Market Discrimination against the Poor and the Impact of Consumer Disclosure Laws: The Used Car Industry," 13 *Law and Society Review* 695 (1979), p. 708. The theoretical foundation for the study, however, is not well defined with respect to price changes.

135 These data were originally collected by the Subcommittee on Commerce and Finance of the House Interstate and Foreign Commerce Committee and by the FTC. The FTC has generously provided the author with copies of both the 1974 and 1978 sets of warranties.

136 See Table 14.3 *infra* and discussion in text.

137 A recent empirical study of the Act's effects confirms this conclusion. Comment, "An Empirical Study of the Magnuson-Moss Warranty Act," 31 *Stanford Law Review* 1117 (1979), p. 1138. The study, however, only compares

pre- and post-Act compliance with the Federal Minimum Standards. Thus, it does not address the specific changes in all warranty provisions observed here.

138 However, for cookware, freezers, and dryers, there was only one firm in the sample.

139 The Stanford study, *supra* note 137, found one firm that eliminated written warranty coverage altogether after the Act became effective.

140 See text preceding notes 52 and 53 *supra*.

141 See, e.g., note 59 *supra*. Donald R. Rothschild, "The Magnuson-Moss Warranty Act: Does It Balance Warrantor and Consumer Interests?" 44 *George Washington Law Review* 335 (1976), pp. 378–80.

15. Commission performance, incentives, and behavior

1 Some of our discussions of Commission activities concern ongoing projects. Although some of the projects will be modified, their major thrust will usually survive.

2 The causality between the complexity of the legal theory and the size of the case may be less apparent than that between factual complexity and size. Although perhaps not a necessary consequence, large FTC cases have involved such complex legal issues as shared monopoly (see Chapter 6) and expansion of the unfairness doctrine (see Chapter 4).

3 The preference for centralized (or large) cases is distinct from a preference for regulatory or deregulatory solutions. Thus, both deregulatory and regulatory activities could take either a centralized or a decentralized approach.

4 Two details of this analysis should be stated. First, the analysis could be extended to a multidimensional plane, reflecting the many agencies and parts of Congress with opinions on the many dimensions of FTC action. Second, we treat the political environment as an exogenous variable in our explanation of FTC behavior, recognizing, of course, that the political environment can influence the attitudes of FTC staff members toward an issue. See, generally, Sections IV and V *infra*.

5 Reorganization Plan No. 8, 64 Stat. 1264 (1950).

6 *Federal Trade Commission Oversight: Hearings before the Senate Commerce Committee*, 93rd Cong., 2d Sess. (May 9 and May 14, 1974), p. 294.

7 *FTC: Watch* (December 16, 1977), p. 3, and Special Supplement.

8 *Federal Trade Commission Regional Office Operations: Hearings before a Subcommittee of the House Committee on Government Operations*, 95th Cong., 1st Sess. (March 15, 1977), p. 159 [hereinafter referred to as 1977 Regional Office Hearings].

9 For example, in fiscal year 1977 the regional offices used about 20 percent of Commission resources, while in fiscal 1979 they used about 15 percent.

10 See *Hearings on FTC Appropriations for 1975 before the House Appropriations Committee*, 93rd Cong., 2d Sess. (1974), p. 190.

11 See 1978 Moss Questionnaire, *supra* Chapter 3, at note 14, question 19.

12 For information on changes that the Pertschuk Administration has implemented, see 1978 Moss Questionnaire, *supra* note 11, questions 14 and 17, and address by Albert Foer, Assistant Director, Bureau of Competition (Columbus, Ohio, June 15, 1979).

13 Robert Pitofsky, ed., "Carter Transition Paper on FTC," (unpublished report, December 1976), p. 3.

14 In 1969, various commissioners used the appointment power to stage a coup

against Chairman Dixon in the highly charged atmosphere within the Commission. See David M. Welborn, *Governance of Federal Regulatory Agencies* (Knoxville, Tenn.: University of Tennessee Press, 1977), pp. 52–54.

15 See, e.g., Mike W. Kirkpatrick, "Dinner Address," 40 *Antitrust Law Journal* 328 (1971), p. 332.

16 See, e.g., Robert J. Mackay and Carolyn L. Weaver, "Monopoly Bureaus and Fiscal Outcomes: Deductive Models and Implications for Reform," in Gordon Tullock and Richard E. Wagner, eds., *Policy Analysis and Deductive Reasoning* (Lexington, Mass.: D. C. Heath and Company, 1978), pp. 141–65.

17 *FTC: Watch* (March 10, 1978), p. 27. The details of the vote underscore the power of the chairman. Except for Pertschuk, the other commissioners did not appear to favor a rule. The "compromise" was to issue only a set of staff proposals; there is no proposed Commission rule. With any other commissioner besides the chairman, rule-making proceedings would not have started.

18 Welborn, *supra* note 14, at 32.

19 See *ABA Report, supra* Chapter 1, note 10, at 13.

20 See *Hearings on Agriculture, Environmental and Consumer Protection Appropriations for 1975 before the Subcommittee on Agriculture, Environmental and Consumer Protection Appropriations of the House Appropriations Committee*, 93rd Cong., 2d Sess. (April 9, 1974). For another view that the Commission has limited control over its activities, see Lawrence G. Meyer, "Some Brief Reflections on Shadows, Mirrors and Revolving Doors: Case Selection at the Federal Trade Commission," 46 *Antitrust Law Journal* 575 (1977), pp. 581–83.

21 See Fairlea Sheehy, *The Federal Trade Commission in the 1970s: An Overview of the Commission from Kirkpatrick to Pertschuk* (May 1, 1978) (unpublished paper written to fulfill Third Year Paper requirement at Harvard Law School), p. 52.

22 Much of this controversy is part of the public record. See 7 *Antitrust Law & Economics Review* No. 2, 59 (1974); *id.*, no. 1, 27 (1974); 635 & 636 *Antitrust and Trade Regulation Report* (BNA) (October 23 and 30, 1973).

23 1975 Moss Questionnaire, *supra* note 11, question 45.

24 *FTC: Watch* (November 4, 1977), p. 9.

25 See 1975 Moss Questionnaire, *supra* note 11, question 44, for a list of the Bureau of Economics' memoranda to the Commission. The role of the evaluation committee (in both bureaus) in planning may decrease under Pertschuk with the new planning apparatus.

26 See Judith A. Hartman, *Representative Bureaucracy: Variations in Specialization and Heirarchy in Sixty Federal Agencies* (unpublished paper delivered at the 1975 Annual Meeting of the Political Science Association), pp. 116–30. This paper studied the relationship between the FTC's lawyers and economists through extensive interviews of individuals working on 31 antitrust cases.

27 *Id.*, at 121.

28 See *Hearings before Ad Hoc Subcommittee on Antitrust, the Robinson-Patman Act and Related Matters of the House Select Committee on Small Businesses*, 94th Cong., 1st Sess. (November and December 1975; January 1976).

29 See the discussion of pre-1970 FTC case selection in Chapter 1 *supra*. National advertising and mergers were exceptions; for both of these activities, complaints were not predominantly used.

30 1975 Moss Questionnaire, *supra* note 11, question 38.

31 As explained in Chapter 6 *supra*, however, the theory underlying PRAM was, and continues to be, extremely influential.

32 See 636 *Antitrust and Trade Regulation Report* (BNA) (October 23, 1973), § D.

33 For discussion of the controversy regarding, and history of, OPPE, see James W. Singer, "FTC Planning Office Plays Larger Role in Decision Making," 7 *National Journal* 1298 (1975); FY 1975 Appropriations Hearings, *supra* note 10, at 201–7.

34 A description of the information system and its history can be found in Touche, Ross & Co., *FTC Management Information Systems Planning Study* (unpublished report to FTC, 1976). See also 1975 Moss Questionnaire, *supra* note 11, question 9.

35 See 1975 Moss Questionnaire, *supra* note 11, question 41, providing information on the budgeting procedure.

36 For example, there were numerous planning sessions held in 1972. See *id.*, question 23.

37 See *Hearings on FTC before Subcommittee on State, Justice, Commerce, the Judiciary and Related Agencies of the House Appropriations Committee*, 95th Cong., 2d Sess. (March 13, 1978).

38 From fiscal year 1975 through fiscal year 1977, the planned resources for the horizontal restraints program increased from about $0.9 million to $2.4 million. The failure of the BC to meet the desire for horizontal cases at the level the Commission wanted can be seen in the 1978 planned decrease to $2 million. For fiscal 1979, this figure was increased to $2.5 million. Source: FTC Budget Justifications to Congress. See Chapter 6 *supra* for a discussion of the agency's failure to increase its horizontal price-fixing efforts.

39 See II Office Policy Planning and Evaluation, Fiscal Year 1976, Mid-year Review (unpublished FTC report, January, 1976, available through Moss subcommittee and BNA).

40 Touche, Ross & Co.'s 1976 report on the FTC's information systems, *supra* note 34, discusses faulty data at 1-6 of the Executive Summary.

41 The 1978 Moss Questionnaire, *supra* note 11, question 14, indicates that the Pertschuk Administration recognized the weak link between case selection and budgeting and planning.

42 See 1978 Moss Questionnaire, *supra* note 11, question 18. A detailed discussion of FTC impact evaluations is Michael B. Mazis, "Evaluation of the FTC: A Status Report and Recommendations for the Future" (*FTC Policy Planning Issues Paper*, April 1978).

43 The neoclassical economic theory of producer behavior has been subject to extensive criticism for several decades. This debate has yet to yield a general theory of producer behavior in profit, nonprofit, and governmental organizations. This lack of agreement has been primarily fueled by dissatisfaction with the wealth-maximization assumption used in conventional theory, and by a failure of ad hoc hypotheses to explain the actions of public and other nonproprietary enterprises. See Kenneth W. Clarkson and Donald L. Martin, eds., *The Economics of Nonproprietary Organizations* (Greenwich, Conn.: JAI Press, 1980) for a review of much of this material.

44 In economics, "proprietary" describes the right to future gains and losses. "Profit" describes the right to the differences between revenues and costs. For simplicity, we assume that "profit" refers to both rights.

45 See, generally, Anthony Downs, *Inside Bureaucracy* (Boston: Little, Brown

and Company, 1966); Gordon Tullock, *The Politics of Bureaucracy* (Washington, D.C.: Public Affairs Press, 1965).

46 See Chapter 5 *supra,* at note 21 and accompanying text.

47 See, generally, Gary S. Becker, *Human Capital* (New York: Columbia University Press, 1964).

48 See, e.g., Meredith Associates, Inc., "Report to the Chairman Federal Trade Commission: Attorney and Attorney Manager Recruitment, Selection and Retention" (July 15, 1976), p. 10.

49 *Id.,* at 14.

50 *Id.,* at 12.

51 See, e.g., 1975 Moss Questionnaire, *supra* note 11, question 13.

52 Of course, the performance of top staff will influence their value in the job market. The consensus of past FTC officials whom we interviewed, however, was that for most individuals their performance probably affects their future income less than whether or not they had the job.

53 In a hostile political environment, expansion of FTC authority could reduce (at least the growth rate of) the agency's budget. See Section V *infra.* Nevertheless, some expansions could still be worth the cost of a lower budget.

54 The increase in FTC authority during the 1970s does not depend upon a change in employee preferences for investing in human capital. See Section V *infra.*

55 We discuss only those economists who interact with the lawyers in case selection and litigation. Other economists engage in more academic activity, such as writing reports on various issues and industries. In addition, we do not consider the incentives of economists who move to the private sector, an option not exercised until recently, when two key Bureau of Economics officials started a successful consulting firm. As this option becomes more attractive, the importance of the FTC as a training ground for economists will increase.

56 Based on interviews with FTC officials.

57 For the leading discussion on the importance of budget maximization, see William A. Niskanen, *Bureaucracy and Representative Government* (New York: Aldine Publishing Company, 1971). Note 59 *infra* discusses the limits of budget maximization for understanding the FTC.

58 A weaker constraint is the extent to which the work of FTC economists has support among academics. Because the theory may be tested in court and because many FTC economists attempt to maintain contacts with the academic community, a theory without support among prestigious academic economists is less desirable.

59 Our approach differs from some other attempts at explaining bureaucratic behavior. For example, Posner assumes that the agency's goal is to maximize utility, defined as "the public benefit." Richard A. Posner, "The Behavior of Administrative Agencies," 1 *The Journal of Legal Studies* 305 (1972). This assumption differs from the assumption that individuals maximize their self-interest that we, and most economists, use. Moreover, Posner's assumption does little to explain many attributes of FTC behavior, such as the adverse consequences of FTC cases and its internal conflicts. Niskanen, on the other hand, argues that bureaus act as if they wish to maximize their budgets. Niskanen, *supra* note 57. In ignoring the importance of human capital (among other reasons), this approach fails to capture the complexity of agency performance. This is not to deny that (even formal) economic analysis has taken important steps to capturing the complexity of government behavior. See, e.g.,

Sam Peltzman, "Toward A More General Theory of Regulation," 19 *Journal of Law and Economics* 211 (1976).

60 The Nader and ABA reports, both discussed in Chapter 1 *supra*, were not better written or more persuasive than previous criticisms of the FTC. Instead, they appeared to be symptomatic of the changing political environment. Although explaining changes in that environment is beyond our purpose, the emergence of consumerism as a political force was undoubtedly important.

61 Of course, producers do not speak with one voice. Regarding the FTC, small and large producers have often differed. Large producers have often felt that the Commission penalizes their efficiency, thereby protecting small producers, especially in RP enforcement. Although the Commission was once believed to be a haven for protection of small producers, many small producers now seem to be critical of the Commission, particularly over the lack of RP enforcement. See Special Subcommittee of the House Small Business Committee, *supra* note 28. In any event, during 1969 and 1970, neither small nor large producers seemed to have vigorously opposed reform of the Commission.

62 Although we have not closely analyzed the internal operation and employment patterns of FTC personnel before 1970, the incentives of FTC employees need not have changed to explain the agency's transformation. Without support from the factions that shape its external constraints, it is very unlikely that the agency could have attained its current prominence.

63 See, generally, the discussion of the legislative veto in Chapter 3 *supra*.

64 Computed from *The Budget of the United States Government*, App. A, fiscal years 1970 through 1981, and *Economic Indicators*, May 1980 (Washington, D.C., U.S. Government Printing Office, 1980).

65 See *FTC: Watch* for the last months of 1979 for an excellent summary of these events.

66 On changes in FTC rule making, see Chapter 10 *supra*. Nevertheless, the agency remains deeply committed to the activist thrust of the activities described in Chapters 6 through 14 *supra*. Changes, to date, have been marginal. On Pertschuk's plans to increase the FTC's scope, plans that contributed to the agency's political troubles, see, e.g., *supra* Chapter 4, at note 41; Michael Pertschuk, "New Direction for the FTC," speech before the Eleventh New England Antitrust Conference, Boston, November 18, 1977, reprinted in *A Dialogue with the Federal Trade Commission* (New York: Harcourt Brace Jovanovich, 1979), pp. 87–107. Moreover, procedurally the FTC under Pertschuk exacerbated its problems: "On the record, this is an agency which lets its own rulemaking staff summarize rulemaking records for the Commissioners, which lets its staff parcel out 'public participation' money almost without exception to groups which favor the staff-proposed rule or advocate *even harsher* drop at regulation, which cuts off outside consultation but preserves the staff's access, and which approves 'blanket subpoenas.'" *FTC: Watch* (September 21, 1979), p. 4.

67 Before 1970, the agency implicitly adopted the market concentration doctrine in its merger program, but did not use the doctrine to attack structure as in the 1970s.

68 Particularly the large cases and rules, moreover, satisfy the demands of an activist political environment. Further, even small cases can occasionally be used for political purposes. For example, during the hostility of the late 1970s,

the Commission somewhat increased Robinson-Patman enforcement, an action that could provide much needed political support.

69 Because both agencies attack mergers, the second point appears less important than the first. Even within mergers, however, the possibility for some complementarity exists.

70 If the FTC develops a separate theory under Section 5 to attack sophisticated price-fixing arrangements, perhaps using its consumer redress power as a remedy and using evidence of economic impact to show the existence of price-fixing, then both FTC lawyers and economists would benefit.

71 Although BCP attorneys overwhelmingly leave the agency, they apparently stay longer than their BC counterparts. The Meredith Report, *supra* note 48, found that in a sample of attorneys who had recently left the agency, about 90 percent of the departing BC attorneys had been with the agency less than five years, compared to only about 70 percent of BCP attorneys. These statistics are consistent with consumer protection attorneys desiring human capital, particularly if BC attorneys acquire the needed experience more quickly than those in BCP. The statistics are also consistent with a greater preference among consumer protection attorneys for "reshaping the world," as discussed in Section III B. See Chapter 1 *supra*, at note 17 and accompanying text for additional evidence of this attribute in FTC consumer protection. Nevertheless, to the extent that BCP attorneys still seek careers in private firms, as the available, but sketchy, evidence indicates, the preference for power appears less important than that for wealth. Moreover, the existence of routine, relatively small cases in both bureaus is more consistent with increasing wealth, particularly for young attorneys, than for increasing power.

72 On the uses and abuses of the concept, see James D. Gwartney and Richard Stroup, *Economics,* 2nd ed. (New York: Academic Press, 1980), ch. 30. Two limits on the theory for FTC use exist. The theory must have some degree of respectability in the academic community. See note 58 *supra.* Moreover, the more stringent the judicial review of rules, the more rigorous the theory and its applications must be.

73 For a chairman with a short time horizon, the costs of reorganization may outweigh the gains. Instead, this chairman might choose another alternative strategy against projects he disapproves. One such strategy would be to use his power to delay projects.

16. What can be done?

1 Because most of the changes discussed here could be the subject of separate articles, we necessarily neglect some of their detail.

2 Several of those whom we interviewed mentioned this argument, including reference to the oil industry, as we discuss below. The "safety valve" is also frequently discussed in *FTC: Watch.* See, e.g., *FTC: Watch* (September 21, 1979), pp. 6–7. See also the conclusion to Chapter 6 *supra.*

3 Government regulation affects the *individual* producers involved more severely than it affects individual consumers, even though the total cost to consumers as a *group* may exceed the benefits to the class of producers. Further, "free-rider" problems deter consumers from successful lobbying. For a detailed treatment of these problems, see George J. Stigler, "The Theory of Economic Regulation," 2 *Bell Journal of Economics and Management Science* 3 (1971).

4 See Chapter 3 *supra,* at note 32. "Consumerist" refers to members of organized groups claiming to represent all (or most) consumers.

5 Although the recent trend in administrative law described in Chapter 4 *supra*
will probably constrain the FTC more than was traditional, cost/benefit analysis appears necessary for a truly effective constraint. See Kenneth W. Clarkson and Timothy J. Muris, "Constraining the Federal Trade Commission: The
Case of Occupational Regulation," *University of Miami Law Review* (forthcoming).

6 The origins, progress, and resolutions of these efforts can be traced in trade
journals that periodically report on the FTC, such as *FTC: Watch* and the *Antitrust and Trade Regulation Report.*

7 As explained in Chapter 3 *supra,* some Section 5 cases are in reality antitrust
cases. We would leave these cases to current law with the reform suggested in
Section III D *infra.* We do not favor an antitrust system with the changes suggested below applied under only Sherman and Clayton Act cases brought by
the FTC, and analysis of how the Sherman and Clayton Act should be re-
drafted is beyond the scope of this study.

8 We are indebted to Mark Grady for suggestions regarding definitions of deception and unfairness.

9 Not all FTC cases need cost/benefit analysis, for two reasons. For cases of
small magnitude, perhaps defined in terms of a dollar threshold, the extra administrative costs of cost/benefit analysis are not worth the effort. More important, under our approach the FTC could avoid cost/benefit analysis under
judicially defined *per se* categories of illegality. When the consensus of economic analysis or when Commission experience with the practice indicate
that the practice could not benefit consumers, it would be *per se* illegal.

10 Aaron Wildavsky, "Rescuing Policy Analysis from PPBS," in Robert Have-
man and Julius Margolis, eds., *Public Expenditures and Policy Analysis*
(Chicago: Markham Publishing Company, 1970), p. 461.

11 When the effect of the remedy could not be reversed, the tougher cost/benefit
standard would apply. The agency might claim that firms subject to the regulation could artificially raise costs during the five years. Five years is a long
time, however, to engage in such unprofitable behavior for an uncertain
payout. Moreover, firms would have an incentive not to raise costs, just as
they have an incentive to cheat on price-fixing cartels. In any event, the FTC
could raise this issue, with the burden of persuasion on the agency.

12 See Chapter 2 *supra,* at note 7 and accompanying text. See also David O.
Bickart, "Civil Penalties under the Section 5(m) of the Federal Trade Commission Act," 44 *University of Chicago Law Review* 761 (1977).

13 Although consumerists have been less guilty of this defect than have business
groups, the consumerists do not always use economic analysis, the only feasible method of determining the economic interests of consumers as a class.

14 The funeral industry has been one of the worst offenders. See, e.g., *FTC:
Watch* (January 27, 1977), pp. 4–5, and *FTC: Watch* (June 30, 1978), p. 16.
Even regarding the two rules studied individually in this book, industry
sources performed neither the cost/benefit analysis for mobile homes nor the
similar analysis for creditors' remedies.

15 E.O. 12044, which calls for semi-annual review of existing rules, is voluntary
for independent regulatory agencies. Further, *OMB Circular A-11,* which gov-
erns budget submission does not formally incorporate cost/benefit analyses
into budget decisions.

16 A further problem is where the devil's advocate will fit organizationally. We regard this as a detail as long as the advocate is not part of the operating bureaus. The advocate could be a separate office or part of the General Counsel's or Executive Director's staffs.

17 As with the devil's advocate, the effectiveness of peer review will depend in part upon the enthusiasm of strategically important individuals, in this case at least the Director of the Bureau of Economics.

18 See, e.g., Peter A. White, "FTC: Wrong Agency for the Job of Adjudication," 61 *American Bar Association Journal* 1242 (1975).

19 As Chapter 15 *supra* notes, however, the staff has the real power in determining what complaints will be issued.

20 Arthur Rosett, "Supreme Court v. the District Court in Antitrust Cases," 26 *Mercer Law Review* 795 (1975).

Selected bibliography

Books and articles

Alexander, George G. *Honesty and Competition: False-Advertising Law and Policy under FTC Administration.* Syracuse, N.Y.: Syracuse University Press, 1967.

American Enterprise Institute. *Government Regulation: Proposals for Procedural Reform.* Washington, D.C.: American Enterprise Institute, 1979.

Ash, Roy L., *et al.* "Ash Report on the FTC: Antitrust Moving to the White House?" 4 *Antitrust Law and Economics Review* 21 (1970).

Auerbach, Carl A. "The Federal Trade Commission: Internal Organization and Procedure." 48 *Minnesota Law Review* 383 (1964).

Cox, Edward F., Robert C. Fellmeth, and John E. Schultz. *The Nader Report on the Federal Trade Commission.* New York: Barron Press, 1969.

Davidson, S. Forrester. "The Place of the Federal Trade Commission in Administrative Law," 8 *George Washington Law Review* 280 (1939).

Dole, Elizabeth H. "Cost–Benefit Analysis versus Protecting the Vulnerable: The FTC's Special Interest Groups." 9 *Antitrust Law and Economics Review,* no. 2, 15 (1977).

"Federal Trade Commission Silver Anniversary Issue," 8 *George Washington Law Review* 249 (1940).

"The Fiftieth Anniversary of the Federal Trade Commission," 64 *Columbia Law Review* 385 (1965).

Fuchs, V., ed. *Industrial Organization.* Washington, D.C.: National Bureau of Economic Research, 1972.

Gardner, Judy. "FTC Seeks Wider Impact in Antitrust Work: Puts New Emphasis on Planning." 4 *National Journal* 1151 (1972).

Gellhorn, Ernest T. "Proof of Consumer Deception before the Federal Trade Commission." 17 *Kansas Law Review* 559 (1969).

Goldschmid, Harvey G., H. Michael Mann, and G. Fred Weston, eds. *Industrial Concentration: The New Learning.* Boston: Little, Brown and Company, 1974.

Green, Mark G., Beverly C. Moore, and Bruce Wasserstein. *The Closed Enterprise System: Ralph Nader's Study Group on Antitrust Enforcement.* New York: Grossman Publishers, 1972.

Henderson, Gerard C. *The Federal Trade Commission.* New Haven, Conn.: Yale University Press, 1924.

Law and Business, a Dialogue with the Federal Trade Commission. New York: Harcourt Brace Jovanovich, 1979.

Liebeler, Wesley G. "Toward a Consumers' Antitrust Law: The Federal Trade Commission and Vertical Mergers in the Cement Industry." 15 *U.C.L.A. Law Review* 1153 (1968).

MacIntyre, A. Everette, and Goachen G. Volhard, "The FTC and Incipient Unfairness." 41 *George Washington Law Review* 407 (1973).

Pitofsky, Robert. "Beyond Nader: Consumer Protection and the Regulation of Advertising." 90 *Harvard Law Review* 661 (1977).

Posner, Richard A. "The Behavior of Administrative Agencies." 1 *Journal of Legal Studies* 305 (1972).

Rockefeller, Edwin S. *Desk Book of FTC Practice and Procedure.* New York: Practicing Law Institute, 1976.

Rothschild, Donald R. "The Magnuson-Moss Warranty Act: Does It Balance Warrantor and Consumer Interests?" 44 *George Washington Law Review* 335 (1976).

Scanlon, Paul D. "FTC and Phase II: The McGovern Papers." 5 *Antitrust Law and Economics Review,* no. 3, 19 (1972).

Stigler, George J. "The Economics of Information." 69 *Journal of Political Economy* 213 (1961).

Stone, Alan. *Economic Regulation in the Public Interest.* Ithaca, N.Y.: Cornell University Press, 1977.

"Symposium on the Federal Trade Commission: A Program of Enforcement," 38 *Indiana Law Journal* 319 (1963).

Wagner, Susan. *The Federal Trade Commission.* New York: Praeger Publishers, 1971.

Welborn, David M. *Governance of Federal Regulatory Agencies.* Knoxville, Tenn: University of Tennessee Press, 1977.

Government publications

Attorney General's Committee on Administrative Procedure. *Part V, Federal Trade Commission,* S. Doc. No. 186, 94th Cong., 3rd Sess. (1976).

Bureau of Consumer Protection. *Funeral Industry Practices: Final Staff Report to the FTC and Proposed Trade Regulation Rule* (June 1978).

Bureau of Consumer Protection. *Proprietary Vocational and Home Study Schools: Final Report to the FTC and Proposed Trade Regulation Rule (December 1976).*

Bureau of Consumer Protection. *Sale of Used Motor Vehicles: Final Staff Report to the FTC and Proposed Trade Regulation Rule* (September 1978).

Cabell, Henry B. *Report of the Presiding Officer on Proposed Trade Regulation Rule Concerning Credit Practices* (August 1978).

Civil Service Commission. *Evaluation of Personnel Management, Federal Trade Commission* (1965).

Commission on Organization of the Executive Branch of the Government (Hoover Commission). *Task Force Report on Regulatory Commissions* (1949).

Federal Trade Commission. *Staff Report on Automobile Warranties* (1970).

Kahn, Jack F. *Report of the Presiding Officer on Proposed Trade Regulation Rule Concerning Funeral Industry Practices* (July 1977).

Magnuson-Moss Warranty – Federal Trade Commission Improvement Act, Pub. L. No. 93-637, Title I, 88 Stat. 2183, 15 U.S.C. §§ 2801-12 (1976).

National Commission on Consumer Finance – Technical Studies. Washington, D.C.: U.S. Government Printing Office, 1973.

Senate Committee on Government Operations. *Study on Federal Regulations: The Regulatory Appointments Process.* S. Doc. No. 25, 95th Cong., 1st Sess. (1977).
Staff of Federal Trade Commission. *Merger Performance: An Empirical Analysis of Nine Corporations* (November 1972).
Staff of Federal Trade Commission. *Statement of Position, Proposed Trade Regulation Regarding Mobile Home Sales and Service* (November 1975).
Subcommittee on Oversight and Investigation of the Senate Committee on Interstate and Foreign Commerce. *Report on Federal Regulation and Regulatory Reform* (Moss Questionnaire), 1975 and 1978.

Miscellaneous

American Bar Association. *Report of the ABA Commission To Study the Federal Trade Commission* (1969).
Antitrust and Trade Regulation Report (Bureau of National Affairs). Various issues, 1970–present.
FTC Budget Justification to Congress, 1970–present.
FTC: Watch. Various issues, 1977–present.
Uniform Commercial Code, Article 2.

Index